Course Taking Sides: Global Issues
10th edition

James Harf, Marie Harf, Mark Lombardi

http://create.mheducation.com

ISBN-10: 130736893X   ISBN-13: 9781307368932

Contents

Credits

Detailed Table of Contents

Unit 1: Global Population and Resources

Richard Jackson, president of the Global Aging Institute (GAI) and formerly of the Center for Strategic and International Studies, argues that demographic trends have affected "the great upheavals of history" from time to time. He points to the upcoming 2020s as a watershed decade when widespread disruptions are likely again to occur. For Jackson, during this next decade, global aging is likely to have a major negative effect on "economic growth, social and political stability, and the shape of the world order." The World Bank study authors call into question the old adage that demographic trends such as global aging, once put into motion, cannot be stopped and typically lead to increased economic costs. They argue instead that individuals and organizations can adjust to these changing trends with a resultant series of more complex outcomes. They suggest, for example, that aging societies "are not destined to experience stagnation or decline in living standards."

Shenggen Fan, director general of the International Food Policy Research Institute, presents a generally positive outlook on the ability of the global food system to provide sufficient food for the world's population despite a number of non-food related intrusions that negatively affect the global capacity of the world's food system. The UN Food and Agriculture Organization report, on the other hand, looks to an increase in the world's chronically undernourished people, from an estimated 717 million in 2015 to 815 million in 2017, as a barometer for revealing a worsening situation, in particular in parts of sub-Saharan Africa, Southeast Asia and West Asia. Given the prevalence of conflict throughout the globe and the increase in climate-related shocks to the food system, two major deterrents to food security, the authors' despair of providing adequate food for all without "renewed efforts through new ways of thinking."

The report suggests that "solutions may be closer than we think" to solving the problem of more than 2 billion people lacking access to safe drinking water and more than double that amount having no access to safe sanitation. The key, according to the Report, is to use nature to create a cost-effective way to address these problems while also providing "environmental, social, and economic benefits." The authors point out that water has been a pressing concern and in some areas of the world, a "critical national concern." They argue that business as usual will result in the failure of the international community to address goals created by international bodies regarding adequate water supplies. The report examines the water crisis from six inter-related contexts "water scarcity and insecurity; water-related disasters; water, sanitation, and health crisis; water infrastructure deterioration and destruction; unsustainable development; and ecosystem degradation."

In this current review of the world's energy outlook, the International Energy Agency, an autonomous UN agency established in 1974, surveys the current global energy system. The report points to four "large-scale shifts" in the system: "the rapid deployment and falling costs of clean energy technologies . . . the growing electrification of energy … the shift to a more service-oriented economy and a cleaner energy mix in China … and the resilience of shale gas and tight oil in the United States." The Report concludes that these are good signs for the world's attempts to address non-renewable energy resources such as oil. Chris Martenson, a fellow at the Post Carbon Institute, presents a forceful argument that within a couple of years, either the world economy will outgrow the supply of oil or the economy will collapse, both undesirable outcomes.

Issue: Is the Paris Climate Change Agreement Working?
Yes: **Todd Stern**, from "Why the Paris Agreement Works," *The Brookings Institution* (2017)
No: **Kelly Levin and Taryn Fransen**, from "Understanding the 'Emissions Gap' in 5 Charts," World Resources Institute (2017)

Todd Stern, a senior fellow at the Brookings Institution, suggests that the negotiated agreement had to clear eight distinct hurdles. He argues that the final agreement was successful in overcoming all of them and provides arguments for his position. He concludes that, unlike all attempts in the previous 20 years, this agreement breaks new ground that "needs to be defended, supported and implemented." His bottom line is that the agreement is working. The World Resources Institute report co-authored by Senior Associate Kelly Levin and Senior Fellow Taryn Fransen uses five charts to explain the "emissions gap,' the "difference between the emissions level countries have pledged to achieve … and the level consistent with limiting warming to well below 2 degrees."

Unit 2: Expanding Global Forces and Movements

Issue: Will The International Community Be Able To Successfully Address The Next Global Pandemic?
Yes: **Arthur G. Fitzmaurice, et al.**, from "Contributions of the US Centers for Disease Control and Prevention in Implementing the Global Health Security Agenda in 17 Partner Countries," *Emerging Infectious Diseases* (2017)
No: **Meera Senthilingam**, from "Seven Reasons We're at More Risk than Ever of a Global Pandemic," *CNN* (2017)

The U.S. Centers for Disease Control and Prevention article describes the efforts of the Global Health Security Agenda, a partnership among a variety of national governments and both international governmental and non-governmental organizations to increase the capacities of countries to respond to infectious disease pandemics around the globe. Launched in 2014, the partnership has made significant progress in helping 17 countries achieve a list of stated objectives. Meera Senthilingam, Editor for CNN Health and Wellness, points to the view of public health experts that the world is at a greater risk than ever before in history of a global pandemic along the magnitude of SARS, swine flu, Ebola, and Zika. Seven major global trends, the author suggests, contribute to the increased likelihood and magnitude of such pandemics.

Issue: Do Adequate Strategies Exist to Combat Human Trafficking?
Yes: **Office to Monitor and Combat Trafficking in Persons**, from "Meeting the Global Challenge: Effective Strategies to Prevent Human Trafficking," *Trafficking in Persons Report 2016*, U.S. Department of State (2016)
No: **United Nations Office on Drugs and Crime (UNODC)**, from "Global Report on Trafficking in Persons 2016," *Austria: United Nations* (2016)

The U.S. Department of State Report describes its two decades effort to combat human trafficking, focusing on the three Ps–prosecution, protection, and protection. While the report discusses challenges to the State Department's efforts, it focuses on success stories and examples in the fight against human trafficking. The 2016 United Nations Office on Drugs and Crime report spells out the magnitude of the problem with the compilation of major data collected about human trafficking. The most worrisome development since the previous report is the increase in the movement of refugees and migrants.

Issue: Is Saudi Arabia Moving toward Increased Democratization and/or Liberalization?
Yes: **Thomas L. Friedman**, from "Saudi Arabia's Arab Spring, At Last," *The New York Times* (2017)
No: "Freedom in the World 2018: Democracy in Crisis," *Freedom House* (2018)

Thomas L. Friedman, a long-time analyst of the Middle East, argues that the most significant reforms taking place in the region today are in Saudi Arabia, mainly due to the efforts of the young, controversial Crown Prince Mohammed bin Salman. Friedman travels to the Kingdom to interview the Crown Prince and Saudi citizens about these religious and economic reforms. He comes away from these conversations convinced the country is moving in a more liberal, open direction. Freedom House is a U.S. government-funded non-governmental organization that annually assesses a country's degree of political freedoms and civil liberties. It relies on a large number of reputable analysts and academic advisors, and subjects its methodology to public examination by experts. Its most recent analysis for Saudi Arabia concludes that the country's status is "Not Free" and documented examples of crackdowns on reform advocates.

Issue: Is Artificial Intelligence a Threat to Humanity?
Yes: Tim Adams, from "Artificial Intelligence: 'We're like Children Playing with a Bomb,' " *The Guardian* (2016)
No: Max Tegmark, from "Benefits and Risks of Artificial Intelligence," *Future of Life Institute* (2018)

Tim Adams, in relaying the thoughts of Oxford philosopher Nick Bostrom, contends that AI represents an existential threat to humanity because AI will develop the ability to replicate its intelligence and learn at a much faster rate than humans. Max Tegmark, an MIT professor, contends that AI can and will be a great boon for humanity and will be shaped by its ability to problem solve and not by some myth regarding its own capacity to "turn on" humanity at some point.

Issue: Is the West Losing the Global Information War?
Yes: Alina Polyakova and Spencer P. Boyer, from "The Future of Political Warfare: Russia, the West, and the Coming Age of Global Digital Competition," *The New Geopolitics* (2018)
No: Molly C. McKew, from "Putin's Real Long Game," *Politico Magazine* (2017)

The authors, both from The Brookings Institution, contend that we are at the nexus of technology, big data and AI such that states and other entities can now engage in political warfare without great consequences and at low cost. They argue that this is exactly what Russia is engaged in right now throughout Europe and the United States. The author, a former advisor to the president of the country of Georgia, argues that the Russian strategy is to so undermine truth and reality in the West so that basic institutions and social order breaks down. The author articulates ways that the West can thwart such actions and win.

Issue: Is Authoritarianism on the Rise or Will Democracy Endure?
Yes: Suzanne Sataline, from "Democracy Under Stress: Is Representative Government in Retreat Worldwide?" *CQ Researcher* (2017)
No: Kurt Weyland and Raúl L. Madrid, from "Liberal Democracy Is Stronger Than Trump's Populism," *The American Interest* (2017)

Suzanne Sataline, a writer based in Hong Kong, contends that if one looks at the past 100 years of development, democracy is clearly in retreat and under attack from a variety of social/political and technological forces. Kurt Weyland and Raúl Madrid, both University of Texas professors, use the growth populism in the West as represented by the election of Donald Trump to argue that democracy is resilient, still strong and capable of thwarting any permanent growth of authoritarianism.

Issue: Is the Power of Social Media Undermining Democracy?
Yes: Erica Chenoweth, from "How Social Media Helps Dictators," *Foreign Policy* (2016)
No: Helen Margetts, from "Of Course Social Media Is Transforming Politics. But It's Not to Blame for Brexit and Trump," *World Economic Forum* (2016)

Erica Chenoweth, University of Denver professor, contends that social media has been hijacked in part by authoritarian and antidemocratic forces to sew doubt and undermine democratic institutions around the globe. Helen Margetts, professor at the Oxford Internet Institute of the University of Oxford, argues that social media has been used for all kinds of reasons both democratic, social justice and authoritarian but sounding the alarm that it is now a force for anti-demotic impulses is overtaking its role and missing the larger context.

Unit 3: The New Global Security Agenda

Issue: Were Efforts to Withdraw the United States from the Iran Nuclear Agreement Misguided?
Yes: Philip Gordon and Richard Nephew, from "The 'Worst Deal Ever' That Actually Wasn't," *The Atlantic* (2017)
No: "Remarks by President Trump on the Joint Comprehensive Plan of Action," The White House (2018)

The authors, both policymakers who were part of the team that negotiated the Iran nuclear deal, argue it is doing what it was supposed to do: prevent Iran from acquiring enough fissile material for a nuclear weapon, demonstrate to the Iranian public the benefits of cooperation with the international community, and buy time for potential changes in Iranian politics and foreign policy – and therefore, efforts to walk away from the agreement are misguided. In announcing that the United States was leaving the Iran nuclear agreement, President Trump argued that the deal "allowed Iran to continue enriching uranium and, over time, reach the brink of a nuclear breakout." He further stated that Iran's claim it desired a peaceful nuclear program "was a lie."

Furthermore, the President also suggested that the deal failed to address Iran's development of ballistic missiles and provides "inadequate mechanisms to prevent, detect, and punish cheating . . . ."

Issue: Has the Assad Regime Won the Syrian Civil War?
Yes: Daniel R. DePetris, from "How Bashar al-Assad Won the War in Syria," *The National Interest* (2017)
No: Krishnadev Calamur, from "No One Is Winning the Syrian Civil War," *The Atlantic* (2018)

Daniel R. DePetris, an analyst at Wikistrat, Inc., suggests that early in the Syrian conflict it appeared that Assad was on his way out. But five years later everything had been turned around and the world came to understand "how wily, clever, and street-smart" the government had been all along, leaving Assad in power with the help of Russian and Iranian support. Krishnadev Calamur, a senior editor at The Atlantic, argues that President Assad and his regime have not won the war. It is more accurate to say that Russian, Iranian, and Kurdish forces have emerged as the victors. He writes that Assad would not be able to survive in power on his own, without Russian and Iranian support. And, while Assad's goal is to regain control of the entire country, Syria as a unified nation has effectively collapsed.

Issue: Is a Two-state Diplomatic Solution to the Israeli-Palestinian Conflict Possible or Likely in the Near Future?
Yes: Mara Rudman and Brian Katulis, from "A Practical Plan on the Israeli–Palestinian Front," *Center for American Progress* (2016)
No: **Nickolay Mladenov**, from "Security Council Briefing on the Situation in the Middle East," *UNESCO* (2018)

The Center for American Progress study, authored by two experienced government analysts who served under Democratic administrations, suggests six building blocks for a two-state solution to the Israeli–Palestinian problem. The study's authors, respected scholars of Middle East affairs, argue that despite a number of factors making a solution more difficult, progress toward a two-state solution can be made if attention is paid to these building blocks. Nicolay Mladenov, the UN Special Coordinator for the Middle East Peace Process, suggests that it is a grim time for those seeking peace in the Middle East. For him, "much of the Middle East continues to be in the grips of an ongoing human tragedy of immense proportions." He argues that those opposed to peace are gaining confidence with each passing day, and they are hindering progress by pushing unilateral facts on the ground that are "blocking the pathway back to the negotiating table."

Issue: Is Russia Increasingly Pursuing a Strategy to Threaten Democratic Regimes Throughout Europe and the Western World?
Yes: Larry Diamond, from "Russia and the Threat to Liberal Democracy," *The Atlantic* (2016)
No: Mark Lawrence Schrad, from "Vladimir Putin Isn't a Supervillain," *Foreign Policy* (2017)

Larry Diamond, a senior fellow at the Hoover Institution and at the Freeman Spogli Institute at Stanford University, argues that Putin "has embraced an opportunistic but sophisticated campaign to sabotage democracy." For Diamond, of greatest danger is the "alarming decay of liberal democracy in Europe and the United States." Mark Lawrence Schrad, a Villanova University professor, suggests that Western commentary on Russia's foreign policy can be placed into two rather extreme camps. One approach calls Putin a global menace while the other sees a country falling apart. Schrad argues that the reality is somewhere in between. "Russia is not nearly the global menace that many fear, nor is it doomed to collapse." Accordingly, he believes that any analysis must be a "sober assessment of the country's capabilities and limitations."

Issue: Will China Be the Next Global Superpower?
Yes: Kenneth Rapoza, from "The Future: China's Rise, America's Decline," *Forbes* (2017)
No: Alan Dupont, from "Will China Rule the World? Asian Superpower Faces Uncertain Future," *The Australian* (2016)

Forbes writer Kenneth Rapoza argues that most economic and social indicators point to both a steady rise for China and a decline for the United States. When the crossover point occurs will be is anyone's guess. Dupont contends that despite China's enormous gifs and potential, it still faces great obstacles in its quest to move from regional dominance to true superpower status.

Issue: Can Diplomacy, Rather than Military Action, Result in North Korea Denuclearizing?
Yes: Uri Friedman, from "Here's What Trump Actually Achieved with North Korea," *The Atlantic* (2018)
No: Brian Barrett, from "All the Times North Korea Promised to Denuclearize," *WIRED* (2018)

Uri Freidman, global affairs staff writer at *The Atlantic*, argues a case can be made that diplomacy might finally work this time in getting North Korea to denuclearize after the latest round of negotiations at the leader level. Among the author's six reasons for optimism is the fact that the two countries are talking to each other at a political decision-maker level—putting the politics first and at a very high level—and that any North Korean denuclearization pledge such as this latest one is significant. Brian Barrett, News Editor at *WIRED*, is not hopeful, suggesting that this is simply another example of the pattern where North Korea promises to "abandon nuclear efforts" with "surprising regularity" and then does not follow through on its promises. He argues that North Korea uses the promise of denuclearization as a "bargaining chip in times of desperation" and details the multiple rounds of negotiations over the past several decades that have all ended in failure.

Rick Stella, Outdoor Editor of *Digital Trends*, makes the argument that in the aftermath of 9/11, innovation and technology in warfare became of paramount importance. As a result, cyber warfare has become the dominant trend in weapons research, development and ultimately application. Daniel Moore, a threat intelligence engineer, makes that case that it is too easy to simply argue that if technology is sophisticated, then it means that all warfare will be cyber. He maintains that one must define one's terms before hitting the default button that all warfare is moving in a cyber direction.

The authors, both writers at *Politico*, through working with former Secretary of Defense Bill Perry paint a pessimistic picture of the likelihood of a nuclear war in the coming years due to issues such as nuclear proliferation, great power rivalry and increasing tensions among key global actors. Stephen Walt, Harvard professor at the JFK School of Government, articulates a nuanced critique of nuclear politics but still maintains that the use of the nuclear deterrent has and will continue to make nuclear war less likely over time despite changes dimensions in the current global landscape.

Preface

This volume reflects the dynamic nature of the contemporary world in which we live. Not only are we now witnessing a dramatic leap in the scope of global change, but we are also experiencing a *rate* of change in the world perhaps unparalleled in recorded history. Change in the international system is not a new phenomenon. Since the Treaty of Westphalia ushered in the concept of the modern sovereign nation-state in 1648, global change has been with us. But earlier manifestations of change were characterized by infrequent bursts of system-altering episodes followed by long periods of "normalcy," where the processes and structures of the international system demonstrated regularity or consistency.

In the early 1800s, the post-Westphalian global system was challenged by a French general turned emperor, Napoleon Bonaparte, who sought to export his newly created utopian vision of the French Revolution beyond the boundaries of France to the rest of the world by force. Napoleon was eventually repelled by a coalition of major powers intent on preserving the world as these countries knew it. Soon nineteenth-century Europe was being transformed by the intrusion of the Industrial Revolution on the daily lives of average citizens and national leaders alike. Technological advances enhanced the capacity of countries to dramatically increase their military capabilities, achieving the ability to project power far beyond their national borders in a much shorter time. Other threats to the existing world order also emerged, the most significant being another failed attempt by a European power, this time Germany, to expand its influence via a major war, later to be called World War I, throughout the continent. The postwar map of Europe reflected major consequences of the abortive German effort.

Almost immediately, the international system was threatened by a newly emergent virulent ideology intent on exporting its tenets throughout the world. Communism had gained a foothold in Russia, and soon its leaders were eager to transport it across the continent, threatening to destroy the existing economic order and, by definition, its political counterpart. Shortly thereafter, a competing virulent ideology, fascism, emerged. Under its manipulation by the Nazis led by a new German leader, Adolf Hitler, and by the militarists in Japan, the international system was once again greatly threatened. Six long years of war and unthinkable levels of devastation and destruction followed, until the fascist threat was turned back. The communist threat persisted, however, until late in the century, when it also virtually disappeared with the collapse of the Soviet Union, felled by its own weaknesses.

In the interim, new challenges to the global order arose in the form of a set of issues like no other during the 500-year history of the nation-state system. The nature of these issues and the pace at which they dominated the global agenda began to quickly reshape the international system. This new agenda took root in the late 1960s, when astute observers began to identify disquieting trends: quickening population growth in the poorer sectors of the globe, growing disruptions in the world's ability to feed its population, increasing shortfalls in required resources, and expanding evidence of negative environmental impacts of human development. Some of these issues—like decreasing levels of adequate supplies of food, energy, and water—emerged as a result of both increased population growth and increased per capita levels of consumption. Dramatic population increases, in turn, resulted in changes in global population dynamics, increasing aged populations or massive new urbanization patterns. The emergence of this new set of issues dovetailed with another phenomenon, globalization, which has emphasized increasing flow of information, goods, and services through innovative technology and a resultant diffusion of regional cultures throughout the globe. Globalization has fundamentally changed how both state and nonstate actors address political, economic, and social issues, including those mentioned above. And the emergence and proliferation of the Internet to every corner of the globe has dramatically affected the ability of individuals to communicate with one another and to influence one another everywhere. This influence may be for good (bringing together people advocating for democratic change) or, conversely, for evil (helping terrorist groups spread their ideologies further and more quickly).

The major consequence of the confluence of these events is that the pace of change has greatly accelerated. No longer is change measured in centuries or even decades; it is now often measured in years or even months. These global issues are characterized by increased complexity, increased geographical impact, increased resistance to solution, and increased fluidity—all presenting new and difficult challenges to the international system.

One only has to compare the world of the 1960s to the world of today to grasp the difference. When students first began to study these issues in the early 1960s, their written analysis was accomplished either by putting pen to pad or by engaging an unwieldy typewriter. Their experience with a computer was limited to watching a moon landing through the eyes of NASA Mission Control. The use of phones was relegated to a location where a cord could be plugged into a wall socket. Their written correspondence with someone beyond their immediate location had a stamp on it. Their reading of news, both serious and frivolous, occurred via a newspaper. Visual news invaded their space in 30-minute daily segments from three major TV networks. Being entertained required some effort, usually away from the confines of their homes or dorm rooms. Today, of course, the personal computer, cell phones, and tablet devices such as iPads have transformed the way students learn, the way they communicate with one another, and the way they entertain themselves. Facebook, Twitter, and YouTube have joined our vocabulary, and humans have at their fingertips more information than at any point in history.

The age of globalization and the instant information age have accelerated, affecting and transforming trends that began several decades ago. No longer are nation-states the most dominant actors on the global stage. Countries are increasingly challenged by an array of other actors—international governmental organizations, private international groups, multinational corporations, and important individuals—who might be better equipped to address newly emerging issues or who might also serve as the source of yet other problems.

The economic collapse of a decade ago, or what some call "the Great Recession," is part of the story of this rapid globalization. Economic shifts were greatly accelerated throughout the global community by technology, interdependence, and connectivity such that governments, analysts, and the public at large were unable to comprehend the destabilizing events as they happened. These shifts are still occurring, and it will take years, if not decades, to emerge from this information revolution with a new set of rules of the road.

As a result in part of this increasingly globalized world, a push for greater and more extreme nationalism, along with threatening echoes of authoritarianism advanced by populist leaders, has recently been sweeping across Western democracies. Relations between states such as Russia, China, and the United States have been shifting as a result of complex economic and political dynamics.

And the Middle East remains unsettled for a number of reasons. First, the ongoing tension between Sunni Arab states and Iran is playing itself out in any number of proxy conflicts. Second, the initial optimism that the Arab Spring might bring a freer and more prosperous life to millions of people across the region has given way to the reality of civil war (in Syria and Yemen), new autocrats (Egypt), or chaos (Libya). Third, add to this terrible mix fact that any number of global and regional powers have entered the fray in the Middle East to advance their own agendas.

The format of *Taking Sides: Clashing Views on Global Issues*, Tenth Edition, follows the successful formula of other books in the Taking Sides series. The book begins with an introduction to the emergence of global issues, the new age of globalization, the effect of 9/11, the recent global economic crisis, a reemerging Russia, and the rise of revolutionary movements throughout North Africa and the Middle East—and the international community's response to these events—that characterize the first quarter of the twenty-first century. This is followed by a discussion of recent trends in the new millennium that seek to challenge the existing global end at the beginning of this new millennium. It then addresses three kinds of global issues. The first set focuses on population-related issues such as an aging population, which represents a global issue by itself, but which also affects the parameters of many other global issues such as food and water, and a range of problems associated with global resources such as energy, and their environmental impact such as climate change. The second set of issues focuses on widely disparate expanding forces and movements across national boundaries brought on by the dramatically increasing ease with which borders may be transgressed such as global pandemics, human trafficking, human rights, antidemocratic movements, and the rising power of social media and the global information war. The third set addresses issues relating to the global security agenda, such as Iran's nuclear program, the civil war in Syria, the Israeli–Palestinian conflict, the threat of Russia against Western democracies, China as the next superpower, how to deal with North Korea's nuclear weapons, and the emergence of cyber-related phenomena that manifest themselves in a variety of ways, from warfare to global crime to economic advantage.

Book Organization

Each issue has two selections, one pro and one con. The readings are preceded by *Learning Outcomes* and an issue *Introduction* that sets the stage for the debate by laying out both sides of the issue and briefly describes the two selections. Each issue concludes with *Critical Thinking and*

Reflection questions, an *Is There Common Ground?* section discussing alternative viewpoints or approaches as well as *Additional Resources* and *Internet References* for further exploration of the issue.

Changes to this edition This 10th edition represents a significant revision. Thirteen of the 21 issues are new issues and all 42 "Yes/No" articles are new readings.

James E. Harf
Maryville University

Marie E. Harf
Department of State (2013–2017)
Central Intelligence Agency (2006–2011)

Mark Owen Lombardi
Maryville University

Editors of This Volume

James E. Harf currently serves as a professor of political science as well as associate vice president and director of the Office of Study Abroad at Maryville University in St. Louis. He spent most of his career at The Ohio State University, where he holds the title of professor emeritus. Among his over three-dozen authored and edited books are *The Wise World Traveler: Becoming a Part of All That You Meet* (Agapy LLC, 2015), *The Unfolding Legacy of 9/11* (University Press of America, 2004), *World Politics and You: A Student Companion to International Politics on the World Stage*, 5th ed. (Brown & Benchmark, 1995), and *The Politics of Global Resources* (Duke University Press, 1986). His first novel, *Memories of Ivy* (Ivy House Publishing Group, 2005), about life as a university professor, was published in 2005. He also coedited a four-book series on the global issues of population, food, energy, and the environment, as well as three other book series on national security education, international studies, and international business. As a staff member on President Jimmy Carter's Commission on Foreign Language and International Studies in the late 1970s, he was responsible for undergraduate education recommendations. He also served 15 years as executive director of the Consortium for International Studies Education. He has been a frequent TV and radio commentator on international issues.

Marie E. Harf is a national security policy and communications strategist who currently serves as a FOX News Channel on-air analyst and cohost of FOX News Radio's "Benson and Harf," a daily two-hour radio show focused on the latest headlines emanating from the nation's capital. Before joining FOX, Marie held a variety of senior roles in government and politics. She began her career at the Central Intelligence Agency as a Middle East Analyst and later served as a key member of Secretary John Kerry's team during his tenure leading the State Department. In 2012, Marie ran all national security and foreign policy issues for President Barack Obama's reelection campaign. In academia, she has served as a fellow at Georgetown University's Institute of Politics and Public Service and currently sits on the Dean's Council of Indiana University's School of Global and International Studies. Marie received a master's degree in foreign affairs from the University of Virginia and a Bachelor of Arts degree in political science with concentrations in Jewish Studies and Russian and Eastern European Studies from Indiana University.

Mark Owen Lombardi is president and chief executive officer of Maryville University in St. Louis, Missouri. Maryville is a comprehensive private university of over 8,000 students and in 2017 was named the third fastest growing university in the United States by the *Chronicle of Higher Education*. In addition to over 13 years as president, Lombardi is coeditor and author of *The Unfolding Legacy of 9/11* (University Press of America, 2004) and coeditor of *Perspectives of Third World Sovereignty: The Post-Modern Paradox* (Macmillian, 1996). Lombardi has authored numerous articles and book chapters on such topics as U.S. foreign policy, African political economy, the cold war, and the revolution in higher education. Lombardi is a member of numerous civic organizations and boards locally and nationally, and he has given over 200 speeches to local and national groups on topics ranging from the revolution in higher education to U.S. politics, international affairs, and U.S. foreign policy. He has also appeared over 75 times as a political commentator for local and national news outlets. He is also author of the forthcoming *Pivot: A Vision for the New University* (2019).

Acknowledgment

We extend our heartfelt thanks to McGraw-Hill editor Mary Foust for her professionalism and flexibility in making the completion of this work possible.

To my daughter, Marie: May your world conquer those global issues left unresolved by my generation. (James E. Harf)

For my parents, Dr. James E. and Jane Ax Harf who made me want to explore and understand the world. (Marie E. Harf)

For Betty and Marty who instilled a love of education and a need to explore the world. (Mark Owen Lombardi)

Editors/Academic Advisory Board

Members of the Academic Advisory Board are instrumental in the final selection of articles for each edition of TAKING SIDES. Their review of articles for content, level, and appropriateness provides critical direction to the editor and staff. We think that you will find their careful consideration well reflected in this volume.

Academic Advisory Board Members

Tahereh Alavi Hojjat
Desales University

Deborah Carter
Coahoma Community College

Dori Danko
Grand Valley State University

V. Daviero
Pasco-Hernando State College

Thomas P. Dolan
Columbus State University

Gary Donato
Bentley University

Tahmineh Entessar
Webster University

Jeffrey Fahrenwald
Rockford University

Mark Fenton
University of Wisconsin, Stout

Ronald Fritze
Athena State University

Ronald Helms
Wright State University

Rolf Hemmerling
Webster University

Samira Hussein
Johnson County Community College

Alexander Katkov
Johnson & Wales University

Sukanya Kemp
University of Akron

Tadesse Kidane-Mariam
Edinboro University of Pennsylvania

Dongho Kim
SUNY Empire State College

Howard Lehman
University of Utah

Christopher Leskiw
University of the Cumberlands

Michael J. Littman
SUNY Buffalo State College

Mike Madaris
William Carey University

Allison McGullion
West Kentucky Community & Technical College

Victoria McKee
University of Oklahoma

Mary K. McManamon
Lake Erie College

Lois McWhorter
Somerset Community College

Ray Melcher
Alvernia University

Mark Mishler
Seton Hall University

Alison Mukweyi
Wiley College

Kay Murnan
Ozarks Technical Community College

Charles Nichols
Kentucky State University

Raphael Chijioke Njoku
Idaho State University

Charles Perabeau
Olivet Nazarene University

Mark Ryan
Hawkeye Community College

Lester Sandres Rapalo
Union County College

Introduction

Threats of the New Millennium

As the new millennium dawned almost two decades ago, the world witnessed two very different events whose impacts have been far reaching, profound, and in many ways have shaped the trajectory of global issues ever since. The first was the era that brought deadly mass terrorism to the shores of the United States with the tragedy of 9/11. This act rocked the international community and shifted the focus of many national and global leaders throughout the world. The aftermath and the forces that it unleashed have shaped many if not all of the global security issues ever since. The focused interest of national policy makers was soon transformed into a war on terrorism, later transformed into a long continuous war on terrorists, while average citizens from the heartland of the United States to the urban centers of Europe, the peoples of North Africa to the Sunni and Shi'ite communities of the Islamic world have been directly impacted. Unfortunately, as the millennium's first decade ended, other challenges to global welfare and security also emerged. At the global level, a severe financial crisis forced world leaders to question the major tenets of contemporary capitalism. At the national level, a reemerging Russian presence, flexing its new economic muscles based on energy and backed by a growing military might, brought back fears of a new Cold War. Several countries long considered part of the developing world made significant strides toward the development of nuclear weapons. And throughout North Africa and the Middle East, citizens took to the streets to protest decades of autocratic rule by despotic rulers and to seek more democratic government.

The second event at the beginning of the millennium was less dramatic and certainly did not receive the same fanfare but still has had both short- and long-term ramifications for the global community in the twenty-first century. This was the creation of a set of ambitious Millennium Development Goals (MDG) by the United Nations. In September 2000, 189 national governments committed to eight major goals in an initiative known as the UN MDG: eradicate extreme poverty and hunger; achieve universal primary education; promote gender equality and empower women; reduce child mortality; improve maternal health; combat HIV/AIDS, malaria, and other diseases; ensure environmental sustainability; and develop a global partnership for development. This initiative was important not only because the United Nations was setting an actionable 15-year agenda against a relatively new set of global issues but also because it signified a major change in how the international community would henceforth address such problems confronting humankind. The new initiative represented recognition of (1) shared responsibility between rich and poor nations for solving such problems, (2) a link between goals, (3) the paramount role to be played by national governments in the process, and (4) the need for measurable outcome indicators of success. The UN MDG initiative went virtually unnoticed by much of the public, although governmental decision makers involved with the United Nations understood its significance. As we approach the 15-year time line for implementation of these millennium goals, the success rate has been mixed at best as the commitments of time and money made earlier have not materialized as planned.

As we are about to enter the third decade of this new millennium, we have begun to witness yet a third event that affects the consequences of the two earlier events just described. In the United States and throughout Europe and parts of Asia, a wave of extreme nationalism and populism has begun to manifest itself in sharp contrast to globalization exemplified by the UN Millennium Goals. Candidate Donald Trump's Make America Great Again and his subsequent movement away from multilateralism in trade, nuclear security, and other issues is but one example of this emerging nationalism. The relatively strong showing of the far-right party in the recent French election and current challenges to the German leader from nationalist forces are other examples of this anti-multilateralism, as are new Russian foreign policy strategies and rise of leaders in Eastern European countries such as Hungary. While nationalism has never been abandoned by national leaders in the post–World War II move toward globalization, extreme variants of the theme are a new challenge to world movers and shakers.

These three major events, although vastly different, symbolize the world in which we now find ourselves, a world far more complex and more violent than either the earlier one characterized by the cold war struggle between the United States and the Soviet Union or the post–cold war era of the 1990s, where global and national leaders struggled to identify and then find their proper place in the post–cold war world order. Consider the first event, the 9/11 tragedy. This act reminds us all that the use of power in pursuit of political goals in earlier centuries is still an option for those throughout the world who believe themselves disadvantaged or under attack, but what is different and profound is the global reach of terrorism and the expanding array of tools available to those groups. Formally, declared wars fought by regular national military forces publicly committed (at least on paper) to the tenets of just war theory have now been replaced by a plethora of "quasi-military tactics" whose defining characteristics are asymmetrical, civilian targeted, and designed to undermine the very foundation of open societies, freedom. At the same time, a few rogue states, Iran and North Korea, for example, have accelerated and in some respects attained the ultimate in weaponry (nuclear) to further their own national goals.

On the other hand, the second event of the new century, the UN MDG initiative, symbolizes the other side of the global coin, the recognition that the international community is also beset with a number of problems that transcend national security and call into question the very viability of the Earth's ecosystem. The past four decades have witnessed the emergence and thrust to prominence of a number of new problems relating to social, economic, and environmental characteristics of the citizens who inhabit this planet. These problems impact the basic quality of life of global inhabitants in ways very different from the scourges of military violence. But their impact is just as profound. At the heart of this global change affecting the global system and its inhabitants for good or for ill is a phenomenon called globalization. Despite the rise of extreme nationalism, globalization still represents the dominant path favored by many of the world's leaders.

The Age of Globalization

The cold war era, marked by the domination of two superpowers in the decades following the end of World War II, has given way to a new era called globalization. This new epoch is characterized by a dramatic shrinking of the globe in terms of travel and communication, increased participation in global policy-making by an expanding array of national and nonstate actors, and an exploding set of integrated problems with ever growing consequences. While the tearing down of the Berlin Wall 21 years ago dramatically symbolized the end of the cold war era, the creation of the Internet, with its ability to

connect around the world, and the fallen World Trade Center, with its dramatic illustration of vulnerability, symbolize the new paradigm of connectivity, impact, cooperation, and violence.

Globalization is a fluid and complex phenomenon that manifests itself in thousands of wondrous and equally disturbing ways. In the past couple of decades, national borders have shrunk or disappeared, with a resultant increase in the movement of ideas, products, resources, finances, and people throughout the globe. This reality has brought with it great advances and challenges. For example, the ease with which people and objects move throughout the globe has greatly magnified fears like the spread of disease. The term "epidemic" has been replaced by the phrase "global pandemic," as virulent scourges unleashed in one part of the globe now have greater potential to find their way to the far corners of the planet. The world has also come to fear an expanded potential for terrorism, as new technologies combined with increasing cultural friction and socioeconomic disparities have conspired to make the world far less safe than it had been. The pistol that killed the Austrian Archduke in Sarajevo in 1914, ushering in World War I, has been replaced by the jumbo jet used as a missile to bring down the World Trade Center, snuffing out the lives of thousands of innocent victims. We now live in an era of global reach for both good and ill, where a small group or a single individual can touch the hearts of people around the world with acts of kindness or can shatter their dreams with acts of terror.

This increase in the movement of information and ideas has ushered in global concerns over cultural imperialism and religious/ethnic wars. The ability both to retrieve and to disseminate information in the contemporary era will have an impact in this century as great as, if not greater than, the telephone, radio, and television in the last century. The potential for global good or ill is mind-boggling. Finally, traditional notions of great power security embodied in the cold war rivalry have given way to concerns about terrorism, genocide, nuclear proliferation, cultural conflict, rogue states, and the diminishing role of international law.

Globalization heightens our awareness of a vast array of global issues that will challenge individuals as well as governmental and nongovernmental actors. Everyone has become a global actor and so each has policy impact. This text seeks to identify those issues that are central to the discourse on the impact of globalization. The issues in this volume provide a broad overview of the mosaic of global issues that will affect students' daily lives.

What Is a Global Issue?

We begin by addressing the basic characteristics of a *global issue*.[1] By definition, the word *issue* suggests disagreement among several related dimensions:

1. Whether a problem exists and how it comes about.
2. The characteristics of the problem.
3. The preferred future alternatives or solutions.
4. How these preferred futures are to be obtained.

These problems are real, vexing, and controversial because policy makers bring to their analyses different historical experiences, values, goals, and objectives. These differences impede and may even prevent successful problem-solving. In short, the key ingredient of an issue is disagreement.

The word *global* in the phrase *global issue* is what makes the set of problems confronting the human race today far different from those that challenged earlier generations. Historically, problems were confined to a village, city, or region. The capacity of the human race to fulfill its daily needs was limited to a much smaller space: the immediate environment. In 1900, 90 percent of all humanity was born, lived, and died within a 50-mile radius. Today, a third of the world's population travel to one or more countries. In the United States, 75 percent of people move at least 100 miles away from their homes and most travel to places their grandparents could only dream about.

What does this mobility mean? It suggests that a vast array of issues are now no longer only local or national but are global in scope, including but not limited to food resources, trade, energy, health care, the environment, disease, natural disasters, conflict, cultural rivalry, populism, rogue states, democratic revolutions, and nuclear Armageddon.

The character of these issues is thus different from those of earlier eras. First, they transcend national boundaries and impact virtually every corner of the globe. In effect, these issues help make national borders increasingly meaningless. Environmental pollution or poisonous gases do not recognize or respect national borders. Birds carrying the avian flu and nuclear radiation leaking from disabled power plants have no knowledge of political boundaries.

Second, these new issues cannot be resolved by the autonomous action of a single actor, be it a national government, international organization, or multinational corporation. A country cannot guarantee its own energy or food security without participating in a global energy or food system. Third, these issues are characterized by a wide array of value systems. To a family in the developing world, giving birth to a fifth or sixth child may contribute to the family's immediate economic well-being. But to a research scholar at the United Nations Population Fund, the consequence of such an action multiplied across the entire developing world leads to expanding poverty and resource depletion.

Fourth, these issues will not go away. They require specific policy action by a consortium of local, national, and international leaders. Simply ignoring the issue cannot eliminate the threat of chemical or biological terrorism, for example. If global warming does exist, it will not disappear unless specific policies are developed and implemented.

These issues are also characterized by their persistence over time. The human race has developed the capacity to manipulate its external environment and, in so doing, has created a host of opportunities and challenges. The accelerating pace of technological change suggests that global issues will proliferate and will continue to challenge human beings throughout the next millennium.

In the final analysis, however, a global issue is defined as such only through mutual agreement by a host of actors within the international community. Some may disagree about the nature, severity, or presence of a given issue. These concerns then become areas of focus after a significant number of actors (states, international organizations, the United Nations, and others) begin to focus systematic and organized attention on the issue itself.

The Nexus of Global Issues and Globalization

Since 1989, the world has been caught in the maelstrom of globalization. Throughout the 1990s and into the twenty-first century, scholars and policy makers have struggled to define this new era. As the early years of the new century ushered in a different and heightened level of violence, a sense of urgency emerged. At first, some analyzed the new era in terms of the victory of Western or American ideals, the dominance of global capitalism, and the spread of democracy versus the use of religious fanaticism by the have-nots of the world as a ploy to rearrange power within the international system. But recent events call into question assumptions about Western victory or the dominance of capitalism. Others have defined this new era simply in terms of the multiplicity of actors now performing on the world stage, noting how states and their sovereignty have declined in importance and impact vis-à-vis . . . others such as multinational corporations and nongovernmental groups like Greenpeace and Amnesty International. Still others have focused on the vital element of technology and its impact on communications; information storage and retrieval; global exchange; and attitudes, culture, and values.

Whether globalization reflects one, two, or all of these characteristics is not as important as the fundamental realization that globalization is the dominant element of a new era in international politics. The globalization revolution now shapes and dictates the agenda. To argue otherwise is frankly akin to insisting on using a rotary phone in an iPhone world. This new period is characterized by several basic traits that greatly impact the definition, analysis, and solution of global issues. They include the following:

- an emphasis on information technology;
- the increasing speed of information and idea flows;
- the ability of global citizens to access information at rapidly growing rates and thus empower themselves for good or for ill;
- a need for greater sophistication and expertise to manage such flows;
- the control and dissemination of technology;
- the cultural diffusion and interaction that comes with information expansion and dissemination.

Each of these areas has helped shape a new emerging global issue agenda. Current issues remain important and, indeed, these factors help us understand them on a much deeper level. Yet globalization has created a new array of problems that is reshaping the international landscape and the dialogue, tools, strategies, and approaches that all global actors will take.

For example, the spread of information technology has made ideas, attitudes, and information more available to people throughout the world. Americans in Columbus, OH, had the ability to log onto the Internet and speak with their counterparts in Kosovo to discover when NATO bombing had begun and to gauge the accuracy of later news reports on the bombing. Norwegian students can share values and customs directly with their counterparts

in South Africa, thereby experiencing cultural attitudes firsthand without the filtering mechanisms of governments or even parents and teachers. Scientific information that is available through computer technology can now be used to build sophisticated biological and chemical weapons of immense destructive capability or equally to promote the dissemination of drugs and medicines outside of "normal" national channels. Ethnic conflicts and genocide between groups of people are now global news, forcing millions to come to grips with issues of intervention, prevention, and punishment. And terrorists in different parts of the globe can communicate readily with one another, transferring plans and even money across national and continental boundaries with ease. And antagonists against autocratic regimes can also communicate with their counterparts within their own society as well as those in neighboring countries, as witnessed by communication flows throughout North Africa and the Middle East among groups and individuals seeking democracy in the early months of 2011.

Globalization is an international system, but it is also a revolutionary force that is rapidly adapting and changing. Because of this fluid nature and the fact that it is both relatively new and largely fueled by the amazing speed of technology, continuing issues are constantly being transformed and new issues are emerging regularly. The nexus of globalization and global issues has now become, in many ways, the defining dynamic of understanding global issues. Whether dealing with new forms of terrorism and new concepts of security, expanding international law, solving ethnic conflicts, dealing with mass migration, coping with individual freedom and access to information, or addressing cultural clash and cultural imperialism, the transition from a cold war world to a globalized world helps us understand in part what these issues are and why they are important. But most importantly, this fundamental realization shapes how governments and people can and must respond.

Identifying the New Global Issue Agenda

The organization of this text reflects the centrality of globalization. The first unit focuses on the continuing global agenda of the post–cold war era. The emphasis is on global population and environmental issues and the nexus between these two phenomena. The next unit addresses the consequences of the decline of national boundaries and the resultant increased international flow of information, ideas, money, and material things in this globalization age, some for good and others for evil. The last unit addresses the new global security dilemma that has developed as a consequence of both the end of the cold war and 9/11.

The revolutionary changes of the last few decades present us with serious challenges unlike any others in human history. However, as in all periods of historic change, we possess significant opportunities to overcome problems. The task ahead is to define these issues, explore their context, and develop solutions that are comprehensive in scope and effect. The role of all is to analyze objectively such problems and search for workable solutions. As students of global issues, your task is to educate yourselves about these issues and become part of the solution.

James E. Harf
Maryville University

Marie E. Harf
U.S. Department of State (2013–2017)
Central Intelligence Agency (2006–2011)

Mark Owen Lombardi
Maryville University

Note

1. The characteristics are extracted from James E. Harf and B. Thomas Trout, *The Politics of Global Resources,* Duke University Press, 1986, pp. 12–28.

Unit 1

UNIT

Global Population and Resources

*I*t is not a coincidence that many contemporary global issues—environmental degradation, resources depletion, global warming and climate change, hunger, energy shortages, and the like—arrived at about the same time as world population growth was exploding, particularly in the developing world, about half a century ago. No matter what the issue was, the resultant presence of a large and fast-growing population occurring simultaneously with initial cracks in the ability of global consumers to easily find required resources not only contributed to the creation of this new set of problems, but it also transformed each of their basic characteristics and exacerbated the ability of national and global policy makers to address them.

As the world entered the new millennium, however, population birth rates, already declining in the developed world, changed again, this time showing declining growth rates caused by lowering birth rates, particularly in the developing world. This, in turn, made the challenge of addressing the newly emerging global agenda initially easier. But these declining rates following decades of significant growth unfortunately led to other problems, such as an aging global population and a declining workforce. The late 20th-century problem of a too large young population vis-à-vis the older generations was reversed as the latter started to grow at a faster pace than the former. The emergence of a growing graying population throughout the globe immediately began to have a significant impact, which has only continued to grow as the demographics of birth and death rates over the past 40+ years play themselves out now and in the coming years and decades. In short, the ability of the global community to respond to any given global issue is diminished by certain population conditions, be it an extremely young consuming population in a poor country in need of producers or an ever-growing senior population for whom additional services are needed.

Nowhere is the problems associated with population more evident than when we consider the planet's resource base. We live on a planet with finite resources, conceptualized in the Spaceship Earth picture taken from outer space. The availability of these resources—water, food, oil, and the like—and the manner in which and the pace at which the planet's inhabitants use them characterize a major component of today's global agenda. Thus, climate change now occupies an extremely important place on the global agenda of nations and nonstate actors alike.

Typically, a wide range of opinion exists about the environment and its resource base—some driven by ideology, some by science, some by economic self-interest, and some by simple noninterest. Disagreements abound about the existence of the problem, the nature of the problem, the scope of the problem, and how to solve the problem. And except for the noninterest group, none are shy about using the media and other venues to advance their own perceptions of what constitutes reality. Nowhere is this more evident, for example, than the debate over climate change and its effects on the ability to take maximum advantage of the planet's resource base.

For some, those "environmentalists" who take a pessimistic view of future resource availability are simply alarmists who have allowed ideology rather than science to drive their convictions. For others, many policy makers and other nonbelievers are to be called out because they chose to ignore overwhelming scientific evidence in order to advance their own political or economic agendas. And among the population are also many uncaring individuals who simply ignore warning signs because they choose to put their heads in the sand out of total noninterest.

Not only does the availability of these resources (production) pose a potential issue, but how we distribute the resources and how we consume them also are thought by many to leave their marks on the planet. A basic set of questions relates to whether these impacts are permanent, too degrading to the planet, too damaging to one's quality of life, or simply beyond a threshold of acceptability.

Selected, Edited, and with Issue Framing Material by:
James E. Harf, *Maryville University*

ISSUE

Is Global Aging a Major Problem?

YES: Richard Jackson, from "Global Aging and the Outlook for Growth and Stability in the Developing World," *Global Aging Institute* (2017)

NO: Maurizio Bussolo, Johannes Koettl, and Emily Sinnott from "Golden Aging: Prospects for Healthy, Active, and Prosperous Aging in Europe and Central Asia," *World Bank Group* (2015)

Learning Outcomes

After reading this issue, you will be able to:

- Gain an understanding of why the 2020s are said to be an upcoming decade of global population aging and population decline.
- Appreciate how a global aging and declining population affect economic growth, living standards, and the shape of the world order.
- Understand how future demographic conditions will especially negatively influence developing societies differently than they have in the developed world.
- Understand why Richard Jackson believes that the decade of the 2020s will be especially disruption for the consequences of global aging.
- Be able to discern the potential for a variety of "demographic storms," in Jackson's words.
- Understand why the World Bank believes that global aging rather than economic stagnation and decline will describe the future.

ISSUE SUMMARY

YES: Richard Jackson, president of the Global Aging Institute (GAI) and formerly of the Center for Strategic and International Studies, argues that demographic trends have affected "the great upheavals of history" from time to time. He points to the upcoming 2020s as a watershed decade when widespread disruptions are likely again to occur. For Jackson, during this next decade, global aging is likely to have a major negative effect on "economic growth, social and political stability, and the shape of the world order."

NO: The World Bank study authors call into question the old adage that demographic trends such as global aging, once put into motion, cannot be stopped and typically lead to increased economic costs. They argue instead that individuals and organizations can adjust to these changing trends with a resultant series of more complex outcomes. They suggest, for example, that aging societies "are not destined to experience stagnation or decline in living standards."

Today more than one in eight inhabitants of this planet is 60 years or older and is growing by 3 percent per year. By 2030, it is projected to be one in six persons, as the elderly population is projected to grow by 56 percent. At that time, there will be more elderly people than persons under the age of nine. Or to put it another way, people 65 and older now outnumber children five years of age and younger. Aging is happening in virtually all regions and all countries of the globe and is especially evident most recently in the developing world as aging rates there surpass those of the developed world. The developed world has been faced with an aging population for some time now as one in five in Europe and North America is aged 60 or older and expected to increase to one in four by 2030 if not higher. By 2050, all regions of the globe except Africa will have about ¼ of their population 60 years old or above, as the number of people aged 60 and older will have doubled from recent levels. This phenomenon has been brought on by declining birth rates and an increasing life expectancy, and it is now being followed by the developing world. Between now and 2030, the number of elderly will grow the fastest in Latin America and the Caribbean, with an estimated 71 percent increase in those over 60 years of age, and the percentages for other regions of the developing world are not far behind.

The phenomenon first appeared during the last quarter of the previous century with the demographic transition from high birth and death rates to lower rates in more affluent countries. The drop in death rates in these countries was a function of two basic factors: (1) the dramatic decline in both infant mortality (within the first year of birth) and child mortality (within the first five years) due to women being healthier during pregnancy and nursing periods and due to the virtually universal inoculation of children against principal childhood diseases and (2) longer life spans, once people reach adulthood, in large part because of medical advances against key adult illnesses, such as cancer and heart disease.

Declining mortality rates yield an aging population in need of a variety of services—heath care, housing, and guards against inflation, for example—provided, in large part, by the tax dollars of the younger, producing sector of society. As the "gray" numbers of society grow, the labor force is increasingly called upon to provide more help for this class.

Declining birth and death rates mean that significantly more services will be needed to provide for the aging populations of the industrialized world, while at the same time, fewer individuals will be joining the workforce to provide the resources to pay for these services. However, some experts say that the new work force will be able to take advantage of the skills of the more aged, unlike previous eras. In order for national economies to grow in the information age, an expanding workforce may not be as important a prerequisite as it once was. Expanding minds, not bodies, may be the key to expanding economies and increased abilities to provide public services.

However, the elderly and the young are not randomly distributed throughout society, which is likely to create a growing set of regional problems. In the United States, for example, the educated young are likely to leave the "gray belt" of the north for the Sun Belt of the south, southwest,

and west. Who will be left in the older, established sectors of the country that were originally at the forefront of the industrial age to care for the disproportionately elderly population? Peter G. Peterson introduces the phrase "the Floridization of the developed world," where retirees continue to flock in unprecedented numbers to more desirable locations, in order to capture the essence of the problems associated with the changing age composition in industrial societies. What will happen 30–40 years from now, when the respective sizes of the young and the elderly populations throughout the developed world will yield a much larger population at the twilight of their existence? Although the trend has been most evident in the richer part of the globe, people are now also living longer in the developing world, primarily because of the diffusion of modern medical practices. But unless society can accommodate their skills of later years, they may become an even bigger burden in the future for their national governments.

A 2001 report, *Preparing for an Aging World: The Case for Cross-National Research* (National Academy of Sciences), identified a number of areas in which policy makers need a better understanding of the consequences of aging and resultant appropriate policy responses. Unless national governments of the developed world can effectively respond to these issues, the economic and social consequences can have a significant negative impact in the aging population cohort as well as throughout the entire society. This theme was reiterated in a major report of the Population Reference Bureau in March 2005 (*Global Aging: The Challenge of Success*), suggesting three major challenges of an aging population: (1) economic development issues, (2) health and well-being issues, and (3) the challenge of enabling and supportive environments.

The issue of the changing age composition in the developed world was foreseen a few decades ago, but its heightened visibility is more recent. This visibility culminated in a UN-sponsored conference on aging in Madrid in April 2002. Its plan of action commits governments to address the problem of aging and provides them with a set of 117 specific recommendations covering three basic areas: older individuals and development, advancing health and well-being into old age, and ensuring enabling and supportive environments.

With the successful demographic transition in the industrial world, the percentage of those older than 60 years is on the rise, whereas the labor force percentage is decreasing. In 1998, 19 percent of the first world population fell into the post-60 category (10 percent worldwide). Children younger than 15 years also make up 19 percent of the developed world's population, whereas the labor force is at 62 percent. With birth rates hovering around 1 percent or less, and life expectancy increasing, the percentages will likely continue to grow toward the upper end of the scale.

Paul Peterson has argued that the costs of global aging will outweigh the benefits, and the capacity of the developed world to pay for these costs is questionable at best. He suggests that the economic burden on the labor force will be "unprecedented" and offers a number of solutions ("Gray Dawn: The Global Aging Crisis" in *Foreign Affairs*, January/February 1999).

A U.S. Department of Commerce study, *An Aging World: 2008*, suggests nine trends that will likely present aging challenges throughout the globe. (1) The population is aging, as people 65 years and older will outnumber those younger than 5 years. (2) Life expectancy is increasing, raising questions about human life span. (3) The number of the oldest, those older than 80 years, is rising and will more than double within 30 years. (4) Some countries are experiencing aging populations, while their total populations decline. (5) Noncommunicable diseases are becoming an increasing burden as they now are the major cause of death among old people. (6) Because of longer life spans and fewer children, family structures are changing and care options for the elderly may change. (7) There are shrinking ratios of workers to pensioners, as people live longer in retirement, taxing health, and pension systems. (8) Social insurance systems are becoming less sustainable. (9) Population aging is having huge effects on social entitlement programs.

A World Bank study (Ronald Lee et al., *Some Economic Consequences of Global Aging*, December 2010) outlines concerns about the effects of aging on societies: slower economic growth, poverty among the elderly, generational equity, inadequate investment in physical and human capital, inefficiency in labor markets, suboptimal consumption profiles, and unsustainable public transfer systems.

Neil Howe and Richard Jackson describe the geopolitical implications of global aging for the highly developed societies in *The Graying of the Great Powers* (Center for Strategic and International Studies, 2008). The first is that both the population and the gross domestic product (GDP) of the developed world will decline as a percentage of global totals, thus leading to a loss of influence. Within the developed world, though, the U.S. share will rise, leading to increased influence. Most nations in Sub-Saharan Africa and those in the Muslim world will experience large youth bulges, leading to a chronically unstable situation until at least the 2030s. Many nations in North Africa, the Middle East, South and East Asia, and the

former Soviet bloc are experiencing rapid demographic change that could lead to either civil collapse or a reactive neo-authoritarianism. The threat of ethnic and religious conflict will continue as a security challenge throughout the world. The 2020s will be a decade of maximum political danger. The aging developed world will have shortages of young–adult man power. And finally, this world may struggle to remain culturally attractive and politically relevant to younger peoples.

Alternatively, some analysts are looking at an aging population from a lens that is not half empty but that has some positive aspects to it. One such positive possibility is a decrease in military conflict throughout the globe as societies face manpower shortages while dealing with social services for the elderly. Another approach is to observe how the experience of age is brought to bear in a productive way in modern societies that can reap the benefits of productive labor achieved through brains rather than brawn.

Finally, the 2015 UN report, *World Population Ageing 2015* (UN Department of Economic and Social Affairs), offered a balanced view of how the world must react to this ever increasing global phenomenon. The report makes the obvious argument that preparing for this change in global age cohorts is critical to the international community's ability to achieve its sustainable development goals. Pension systems are particularly at risk as old-age support ratios decline. Health-care systems represent another important area that must adjust to the needs of the growing numbers of the elderly, including lifelong health and preventive care. The very elderly will be in greater need of home-based and facility-based around-the-clock care. And the increasing need to eliminate age-related discrimination will become more pressing. Easier access to infrastructure and services will remain a taunting challenge to governments. The UN report concludes with the belief that governments have the capacity to determine current and future needs and thus will be able to "ensure the well-being and full socioeconomic integration of older persons while maintaining the fiscal solvency of pension and health-care systems and promoting economic growth."

The YES selection by Richard Jackson summarizes the economic, social, and geopolitical problems that global aging will present over the next several decades. His emphasis is on the developing world because that is where the greatest changes will occur, changes that are, is his words, both more complicated and less understood than those for the developed world. Jackson does observe some aspects of the demographic situation that might yield a cause for optimism. He points out how the upcoming stages of the demographic transition in the developing world could be constructive rather than disruptively negative. He sees a decline in the "large youth bulges," which should lead to more societal stability and institution building for facilitating "the creation and protection of wealth." In addition, Jackson foresees a "decline in society's dependency burden," leading to a rise in the ratio of producers to consumers. However, there are several causes for concern, which Jackson is quick to point out. Demographic trends could result in major disruptions as happened in the developed world. Moreover, it is possible that the elderly class could reach such a large size, so as to end the demographic dividend assumed to occur in the latter stages of the demographic transition. As well, favorable demographics alone are not enough. Societies must still access resources and then allocate them appropriately. That is, they must also grow rich as they grow old. A fourth concern is the stress of the development process. It must be met head-on and managed. Finally, when the day comes when the demographic transition has moved through its various stages in the developing world, the latter must have been able to have created a modern welfare state that can provide "full protection" for the elderly. Without this cultural change, society will likely fall short of benefiting from the aging of its population.

The NO selection, a World Bank report, takes its title from a time in Greek mythology where there was "peace, harmony, stability, and prosperity when humans lived to a very old age." Its bottom line is "although many challenges are real and urgent, aging also creates opportunities, including opportunities to increase labor productivity and the quality of education." The report outlines policies in two major areas that, if implemented, could result in "Golden Aging." These include rebalancing demographic trends and tackling economic challenges and opportunities associated with demographic changes. The former include a focus on preventive health care and more diagnostics rather than hospital care, labor-market policies focusing on women that result in an increase in fertility rates toward replacement levels, and encouraging policies that lead to more flexibility in labor markets (lifelong learning, mobility, and migration). Economic policies include (1) fiscally responsible reforms to pension systems, health care, and long-term care; (2) reforms in labor and pension laws and improved incentives "to keep investing in human capital" throughout one's lifetime, which should lead to increased participation and productivity on the part of the elderly; and (3) "appropriate safety nets regarding health care so that poverty does not result.

YES

Richard Jackson

Global Aging and the Outlook for Growth and Stability in the Developing World

When people think of disruptive forces, demography may not leap to mind as readily as technology, ideology, or climate change. Yet from the fall of the Roman and Mayan empires to the Black Death and the youth-driven revolutions of the twentieth century, demographic trends have often played a decisive role in precipitating the great upheavals of history. By the 2020s, an ominous new conjuncture of these trends may once again threaten widespread disruption. We're talking about global aging, which is likely to have a profound effect on economic growth, social and political stability, and the shape of the world order.

For most of the world's developed countries, the next few decades are set to be one of rapid population aging and population decline.[1] The developed world is of course already aging, due to falling birth rates and rising life expectancy. But beginning in the 2020s, this aging will get an extra push as large postwar baby boom generations move fully into retirement. By 2050, the elderly share of the U.S. population, which was 12 percent as recently as 2000, will climb to 22 percent. In Western Europe, the share will reach 30 percent, and in Japan, which is ground zero for global aging, it will reach 36 percent.

Falling birth rates are not only transforming traditional population pyramids, leaving them top-heavy with elders, but are also ushering in a new era of population stagnation and decline. The working-age population has already begun to contract in several large developed countries, including Germany and Japan. By 2030, it will be stagnant or contracting in nearly all of them, the only major exception being the United States, which benefits from its relatively high birth rate and substantial net immigration. In a growing number of countries, total population will begin a gathering decline as well. Unless birth rates or immigration surge, Japan and some European countries are on track to lose nearly ½ of their total current population by the end of the century.

The aging of the developed world threatens to erode its economic and geopolitical stature. Rising pension and health-care costs will put intense pressure on government budgets, potentially crowding out spending on other priorities, from education and the environment to national defense and foreign assistance. Economic performance may suffer as workforces gray and rates of savings and investment decline. With electorates increasingly dominated by older voters, the social and political mood may become more risk-averse and inward-looking. In terms of sheer demographic and economic size, the developed world will shrink dramatically relative to a faster-growing developing world.

The weakening of the developed world might be less worrisome if demographic trends were at the same time rendering the developing world more peaceful and stable. Some optimists argue that this will indeed be the case.[2] Like the developed world before it, the developing world is in the midst of the "demographic transition"—the shift from high fertility and high mortality to low fertility and low mortality that accompanies development and modernization. Although this shift will ultimately result in a graying population and a rising old-age dependency burden, it first opens up a window of opportunity for economic and social development. With population growth rates slowing, median ages rising, and youth bulges fading throughout most of the developing world, the optimists predict that the demographic weather will be increasingly sunny over the next few decades.

While the case for optimism has some merit, there are also major causes for concern. To begin with, the pace and timing of the demographic transition are highly uneven. In many of the poorest and least stable countries (especially in Sub-Saharan Africa and the Greater Middle East), the demographic transition has stalled in its early stages, while in many of the most economically successful countries (especially in East Asia), the entire demographic shift from young and growing to old and stagnant or declining is occurring at a breathtaking pace—far more rapidly than it did in any of today's developed countries. The former will continue to be wracked by large youth bulges for decades to come, while the latter will have to cope with premature aging.

Moreover, even in those countries where population trends are favorable, the demographic transition merely creates an opportunity, and opportunities must be seized. Many emerging markets lack the institutional capacity to translate their favorable demographics into faster economic growth and greater social and political stability. Economists, sociologists, and historians who have studied the development process also agree that societies are buffeted by tremendous stresses as they move from traditional to modern.[3] Many of these stresses, from rapid urbanization to growing income inequality, become most acute midway through the demographic transition and the development process. While it may be true that development ultimately leads to greater stability, it is also true that journeys can be more dangerous than destinations. The risk of social and political upheaval could grow throughout the developing world—even as the developed world's capacity to deal with the potential threats diminishes.

This issue brief explores the disruptive economic, social, and geopolitical shifts that are likely to arise from global demographic change over the next few decades, identifies some of the most significant risks, and draws a few critical lessons for policy makers and business leaders. It focuses on the outlook for the developing world, where the impact of global aging is both more complicated and less well understood.

The Case for Optimism

While demographic change in the developing world was a highly disruptive force during much of the twentieth century, there is a school of thought which holds that it will become a constructive one in the twenty-first. The case for optimism is rooted in the dynamics of the demographic transition, which unfolds in a series of distinct phases, each of which has very different implications for growth and stability.

During the first phase of the transition, which got under way in the developing world in the early postwar decades, mortality rates fell, especially those for infants and children, while birth rates remained high. The result was a spectacular surge in population growth. From 1950 to 1975, the global population grew at an average annual rate of 2 percent, faster than it had ever grown at any time in recorded history. Economically, the demographic

transition seemed to be pushing the developing world toward a Malthusian resource crisis—or at least so warned Paul Ehrlich and David Brower in their 1968 bestseller, *The Population Bomb*, and the Club of Rome in its 1972 report, *The Limits to Growth*.[4] Meanwhile, the large youth bulges that the transition spawned became a driving force behind social and political upheaval, from China's Cultural Revolution starting in the late 1960s to the Muslim world's radical Islamist movement starting in the late 1970s.

Just as fears about the "population bomb" were peaking, however, most of the developing world entered a new phase in the demographic transition. Beginning in the 1970s and 1980s, birth rates suddenly began to fall. Indeed, they plummeted, putting a break on runaway population growth and shifting age structures steadily upward. Fertility is now beneath the so-called 2.1 replacement level needed to maintain a stable population from one generation to the next throughout East Asia, the only exception being Mongolia, as well as throughout Eastern Europe, with no exceptions at all. It is near, at, or beneath replacement in all of Latin America's major economies. And it is falling like a stone in South Asia and much of the Greater Middle East.

The dramatic decline in birth rates has in turn triggered two demographic shifts that can have a positive impact on economic growth and social and political stability. The first shift is the decline of large youth bulges. Throughout history, people have observed that young men are responsible for most of the world's mayhem. Since the mid-1990s, a substantial body of research has confirmed that there is a close correlation between the size of a society's youth bulge, which is usually defined as the ratio of youth aged 15–24 to the entire adult population aged 15 and over, and the incidence of conflict and instability, especially civil unrest and state failure.[5] The good news is that youth bulges have peaked in most regions of the developing world and are projected to decline steeply over the next few decades. As the overall age structure of the population shifts upward, societies should not only become more stable but also more focused on building institutions that facilitate the creation and protection of wealth.

The second, and economically more important, shift is the decline in society's dependency burden. To measure the size of this burden, demographers look at a country's "total dependency ratio"—that is, the ratio of children plus elderly to working-age adults. When the developing world's demographic transition first got under way, the explosive growth in the number of children pushed up the total dependency ratio and put downward pressure on living standards. But once fertility fell, the total dependency ratio began to decline, tending to buoy up living standards. Another way to understand the dynamic is to look at the share of a country's population, that is, in the traditional working years. As dependency ratios have declined during the second phase of the demographic transition, the share of the population in the working years has risen, often dramatically. In effect, the ratio of producers to consumers has gone up.

Beyond this simple arithmetic, declining dependency burdens can also alter economic behavior in ways that further accelerate the pace of living-standard growth. Labor force participation rates may increase because fewer children free up adult time, and especially the time of women, for participation in the market economy. Over time, savings rates may increase as well as more of the working-age population ages into the high-saving middle years. Declining family size, together with rising life expectancy, also increases incentives to invest more in the "quality" of children and thus of the future workforce. The overall dynamic is called the "demographic dividend," and it opens up a window of opportunity for economic and social development.

The dynamic is not merely theoretical. Development economists who have studied the demographic transition agree that it has given a powerful boost to economic growth in emerging East Asia, first underpinning the stunning rise of the Tigers, and then, more recently, of China. Since 1975, the total dependency ratio in emerging East Asia has fallen from 116 to 49, the largest drop of any region in the world. Meanwhile, the share of the population in the working years has risen from 46 percent to 67 percent. Several studies have concluded that the shift in the age structure of East Asia's population accounts for between ¼ and ⅖ of the growth in the region's living standards since the mid-1970s.[6]

Much of the rest of the developing world, including Latin America, South Asia, and large parts of the Greater Middle East, has now entered this demographic sweet spot and will continue to traverse it over the next few decades. As it does, the hope is that a growing number of countries will follow East Asia's lead.

Causes for Concern

In recent years, this upbeat demographic narrative has underpinned predictions about the inevitable rise of the BRICs as well as broader expectations about the growth of the global middle class. While there is indeed room for optimism about the future, there are also causes for concern. The demographic transition may ultimately push the developing world toward greater prosperity, stability, and peace, but it is highly unlikely that the progress will be linear. Indeed, demographic trends in the developing world may prove to be every bit as disruptive in this century as they were in the last.

To begin with, not all countries are progressing in tandem through the demographic transition. The transition has failed to gain traction in much of Sub-Saharan Africa, where the fertility rate remains stuck at 5.1, twice the developing-world average. The average youth bulge is 35 percent, about what it has been since the 1970s, and is projected to remain at elevated levels for decades to come. The transition has also failed to gain traction in parts of the Greater Middle East, including such chronically unstable countries as Afghanistan, Iraq, Somalia, Sudan, and Yemen. In recent years, these countries have amply demonstrated the correlation between extreme youth and violence. If that correlation endures, chronic unrest and state failure could persist through at least the 2020s and 2030s. Here, the demographic window of opportunity for rapid economic and social development still lies well over the horizon—and may not materialize at all unless birth rates fall.

Meanwhile, the countries of emerging East Asia, where birth rates fell sooner and farther than anywhere else in the developing world except Eastern Europe, are already reaching a new tipping point, where rapidly aging populations are beginning to lean against economic growth. The demographic transition, after all, has a third and final phase. Eventually, the growth in the number of elderly overtakes the decline in the number of children, dependency burdens once again rise, and the period of demographic dividend comes to an end. Within a few decades, China will be older than the United States, and South Korea, Singapore, and Taiwan will be vying with Italy, Germany, and Japan for the title of oldest country on earth. As they enter the final stage of the demographic transition, these countries will encounter many of the same difficulties now confronting today's developed economies, from rising fiscal burdens to graying workforces and declining rates of savings and investment. Here, the demographic window of opportunity for rapid development is already closing.

Nor is there any guarantee that those countries which now find themselves in the middle of the demographic transition will succeed in leveraging their demographic dividends. The reality is that favorable demographics only help to the extent that societies are capable of mobilizing economic resources and allocating them to productive activities. If demography were all that mattered, most emerging markets would have been growing as fast, or nearly as fast, over the past few decades as those in East Asia have. Although East Asia is leading the way through the demographic transition, total dependency ratios have also been falling and the working-age share of the population has been rising since the mid-1970s in every region of the developing world except Sub-Saharan Africa. Yet no other region has managed to achieve sustained growth rates in living standards that even approach East Asia's. Since 1975, real GDP per capita in emerging East Asia has risen by a staggering 1,513 percent. In South Asia, it has risen by 326 percent, in Latin America by 64 percent, and in the Greater Middle East by 37 percent.

East Asia's emerging markets have succeeded so spectacularly because they got everything, or nearly everything, right. They all benefited from sound macroeconomic management, progrowth business and labor-market regulation, and, to varying degrees, good governance and the rule of law. Crucially, governments pursued export-led growth strategies that facilitated the movement of unskilled labor from the unproductive rural sector into basic manufacturing. At the same time, they made or encouraged the private sector to make massive investments in infrastructure, R&D, and, above all, human capital that allowed their economies to gradually move up the global value-added scale. When its demographic transition got under way in the 1950s and 1960s, South Korea was still a predominantly agrarian society of peasant farmers. Today, it is a high-income country with the highest secondary school and university graduation rates in the Organisation for Economic Co-operation and Development. Quite simply, many of the conditions that explain East Asia's success do not yet exist in large parts of the developing world.

When these conditions are absent, the demographic dividend can become a demographic liability. Unless there are sufficient employment opportunities for the surging number of working-age adults, unemployment will rise as countries move through the demographic transition—and along with it, popular resentment and unrest will grow. In parts of the Greater Middle East, the failure to create jobs has helped to trigger social revolution and played a role in fomenting religious extremism. In parts of Latin America, it has led to massive out-migration.

Along with leveraging their demographic dividends, emerging markets face another hurdle as they move through the demographic transition: managing the stresses of development. As countries are integrated into the global marketplace and the global culture, traditional economic and social structures are overturned and traditional value systems are challenged. Meanwhile, along with the economic benefits of rising living standards, development also brings the social costs of rapid urbanization, growing income inequality, and environmental degradation. When plotted against stage of development and demographic transition, many of these stresses exhibit a hump-shaped or "inverted-U" pattern, meaning that they become most acute midway through the demographic transition and the development process.

Ironically, the countries that are undergoing the most rapid demographic transitions and the most rapid development may be the most at risk of social and political crisis or even chaotic collapse. After all, the more rapid the pace of demographic and economic change is, the less time political systems, social institutions, and cultural attitudes have to adapt. It is no accident that the Chinese government's renewed authoritarianism coincides with mounting popular discontent over the rural–urban income gap, the inadequate social safety net, and the deteriorating environment. Nor is it an accident that many other emerging markets, from Iran and Turkey to Venezuela and Vietnam, find the China model attractive. Neo-authoritarian regimes like China's have a twofold appeal to some developing countries. One appeal is their reputation for promoting economic growth (the upside of development) better than democracies. The other appeal is as a means of staving off the social and political upheaval that can be triggered by rapid demographic, economic, and cultural change (the downside).

There is another challenge that most emerging markets will ultimately face—namely, coping with the rapid aging of their populations when the demographic transition enters its final phase. The developing world's age waves will be arriving in societies that in most cases are not only less affluent than those in the developed world, but that have not yet put in place the full social protections of a modern welfare state. In most emerging markets, only a fraction of the workforce is earning a benefit under any type of pension system, either public or private. From China and India to Brazil and Mexico, the majority of the elderly still depend heavily on the extended family for economic support. Yet traditional family support networks are already under stress as countries urbanize and modernize and will soon come under intense new demographic pressure as family size declines. An aging crisis of potentially immense dimensions looms in the future of many emerging markets if they fail to construct adequate old-age safety nets.

Demographic Storms

Global aging is in many ways a benign development. No one wants to see life expectancy fall, and many of us would agree that higher birth rates, and hence faster population growth, would create its own set of problems. Yet global aging is also a development that will pose serious economic and geopolitical risks in decades to come.

To the extent that policy makers and business leaders consider demographic risks at all in their long-term planning, they tend to focus on the familiar one of large youth bulges and state failure in low-income countries. As we have seen, this risk is not going to disappear any time soon. Lingering youth bulges could continue to foster instability and blight development prospects in much of Sub-Saharan Africa and parts of the Greater Middle East through at least the 2020s and 2030s. Yet it is the less familiar risks faced by middle-income countries that are midway through the demographic transition and the development process that may prove the most serious. State failure in a country like Somalia or Yemen is a humanitarian tragedy. State failure in a populous and economically important middle-income country would be a geopolitical catastrophe. The consolidation of neo-authoritarian regimes, which often gain legitimacy by promising to prevent just such an outcome, may be less dramatic but is no less disruptive to the rules-based world order.

There is no way to know which of the demographic storms that are now brewing in the developing world will intensify and become destructive. Many of today's emerging markets, and perhaps most of them, will manage to navigate their demographic transitions and move up and over the so-called development hump without experiencing a major social and political crisis, much less a chaotic collapse. It is certainly encouraging that economic performance in most of the developing world has improved markedly over the past 15 years. A record number of countries have experienced at least modest growth in real per capita income, and a significant number have experienced rapid growth. From Latin America to South Asia, many emerging markets that were riven by social unrest and political strife a generation ago have now become stable democracies.

What we know about the demographic transition and the development process, however, suggests that most emerging markets, even the very largest, face significant risks. Russia is on the cusp of what is likely to be the fastest and most extended population implosion of any great power since the plague-ridden Middle Ages.

Unless reversed, it will progressively weaken the country's already fragile economy. India's demographics are relatively favorable. But despite its large English-speaking middle-class and world-class high-tech and outsourcing sectors, it must cope with large deficits in infrastructure and human capital as well as deep ethnic and religious divisions. China, which may be the first country to grow old before it grows rich, has been "peacefully rising." But its massive age wave and huge gender imbalance threaten to act as multipliers on the economic and social stresses arising from rapid development. By the 2020s, demographic trends, which up to now have helped to propel China's rise, could be weakening the twin pillars of the current regime's legitimacy: rapidly rising living standards and social stability.

Notes

1. All demographic data in this issue brief come from *World Population Prospects: The 2015 Revision* (New York: UN Population Division, 2015). Projections refer to the UN's "medium variant." However, country groups are defined by the author and differ in some respects from UN definitions. For details, see the Note on Country Groups at the end of the issue brief.

2. See, most importantly, Richard P. Cincotta, Robert Engelman, and Daniele Anastasion, *The Security Demographic: Population and Civil Conflict After the Cold War* (Washington, DC: Population Action International, 2003); Elizabeth Leahy et al., *The Shape of Things to Come: Why Age Structure Matters to a Safer, More Equitable World* (Washington, DC: Population Action International, 2007); and Mark L. Haas, "A Geriatric Peace? The Future of U.S. Power in a World of Aging Populations," *International Security* 32, no. 1 (Summer 2007).

3. For a discussion of the literature, see Richard Jackson and Neil Howe, *The Graying of the Great Powers: Demography and Geopolitics in the 21st Century* (Washington, DC: CSIS, 2008), 142–150.

4. Paul R. Ehrlich and David Brower, *The Population Bomb* (New York: Ballantine Books, 1968); and Donella H. Meadows et al., *The Limits to Growth* (New York: Universe Books, 1972).

5. See, among others, Daniel C. Esty et al., *State Failure Task Force Report: Phase II Findings* (McLean, VA: Science Applications International Corporation, 1998); Cincotta, Engelman, and Anastasion,

The Security Demographic: Population and Civil Conflict After the Cold War; Henrik Urdal, "A Clash of Generations? Youth Bulges and Political Violence," *International Studies Quarterly* 50, no. 3 (2006); and Leahy et al., *The Shape of Things to Come: Why Age Structure Matters to a Safer, More Equitable World.*

6. See, for example, David E. Bloom and Jeffrey Williamson, "Demographic Transitions and Economic Miracles in Emerging Asia," *World Bank Economic Review* 12, no. 3 (September 1998); David E. Bloom, David Canning, and Pia N. Malaney, "Demographic Change and Economic Growth in Asia," CID Working Paper no. 015 (Cambridge, MA: Center for International

Development at Harvard University, May 1999); and Jeffrey Williamson, "Demographic Change, Economic Growth, and Inequality," in *Population Matters: Demographic Change, Economic Growth, and Poverty in the Developing World*, eds. Nancy Birdsall, Allen C. Kelley, and Steven Sinding (New York: Oxford University Press, 2001).

RICHARD JACKSON is a president and founder of the Global Aging Institute (GAI) and a senior associate at the Center for Strategic and International Studies (CSIS). He is an author of numerous policy studies on global aging. He has a PhD in history from Yale University.

**Maurizio Bussolo, Johannes Koettl, and
Emily Sinnott**

Golden Aging

Prospects for Healthy, Active, and Prosperous Aging in Europe and Central Asia

Overview: Golden Aging

The Golden Age in Greek mythology was a time of peace, harmony, stability, and prosperity when humans lived to a very old age.

Introduction

The countries of Europe and Central Asia (ECA) are aging. The average age of the population increased from 29 years in 1950 to 37 years in 2015, and the share of people 65 and older in the total population rose from 6 percent in 1950 to 12 percent in 2015. According to simple extrapolations based on the United Nations' medium-fertility demographic scenario, by 2050, the share of older people could reach 21 percent. This process is most advanced in Central Europe, the Western Balkans, the Eastern Partnership, and the Russian Federation. The populations of Turkey and Central Asia are much younger, but in coming decades, they may age even faster than European countries did in previous decades. Aging in Europe and Central Asia is different from that in Western Europe and East Asia, two other regions that are already advanced in the aging process. Whereas aging is often driven by a fall in both fertility rates and mortality at old age, the rise in the average age in Europe and Central Asia is largely attributable to low and declining fertility rates rather than to increases in longevity. Thus, population growth has slowed sharply. Indeed, in more than half the countries in Europe and Central Asia, the population is already shrinking. In several countries, emigration has accelerated population declines.

This remarkable aging is generally seen as a grave threat to social welfare. Among other issues, if older people eventually cease to work and begin to dissave, then increases in the relative size of older cohorts will reduce productive capacity, while government revenues will not be enough to meet obligations to older generations. It is not the first time that demographic trends have triggered serious concerns. During the 1970s, the opposite trend—high fertility rates and rapidly growing populations in many developing countries—was a reason for alarm.

Why have opposite demographic trends triggered similar gloomy forecasts for growth, welfare, and fiscal sustainability? One reason is the daunting challenges involved in providing education, jobs, equipment, and infrastructure for large and fast-growing younger cohorts and in providing health care, jobs, and pensions for large and fast-growing older cohorts. A second reason is that many analyses focus on the challenges but much less on the opportunities inherent in demographic trends.

And, significantly, these concerns also often reflect the mistaken assumption that individuals' behavior will remain constant in the face of demographic change. In reality, people do change their behavior to cope with aging, and there is considerable scope for government policy to encourage changes that will mitigate both the demographic drivers and the economic consequences of aging.

This report aims to take a broader perspective than many other publications, going well beyond a discussion of the macroeconomic challenges and the necessary fiscal responses. It concludes that, although many challenges are real and urgent, aging also creates many opportunities, including opportunities to increase labor productivity and the quality of education. The report emphasizes that behavioral responses, by individuals and firms, will result in a markedly different reality from the one implied by simple extrapolations.

. . .

The report concludes by outlining policy reforms that could support the region in achieving a period of "Golden Aging," with relatively stable populations where people live long, healthy, active, and prosperous lives:

- *Policies for rebalancing demographic trends*

  - A focus on preventive care, primary care, and more diagnostics, instead of the predominant model of hospital care, could reduce mortality rates.
  - Labor-market policies that help women reconcile family, and career goals could encourage a rebound in fertility rates toward replacement levels.
  - Encouraging lifelong learning, mobility, and migration, both domestically and internationally, could improve the flexibility of labor markets.

- *Policies to tackle economic challenges and opportunities*

  - Reforms are required to place pension systems, health care, and long-term care on fiscally sustainable paths.
  - Adjustments in labor and pension laws and improved incentives to keep investing in human capital throughout an individual's working life would facilitate increased participation and productivity of the elderly in the labor market.
  - Appropriate social safety nets could ensure that health care and long-term care are affordable and support the elderly who are most at risk of poverty.

. . .

Mixed Economic Consequences

From a demographic perspective, aging could be a positive development, with promising opportunities. But is aging from an economic perspective also a largely positive development, with promising opportunities? This report relies on the analysis of recent data and model-based simulations to answer this question. Aging societies are seriously concerned about slowing economic growth, exploding health-care costs for the elderly, insolvent pension systems, large inequalities among old people, and lack of dynamism in labor markets. Young, fast-growing populations have been very successful at generating high growth of gross domestic product (GDP) in recent decades. The aging and stagnating population of Japan has experienced a stagnating economy for the past 25 years. Japan has accumulated large fiscal deficits, has been stuck in a deflationary environment, and seems unable to generate economic growth once again. Does stabilization of the population inevitably lead to stagnant economies?

The answer to that question is no. Economic growth, and especially per capita economic growth, is only to a limited extent directly influenced by demographics. Many factors other than aging are substantially more important in driving economic changes. Technological catching up to Western European countries is important in boosting productivity and per capita income growth. Technological innovation and perverse incentive structures can push up health-care costs. High generosity in pension eligibility and benefits during the past decades was much more important than increased life expectancy in threatening the solvency of pension systems: some countries in Europe and Central Asia spend a larger share of GDP on pensions than the already aging and high-income Western European countries do. Although inequality in older age groups tends to be larger than inequality in younger age groups, factors other than aging heavily influence changes in overall inequality.

This report concludes that the economic consequences of aging are much more mixed than sometimes feared. Some of the consequences indeed pose significant challenges, but other economic effects of aging can be positive. In most countries in the region, where aging is already advanced, aging does present considerable fiscal challenges, which many governments are already confronting. Many individuals are already adjusting their participation in the labor force in response to changed pension entitlements and longer lives. Interesting efforts are under way by firms to learn how to take advantage of the specific skills of an older labor force. Although high average age levels still lie in the future for Central Asia, the future is much nearer than many expect and now is the time to prepare for a very different age structure. Increasing the quality of education and investing in the health of the current young generation would lay the foundation for healthy and active aging. Designing sustainable and equitable pension and health-care systems now would provide a safety net for those who need it but also create flexibility and incentives for those who want additional coverage.

Examining the concerns expressed during the past century about the macroeconomic consequences of fast population growth and young populations will lead to a better understanding of the macroeconomic effects of aging. Those concerns came down to the problem of providing a rapidly increasing population with sufficient resources to become prosperous. How can countries accumulate enough capital to support fast economic growth? High population growth requires a higher investment rate to maintain the existing capital intensity of an economy. How can enough education be supplied to large cohorts of young people, even to maintain existing educational levels? How can natural resource constraints be overcome in increasingly densely populated areas?

These concerns were grounded in the problems that countries with young, fast-growing populations were facing.[1] They were often characterized by labor-intensive production, low educational levels, insufficient infrastructure, and severe environmental stress. In that sense, low fertility was more a part of the solution than a part of the problem. In countries with aging, stable populations, less investment is needed to maintain sufficient capital per person. At the danger of an overly simplistic analysis, it is indeed true that the specialization patterns in the older societies of Europe and Central Asia are more capital-intensive than the younger societies of Central Asia and Turkey. And, consistent with the expected pattern, educational levels are also higher in the older part of ECA than in Central Asia. Thus, an important macroeconomic impact of lower fertility and slowing population growth is the possibility for increased human and physical capital per worker, while production per worker tends to increase as production becomes more capital intensive. And there is evidence that that is exactly what is happening in the region.

Increasing production per worker does not mean, however, that income per capita is also increasing. The share of workers in the population might decline as the share of the elderly, who no longer participate in the labor force, rises. At least until now, this potentially negative impact on per capita income has not materialized. The increasing share of elderly has been offset—and in many countries in Central Europe more than offset—by a declining share of young people who also do not participate in the labor force. While demographic forces may tend to increase dependency ratios in the future (as the share of elderly increases further and the share of young people stays more or less constant), behavioral responses that result in increased and longer labor force participation can be expected to reduce dependency ratios. On balance, the number of inactive people per worker will not necessarily increase.

This positive macroeconomic impact of lower fertility on per capita incomes could well remain if changes in the saving rate are taken into account. As the elderly tend to dissave—that is, they consume by drawing down their past savings—the economy's saving rate can be expected to decline if the share of elderly increases. However, the simulations indicate that workers, who benefit from higher wage incomes when population growth declines, may increase their savings. As a result, the total drop in savings is lower given the increase in capital intensity caused by lower population growth.

Thus, lower fertility may reduce the size of the population but can increase per capita income by increasing capital per worker. By contrast, aging caused by increased life expectancy, which has already been observed in Western Europe and many countries in East Asia and is anticipated in many countries in Europe and Central Asia as they improve their preventive health care, has different macroeconomic effects. As increased life expectancy does not lead to slower population growth—on the contrary, it temporarily leads to higher population growth—there is, unlike the case of reduced fertility, no automatic tendency toward increased capital intensity of production and increased labor productivity. However, if a rise in life expectancy is anticipated by current workers, then they could, theoretically, save to prepare for longer retirement. That could lead, at least for some time, to increased capital intensity and thus to increased labor productivity if those additional savings are not all invested abroad. However, that positive impact will not last. Once the share of elderly in the population increases, the positive impact will dissipate.

The conclusion of model simulations is that declining mortality rates at older age may ultimately reduce per capita income, despite higher savings by workers and thus higher capital accumulation, if people spend more time in retirement without working longer. However, the story changes completely if people work longer. If the additional life expectancy were proportionally allocated to working time and time spent in retirement, the impact on per capita income would become positive again.[2] And that is exactly what is already happening in many countries in Europe and Central Asia. As life expectancy increases, the labor participation rates of older people also increase, and the gap in participation rates between the young and the older age groups is starting to decline. This positive correlation can be a result of many economic and policy factors, but it is important to note that the rise in labor participation means that the ratio of inactive to active population need not increase in aging economies.

Apart from increased participation rates, there are other mechanisms through which effective labor supply will likely increase more than is suggested by pure extrapolation of demographic trends. One such mechanism is that younger age groups may be better educated than older age groups. This implies that the increase in human capital could exceed the increase in the number of workers. However, major policy efforts would be required to realize these projections. Currently, in several countries, the quality of education is not increasing, even if enrollment rates are rising.

Four Areas of Uncertainty

From a macroeconomic perspective, the aging currently observed in most of Europe and Central Asia and that expected in Central Asia and Turkey could have positive effects. However, the impact of aging on labor force participation and individual productivity will depend critically on attitudes and behaviors that are difficult to anticipate, much less quantify, in model simulations. Among the many issues involved, four are subject to considerable uncertainty and will be reviewed in turn:

- Will the older people of the future be inclined to work longer as they live longer?
- Will the older people of the future be as productive, mobile, innovative, and entrepreneurial as young people?
- Will the rise in the average age of physical and human capital—which could imply outdated education, infrastructure that does not meet current needs, and factories that fail to employ the newest technologies—mean that the total impact of aging is negative, despite the modestly positive effects that can come through the key macroeconomic transmission channels?
- Will an aging society imply a rise in inequality?

Aging and Labor Force Participation

One of the startling conclusions of this report is that dependency ratios need not increase in an aging economy. The conventional definition of dependency ratio has often relied on a fixed chronological age of 65 to distinguish between working and retired. This arbitrary cutoff may no longer be relevant because, as further elaborated in the report, many people above 65 are willing—and expected—to work. This report defines a novel dependency ratio as the number of inactive to active people in the adult population (aged 15 and older), which should better capture the true state of dependency of the economy, that is, how many inactive people that each worker and tax contributor is supporting. If past trends continue, projections of the International Labour Office (ILO) to 2030 suggest that dependency ratios, with the new definition, will only increase slightly in most of the region (ILO Stats). In the Western Balkans, the dependency ratio is actually projected to decline somewhat. This projection realistically assumes that the positive trend of longer work

lives and increased labor force participation, especially of women, that was observed in most countries in the past will continue until 2030.

Beyond 2030, pure demographics point to a worsening of the dependency ratios, especially in the Western Balkans and the young countries. But with continued trends toward greater female labor force participation and longer work lives, the dependency ratio could remain fairly stable or even improve. The scenarios developed in this report show that a female-to-male convergence in participation rates, which would require favorable workplace environments and better work–life balance, would be sufficient to keep dependency ratios more or less constant. This would actually lead to a considerable improvement in the dependency ratio in the young countries of Europe and Central Asia. A convergence to participation profiles as observed in Iceland—a benchmark country with the highest overall participation rates—would actually decrease dependency ratios considerably in all subregions. Combining all these positive developments (admittedly an extreme assumption) could potentially decrease dependency ratios to between a half and a third of today's levels.

In countries in the Organisation for Economic Co-operation and Development (OECD), the time people spend in retirement has risen significantly during the past decades. But more than half of that increase was due to earlier retirement. On average, men retired at age 68.7 and had a remaining life expectancy of about 10.6 years in 1970; in 2012, men retired at age 64.2, with a remaining life expectancy of 18 years. In other words, people nowadays not only live longer, but—as pension systems became more generous—also retire earlier. In OECD countries, the trend is already reversing: since the 1990s, the average effective retirement age has started to increase and people have begun working longer. If this trend continues, gains in life expectancy will indeed be translated into longer work lives. Decreasing the possibilities for early retirement, further increases in statutory retirement ages, and making the retirement age flexible are prerequisites for this.

Aging and Productivity

Is downward pressure on overall productivity likely in an aging workforce because people become less productive when they age? Again, the evidence provided in this report sketches a mixed picture. What is clear, though, is that as some functions of cognitive performance decline with age, the brain has a remarkable ability to compensate with improvements in other functions. For example, brain scans show that aging brains access less new information than younger brains, but that they compensate for that with a much larger amount of experience and knowledge. Moreover, aging also affects personality traits and non-cognitive skills, both of which are also highly relevant for labor-market outcomes. Conscientiousness, agreeableness, and emotional stability improve with age, while openness and extroversion decline (Wieczorkowska-Wierzbińska 2014).

Finally, the literature provides ample evidence for the declining physical strength of older people, suggesting that older workers are less suitable for physically demanding jobs. At the same time, key strengths can be maintained through regular use. A good example is grip strength: while in the general population, grip strength peaks at the age of 35 and declines quickly thereafter, this might not be true for workers who rely on their grip strength every day. In fact, the grip strength of assembly-line workers has been shown to remain constant until the age of 65 (Spirduso, Francis, and MacRae 1995).

In conclusion, the effects of aging on the brain, the body, and personality are diverse. This begs the question of whether firms can take advantage of these shifts and new strengths. Given that certain skills appreciate with age (such as speech and language), aging economies can capitalize on this comparative advantage and shift toward industries that use the skills more intensively (e.g., printing and sales; Cai and Stoyanov 2014). Using data on international trade and industry-level skill intensity, this report finds evidence that endowments shift with an aging workforce and that firms are taking advantage of these changing skills.

In contrast, and counteracting this positive finding, there is empirical evidence that older people are less mobile, less innovative, and less entrepreneurial. Experience is often job specific and becomes less valuable if workers have to change firms or deal with new technologies. Older workers are less mobile because they have established a family, own a house, or accumulated job-specific benefits. Older people become less entrepreneurial because risk-taking becomes more costly as they have more to lose. Especially when economic growth requires substantial change, an aging society can become a disadvantage. Governments, firms, and individuals can increase mobility and flexibility by educating young people to lay the foundation for lifelong learning, encouraging both domestic and international migration, making benefits less job dependent (e.g., encouraging portable pensions), and increasing mobility in housing markets.

Aging of Capital

Human and physical capital, including infrastructure, may become outdated in an aging society. When the population is no longer growing, or is even shrinking, then the average age of human and physical capital will rise with the average age of people. This could depress productivity if a significant part of technological progress is embedded in new vintages of knowledge and capital. However, it is not easy to uncover empirical evidence of the size of these effects. Moreover, slower population growth provides the opportunity to improve the quantity and quality of education and to increase capital-to-output ratios, which can counteract the effects of an aging capital stock.

Aging and Economic Inequality

The impact of aging on the average income—even after considering the above qualifications—may not necessarily be negative; however, aging also influences its distribution. Many studies have shown that income inequality within older age cohorts is greater than within young cohorts (see, e.g., Attanasio, Hurst, and Pistaferri 2014; Deaton and Paxson 1994; Ohtake and Saito 1998). Three mechanisms are responsible for this phenomenon. First, the disadvantages in early years can be exacerbated at old age. Around the world, mortality rates are inversely correlated with education and income, but the differentiation in mortality rates is especially large in Europe and Central Asia. In Central Europe, the Eastern Partnership, and Russia, life expectancy at age 50 for males with tertiary education is around 10 years higher than for males without upper-secondary education. In comparison, that difference is about 6 years in the United States. Not only dying at a younger age, people with lower education and income would also be less healthy in their last years, which may imply higher health-care costs that drive many into impoverishment. Second, people gradually accumulate wealth over time, so that the inequality in wealth accumulated at retirement age is much larger than income inequality. That also implies high inequality in income derived from accumulated wealth during retirement. Third, skill premiums rise with age. The combination of education and experience makes people more productive or at least makes it possible to get promoted into positions with higher salaries. By contrast, experience hardly increases the wages of unskilled workers. That means that the wage gap between skilled and unskilled workers is greater among older workers than among younger workers. For example, in Romania, 25- to 29-year-old tertiary education graduates earn on average 50 percent more than their lower-skilled counterparts. At ages 50–64, the difference is expected to rise to more than 70 percent. Nevertheless, with a combination of improved education of the young and social safety nets for the old, this growing divide among older age groups can be mitigated.

Notes

1. The discussion in the following paragraphs about the impact of aging (or more stable populations) on economic growth is in line with what the literature often labels the second demographic dividend. The literature refers to a first demographic dividend as the boost that the decline of fertility brings to income growth. As the population born during the high-fertility years enters the labor force and the number of children decreases, the dependency ratio temporarily goes down, so that other things being equal, per capita income grows. The dependency ratio begins increasing again as the old-age mortality is reduced. However, this transition could lead to a second dividend if improved longevity generates incentives to work longer and accumulate more assets. With fewer children to care for, there can be more investments in human capital. These factors will be beneficial to the growth of per capita income (Lee and Mason 2006).

2. This implies that for every year that people live longer, roughly three months could be spent in retirement and nine months in the active labor force.

MAURIZIO BUSSOLO is a lead economist in the office of the Chief Economist for Europe and Central Asia at the World Bank.

JOHANNES KOETTL is a senior economist in the Social Protection and Labor Global Practice of the World Bank.

EMILY SINNOTT is a senior economist in the Europe and Central Asia Region of the World Bank.

EXPLORING THE ISSUE

Is Global Aging a Major Problem?

Critical Thinking and Reflection

1. What do analysts really mean when they talk about a global aging population?
2. Why is the 2020s considered to be a decade of reckoning because of an aging global population?
3. Are the major problems associated with aging going to be concentrated in the developing world rather than across the entire globe during the next 50 years?
4. Is there a role for both government policy makers and the private business sector in addressing the issues associated with global aging?
5. Will an aging population lead to economic stagnation or growth over the coming decades, particularly in the developed world?

Is There Common Ground?

There is now a consensus that demographic trends matter with respect to a wide range of public policy issues. There is also agreement on the nature of future trends, particularly as they relate to global aging. And societies are coming to agree on the economic implications of such aging.

Additional Resources

Kunkel, Suzanne R., *Global Aging: Comparative Perspectives on Aging and the Life Course* (Springer Publishing Company, 2013)

Rowland, Donald T., *Population Aging: The Transformation of Societies* (Springer, 2012)

United Nations Department of Economic and Social Affairs, *World Population Ageing 2015* (United Nations, 2015)

World Health Organization, *World Report on Ageing and Health* (Geneva, 2015)

Zimmer, Zachary, and McDaniel, Susan A., *Global Ageing in the twenty-First Century: Challenges, Opportunities and Implications* (Routledge, 2013)

Internet References . . .

Global Action on Aging

www.globalaging.org

Population Reference Bureau

www.prb.org

The CSIS Global Aging Initiative

www.csis.org/gai/

The Population Council

www.popcouncil.org

UN Program for Ageing

www.un.org.development/desa/agency/

Selected, Edited, and with Issue Framing Material by:
James E. Harf, *Maryville University*

ISSUE

Will the World Be Able to Feed Itself in the Foreseeable Future?

YES: Shenggen Fan, from "Progress, Uncertainty, and Rising Antiglobalism," *2018 Global Food Policy Report*, International Food Policy Research Institute (2018)

NO: Food and Agriculture Organization of the United Nations, IFAD, UNICEF, WFP, and WHO, from "2017: The State of Food Security and Nutrition in the World: Building Resilience for Peace and Food Security," Food and Agriculture Organization of the United Nations (2018)

Learning Outcomes

After reading this issue, you will be able to:

- Gain an understanding of the extent of undernourishment and hunger globally.
- Describe progress made in addressing global undernourishment in the past 25 years.
- Be able to describe why the year 2017 brought a sense of optimism to those who seek to reduce global hunger.
- Understand how the prevalence of conflict throughout the globe and increasing climate-related shocks adversely affect the global food system.
- Understand why pessimists point to a litany of negative characteristics of the recent global food system to suggest that the future glass is only half-full.
- Discuss why policy makers must look at the entire food system and its uniqueness when considering action.

ISSUE SUMMARY

YES: Shenggen Fan, director general of the International Food Policy Research Institute, presents a generally positive outlook on the ability of the global food system to provide sufficient food for the world's population despite a number of nonfood-related intrusions that negatively affect the global capacity of the world's food system.

NO: The UN Food and Agriculture Organization report, on the other hand, looks to an increase in the world's chronically undernourished people, from an estimated 717 million in 2015 to 815 million in 2017, as a barometer for revealing a worsening situation, in particular, in parts of sub-Saharan Africa, Southeast Asia, and West Asia. Given the prevalence of conflict throughout the globe and the increase in climate-related shocks to the food system, two major deterrents to food security, the author's despair of providing adequate food for all without "renewed efforts through new ways of thinking."

The lead editorial in *The New York Times* on March 3, 2008, began with the sentence: "The world's food situation is bleak. . . ." The primary culprit, according to the editorial, is the rising cost of wheat. The blame, in turn, was placed on the growing impact of biofuels. Others echoed the same message, adding climate change and the rising cost of shipping to the list of culprits. The UN Food and Agricultural Organization (FAO) also issued a series of warnings in late 2007 and early 2008 about the growing food crisis. Nine days later, UN Secretary-General Ban Ki-moon in *The Washington Post* also sounded the global food alarm, alluding to high food costs and food insecurity.

Nineteen months later in October 2009, the UN FAO Director-General Jacques Diouf in a major speech suggested that agriculture would have to become more productive if the globe's growing population was to be fed. He suggested that future production growth would be found in increased yields and better crop intensity. Further, he argued that a major problem was that food was not being produced by 70 percent of the world's poor who worked in agriculture.

A year later, FAO issued another edition of *Food Outlook*. In it, the UN organization suggested that another food crisis was upon us, caused primarily by less than anticipated food production. At the same time, FAO also targeted higher grain prices. The International Food Policy Research Institute (IFPRI) echoed the need for more production, blaming growing world population and negative production results because of climate change and suggesting that rising food prices were simply a result of the increased demand.

In 2013, the UN FAO reported that one in eight individuals suffered from chronic undernourishment. And as 2015 ended, concerns of international governmental organizations continued. The UN Food Programme revealed that approximately 800 million people throughout the globe, 98 percent of whom were in the developing world, were suffering from hunger as a result of global conditions. FAO also issued dire warnings about the effect of weather on the global food situation.

Private individuals like Robert G. Lewis and Lester Brown shared the same view as government officials during this period, particularly relating to the observation that the culprit was increased demand. And this demand is occurring in places whose population can less afford to purchase food. Respected observers of the global food problem echo this message. Lester Brown argued recently in a new book that the world is undergoing a major transition from food abundance to food scarcity. Several

bloggers have picked up a common theme, suggesting 20 signs that a terrible food crisis is just on the horizon.

Of course, not everyone believed that for whatever the reason, food shortage was a myth despite the fact that one in six people were going hungry. While a 2012 report by the IFPRI echoed these dire statements, spelling out serious weaknesses that continue to plague the global food system—"lack of ability to respond to volatile food prices, extreme weather, and inadequate response to food emergencies" it also revealed some encouraging signs. After years of neglect, both agriculture and food security were back on the world's political agenda. China and India were increasing spending in these two areas. About 20 African countries adopted national investment plans, where 10 percent of their budgets were being devoted to achieving an annual agricultural growth rate of 6 percent.

And the world is finally beginning to see positive results. World hunger declined somewhat, although the situation remained serious. Fifteen countries made substantial progress, with the largest improvements in Angola, Bangladesh, Ethiopia, Malawi, Nicaragua, Niger, and Vietnam, according to the 2012 Global Hunger Index.

Visualize two pictures. One is a group of people in Africa, including a significant number of small children, who show dramatic signs of advanced malnutrition and even starvation. The second picture shows an apparently wealthy couple finishing a meal at a rather expensive restaurant. The waiter removes their plates still half-full of food and deposits them in the kitchen garbage can. These scenarios once highlighted a popular film about world hunger. The implication was quite clear. If only the wealthy would share their food with the poor, no one would go hungry. Today the simplicity of this image is obvious. Yet recent food crisis said nothing about an inadequate or maldistributed supply of food.

This issue addresses the question of whether or not the world will be able to feed itself by the middle of the twenty-first century. A prior question, of course, is whether or not enough food is grown throughout the world today to handle current nutritional and caloric needs of all the planet's citizens. News accounts of chronic food shortages somewhere in the world seem to have been appearing with regular consistency for close to 40 years. This time has witnessed graphic accounts in news specials about the consequences of insufficient food, usually somewhere in sub-Saharan Africa. Also, several national and international studies have been commissioned to address world hunger. An American study organized by President Carter, for example, concluded that the root cause of hunger was poverty.

One might deduce from all of this activity that population growth had outpaced food production and that the planet's agricultural capabilities are no longer sufficient, or that the poor have been priced out of the marketplace. Yet the ability of most countries to grow enough food has not yet been challenged. During the 1970–2000 period, only one region of the globe, sub-Saharan Africa, was unable to have its own food production keep pace with population growth.

This is instructive because, beginning in the early 1970s, a number of factors conspired to lessen the likelihood that all humans would go to bed each night adequately nourished. Weather in major food-producing countries turned bad; a number of countries, most notably Japan and the Soviet Union, entered the world grain-importing business with a vengeance; the cost of energy used to enhance agricultural output rose dramatically; and less capital was available to poorer countries as loans or grants for purchasing agricultural inputs or the finished product (food) itself. Yet the world has had little difficulty growing sufficient food, enough to provide every person with two loaves of bread per day as well as other commodities.

Why then did famine and other food-related maladies appear with increasing frequency? The simple answer is that food has been treated as a commodity, not a nutrient. Those who can afford to buy food or grow their own do not go hungry. However, the world's poor became increasingly unable to afford either to create their own successful agricultural ventures or to buy enough food.

The problem for the next half-century, then, has several facets to it. First, can the planet physically sustain increases in food production equal to or greater than the ability of the human race to reproduce itself? This question can only be answered by examining both factors in the comparison—likely future food production levels and future fertility scenarios. A second question relates to the economic dimension—will those poorer countries of the globe that are unable to grow their own food have sufficient assets to purchase it, or will the international community create a global distribution network that ignores a country's ability to pay? And third, will countries that want to grow their own food be given the opportunity to do so?

Let's look at the recent set of facts relating to world food and hunger. The FAO source used in this issue outlined some key findings. World hunger is on the rise again to over 815 million as compared to 777 million three years ago. Most of the increase can be traced to the two principal factors of rising conflicts and climate-related shocks.

Economic slowdowns have also contributed to the dire situation. Children have suffered as stunting continued to affect one of four children. And $1/3$ of women of reproductive age suffer from anemia. Other problems relating to these two cohort groups are also evident.

Three alternative perspectives are relevant to a discussion over the world's future ability to feed its population. The most basic alternative is the question of the target of international action. At its most basic, the root cause of hunger is poverty, first suggested decades ago by President Jimmy Carter's hunger commission. If the truth is in the ability to afford to pay for food, why not simply focus on eliminating poverty, hence solving the food problem?

Two other alternative perspectives are found in the literature. One is a report by the Rabobank group, "Sustainability and Security of the Global Food Supply Chain" (undated). Although it concluded that there was sufficient global potential to produce the 70 percent more food needed for 2050, the key factor was the global food system, a long supply chain that "encompasses different countries and numerous participants and stakeholders." To this group, less important are balancing food shortages across regions/countries and changing dietary habits and needs.

A very different alternative approach was advanced by the Worldwatch Institute in 2011 (*The State of the World*). Instead of growing more food, the key to addressing the food crisis was to "encourage self-sufficiency and waste reduction." That is, the emphasis should not be on the food production side of the equation but, rather, on the food consumption side. This was earlier seen in the energy issue where attention away from production to consumption changed the entire global mind-set in the mid-1970s. This view was shared by Julian Cribb, award-winning journalist, who suggested that rarely had we been advised "of the true ecological costs of eating" (*The Coming Famine*, 2010). He argued the need for a world diet that "is sparing of energy, water, land, and other inputs and has minimal impact on the eider environment." He added other "big-picture solutions": curbing waste, sharing knowledge, recarbonizing, and movement toward a world farm.

The selections for this issue address the specific question of the planet's continuing ability to grow sufficient food for its growing population.

In the YES selection, Shenggen Fan presents a balances view of the future food situation. Acknowledging recent problems, he nonetheless sees "strong food production and declining food prices." More importantly, he observed several policy developments during the recent past that should result in "a sustainable future." In short, he observes a food systems approach at work that integrates the global approach to the multiple challenges of "hunger, climate change, inequality, jobs, and growth." And he also observed increased national commitments to the problems associated with global food issues. These renewed commitments coupled with accelerating technological advances bode well for the future.

In the NO selection, the report from the UN Food and Agriculture Organization suggests that world hunger, declining the near past, has begun to rise again throughout the globe. It argues that much of this increase is due to an increase in the number of conflicts, but it is also exacerbated by what the report calls "climate-related shocks." Economic showdowns have also contributed to increasing global hunger.

YES ↵

Shenggen Fan

Progress, Uncertainty, and Rising Antiglobalism

The year 2017 was marked by increasing uncertainty amid mixed signs of progress. The world enjoyed a strong economic recovery following a period of stagnation, but global hunger increased as conflicts, famine, and refugee crises persisted. The global landscape continued to change, as anti-globalization sentiment threatened international trade and investment as well as the flow of people and knowledge. Major global events evidenced a shift away from the decades-long trend toward greater global integration. These events included the failure to reach agreement at the World Trade Organization (WTO) Ministerial Conference as well as bilateral actions of the United States and the United Kingdom, all signaling the potential rise of isolationism and protectionism. These changes create uncertainties for global food security and nutrition.

Looking Back at 2017

Economic Recovery, Yet Rising Inequality

Following weak global economic growth in 2016, the weakest since the 2008 global financial crisis, 2017 saw an economic turnaround. Strong economic growth and recovery were supported by a positive global financial environment and the momentum of recovery in advanced economies and several emerging economies.

While it is too early to measure changes in poverty in 2017, the global recovery bodes well for the world's poorest. However, rising inequality within countries may dampen the prospects for poverty reduction. Over recent decades, income inequality within almost all countries increased, although at different speeds, with the lowest levels of inequality in Europe and the highest levels in the Middle East. Global inequality has risen sharply since 1980, as the income of the richest individuals in the world—the top 1 percent—has grown twice as much as that of the bottom 50 percent. Despite promising growth in emerging economies, global inequality is expected to continue increasing if countries hold to "business as usual" policies.

Upward Trend in Hunger and Food Insecurity

Global hunger increased after nearly a decade of prolonged decline. The number of undernourished people globally rose from 777 million in 2015 to 815 million in 2016. Much of the worsening trend in global hunger can be linked to persistent conflicts, which have been exacerbated by climate shocks. The global community dealt with famine as an estimated 38 million people in Nigeria, Somalia, South Sudan, and Yemen faced severe food insecurity, and Ethiopia and Kenya suffered significant droughts. While the global prevalence of stunting among children under age five fell from almost 30 percent in 2005 to 23 percent in 2016, stunting remained a significant issue, with 155 million children affected. If the current trend continues, 130 million children will be stunted in 2025, 30 million above the World Health Assembly target. To significantly reduce stunting and hunger by 2030 if not sooner, many countries will need to accelerate progress. At the same time, overnutrition continues to be a growing concern, for example, in Central Asia, where all countries saw increases in overweight and obesity.6

Strong Food Production and Declining Food Prices

Global food prices remained relatively high for most of 2017, largely driven by higher prices of meat, dairy, and sugar, following low prices in 2015 and 2016. After three months of consecutive increases around midyear, prices declined steadily in the last months of 2017, with a steep decline in December from falling dairy, vegetable oil, and sugar prices. Global cereal production for 2017 is projected at 2,627 million metric tons, a 0.6 percent increase over 2016. Much of the increase is from higher production of coarse grains, forecast at 1,371 million metric tons, a 24-million-ton increase for the year. Contributing to this growth were record high production in Indonesia and increases in US maize production. Global wheat and rice production are forecast to be marginally lower than 2016 levels. With global food commodity prices expected to remain low as a result of strong production and slowing demand growth in emerging economies, much of the world's poor population, who spend a large portion of their income on food, may experience improvements in food security and reductions in poverty.

Antiglobalism on the Rise

Major events in 2017 pointed to a rise in anti-globalization sentiment in the international community. The United States announced its withdrawal from the Trans-Pacific Partnership trade agreement early in the year and later from the Paris Agreement on climate change, marking a shift away from multilateral and international agreements. In Europe, the United Kingdom continued its "Brexit" process, introducing the "Great Repeal Bill" and beginning negotiations for withdrawal from the European Union in 2019. Further, the failure to reach an agreement on a joint Ministerial Declaration at the Eleventh WTO Ministerial Conference in Buenos Aires highlighted critical setbacks, including for agriculture in terms of addressing domestic subsidies, public food stocks, and special safeguard mechanisms, which may presage a new era of isolationism and protectionist policies.

Nevertheless, growth in international trade and investment indicated a continued overall trend toward global integration. World trade grew by 3.6 percent in 2017, a substantial increase from the 1.3 percent growth of 2016. Trade growth was largely driven by recovering import demand in Asia and North America. Global investment flows saw a modest recovery and were forecast to increase to US$1.8 trillion in 2017. While foreign direct investment to developing economies fell by 14 percent, flows to developed economies increased by 5 percent, and flows to transition economies nearly doubled.

Continued Momentum for Sustainable Development

Several major global policy developments in 2017 helped to maintain momentum toward creating a sustainable future and were marked by an increased focus on using a food systems approach to tackle the multiple challenges of hunger, climate change, inequality, jobs, and growth.

G20 leaders committed to the sustainable use of water in food and agricultural production at the 2017 Agriculture Ministers' Conference in Berlin, with an emphasis on governance and coherence of water-related policies; water-use efficiency and resilience; water quality; and information, innovation, and collaboration. The G7 Agriculture Ministerial Meeting focused on protecting farmers' incomes from market crises, natural disasters, and climate change and noted the links between agriculture, migration, and rural development. The meeting in Milan called on governments not only to safeguard farmers' incomes but also to promote cooperation among farmers and diversification of production. The discussions highlighted the importance of providing concrete financial tools for farmers, such as risk management strategies, through investments in research, innovation, information, communication, and training.

The Global Nutrition Summit galvanized governments and donors together to pledge US$640 million in new funding to address the challenges in nutrition facing nearly every country. The summit brought together a wide range of stakeholders to accelerate the global response to malnutrition and launched the *Global Nutrition Report 2017*.

Progress toward the 2030 Agenda for Sustainable Development continued, as the United Nations Statistical Commission formally adopted the indicator framework to track progress on meeting the Sustainable Development Goals (SDGs). This coincided with the adoption of the Cape Town Global Action Plan for Sustainable Development Data, which calls on governments, policy leaders, and the international community to work collectively toward improving data for the SDGs. Countries continued to work together to increase climate action under the Paris Agreement, with the 2017 United Nations Climate Change Conference held against a backdrop of extreme weather events, including hurricanes in the United States and Caribbean, drought in Africa, and floods in South Asia.

Increased National Commitments

At the national level, countries made progress on environmental sustainability as well as nutrition. Norway launched a US$400 million fund to reduce deforestation through agriculture. China issued a new National Nutrition Plan for 2017–2030 that sets nutrition and health goals for anemia, stunting, and breastfeeding for 2020 and 2030. The plan also highlights the importance of regulations, research, and monitoring for nutrition and health outcomes. Bangladesh launched its Second National Plan of Action on Nutrition (2016–2025), outlining efforts to reduce all forms of malnutrition, especially for children, adolescent girls, pregnant women, and lactating mothers.

India launched its National Nutrition Strategy, which commits to ensuring that every child, adolescent girl, and woman attain optimal nutritional status by 2022. Some countries undertook agricultural reforms, such as the expansion of irrigated areas and improved distribution of fertilizers and seeds in Algeria and enhanced water access in Djibouti. Many others—including Ghana, India, and Nigeria—reconfirmed their commitments to Zero Hunger and second Sustainable Development Goal (SDG 2) on ending hunger and malnutrition by 2030.

Looking Forward to 2018

Antiglobalism and the changing global landscape may create further political and economic uncertainties and continue to impact trade, investment, and migration. In particular, the threatened retreat of the United States from international agreements and institutions, including the United Nations, may add to global uncertainties. As many emerging challenges faced by the international community transcend national borders, global governance will be evermore crucial to guide global norms and galvanize collective commitment and action. Whether European countries and emerging economies will step up to lead global governance efforts is an important question for the years ahead.

Global growth is projected to strengthen to 3.1 percent in 2018, which could translate to improvements in livelihoods, poverty status, and food security. Strong global manufacturing and trade, a benign financial environment, and largely stabilized commodity prices support these positive projections. Growth in emerging and developing economies is expected to be strong, with projected growth of 4.5 percent in 2018. East Asian growth is projected to slow slightly in 2018 to 6.2 percent, as China gradually slows, but the rest of the region picks up modestly. The Europe and Central Asia region is forecast to accelerate to 2.9 percent in 2018, and Latin America and the Caribbean to 2.0 percent. After a slight decline in the Middle East and North Africa, growth is expected to rebound to 3.0 percent, assuming a moderation in geopolitical tensions and a rise in oil prices. South Asian growth is projected to accelerate to 6.9 percent in 2018, driven by expansion of domestic demand and exports. Projections for Africa south of the Sahara are a modest 3.2 percent for 2018.

Despite this relatively positive economic outlook, adjustments in the global economy are expected to continue as national economies deal with shrinking workforces and diminished productivity gains while still recovering from the 2008 financial crisis. Growing tendencies toward protectionism, evidenced by changes in US and UK trade policies, also create further economic uncertainties.

However, technological advances will continue to accelerate rapidly, especially in automation and artificial intelligence. While this has the potential to threaten economies and industries that are not able to adjust to the rapid change, technological innovations, coupled with the global flow of knowledge, can be game changers for agriculture and food systems. For example, innovations in information and communication technologies, especially through mobile phones, together with open access data can put vital information in the hands of farmers.

In 2018, the international community is expected to face persistent threats to food security, especially hunger fueled by conflict and compounded by drought. International support will continue to be important for African countries that suffered famine and drought, as much of their populations will remain vulnerable to food insecurity, including 6 million people in South Sudan. In Africa, growth will also remain vulnerable to debt-related fiscal risks, especially in natural resource–exporting countries. Specific challenges will also require international attention, particularly the troubling outlook in Venezuela, where gross domestic product per capita declined for the fourth consecutive year and conditions worsened with acute shortages in food, medicine, and other basic products.

Climate change will continue to pose immediate and long-term threats, particularly extreme weather events, water and soil stress, and food insecurity. Global cooperation will be essential as tensions over climate change grow. Building resilience to climate shocks and strengthening climate-smart agriculture will be increasingly critical.

A renewed commitment to working together will be the key to achieving food security and better nutrition in a sustainable way. At the global, regional, and national levels, data and evidence must remain at the heart of more open, transparent, and inclusive food systems. Current discussions on food systems and commitments to ending hunger must be moved forward to action. Enacting policies to garner the benefits of globalization while minimizing the risks that fuel antiglobalism will be a critical priority in 2018 and beyond.

Shenggen Fan has served as a director general of the International Food Policy Research Institute since 2009.

Food and Agriculture Organization of the United Nations

2017 The State of Food Security and Nutrition in the World

Building Resilience for Peace and Food Security

Key messages

→ After a prolonged decline, world hunger appears to be on the rise again. The estimated number of undernourished people increased to 815 million in 2016, up from 777 million in 2015.

→ Much of the recent increase in food insecurity can be traced to the greater number of conflicts, often exacerbated by climate-related shocks.

→ Even in some peaceful settings, food security has deteriorated as economic slowdowns challenge access to food for the poor.

→ The worrying trend in undernourishment is not yet reflected in levels of chronic child malnutrition (stunting), which continue to fall—but at a slower rate in several regions.

→ Despite the decline, in 2016, stunting still affected one of the four children under the age of five years, or 155 million children. In some regions, stunting affects $1/3$ of children under five years.

→ Wasting continues to threaten the lives of almost 52 million children (8 percent).

→ Almost $1/3$ (33 percent) of women of reproductive age worldwide suffer from anemia, which also puts the nutrition and health of many children at risk.

→ Child overweight and adult obesity are on the rise, including in low- and middle-income countries.

→ Multiple forms of malnutrition are coexisting, with countries experiencing simultaneously high rates of child undernutrition and adult obesity.

After a Prolonged Decline, World Hunger Appears to Be on the Rise Again

In 2016, the number of undernourished people in the world increased to an estimated 815 million, up from 777 million in 2015 but still down from about 900 million in the year 2000. Similarly, while the prevalence of undernourishment (PoU) is projected to have increased to an estimated 11 percent in 2016, this is still well below the level of a decade ago. Nonetheless, the recent increase is caused for great concern and poses a significant challenge for international commitments to end hunger by 2030.

It is not yet clear whether this recent uptick in hunger and food insecurity levels signals the beginning of an upward trend, or whether it reflects an acute transient situation. However, reductions in the levels and degree of undernourishment have slowed significantly since 2010. This sobering news comes in a year in which famine was declared in one country (South Sudan), and crisis-level food insecurity situations at risk of turning into famines were identified in several others (including Nigeria, Somalia, and Yemen).

The food security situation has visibly worsened in parts of sub-Saharan Africa and South-Eastern and Western Asia, as detailed in part 1 of this report. Deteriorations have been observed most notably in situations of conflict, often compounded by droughts or floods (linked in part to the El Niño phenomenon). Part 2 of this report analyzes in depth how conflict affects food security and how food insecurity itself can become a trigger for conflict. Over the past 10 years, the number of violent conflicts around the world has increased significantly, hitting rural communities the hardest. More conflict is thus driving greater food insecurity, fueling hotbeds of violence and creating new ones. The situation has also deteriorated in some peaceful settings, particularly those affected by economic slowdowns. A number of countries heavily dependent on commodity exports have suffered dramatically reduced export and fiscal revenues in recent years, which has affected both food availability through reduced import capacity and food access through reduced fiscal potential to protect poor households against rising domestic food prices.

Child Undernutrition Continues to Decline, But Levels of Overweight Are Increasing

The worrisome trend in undernourishment indicators is, however, not reflected in nutritional outcomes. Evidence on various forms of malnutrition (outlined further below) points to continued decreases in the prevalence of child stunting, as reflected in global and regional averages. However, stunting still affects almost one in four children under the age of five, increasing their risk of impaired cognitive ability, weakened performance at school and work, and dying from infections. At the same time, overweight among children under five is becoming more of a problem in most regions, and adult obesity continues to rise in all regions. Multiple forms of malnutrition therefore coexist, with countries experiencing simultaneously high rates of child undernutrition and adult obesity.

It may be difficult to make sense of a situation in which food security in terms of the estimated adequacy of dietary energy intake is deteriorating globally, though child undernutrition (stunting) is falling and adult obesity is rising. However, food security is but one determinant of nutritional outcomes, especially for children. Other factors include women's educational level; resources allocated to national policies and programs for maternal, infant, and young child nutrition; access to clean water, basic sanitation, and quality health services; lifestyle; food environment; and culture. More context-specific assessments are needed to identify the links between household food security and nutrition and the causes underlying the apparent divergence in the most recent food security and nutritional trends. However, overall, these recent estimates are a warning signal that achieving the goal of a world without hunger and malnutrition by 2030 will be challenging. Accomplishing it will require sustained commitment and efforts to promote adequate availability of and access to nutritious food.

A New Era: Food Security and Nutrition in the 2030 Agenda for Sustainable Development

The State of Food Security and Nutrition in the World 2017 marks the start of a new era in monitoring progress toward achieving a world without hunger and malnutrition—an aim set by the 2030 Agenda for Sustainable Development (2030 Agenda). The SDG 2 calls on countries to "end hunger, achieve food security and improved nutrition, and

promote sustainable agriculture" by 2030. Composed of eight targets, SDG 2 unites hunger, food security, nutrition, and sustainable agriculture under a single objective, compelling the international community to move toward an understanding of how they are interrelated and promoting integrated policy approaches and actions. The start of the 2030 Agenda coincided with the launch of the United Nations Decade of Action on Nutrition (2016–2025), adding impetus to joint efforts at eradicating hunger and preventing all forms of malnutrition worldwide.

Recent Trends in Hunger and Food Insecurity

Target 2.1

> By 2030, end hunger and ensure access by all people, in particular the poor and people in vulnerable situations, including infants, to safe, nutritious, and sufficient food all year round.

PoU

The most recent PoU estimates show that, despite significant population growth, the share of undernourished people in the world decreased from 14.7 percent in 2000 to 10.8 percent in 2013. However, this rate of reduction has slowed significantly recently, coming to a virtual halt between 2013 and 2015. Most worryingly, FAO estimates for 2016 indicate that the global PoU in 2016 may have actually risen to 11 percent, implying a return to the level reached in 2012 and suggesting a possible reversal of the downward trend sustained over recent decades.

The absolute number of people in the world affected by chronic food deprivation began to rise in 2014—going from 775 million people to 777 million in 2015—and is now estimated to have increased further to 815 million in 2016.

The stagnation of the global average of the PoU from 2013 to 2015 is the result of two offsetting changes at the regional level: in sub-Saharan Africa, the share of undernourished people increased, while there was a continued decline in Asia in the same period. However, in 2016, the PoU increased in most regions except Northern Africa, Southern Asia, Eastern Asia, Central America, and the Caribbean. The deterioration was most severe in sub-Saharan Africa and South-Eastern Asia.

Sub-Saharan Africa also remains the region with the highest PoU, affecting an alarming 22.7 percent of the population in 2016. The situation is especially urgent in

Eastern Africa, where $1/3$ of the population is estimated to be undernourished—the subregion's PoU increased from 31.1 percent in 2015 to 33.9 percent in 2016. The Caribbean (17.7 percent) and Asia (11.7 percent overall, with peaks of 14.4 percent in Southern Asia) also continue to show a high PoU. In Asia, the most visible uptick in undernourishment was in South-Eastern Asia, increasing from 9.4 percent to 11.5 percent from 2015 to 2016 to return near levels reached in 2011. In contrast, levels remain low in Latin America, although there are signs that the situation may be deteriorating, especially in South America, where the PoU climbed from 5 percent in 2015 to 5.6 percent in 2016.

Owing in part to the size of its population, the highest number of undernourished people is in Asia. FAO estimates that in 2016 almost 520 million people in Asia, more than 243 million in Africa, and more than 42 million in Latin America and the Caribbean did not have access to sufficient food energy.

The recent increase in the PoU is also confirmed by other data sources. It can be attributed to a variety of factors. New information from food commodity balances for many countries points to recent reductions in food availability and increases in food prices in regions affected by El Niño/La Niña–related phenomena—most notably in Eastern and Southern Africa and in South-Eastern Asia. In addition, the number of conflicts has increased in the past decade, in particular in countries already facing high food insecurity and with much of the related violence affecting rural areas and having a negative impact on food production and availability. This surge in conflicts has affected African and Near East nations the most and led to food-crisis situations, especially where compounded by droughts or other weather-related events and fragile response capacities.

Worsening food security conditions have also been observed in more peaceful settings, particularly where economic slowdowns have drained foreign exchange and fiscal revenues. This has affected both food availability by reducing import capacity and food access owing to more limited fiscal space to protect poor households against rising domestic food prices, as seen, for example, in parts of Latin America and Western Asia. Costs have risen significantly in countries that typically rely on revenues from oil and other primary commodity exports to finance food imports and subsidies. Lower oil and mineral prices have limited governments' spending capacity, contributing to slowdowns, stagnation, or outright recessions in the real sector of some economies, leading to increased unemployment and declines in incomes. In addition, such economic downturns have reduced fiscal revenue and eroded resources available to sustain subsidies on basic needs and support through social protection programs.

Prevalence of Severe Food Insecurity in the Population, Based on the FIES

The FIES is a new source of additional evidence on the state of food security. Data collected by FAO in 2014, 2015, and 2016 in almost 150 countries reveal that nearly 1 in 10 people in the world (9.3 percent) suffered from severe food insecurity, corresponding to about 689 million people.

Pronounced differences in the prevalence of severe food insecurity are observed across continents, largely paralleling those for undernourishment. Africa has the highest levels of severe food insecurity, reaching 27.4 percent of the population—almost four times that of any other region in 2016. It is also one of the regions where food insecurity is on the rise, particularly in sub-Saharan Africa, with an increase of almost 3 percentage points from 2014 to 2016. Higher food insecurity was also observed in Latin America over the three-year period, rising from 4.7 percent to 6.4 percent.

In Asia, the prevalence of severe food insecurity decreased slightly between 2014 and 2016, from 7.7 percent to 7.0 percent overall, driven mainly by the reduction observed in Central Asia and Southern Asia.

As the FIES survey was administered to individual respondents, one important feature is that the results can be analyzed at the individual level. This makes it possible to compare food insecurity levels among men and women, inter alia, with three-year averages showing that the prevalence of food insecurity was slightly higher among women at the global level as well as in every region of the world.

Trends in All Forms of Malnutrition

Target 2.2

> By 2030, end all forms of malnutrition, including achieving, by 2025, the internationally agreed targets on stunting and wasting in children under five years of age, and address the nutritional needs of adolescent girls, pregnant and lactating women, and older persons.

SDG 2, Target 2.2, calls for an end to "all forms of malnutrition" by 2030, as does the UN Decade of Action on Nutrition. Malnutrition ranges from severe undernutrition to overweight and obesity. It affects populations throughout the life cycle, from conception through childhood, into adolescence, adulthood, and older age. Malnutrition may be a reflection of deficiencies in macronutrients (carbohydrates, fats, or proteins) or micronutrients (vitamins and minerals). It can be acute—resulting from an immediate crisis in food accessibility, inadequate nutrient intake, and/or infection—or chronic, with cumulative deleterious effects over sustained periods. On the other hand, an excessive intake of food and calories and/or limited energy expenditure results in increased body weight and fat accumulation, which can lead to diet-related noncommunicable diseases and other health problems. Undernutrition, overweight, and their associated noncommunicable diseases now coexist in many regions, countries, and even households. Six nutrition indicators—three that form part of the SDG monitoring framework and three that refer to global nutrition targets agreed by the World Health Assembly (WHA)—are described below to better understand the multiple burden of malnutrition, which affects all regions in the world.

Stunting among Children under Five Years of Age

Children's linear growth in the first five years of life is assessed by the stunting indicator. Stunting is evidence that children are too short for their age, which in turn is a reflection of a chronic state of undernutrition. When children are stunted before the age of two, they are at higher risk of illness and more likely than adequately nourished children to develop poor cognitive skills and learning abilities in later childhood and adolescence. This will affect labor productivity, income-earning potential, and social skills later in life, with consequences beyond the individual level. If widespread, stunting also drags down the economic development of entire communities and nations.

Stunting impedes the achievement of other SDG targets related to child health, educational attainment, and economic growth. Thus, SDG Target 2.2 aims to reduce its prevalence by 2025. Whereas the global nutrition target for stunting adopted in 2012 by the WHA is expressed in terms of the total number of stunted children, the SDG indicator measures the prevalence of stunting: owing to population growth, the number of stunted children can increase even as there is a decrease in the prevalence of stunting. Hence, it is important to assess trends in both relative and absolute terms.

According to the latest estimates for 2016, 155 million children under five years across the world suffer from stunted growth. Globally, the prevalence of stunting fell from 29.5 percent to 22.9 percent between 2005 and 2016. However, at current trends, there would be 130 million stunted children by 2025, which would be 30 million

above the global WHA target and despite a 40 percent reduction from 2012 levels.

The prevalence of stunting is currently highest in Eastern Africa, Middle Africa, Western Africa, Southern Asia, and Oceania (excluding Australia and New Zealand), where more than 30 percent of children under five are too short for their age. From 2005 to 2016, most regions achieved reductions in stunting, with the rate of improvement fastest in Asia (particularly Eastern and Central Asia) and Latin America and the Caribbean. The prevalence of stunting also declined in all subregions in Africa, but at a much slower rate. In fact, the rate of decline in stunting in Africa has not kept pace with population increases, resulting in a higher number of stunted children overall. In absolute terms, Africa is the only region where the number of stunted children has risen, with Western Africa accounting for half of this increase. The vast majority of stunted children live in Asia (87 million) and Africa (59 million).

Among the key determinants of stunting are compromised maternal health and nutrition before and during pregnancy and lactation, inadequate breastfeeding, poor feeding practices for infants and young children, and unhealthy environments for children, including poor hygiene and sanitation.

Accordingly, stunting (as well as wasting, overweight, and micronutrient deficiencies) can be addressed through preventive actions, including by ensuring that pregnant and lactating mothers are adequately nourished, that infants receive exclusive breastfeeding during the first six months of life, and that complementary foods are available in adequate quantities, quality, and variety for children aged 6–23 months. To reduce stunting, it is essential to focus nutrition interventions on the first 1,000 days of life—from conception to the age of two years—and improve access to quality health services for maternal and child health. Other steps may be needed to prevent infections and illnesses from negatively affecting nutritional status, such as improving access to safe water, awareness of safe disposal of child feces, and basic hygiene (e.g., access to soap).

Wasting among Children under Five Years of Age

Childhood wasting, or being too thin for one's height, reflects a recent and acute process that leads to weight loss and/or poor weight gain. Wasting usually results from low birth weight, inadequate diet, poor care practices, and infections. It is of critical importance due to the consequent heightened risk of disease and death. It will be difficult to continue improving child survival without investing in preventive interventions to reduce the number of children suffering from wasting, while ensuring timely and appropriate life-saving treatment for children affected by severe wasting.

The internationally agreed global nutrition target is to reduce and maintain childhood wasting to below 5 percent by 2025. In 2016, wasting affected 7.7 percent (51.7 million) of children under five years of age worldwide. About 17 million children suffered from severe wasting. Southern Asia stands out with a high prevalence of 15.4 percent—well above that of any other subregion. At 8.9 percent, South-Eastern Asia is also far off target. While the prevalence is somewhat lower in Africa, it still stands above the global nutrition target.

Overweight among Children under Five Years of Age

Childhood overweight, or being too heavy for one's height, reflects a chronic process of excessive weight gain. Overweight children are at a higher risk of developing serious health problems, including type 2 diabetes, high blood pressure, asthma and other respiratory problems, sleep disorders, and liver disease. Childhood overweight also increases the risk of obesity, diet-related noncommunicable diseases, premature death, and disability in adulthood. The economic costs of the rising epidemics of childhood overweight and obesity are considerable, both in terms of the enormous financial strains on health-care systems and of lost productivity. Reversing obesity and overweight is a serious challenge: the emphasis must be on prevention.

Worldwide, an estimated 41 million children (about 6 percent) under five were considered overweight in 2016, up from 5 percent in 2005. While this may seem a small increase, most subregions show an upward trend. In 2016, the prevalence of childhood overweight reached almost 12 percent in Southern Africa, 11 percent in Central Asia, 10 percent in Northern Africa, 8 percent in Northern America, and 7 percent in South-Eastern Asia and South America. Only Western Africa, South America, and Eastern Asia recorded slight declines between 2005 and 2016. In Eastern Africa, the prevalence remained constant at 4.7 percent. All other regions registered increases in the prevalence of childhood overweight, the fastest rising being in South-Eastern Asia and Oceania.

Many children today are growing up in obesogenic environments that encourage unhealthy food preferences and inadequate physical activity patterns, which in turn lead to weight gain and obesity. Energy imbalances have resulted from changes in the availability, affordability, and marketing of highly processed foods that are high in sugar and fats, often combined with a decline in physical activity owing to more sedentary lifestyles.

Obesity among Adults

Obesity in adults, or having more weight than considered healthy, is a long-term consequence of consuming more energy than is expended. It is a major risk factor for noncommunicable diseases, including cardiovascular disease, diabetes, and some cancers. Noncommunicable diseases represent the leading causes of death and illness worldwide and contribute to social inequities. Available cost estimates also indicate overweight and obesity pose increasing burdens on individuals, families, and societies.

While the SDG framework does not include a specific indicator for adult obesity, eliminating it is included in the target to end all forms of malnutrition. Reducing obesity will be important for achieving other SDG targets—such as ensuring healthy lives and promoting well-being for all (Target 3.4)—as well as for reducing death rates from noncommunicable diseases through prevention and treatment.

The global prevalence of obesity more than doubled between 1980 and 2014. In 2014, more than 600 million adults were obese, equal to about 13 percent of the world's adult population. The prevalence is higher on average among women (15 percent) than men (11 percent). While it varies widely across regions of the world, the problem is most severe in Northern America, Europe, and Oceania, where 28 percent of adults are classified as obese, compared with 7 percent in Asia and 11 percent in Africa. In Latin America and the Caribbean, roughly ¼ of the adult population is currently considered obese.

Obesity has steadily increased in all regions since 1975, and the pace has accelerated in the past 10 years. Global adult obesity rates increased by an average of 1 percentage point every three years between 2004 and 2014. Historically, the prevalence of adult obesity has been much lower in Africa and Asia, where only moderate increases were observed in the 1980s and 1990s. More recently, however, obesity has spread rapidly among larger parts of the population in these regions as well. Hence, while many low- and middle-income countries still face high levels of undernutrition and prevalence of infectious, communicable diseases, they are now also experiencing an increasing burden of people suffering from overweight and obesity and an associated rise in certain noncommunicable diseases such as diabetes.

Changes in dietary patterns and food systems have led to increasing consumption of highly processed foods across the world. While processed foods are not necessarily unhealthy, many contain high levels of saturated fats, salt, and sugars and tend to be low in vitamins and minerals. As a result, diets have become less healthy. At the same time, income growth and urbanization have led to more sedentary lifestyles, exacerbating imbalances in food energy intake and energy use. Poor nutrition in this sense of the word is now considered the major risk factor for the global burden of disease.

Anemia in Women of Reproductive Age

Anemia occurs when red blood cells are low in number and size, resulting in a state of hemoglobin concentration that limits the blood's ability to transport oxygen around the body. This can be due to eating a diet that is low in micronutrient content (e.g., iron, folate, riboflavin, and vitamins A and B12), acute and/or chronic infections (e.g., malaria, tuberculosis, and HIV), other chronic diseases and cancer, or inherited genetic disorders that affect hemoglobin synthesis, red blood cell production or red blood cell survival. Anemia is thus an indicator of both poor nutrition and poor health. Children and women are particularly vulnerable to anemia.

SDG Target 2.2 explicitly calls for the nutritional needs of adolescent girls and pregnant and lactating women to be addressed, as anemia in women of reproductive age is a public health concern. The condition not only has significant adverse health consequences for women and their offspring, it can also affect social and economic development. When anemia occurs during pregnancy, it causes fatigue, lowered productivity, increased risk of maternal and perinatal mortality, low birth weight, and anemia and poor growth and development in young children. Anemia is therefore closely linked to other SDG targets—lowering its prevalence will help to reduce maternal mortality (Target 3.1) and improve levels of economic productivity (Target 8.2). Meanwhile, achieving universal health coverage (Target 3.8) and increasing access to sexual and reproductive health care (Target 5.6) would also contribute to reducing the prevalence of anemia.

The most recent estimates for 2016 indicate that anemia affects 33 percent of women of reproductive age globally (about 613 million women between 15 and 49 years of age). In Africa and Asia, the prevalence is highest at over 35 percent. It is lowest in Northern America and Europe, and Oceania (below 20 percent).

The global average of the prevalence of anemia in women of reproductive age increased slightly between 2005 and 2016, although the increase was not statistically significant. It declined from 42 percent to 38 percent in

Africa and from 25 percent to 22 percent in Latin America and the Caribbean, although this was offset by slight increases in all other regions. In 2012, the WHA set the target of halving the prevalence of anemia in women of reproductive age by 2025. Progress so far has clearly been off track.

Exclusive Breastfeeding for Infants under Six Months of Age

Improved rates of breastfeeding directly contribute to ending hunger and child malnutrition, and increasing the rate of exclusive breastfeeding by up to 50 percent in the first six months of life is one of the global nutrition targets endorsed by the WHA. Exclusive breastfeeding is part of optimal breastfeeding practices, which also include initiation within the first hour of life and continued breastfeeding up to two years old or beyond. Breastfeeding is a cornerstone of child survival and development as it provides essential irreplaceable nutrition for a child's physical and cognitive growth. Breastfeeding helps to reduce child mortality, improve nutritional status, prevent common childhood illnesses and noncommunicable diseases, and improve development and learning. It is considered to be the preventive intervention with the single largest impact on child survival. Breastfeeding also benefits mothers as it promotes uterine contraction, helps prevent postpartum hemorrhage, decreases the likelihood of developing iron-deficiency anemia, and reduces the risk of various types of cancer.

According to a recent estimate, improving breastfeeding rates could prevent 820,000 child deaths and an additional 20,000 maternal cancer-related deaths each year. Moreover, there is increasing evidence that breastfeeding decreases the risk of overweight and obesity later in life.

Globally, 43 percent of infants younger than six months were exclusively breastfed in 2016, up from 36 percent in 2005. The prevalence of exclusive breastfeeding was highest in Southern Asia (59 percent) and Eastern Africa (57 percent). It is much lower in Latin America and the Caribbean (33 percent), Eastern Asia (28 percent), Western Africa (25 percent), and Western Asia (21 percent). Too few countries provided data on exclusive breastfeeding to report a regional average for Europe, North America, or Oceania.

Between 2005 and 2015, the practice of exclusive breastfeeding increased by at least 10 percentage points in 36 out of 82 countries for which comparable data were available. In some countries (e.g., Burkina Faso, Guinea-Bissau, Kenya, and Turkmenistan), the prevalence increased by more than 35 percentage points, providing evidence that it is feasible to achieve significant gains in exclusive breastfeeding in a short period of time. Overall, half of all countries in Africa with trend data exhibited an increase of 10 percentage points or more, and a greater proportion of countries in that region made increases in excess of 20 percentage points when compared to Europe or Latin America and the Caribbean. However, in many countries, more still needs to be done to improve breastfeeding practices.

Toward an Integrated Understanding of Food Security and Nutrition

So far, this report has provided an assessment of the state of food security and nutrition in the world based on an examination of two indicators of food security and six indicators on nutrition. However, fulfilling the ambitions of the 2030 Agenda requires a proper understanding of the interrelationships among these indicators. Balanced diets are essential for improved nutrition, health, and well-being. The success of efforts to improve diets will depend on a better understanding of the complex relationships between food security and nutrition, the food systems in which they are embedded and the social, political, and economic forces shaping them. The preliminary analyses in this section are intended to promote more integrated and critical thinking on these issues.

There is ample evidence that food insecurity and malnutrition in all its forms have multiple and diverse negative effects on health and well-being. Adverse impacts on mental health and cognitive and behavioral effects in children are also well documented. The nutrition indicators discussed in the previous section refer to different moments in the human life cycle, helping to shed light on the consequences of food insecurity and malnutrition for health and development before birth, into infancy and on to adulthood.

The coexistence of food insecurity and obesity—even in the same household—is often seen as paradoxical, but there are many explanations for this. As resources for food become scarce, people often choose to eat lower-cost, less-healthy, more energy-dense foods, choices that can lead to people becoming overweight and obese as their means to access healthy food diminish.

Periodic episodes of food insecurity and deprivation can also lead to eating disorders and stress-related metabolic responses. This can in turn increase the risk of obesity and noncommunicable chronic diseases such as cancer, diabetes, hypertension, and heart disease. Food insecurity and poor nutrition during pregnancy and childhood are also associated with metabolic adaptations that increase the risk of obesity and associated noncommunicable chronic diseases in adulthood. Readily available and accessible highly processed foods that are high in fat, sugar and salt, and shifts away from traditional diets toward convenience foods further help explain the coexistence of multiple forms of malnutrition within the same communities and households.

While food insecurity at the household or individual level increases the risk of developing various forms of malnutrition, there are many mediating factors. All of the nutritional outcomes analyzed here are affected in important ways by other elements, such as educational level, lifestyle, food environment, and habits, and access to clean water, basic sanitation, and quality health services. In turn, undernutrition negatively affects cognitive development and child growth, leading to reduced levels of productivity and economic development.

As more and improved data become available in the years ahead, it will be possible to enhance knowledge of the links between the food security and nutrition indicators analyzed below, the factors that mediate these links, and the actions needed to simultaneously promote both food security and better nutrition.

The Multiple Burden of Malnutrition

No country is free from malnutrition, and most countries experience multiple burdens of malnutrition. Typically, data on child undernutrition, micronutrient deficiencies, child overweight, and adult obesity are presented separately. This section aims to shed some light on the overlaps, as they reflect the numerous issues that countries are facing.

Out of 119 countries with comparable data for at least three of the six nutrition indicators, only two (Japan and the Republic of Korea) experienced just one single form of malnutrition. Rates of prevalence of childhood stunting are positively correlated with childhood wasting and anemia among women. Similarly, countries with a high prevalence of childhood overweight also tend to have a high prevalence of adult obesity, while in countries that still have high rates of child stunting, adult obesity tends to be lower.

Although this cross-country analysis indicates that lower prevalence of childhood stunting tends to be found in countries with a higher rate of adult obesity, many countries have high rates of both. For example, of the 107 countries with data on both stunting in under-five year olds and adult obesity, 35 have a prevalence of more than

10 percent in under-five stunting as well as more than 10 percent in adult obesity. In three countries (Egypt, Iraq, and Vanuatu), more than 20 percent of the under-five population is stunted and more than 20 percent of adults are obese.

Therefore, tackling malnutrition in all its forms requires a country-specific combination of measures that leverage multiple sectors to address the underlying determinants of malnutrition and target nutrition interventions to prevent or treat the direct determinants of malnutrition. Countries make progress when initiatives from multiple levels and sectors converge and reinforce each other.

Food Insecurity and the Multiple Burden of Malnutrition

Food insecurity, or the inability of households and individuals to access food of adequate quantity and quality, is an important determinant of malnutrition. However, exploring the causal relationships between food insecurity and nutrition outcomes requires detailed information at the household—or even better, individual—level. As a preliminary step, a simple cross-country analysis was performed to explore the relationships between PoU and nutritional indicators.

Presents the results of country-specific fixed effects logistic regressions using all available country-level data from 1990 to 2015. The results control for the income level in each country. Country dummies were introduced to control for specific country characteristics that do not vary with time.

The results show that countries with higher levels of undernourishment also show higher levels of stunting and wasting. In contrast, higher levels of undernourishment are associated with lower levels of child overweight and adult obesity.

The results suggest that adult obesity is more prevalent in countries with a low PoU. Many Pacific Island countries and territories are outliers, showing much higher adult obesity rates (in the range of 40–50 percent) than those of other countries with a similar PoU.

The negative association between food insecurity and obesity is confirmed when using cross-country data for the prevalence of severe food insecurity in the population as measured with the FIES. However, the findings differ when countries are grouped by income level. This is consistent with the growing body of literature showing that food insecurity at the household level is associated with obesity. Among high- and upper-middle–income countries, the adult obesity rates are higher in countries

where the prevalence of severe food insecurity (measured by the FIES) is also comparatively higher. Understanding the reasons for this requires an analysis of the association between food security and obesity at the household and individual level, as well as of the multiple mediating factors. This is possible when the FIES survey module is included in national health and nutrition surveys or in household consumption and expenditure surveys. Existing evidence from higher-income countries suggests that food insecure people rely on lower-cost, less-healthy, energy-dense foods and are also at higher risk of eating disorders and stress-related metabolic responses, all of which can lead to obesity.

Strengthening the Evidence Base to Monitor Food Security and Nutrition

Bringing food security and nutrition under one single goal in the 2030 Agenda has catalyzed efforts at coming to an integral understanding of these fundamental ingredients of human well-being. While ample data are already available, many more are needed in order to come to a fuller understanding. In particular, improved coordination is needed at the national, regional, and global levels to produce data capable of shedding more light on the links between food insecurity and malnutrition and their determinants.

The simple correlates presented in the previous section suggest that when people face food insecurity, they are also likely to be at risk for various forms of malnutrition. However, nutritional outcomes are influenced by many other factors as well, such as physical activity, lifestyle, food preferences, food environments, women's education, and access to clean water, basic sanitation, and quality health services.

Incongruent timing in data collection is one of the limitations of such country-level analysis of food insecurity and nutrition indicators. For example, available data on child stunting and wasting for many countries were collected in years prior to the collection of FIES data. This complicates analysis of the association between food insecurity and these two indicators. This limitation may explain in part why the prevalence of child stunting continues to show a decline even as food insecurity appears to be on the rise.

National surveys that integrate the collection of food insecurity and nutrition data as well as data on potential drivers and mediating factors are essential to understanding the true relationship between food insecurity and malnutrition. Such integrated surveys, if conducted regularly and according to internationally agreed standards, can provide more detailed information at the subnational level, identifying the sociodemographic groups at greatest risk of food insecurity and malnutrition, and helping to guide actions to meet the challenge of leaving no one behind.

More research into the long-term effects of food insecurity on nutritional outcomes is also needed in order to strengthen the evidence base. The hope is that including food insecurity and nutrition indicators in the SDG monitoring framework will provide the necessary impetus for national governments, international donors, and development partners to prioritize such data-collection efforts to build a stronger evidence base.

Progress Has Slowed, New Concerns Have Emerged

In summary, the evidence presented in part 1 reveals a global scenario of a possible recent uptick in hunger. Child undernutrition has continued to decline, but rates are still unacceptably high in some regions. The increasing prevalence of overweight among children and the accelerated rise in obesity among adults are of major concern. Almost all countries in the world are experiencing multiple forms of malnutrition simultaneously, and food insecurity often coexists with obesity.

Globally, cross-country analysis shows that rates of adult obesity are lower in countries with higher rates of food insecurity. However, within the group of upper-middle- and high-income countries, where more than ¼ of the adult population are obese, the highest rates of obesity are associated with relatively higher rates of severe food insecurity. Childhood overweight is highest in Central Asia and Northern Africa, suggesting future problems with adult obesity in these regions as well. The regions most affected by nutritional deficiencies are Africa and Asia, where more than one in three women suffer from anemia and almost ¼ of the population of children under-five are stunted.

The drivers behind these trends in food insecurity and malnutrition differ from country to country and even within countries. Food systems and diets are changing. As large companies increasingly dominate markets, highly processed foods become more readily available, and traditional foods and eating habits are displaced. Weather-related events—in part linked to climate change—have affected food availability in many countries and contributed to the rise in food insecurity. Economic slowdowns in countries highly dependent on oil and other primary commodity export revenues have also had an impact on food availability and/or reduced people's ability to access food.

Malnutrition is not only the result of a lack of access to sufficient, nutritious, and safe food. It also derives from a series of interlinked factors related to inadequate access to resources and services, such as quality health care, education, drinking-water, sanitation, and hygiene. Poor women often face additional hurdles to access resources and services. Compelling evidence shows that improving women's education and status within their households and communities has a direct positive impact on food nutrition and security, in particular child nutrition.

Another increasingly important cause of food insecurity and malnutrition is conflict. People living in countries affected by conflict and violence are more likely to be food insecure and malnourished, particularly in those countries characterized by protracted conflict and fragile institutions.

Part 2 of this report takes a closer look at the specific challenges facing these countries, and the relationship between hunger, conflict, and peace. It highlights the need for conflict-sensitive approaches to improving food security and nutrition, based on a deeper understanding of the dynamics of conflict in each context. More fundamentally, it points to a need to find lasting solutions to conflict if the world is to end hunger and achieve food security and improved nutrition for all.

THE FOOD AND AGRICULTURE ORGANIZATION OF THE UNITED NATIONS, headquartered in Rome, Italy, is a governmental organization with 195 nation members and present in 130 countries. Among its functions is to help eliminate hunger, food insecurity, and malnourishment, and to make agriculture, forestry, and fisheries more productive and sustainable.

EXPLORING THE ISSUE

Will the World Be Able to Feed Itself in the Foreseeable Future?

Critical Thinking and Reflection

1. Do the data from the past decade regarding possible progress in addressing global undernourishment and hunger show the glass to be half-full or half-empty?
2. Is the real problem of undernourishment and hunger due to factors unrelated to the actual growing of food?
3. Is the wide range of pressures adversely affecting food production simply too daunting to allow for dramatic increases in production?
4. What effect will economic development in the poorer regions of the globe have on the capacity of the future world to feed itself?
5. Is it realistic to think that people will unilaterally choose to become self-sufficient (grow their own food) and practice better food anti-waste patterns of behavior?

Is There Common Ground?

Analysts are in agreement that increased population and increased affluence among the currently less-affluent peoples of the world will increase the demand for food in the next 50 years. At the same time, most believe that increased conflicts and climate-related shocks will adversely affect the food supply and demand balance. There is also significant agreement that enough food is currently produced but that the distribution system is flawed for whatever reason. There is also agreement that real progress has been made over the past few decades in lowering the percentage of undernourishment and hunger in the world.

Additional Resources

Food and Agriculture Organization of the United Nations, *Food Outlook: Biannual Report on Global Markets* (November 2017)

Food and Agriculture Organization of the United Nations, *The Future of Food and Agriculture: Trends and Challenges* (2017)

Food and Agriculture Organization of the United Nations, *2017 The State of Food and Agriculture: Leveraging Food Systems for Inclusive Rural Transformation* (2017)

Food Security Information Network, *Global Report on Food Crises 2017* (March 2017)

Global Harvest Initiative, 2017 Global Agricultural Productivity Report, *A World of Productive Sustainable Agriculture* (October 2017)

Internet References . . .

Food First

www.foodfirst.org

International Food Policy Research Institute

www.ifpri.org

The Hunger Project

www.thp.org

UN Food and Agriculture Organization

www.fao.org

UN World Food Programme

www.wfp.org

Selected, Edited, and with Issue Framing Material by:
James E. Harf, *Maryville University*

ISSUE

Can the Global Community Successfully Confront the Global Water Shortage?

YES: "The United Nations World Water Development Report 2018: Nature-Based Solutions for Water," United Nations World Assessment Programme (2018)

NO: Lisa Guppy and Kelsey Anderson, from "Global Water Crisis: The Facts," United Nations University Institute for Water, Environment, and Health (2017)

Learning Outcomes

After reading this issue, you will be able to:

- Understand the evolution of the global community's concern about global water issues.
- Understand the many dimensions associated with the global water crisis.
- Understand the factors associated with increased global water demand.
- Understand the relationship between water and the dimensions of sustainable development.
- Understand why experts predict that the global water crisis threatens the stability of nations and the health of billions of people.

ISSUE SUMMARY

YES: The report suggests that "solutions may be closer than we think" to solving the problem of more than 2 billion people lacking the access to safe drinking water and more than double that amount having no access to safe sanitation. The key, according to the Report, is to use nature to create a cost-effective way to address these problems while also providing "environmental, social, and economic benefits."

NO: The authors point out that water has been a pressing concern and in some areas of the world a "critical national concern." They argue that business as usual will result in the failure of the international community to address goals created by international bodies regarding adequate water supplies. The report examines the water crisis from six interrelated contexts: "water scarcity and insecurity; water-related disasters; water, sanitation, and health crisis; water infrastructure deterioration and destruction; unsustainable development; and ecosystem degradation."

In March 2018, The World Bank and the United Nations issued a joint report sounding the alarm once again about the growing global water situation. *Making Every Drop Count: An Agenda for Water Action* outlined global water problems and laid out a series of recommendations for addressing these problems. The issue was summed up by World Bank President Jim Yong Kim: "The ecosystems on which life is based—our food security, energy sustainability, public health, jobs, cities—are all at risk because of how water is managed today." He continued: "The world today can no longer take water for granted." UN Secretary-General António Guterres echoed that "world leaders now recognize that we face a global water crisis and that we need to reassess how we value and manage water." The

Report was the product of two years of research under the leadership of a panel of 11 heads of state.

The Report highlighted the current dimensions of the global water problem and the accompanying data spelled it out in stark detail. Over 2 billion people drink contaminated water, leading to a child dying every minute of the day. Additionally, 4.5 billion people lack satisfactory sanitation services. The Report continued with the revelation that 2.3 billion people or 36 percent of the global population live in "water-scarce regions" where more than a fifth of the global GDP is produced. The percentage is expected to increase to over 50 percent by 2050. And ironically, water is more likely to be wasted in water-scarce areas than in water-abundant areas. The Report also revealed that over the past 20 years, 90 percent of disasters have been caused by water-related situations. By 2050, desertification will threaten almost 1 billion people's ability to function economically. As more and more people throughout the globe flock to towns and cities, the demand for water will only increase in the coming decades. At the same time, the lack of investment in water infrastructure continues. As the Report relates, "Water crises are usually governance crises." Translating known technical solutions into public policy has been the difficult if not impossible task.

This Report was not the first to sound the alarm. As early as 1964, the United Nations Environmental Programme (UNEP) revealed that close to a billion people were at risk of desertification. At the Earth Summit in Rio de Janeiro in 1992, world leaders reaffirmed that desertification was of serious concern. In March 2011, high-level experts from around the globe met at the invitation of the InterAction Council, an international organization of former heads of government, to discuss the status of the world's freshwater supply as it related to global security. The main conclusion of the group was that the global water crisis is both real and urgent, as 1 billion people were without reliable water sources and 2 billion were without adequate sanitation. Their conclusions mirrored those of others. As the World Water Council suggests, the times of "easy water" are long gone. Water shortages and other water problems are occurring with greater frequency, particularly in large cities. Some observers have speculated that the situation is reminiscent of the fate that befell ancient glorious cities such as Rome.

A 2015 White Paper Prepared by the United Nations Food and Agricultural Organization, *Towards a Water and Food Secure Future: Critical Perspectives for Policy-Makers*, built on these views, suggesting that while the outlook for 2050 "is encouraging, [. . .] much work is needed to achieve sustainable water use [. . .]." While the report suggested that at the global level, sufficient water will exist

for food production, an increasing number of regions will "face growing water scarcity." Urban demands for water will increase in the developing world because of increased population in the coming decades. By 2050, agriculture will continue to be the biggest user of water globally. And climate change is expected, according to the white paper, to bring greater challenges to water management.

A much more stark assessment appeared in February 2016 in the journal *Science Advances*, with the claim that global water shortages are worse than previously thought. Recognition that the supply of water is a growing problem is not new. Moreover, since these early warnings about global water, in conference after conference and study after study, increasing population growth and declining water supplies and quality are being linked together, as is the relationship between the planet's ability to meet its growing food needs and available water. Lester R. Brown, in "Water Deficits Growing in Many Countries: Water Shortages May Cause Food Shortages," *Eco-Economy Update 2002–2011* (August 6, 2002), summed up the problem this way: "The world is incurring a vast water deficit. It is largely invisible, historically recent, and growing fast." The World Water Council's study, "World Water Actions Report, Third Draft" (October 31, 2002), described the problem in much the same way: "Water is no longer taken for granted as a plentiful resource that will always be available when we need it." The report continued with the observation that increasing numbers of people in more and more countries are discovering that water is a "limited resource that must be managed for the benefit of people and the environment, in the present and in the future." In short, water is fast becoming both a food-related issue and a health-related problem. Some scholars are now arguing that water shortage is likely to become the twenty-first century's analog to the oil crisis of the last half of the previous century. The one major difference, as scholars are quick to point out, is that water is not like oil; there is no substitute.

Proclamations of impending water problems abound in the literature. Peter Gleick, in *The World's Water 1998–1999: The Biennial Report on Freshwater Resources* (Island Press, 1998), reported that the demand for freshwater increased six-fold between 1900 and 1995, twice the rate of population growth. The UN study *United Nations Comprehensive Assessment of Fresh-water Resources of the World* (1997) suggested that $1/3$ of the world's population lives in countries having medium to high water stress. One 2001 headline reporting the release of a new study proclaimed that "Global thirst 'will turn millions into water refugees'" (*The Independent*, 1999). News reports released by the UN Food and Agricultural Organization in conjunction with

World Food Day 2002 asserted that water scarcity could result in millions of people having inadequate access to clean water or sufficient food. And the World Meteorological Organization predicts that two of every three people will live in water-stressed conditions by 2050 if consumption patterns remain the same.

Sandra Postel, in Pillar *of Sand: Can the Irrigation Miracle Last?* (W. W. Norton, 1999), suggested another variant of the water problem. For her, the time-tested method of maximizing water usage in the past, irrigation, may not be feasible as world population marches toward 7 billion. She points to the inadequacy of surface water supplies, increasing depletion of groundwater supplies, the salinization of the land, and the conversion of traditional agricultural land to other uses as reasons for the likely inability of irrigation to be a continuing panacea. Yet the 1997 UN study concluded that annual irrigation use would need to increase 30 percent for annual food production to double, necessary for meeting food demands of 2025.

The issue of water quality has also been in the news. The World Health Organization earlier reported that in some parts of the world, up to 80 percent of all transmittable diseases were attributable to the consumption of contaminated water. Also, a UNEP-sponsored study, *Global Environment Out-look 2000,* reported that 200 scientists from 50 countries pointed to the shortage of clean water as one of the most pressing global issues.

Other studies within the past decade brought the same message. The UN *World Water Development Report* 2009 laid out the problems and the challenges of global water and suggested that current decision-making processes are not up to the challenge of addressing these problems. The report outlined major issues in the areas of access to drinking water infrastructure, sanitation infrastructure, effects of population growth, agriculture and livestock, energy, sanitation treatment of waste water, climate change, and migration issues related to water scarcity.

In 2010, the World Water Council, an international water think tank sponsored by the World Bank and the UN, also sounded the alarm, suggesting that more than one of six humans lack access to safe drinking water, while more than two of six lack adequate sanitation. The Council suggested that during the next 50 years, population growth coupled with industrialization and urbanization would dramatically increase the demand for safe water.

Studies show a continuation of major problems relating to water scarcity and insecurity, water-related disasters, water-related sanitation and health issues, and water infrastructure deterioration and destruction. One of the attached articles to this issue outlines the specific problems in each of these areas. For example, the authors suggest that there has been a 55 percent drop in globally available fresh water per capita since 1960, while the global demand is expected to grow by 50 percent by 2030. And 40 percent of the global population is affected as a consequence. They predict that by 2050, 2.3 billion people will likely living in areas with severe water stress. The cost of this water insecurity is estimated at $500 billion annually by that time. Water disasters cost $50 billion annually. It is estimated that by 2050, 150–200 million people will be displaced because of water-related natural phenomena, such as desertification, sea-level rise, and increased extreme weather activities. Regarding drinking water, 1.8 billion people now drink contaminated water by faeces. And 3.5 million individuals die annually from unsafe water and poor sanitation. The news about water infrastructure is not any better. At least 80 percent of wastewater is returned to the environment without adequate treatment. And 30 percent of global water abstraction is lost through leakage. Finally, water-related issues for sustainable development and ecosystem degradation appear daunting as well.

The World Water Council recently suggested a comprehensive plan of action that focused on four major initiatives: supporting political action to improve water and sanitation services and water management, deepening the involvement of major water users, strengthening regional cooperation to achieve water security and economic development, and mobilizing citizens and consumers to address the global water crisis. Twelve specific steps were recommended for the policy community by the Council following the March 2011 meeting:

- Continue the dialogue on the water crisis.
- Endorse the human right to water.
- Support ratification of the UN Watercourses Convention.
- Encourage the UN Security Council to focus on water security.
- Support increased universal sanitation coverage and safe water supply.
- Facilitate links between national and global water, agricultural, and energy policies.
- Support necessary hydroclimatic monitoring.
- Support protection of ecological sustainability boundaries and investment in ecosystem restoration.
- Encourage cooperation and act as a mediator in water conflicts.
- Call on national governments to strengthen water education programs.
- Involve the private sector.
- Create a white paper supporting the above recommendations.

Making Every Drop Count: An Agenda for Water Action built on this plan and laid out a foundation for action. It focused on understanding water, valuing water, and managing water. From this flows, an integrated agenda (1) ensure universal access to safe water and sanitation; (2) build resilient societies and economies, reducing disaster risk; (3) increase water infrastructure investment; and (4) nurture environmental water and develop sustainable cities. All of these steps are to be undertaken through promoting innovation, strengthening partnerships, and increasing global water cooperation.

Although most alluded to a current water shortage that will only worsen, a few analysts suggested otherwise. Bjørn Lomborg, the "skeptical scientist," took this issue in *The Skeptical Environmentalist: Measuring the Real State of the World* (2002) with the opposing view in the global water debate. His argument can be summed up in his simple quote: "Basically we have sufficient water." Lomborg maintained that water supplies rose during the twentieth century and that we have gained access to more water through technology. Benjamin Radford suggested that when one distilled the evidence behind the dire headlines, there is "one little fact. There is no water shortage."

Although most of the discussion and debate has centered on either the dwindling fresh water supply or unequal access thereto, an alternative view suggested that the real issue may be corporate control of water. Maude Barlow, in *Blue Covenant* (2007), made the case that it is privatization of fresh water and other corporate behavior that has contributed significantly to the global water crisis. From putting massive amounts of water into bottles for sale to individuals to controlling large amounts of water used in industry to controlling the world water trade, for-profit private corporations have used supply/demand and other economic principles to undercut the global community's ability to address the global water crisis.

In the YES selection, the 2018 UN World Water Development Report suggests that the solutions to the increased demand for water "may be closer than we think." The strategy is "working with nature" to find nature-based solutions (NBSs) that will lead to a set of interwoven benefits that "are central" to meeting future water needs. The bottom line, according to the report, is that NBS offer "high potential" to meeting future water targets.

In the NO selection, the UN University study argues that the difficulty in meeting the demand for global water is a "pressing societal and geopolitical issue" and of a "critical national concern" is some regions of the planet. The increased nature of the problem is due not only to an increased population but also to an excessive use. By 2015, water demands are expected to increase by 400 percent from manufacturing and 130 percent from household usage.

YES

The United Nations World Water Development Report 2018

Nature-Based Solutions (NBS) for Water

NBS are inspired and supported by nature and use, or mimic, natural processes to contribute to the improved management of water. An NBS can involve conserving or rehabilitating natural ecosystems and/or the enhancement or creation of natural processes in modified or artificial ecosystems. They can be applied at micro- (e.g., a dry toilet) or macro- (e.g., landscape) scales.

Attention to NBS has significantly increased in recent years. This is evidenced through the mainstreaming of NBS into a wide range of policy advances, including in water resources, food security and agriculture, biodiversity, environment, disaster risk reduction, urban settlements, and climate change. This welcome trend illustrates a growing convergence of interests around the recognition of the need for common objectives and the identification of mutually supporting actions—as illustrated best in the 2030 Agenda for Sustainable Development through its acknowledgment of the interdependency of its various Goals and targets.

Upscaling NBS will be central to achieving the 2030 Agenda for Sustainable Development. Sustainable water security will not be achieved through business-as-usual approaches. NBS work with nature instead of against it and thereby provide an essential means to move beyond business-as-usual to escalate social, economic, and hydrological efficiency gains in water resources management. NBS show particular promise in achieving progress toward sustainable food production, improved human settlements, access to water supply and sanitation services, and water-related disaster risk reduction. They can also help to respond to the impacts of climate change on water resources.

NBS support a *circular economy* that is restorative and regenerative by design and promotes greater resource productivity aiming to reduce waste and avoid pollution, including through reuse and recycling. NBS also support the concepts of *green growth* or the *green economy*, which promote sustainable natural resource use and harness natural processes to underpin economies. The application of NBS for water also generates social, economic, and environmental cobenefits, including improved human health and livelihoods, sustainable economic growth, decent jobs, ecosystem rehabilitation and maintenance, and the protection and enhancement of biodiversity. The value of some of these cobenefits can be substantial and tip investment decisions in favor of NBS.

However, despite a long history of and growing experience with, the application of NBS, there are still many cases where water resources policy and management ignore NBS options—even where they are obvious and proven to be efficient. For example, despite rapidly growing investments in NBS, the evidence suggests that this is still well below 1 percent of total investment in water resources management infrastructure.

The World's Water: Demand, Availability, Quality, and Extreme Events

The global demand for water has been increasing at a rate of about 1 percent per year as a function of population growth, economic development, and changing consumption patterns, among other factors, and it will continue to grow significantly over the next two decades. Industrial and domestic demand for water will increase much faster than agricultural demand, although agriculture will remain the largest overall user. The vast majority of the growing demand for water will occur in countries with developing or emerging economies.

At the same time, the global water cycle is intensifying due to climate change, with wetter regions generally becoming wetter and drier regions becoming even drier. At present, an estimated 3.6 billion people (nearly half the global population) live in areas that are potentially water-scarce at least one month per year, and this population could increase to some 4.8–5.7 billion by 2050.

Since the 1990s, water pollution has worsened in almost all rivers in Africa, Asia, and Latin America. The deterioration of water quality is expected to further escalate over the next decades, and this will increase threats to human health, the environment, and sustainable development. Globally, the most prevalent water quality challenge is nutrient loading, which, depending on the region, is often associated with pathogen loading. Hundreds of chemicals are also impacting on water quality. The greatest increases in exposure to pollutants are expected to occur in low- and lower-middle income countries, primarily because of higher population and economic growth and the lack of wastewater management systems.

The trends in water availability and quality are accompanied by projected changes in flood and drought risks. The number of people at risk from floods is projected to rise from 1.2 billion today to around 1.6 billion in 2050 (nearly 20 percent of the world's population). The population currently affected by land degradation/desertification and drought is estimated at 1.8 billion people, making this the most significant category of "natural disaster" based on mortality and socioeconomic impact relative to gross domestic product (GDP) per capita.

Ecosystem Degradation

Ecosystem degradation is a leading cause of increasing water resources management challenges. Although about 30 percent of the global land remains forested, at least 2/3 of this area are in a degraded state. The majority of the world's soil resources, notably on farmland, are in only fair, poor, or very poor condition; and the current outlook is for this situation to worsen, with serious negative impacts on water cycling through higher evaporation rates, lower soil water storage, and increased surface runoff accompanied by increased erosion. Since the year 1900, an estimated 64–71 percent of the natural wetland area worldwide has been lost due to human activity. All these changes have had major negative impacts on hydrology, from local to regional and global scales.

There is evidence that such ecosystem change has over the course of history contributed to the demise of several ancient civilizations. A pertinent question nowadays is whether we can avoid the same fate. The answer to that question will depend at least partly on our ability to shift from working against nature to working with it—through, for example, better adoption of NBS.

The Role of Ecosystems in the Water Cycle

Ecological processes in a landscape influence the quality of water and the way it moves through a system as well as soil formation, erosion, and sediment transport and deposition—all of which can exert major influences on hydrology. Although forests often receive the most attention when it comes to land cover and hydrology, grasslands and croplands also play important roles. Soils are critical in controlling the movement, storage, and transformation of water. Biodiversity has a functional role in NBS whereby it underpins ecosystem processes and functions and, therefore, the delivery of ecosystem services.

Ecosystems have important influences on precipitation recycling from local to continental scales. Rather than being regarded as a "consumer" of water, vegetation is perhaps more appropriately viewed as a water "recycler." Globally, up to 40 percent of terrestrial rainfall originates from upwind plant transpiration and other land evaporation, with this source accounting for most of the rainfall in some regions. Land-use decisions in one place may therefore have significant consequences for water resources, people, the economy, and the environment in distant locations—pointing to the limitations of the watershed (as opposed to the "precipitationshed") as the basis for management.

Green infrastructure (for water) uses natural or semi-natural systems such as NBS to provide water resources management options with benefits that are equivalent or similar to conventional gray (built/physical) water infrastructure. In some situations, nature-based approaches can offer the main or only viable solution (e.g., landscape restoration to combat land degradation and desertification), whereas for different purposes only a gray solution will work (e.g., supplying water to a household through pipes and taps). In most cases, however, green and gray infrastructure can and should work together. Some of the best examples of the deployment of NBS are where they improve the performance of gray infrastructure. The current situation, with aging, inappropriate, or insufficient grey infrastructure worldwide, creates opportunities for NBS as innovative solutions that embed perspectives of ecosystem services, enhanced resilience, and livelihood considerations in water planning and management.

A key feature of NBS is that they tend to deliver groups of ecosystem services together—even if only one is being targeted by the intervention. Hence, NBS usually offer multiple water-related benefits and often help address water quantity, quality, and risks simultaneously.

Another key advantage of NBS is the way in which they contribute to building overall system resilience.

NBS for Managing Water Availability

NBS mainly address water supply through managing precipitation, humidity, and water storage, infiltration and transmission, so that improvements are made in the location, timing, and quantity of water available for human needs.

The option of building more reservoirs is increasingly limited by silting, decrease in available runoff, environmental concerns and restrictions, and the fact that in many developed countries, the most cost-effective and viable sites have already been used. In many cases, more ecosystem-friendly forms of water storage, such as natural wetlands, improvements in soil moisture and more efficient recharge of groundwater could be more sustainable and cost-effective than traditional gray infrastructure such as dams.

Agriculture will need to meet projected increases in food demand by improving its resource use efficiency while simultaneously reducing its external footprint, and water is central to this need. A cornerstone of recognized solutions is the "sustainable ecological intensification" of food production, which enhances ecosystem services in agricultural landscapes, for example, through improved soil and vegetation management. "Conservation agriculture," which incorporates practices aimed at minimizing soil disturbance, maintaining soil cover, and regularizing crop rotation, is a flagship example approach to sustainable production intensification. Agricultural systems that rehabilitate or conserve ecosystem services can be as productive as intensive, high-input systems, but with significantly reduced externalities. Although NBS offer significant gains in irrigation, the main opportunities to increase productivity are in rainfed systems that account for the bulk of current production and family farming (and hence provide the greatest livelihood and poverty reduction benefits). The theoretical gains that could be achievable at a global scale exceed the projected increases in global demand for water, thereby potentially reducing conflicts among competing uses.

NBS for addressing water availability in urban settlements are also of great importance, given that the majority of the world's population is now living in cities. Urban green infrastructure, including green buildings, is an emerging phenomenon that is establishing new benchmarks and technical standards that embrace many NBS.

Business and industry are also increasingly promoting NBS to improve water security for their operations, prompted by a compelling business case.

NBS for Managing Water Quality

Source water protection reduces water treatment costs for urban suppliers and contributes to improved access to safe drinking water in rural communities. Forests, wetlands, and grasslands, as well as soils and crops, when managed properly, play important roles in regulating water quality by reducing sediment loadings, capturing and retaining pollutants, and recycling nutrients. Where water becomes polluted, both constructed and natural ecosystems can help improve water quality.

Nonpoint (diffuse) source pollution from agriculture, notably nutrients, remains a critical problem worldwide, including in developed countries. It is also the one most amenable to NBS, as these can rehabilitate ecosystem services that enable soils to improve nutrient management and hence lower fertilizer demand and reduce nutrient runoff and/or infiltration to groundwater.

Urban green infrastructure is increasingly being used to manage and reduce pollution from urban runoff. Examples include green walls, roof gardens, and vegetated infiltration or drainage basins to support wastewater treatment and reduce stormwater runoff. Wetlands are also used within urban environments to mitigate the impact of polluted stormwater runoff and wastewater. Both natural and constructed wetlands also biodegrade or immobilize a range of emerging pollutants, including certain pharmaceuticals, and often perform better than gray solutions. For certain chemicals, they may offer the only solution.

There are limits to how NBS can perform. For example, NBS options for industrial wastewater treatment depend on the pollutant type and its loading. For many polluted water sources, gray-infrastructure solutions may continue to be needed. However, industrial applications of NBS, particularly constructed wetlands for industrial wastewater treatment, are growing.

NBS for Managing Water-Related Risks

Water-related risks and disasters, such as floods and droughts associated with an increasing temporal variability of water resources due to climate change, result in immense and growing human and economic losses globally. Around 30 percent of the global population is estimated to reside in areas and regions routinely impacted by either flood or drought events. Ecosystem degradation is the major cause of increasing water-related risks and extremes, and it reduces the ability to fully realize the potential of NBS.

Green infrastructure can perform significant risk reduction functions. Combining green and gray infrastructure approaches can lead to cost savings and greatly improved overall risk reduction.

NBS for flood management can involve water retention by managing infiltration and overland flow and thereby the hydrological connectivity between system components and the conveyance of water through it, making space for water storage through, for example, floodplains. The concept of "living with floods," which, among other things, includes a range of structural and nonstructural approaches that help to "be prepared" for a flood, can facilitate the application of relevant NBS to reduce flood losses and, most importantly, flood risk.

Droughts are not limited to dry areas, as is sometimes portrayed, but can also pose a disaster risk in regions that are normally not water-scarce. The mix of potential NBS for drought mitigation is essentially the same as those for water availability and aim to improve water storage capacity in landscapes, including soils and groundwater, to cushion against periods of extreme scarcity. Seasonal variability in rainfall creates opportunities for water storage in landscapes to provide water for both ecosystems and people over drier periods. The potential of natural water storage (particularly subsurface, in aquifers) for disaster risk reduction is far from being realized. Storage planning at river basin and regional scales should consider a portfolio of surface and subsurface storage options (and their combinations) to arrive at the best environmental and economic outcomes in the face of increasing water resources variability.

NBS for Enhancing Water Security: Multiplying the Benefits

NBS are able to enhance overall water security by improving water availability and water quality while simultaneously reducing water-related risks and generating additional social, economic, and environmental cobenefits. They allow for the identification of win–win outcomes across sectors. For example, NBS in agriculture are becoming mainstream because they deliver increased sustainable agricultural productivity and profitability but also enhance overall system-wide benefits, such as improved water availability and reduced downstream pollution. Watershed restoration and protection have become increasingly important in the context of meeting multiple

challenges in sustaining water supplies to rapidly growing cities and reducing risks in them. Urban green infrastructure can yield positive results in terms of water availability, water quality, and flood and drought reduction. In the context of water and sanitation, constructed wetlands for wastewater treatment can be a cost-effective NBS that provides effluent of adequate quality for several nonpotable uses, including irrigation, as well as offering additional benefits, including energy production.

Challenges and Limitations

Challenges to upscaling NBS so that they reach their full and significant potential are somewhat generic across the sectors and at global, region-specific, or place-based scales. There remains a historical inertia against NBS due to the continuing overwhelming dominance of gray infrastructure solutions in the current instruments of the Member States—from public policy to building codes and regulations. This dominance can also exist in civil engineering, market-based economic instruments, the expertise of service providers, and consequentially in the minds of policy makers and the general public. These and other factors collectively result in NBS often being perceived to be less efficient, or riskier, than built (gray) systems.

NBS often require cooperation among multiple institutions and stakeholders, something that can be difficult to achieve. Current institutional arrangements did not evolve with cooperation on NBS in mind. There is a lack of awareness, communication, and knowledge at all levels, from communities to regional planners and national policy makers, of what NBS can really offer. The situation can be compounded by a lack of understanding of how to integrate green and gray infrastructure at scale, and an overall lack of capacity to implement NBS in the context of water. Myths and/or uncertainty remain about the functioning of natural or green infrastructure, and about what ecosystem services mean in practical terms. It is also not entirely clear, at times, what constitutes a NBS. There is a lack of technical guidance, tools, and approaches to determine the right mix of NBS and gray-infrastructure options. The hydrological functions of natural ecosystems, such as wetlands and floodplains, are much less understood than those provided by gray infrastructure. Consequently, NBS are even more neglected in policy appraisal and in natural resource and development planning and management. This situation is partly compounded by insufficient research and development in NBS and particularly by the lack of impartial and robust assessments of current NBS experience, especially in terms of their hydrological performance, and cost–benefit analyses in comparison or conjunction with gray solutions.

There are limits to what ecosystems can achieve and these need much better identification. For example, "tipping points" beyond which negative ecosystem change becomes irreversible are well theorized but rarely quantified. It is therefore necessary to recognize the limited carrying capacity of ecosystems and determine the thresholds where any additional stresses (e.g., the addition of contaminants and toxic substances) will lead to irreversible damage to the ecosystem.

The high degree of variation in the impacts of ecosystems on hydrology (depending on ecosystem type or subtype, location and condition, climate and management) cautions to avoid generalized assumptions about NBS. For example, trees can increase or decrease groundwater recharge according to their type, density, location, size, and age. Natural systems are dynamic and their roles and impacts change over time.

An often overstated assumption about NBS is that they are "cost-effective," whereas this should be established during an assessment, including consideration of cobenefits. While some small-scale NBS applications can be low- or no-cost, some applications, particularly at scale, can require large investments. Ecosystem restoration costs, for example, can vary widely from a few hundred to several millions of US dollars per hectare. Site-specific knowledge on the field deployment of NBS is essential yet often inadequate. Now that attention to NBS has increased, NBS practitioners need to greatly increase the knowledge to support decision-making and avoid overstating NBS performance if this new impetus is not to be squandered.

Responses—Creating the Enabling Conditions for Accelerating the Uptake of NBS

The required responses to these challenges essentially involve creating enabling conditions for NBS to be considered equitably alongside other options for water resources management.

Leveraging Financing

NBS do not necessarily require additional financial resources but usually involve redirecting and making more effective use of existing financing. Investments in green infrastructure are being mobilized, thanks to the increasing recognition of the potential of ecosystem services to provide system-wide solutions that make investments more sustainable and cost-effective over time. Assess-

ments of the returns on investments in NBS often do not factor in these positive externalities, just as those for gray infrastructure often do not take all negative environmental and social externalities into account.

Payment for environmental services schemes provide monetary and nonmonetary incentives to upstream communities, farmers, and private land owners to protect, restore, and conserve natural ecosystems and to adopt sustainable agricultural and other land-use practices. These actions generate benefits to downstream water users in the form of water regulation, flood control, and erosion and sediment control, among others, thus ensuring a constant, high-quality water supply, and helping reduce water treatment and equipment maintenance costs.

The emerging "green bond" market shows promising potential for mobilizing NBS financing and, notably, demonstrates that NBS can perform well when assessed against rigorous standardized investment performance criteria. The private sector can also be further stimulated and guided to advance NBS in the areas in which it operates. Building in-house expertise and awareness of the effectiveness of NBS will facilitate this.

Transforming agricultural policy represents a significant pathway for financing the further uptake of NBS. This requires overcoming the fact that the vast majority of agricultural subsidies, and probably the majority of public funding and almost all private sector investment in agricultural research and development, support the intensification of conventional agricultural, which increases water insecurity. Mainstreaming the concept of sustainable ecological intensification of agricultural production, which essentially involves deploying NBS (e.g., improved soil and landscape management techniques), is not only the recognized way forward in order to achieve food security but would also be a major advance in NBS financing for water.

Assessing cobenefits of NBS (through a more holistic cost–benefit analysis) is an essential step in achieving efficient investments and tapping into financial resources across multiple sectors. All benefits, not just a narrow set of hydrological outcomes, need to be factored into an assessment of investment options. This requires a detailed systematic approach, but evidence shows it will lead to significant improvements in decision-making and overall system performance.

Creating an Enabling Regulatory and Legal Environment

The vast majority of current regulatory and legal environments for water management were developed largely with gray-infrastructure approaches in mind. Consequently, it can often be challenging to retrofit NBS into this framework. However, rather than expecting drastic changes in regulatory regimes, much can be achieved by promoting NBS more effectively through existing frameworks. In places where enabling legislation does not yet exist, identifying where and how NBS can support existing planning approaches at different levels can be a useful first step in this process.

National legislation to facilitate the implementation of NBS at the local level is particularly crucial. A small but growing number of countries have adopted regulatory frameworks promoting NBS at the national level. In Peru, for example, a national legal framework was adopted to regulate and monitor investment in green infrastructure. Regional frameworks can also stimulate change. The European Union, for instance, has significantly increased opportunities for NBS deployment through the harmonization of its legislation and policies regarding agriculture, water resources, and the environment.

At the global level, NBS offer Member States a means to respond to and use the various multilateral environmental agreements (especially the Convention on Biological Diversity, the United Nations Framework Convention on Climate Change, the Ramsar Convention on Wetlands, the Sendai Framework on Disaster Risk Reduction, agreed frameworks for food security, and the Paris Agreementon Climate Change), while also addressing economic and social imperatives. An overarching framework for promoting NBS is the 2030 Agenda for Sustainable Development with its Sustainable Development Goals (SDGs).

Improving Cross-Sectoral Collaboration

NBS can require much greater levels of cross-sectoral and institutional collaboration than gray-infrastructure approaches, particularly when applied at landscape scale. However, this can also open opportunities to bring those groups together under a common approach or agenda.

In many countries, the policy landscape remains highly fragmented. Better harmonization of policies across economic, environmental, and social agendas is a general requirement in its own right. NBS are not only a beneficiary of such harmonization but also a means to achieve it because of their ability to deliver multiple, and often significant, cobenefits beyond just hydrological outcomes. Clear mandates from the highest policy level can significantly accelerate NBS uptake and foster improved intersectoral cooperation.

Improving the Knowledge Base

Improving the knowledge base on NBS, including in some cases through more rigorous science, is an essential

overarching requirement. Established evidence helps convince decision makers of the viability of NBS. For example, a frequently raised concern is that NBS take a long time to achieve their impact, implying that gray infrastructure is quicker. However, the evidence shows that this is not necessarily the case and timescales to deliver benefits can compare favorably to those of gray-infrastructure solutions.

Traditional or local-community knowledge of ecosystem functioning and the nature–society interaction can be a significant asset. Improvements need to be made in the incorporation of this knowledge into assessments and decision-making.

A priority response is the development and implementation of common criteria against which both NBS and other options for water resources management can be assessed. Common general criteria for an assessment of water resources management options (e.g., green vs. gray solutions) can be developed on a case-by-case basis. The full inclusion of all hydrological benefits, other cobenefits, and the entire range of the costs and benefits of ecosystem services (for any option) is a key requirement. This in turn will require consensus building across the various relevant stakeholder groups.

The Potential Contribution of NBS for Water Management to Achieving the 2030 Agenda for Sustainable Development

NBS offer high potential to contribute to the achievement of most of the targets of SDG 6 (on water). Areas in which this contribution translates into particularly striking positive direct impacts on other SDGs are with regard to water security for underpinning sustainable agriculture (SDG 2, notably Target 2.4), healthy lives (SDG 3), building resilient (water-related) infrastructure (SDG 9), sustainable urban settlements (SDG 11), and disaster risk reduction (SDG 11 and, as related to climate change, SDG 13).

The cobenefits of NBS are particularly significant in relation to the ecosystem/environment-related SDGs, including the reduction in land-use pressures on coastal areas and the oceans (SDG 14) and the protection of ecosystems and biodiversity (SDG 15). Some other areas where the cobenefits of NBS deliver particularly high rewards in terms of achieving the SDGs include other aspects of agriculture; energy; inclusive and sustainable economic growth; full and productive employment and decent work for all; making cities and human settlements inclusive, safe, resilient and sustainable; ensuring sustainable consumption and production patterns; and combating climate change and its impacts.

Moving Forward

Increased deployment of NBS is central to meeting the key contemporary water resources management challenges of sustaining and improving water availability and quality, while reducing water-related risks. Without a more rapid uptake of NBS, water security will continue to decline and probably rapidly so. NBS offer a vital means to move beyond business-as-usual. However, the necessity and opportunities for increased deployment of NBS remain underappreciated.

World Water Development Reports have consistently argued for transformational change in how water is managed. The inadequate recognition of ecosystems' roles in water management reinforces the need for transformational change, and increased uptake of NBS provides a means to achieve it. This transformational change can no longer just be aspirational—the shift needs to rapidly accelerate and, more importantly, translate into fully operationalized policy, with improved action at site level. The objective needs to be to minimize costs and risks, and

maximize system returns and robustness, while providing optimal "fit-for-use" performance. A role of policy should be to enable the right site-level decisions to be taken in these regards. We have made a good, if somewhat belated, start in this process, but there is a long way yet to go.

Coda

As humankind charts its course through the Anthropocene and tries to avoid the tragedies of the past, adopting NBS is not only necessary for improving water management outcomes and achieving water security, it is also critical for ensuring the delivery of cobenefits that are essential to all aspects of sustainable development. Although NBS are not a panacea, they will play an essential role in building a better, brighter, safer, and more equitable future for all.

HOSTED AND LED BY UNESCO, the United Nations World Water Assessment Programme (WWAP) coordinates the work of 31 UN-Water members and partners in the World Water Development Report (WWDR).

Lisa Guppy and Kelsey Anderson

 **NO**

Global Water Crisis

The Facts

Water is a foundation of life and livelihoods and is key to sustainable development. Successful water management will serve as a foundation for the achievement of many of the 17 Sustainable Development Goals (SDGs), as well as for SDG 6—which is to "Ensure availability and sustainable management of water and sanitation for all."

Despite this, water is becoming a pressing societal and geopolitical issue—in some regions, it is already of critical national concern. "Business as usual" will mean the world will miss water-related SDGs by a wide margin; up to 40 percent of the world's population will be living in seriously water-stressed areas by 2035; and the ability of ecosystems to provide fresh water supplies will become increasingly compromised.

A total of 60 percent of fresh water comes from river basins that cross national borders. Transboundary water agreements need to be robust enough to deal with increasingly uncertain environmental and climatic conditions, and the social and demographic changes that will raise global population to 9.7 billion by 2050 and double the number of people who live in urban areas.

Different conceptualizations of water can and have led to conflict. The perception of water as a human right and a common public and environmental good is often opposed by the view of water as a commodity that needs to be priced to ensure efficient and sustainable use. Not only nations but provinces and communities will need to align water perspectives to allow for peaceful and effective integrated water resource management and sustainable use.

Effective management will mean tackling neglected issues such as water wastage in current systems, which has been estimated to be up to 30 percent; common institutional dysfunction, unethical practices, poor accountability, and corruption in the water sectors of many countries.

This report highlights looming water crises from six interrelated contexts: water scarcity and insecurity, water-related disasters, water, sanitation and health (WASH) crisis, water infrastructure deterioration and destruction, unsustainable development, and ecosystem degradation.

UN agencies, governments, and civil societies have made clear that radical new approaches to water are needed to reverse these sobering water trends. Only by facing these crises in an intelligent and cohesive way will water continue to support life, development, and biodiversity for our children and our future.

A total of 112 million people were affected by floods 2005–2015, 1.8 billion people now use a source of drinking water contaminated by faces 40 percent gap between water demand and water available by 2030, 80 percent or more wastewater returns to the environment without adequate treatment, 30 percent of global water abstraction is lost through leakage.

US$114 billion per year or more than three times the current level of capital investment is needed to achieve the Sustainable Development Goal 6 targets on water supply, sanitation, and hygiene (6.1 and 6.2). The amount of money needed to meet the other targets of the "water goal" is currently unknown.

12.6 million deaths were attributable to the environment globally in 2012.

Water Scarcity and Insecurity

The notion that water is plentiful—it covers 70 percent of the planet—is false, as only 2.5 percent of all water is freshwater. This limited resource will need to support a projected population of 9.7 billion in 2050; and by that date, an estimated 3.9 billion—or over 40 percent of the world's population—will live in severely water-stressed river basins.

It is not just population that is pressuring water resources. Excessive use is also evident: the global population tripled in the twentieth century, but the use of water increased six-fold. Between now and 2050, water demands are expected to increase by 400 percent from manufacturing and by 130 percent from household use.

As water availability decreases, competition for access to this limited resource will increase. A total of 60 percent of all surface freshwater comes from internationally shared river basins, and there are an estimated 592 transboundary aquifers. Continuing cooperation and coordination between nations is crucial to ensuring water is available for human, economic, and environmental needs. Although hundreds of international water agreements have been signed over time, how countries will cooperatively manage growing resource pressures so that they do not lead to more conflicts over water is not often clear.

Water insecurity can be exacerbated by drought. More people are affected by drought than any other disaster type. In 2016, 411 million people in total were affected by disasters and 94 percent of those were drought affected. Droughts are also the costliest disasters, with significant impacts on agriculture in particular; droughts cause an average US$6–8 billion worth of losses in agriculture in the United States annually. In China, drought has resulted in an annual grain production loss of more than 27 million tons over the last two decades; and from the 1950s to the beginning of this century, the annual average crop area suffering from drought has expanded from 11.6 million hectares to 25.1 million hectares, an increase of 116 percent.

If water were secured for irrigated agriculture, the potential global welfare gain for reduced risk in 2010 would have been US$94 billion. Findings also show that enhanced water security can help stabilize food crop production and prices. In a water secure scenario, the probability of global wheat production falling below 650 million tons per year is reduced from 83 percent to 38 percent.

There has been a drop 55 percent in globally available freshwater per capita since 1960.

By 2030, global demand for water is expected to grow by 50 percent.

Water scarcity currently affects more than 40 percent of the global population.

By 2050, an additional 2.3 billion people can be expected to be living in areas with severe waterstress, especially in North and South Africa and South and Central Asia. Seventy percent Agriculture accounts for of all water withdrawals globally and for over 90 percent in the majority of least developed countries and 70 percent more food will be needed by 2050. Water scarcity, exacerbated by climate change, could cost some regions up to 6 percent of their gross domestic product (GDP).

The 5th assessment of the Intergovernmental Panel on Climate Change projects that for each degree of global warming, approximately 7 percent of the global population will be exposed to a decrease in renewable water resources of at least 20 percent.

Worldwide, the total cost of water insecurity to the global economy is estimated at US$500 billion annually. Including environmental impacts, this figure may rise to 1 percent of global GDP.

Water-Related Disasters

It is vital to protect investments in water-related infrastructure from shocks and stresses. In 2009, the World Bank estimated that by 2030, around half the Bank's water sector portfolio—which was then US$8.8 billion committed and US$11.3 billion in pipeline—would be at high to medium risk of exposure to climate change impacts.

In addition, hydrologic hazards are leading to significant deaths, displacements, and injuries. Up to 90 percent of all disasters are water-related, and over the last two decades, floods have been the most frequent global natural disaster; in 2016, 50 percent of all recorded events were related to flooding. The total value of all assets that are at risk of flooding by 2050 is predicted to be US$45 trillion: a rise of over 340 percent from 2010.

Between 1970 and 2010, the world's population increased by 87 percent, from 3.7 billion to 6.9 billion. During the same period, the annual average population exposed to flood increased by 112 percent—from 33.3 to 70.4 million per year.

By 2050, rising populations in flood-prone lands, climate change, deforestation, loss of wetlands, and rising sea levels can be expected to increase the number of people vulnerable to flood disaster to 2 billion.

The UN was prompted to release warnings about urban flash floods after hundreds died in Guatemala, the United States, and southern France in 2015—stating that under a changing climate, intense rainfall, and urbanization have made these disasters more common in the last two decades.

Water-related ecosystems can mitigate water-related disasters. Every hectare of mangrove and coastal marsh is worth up to US$15,161 a year in disaster-related services, and coastal wetlands helped to avoid more than US$625 million in damages from Hurricane Sandy in 2012. Coral reefs act as wave barriers, and as an example of their effectiveness in risk reduction, spending US$1 million a year on restoring reefs at the Folkestone Marine Park on the west coast of Barbados could lower annual storm losses there by US$20 million.

Despite these risk reduction benefits, water-related ecosystems globally are in decline. In parts of Asia and the

Americas, up to half of all coastal mangrove ecosystems have been degraded or destroyed.

Water-related disasters account for 70 percent of all deaths related to natural disasters.

Worldwide flood damage amounted to over US$50 billion in 2013 and is increasing.

More than 107,000 people died due to hydrological disasters (floods and landslides) between 2000 and 2016.

Several studies estimate that by 2050 between 150 and 200 million people could be displaced as a consequence of phenomena, such as desertification, sea-level rise, and increased extreme weather events.

Floods and landslides have cost an estimated US$453,000,000 between 2000 and 2016.[35]

Water, Sanitation, and Health (WASH) Crisis

Although progress has been made in supplying drinking water to more people year on year, 663 million people still lack "improved" drinking water sources in 2015—and for many people, this "improved" water is not always safe, reliable, affordable, or accessible with equity. For example, around 45 million people in Bangladesh drink water that contains arsenic concentrations greater than WHO standards allow.

Sanitation and hygiene have made less progress, with 2.4 billion people lacking improved sanitation facilities. Equity in sanitation and hygiene access is of particular concern. Seven of 10 people without improved sanitation facilities, and nine of 10 people still practicing open defecation, live in rural areas; and a lack of these services often disproportionately affect women and girls who can not only suffer health repercussions but personal danger when services are not available and not secure. Diarrheal diseases, long associated with poor water and sanitation, account for one in nine child deaths worldwide, making diarrhea the third leading cause of death among children under the age of five. Poor water, sanitation, and hygiene are major contributors to neglected tropical diseases such as schistosomiasis, trachoma, and intestinal worms, which affect more than 1.5 billion people every year.

It is not only households that lack adequate services: in low- and middle-income countries (LMICs), workplaces, schools, and health facilities also lack WASH. In a 2015 survey of LMICs, 38 percent of health facilities did not have an improved water source, 35 percent did not have soap and water for handwashing and 19 percent did not have improved sanitation. The lack of universal WASH in schools costs an estimated 1,863 million days of school attendance globally.

The WASH crisis does not only affect low-income countries. In Canada, there are approximately 5,000 homes in First Nations communities that lack basic water and sewage services. Compared to other Canadians, First Nations' homes are 90 times more likely to be without running water.

If radical change is not affected, universal water, sanitation, and hygiene—as described in SDG targets 6.1 and 6.2—will not be reached. A World Bank report found that capital investments must increase by approximately three times to achieve the water supply, sanitation, and hygiene (WASH) targets globally. Another study has estimated that WASH efforts will need to exceed current trends by almost four times to achieve SDG 6.1 and 6.2 by 2030.

Unsafe water, poor sanitation, and hygiene cause approximately 3.5 million deaths worldwide; the latter estimate represents 25 percent of the deaths of children younger than 14.

2.4 billion people—more than $1/3$ of the global population—do not use improved sanitation facilities.

One in 10 people has no choice but to defecate in the open.

Globally, approximately US$260 billion is lost each year to the effects of poor sanitation and unsafe water on many aspects of the economy but most significantly on health care.

In India, the time spent looking for a toilet or finding some where to go in the open costs the economy over US$10 billion every year in lost productivity—20 percent of GDP.

One thousand children die each day due to preventable water and sanitation-related diseases.

Water Infrastructure Deterioration and Destruction

Under the Millennium Development Goals, many populations counted as being "served" by water supply actually were allocated to systems that had failed. Although there may be as many as 60,000 new handpumps being constructed in Africa every year, a 2007 study found 36 percent of hand pumps across 21 countries in sub-Saharan Africa were not functional. This represents a loss of between US$1.2 and 1.5 billion in investments.

The total cost to water utilities worldwide caused by "nonrevenue water"—a combination of physical and commercial losses—has been conservatively estimated at US$141 billion per year. In developing countries, approximately 45 million cubic meters per day are lost through water infrastructure leakage—enough to serve nearly 200 million people. This problem will only get worse if water infrastructure is not maintained properly, even for high-income countries; for example, the capital investment needed to maintain aging water infrastructure in the United States will reach an estimated US$195 billion in 2040, but if current funding trends continue, needs will be underfunded by US$144 billion.

Until the SDGs began in 2015, there was far less international focus on infrastructure and processes for wastewater treatment, water recycling, and water efficiency, with significant negative impacts in many areas. For example, poorly treated wastewater is used for agriculture in many low-income countries, but children (8–12 years) in areas using wastewater have been shown to have a 75 percent prevalence rate for gastroenteritis, compared to 13 percent in areas using freshwater, bringing a 73 percent higher health cost per child in areas using wastewater.

The failure of water systems is often considered a governance issue. In the water sector, the fragmentation of actors and of accountabilities hinders and undermines transparency and economic efficiency and opens doors for corruption. Institutional dysfunction, unethical practices, opaque decision-making, poor accountability, and corruption are reportedly common, but difficult to quantify.

Water infrastructure that is damaged deliberately can also have tremendous local impacts. For example, one air strike in December 2016 in Syria cut water supplies for 3.5 million people and, while some pumping was restored relatively quickly, 1.4 million had continued reduced supply. Since 2011, water and water infrastructure have been used as a military target in Syria, Ukraine, India, Israel, Yemen, Libya, Afghanistan, Somalia, the Democratic Republic of Congo, South Sudan, Sudan, and Iraq.

In low-income countries, only 8 percent of industrial and municipal wastewater undergoes treatment of any kind.

In lower middle-income countries, only 28 percent of wastewater is treated.

Globally, it has been estimated that between 5 and 20 million hectares of land are irrigated with untreated wastewater.

Unsustainable Development

While the effectiveness of water management varies dramatically between countries, a rapid scale-up in effort and resources will be needed for most countries to achieve Sustainable Development Goal 6 and to support other water-related or water-impacted SDGs. A 2016 study wrote that "the longer governments take to act, the harder it will be

to deliver on their promises by 2030," and that overall, every 3 years of inaction will mean that the amount of effort needed to succeed will increase exponentially.

Beyond SDG 6—the "water goal"—water is fundamental to life and livelihoods. The success of SDG 6 will underpin progress in many other goals, including those for human health, universal education, and urban progress. Water security is fundamental to poverty alleviation, and water resource management impacts almost all aspects of economic activity, including food production and security, industry, energy production, and transport.

However, these human activities often degrade water resources. Two million tons of human waste are disposed of in water courses every day; 15–18 billion m^3 of freshwater resources are contaminated by fossil fuel production every year; and the food sector contributes 40 and 54 percent to the production of organic water pollutants in high-income and low-income countries, respectively. Severe pathogenic pollution affects around $1/3$ of all rivers, severe organic pollution around $1/7$ of all rivers, and severe and moderate salinity pollution around $1/10$ of all river stretches in Latin America, Africa, and Asia.

To move beyond simply "ticking off" sustainability indicators to true sustainability in the water sector, Member States must consider the full cost of water and the services it provides.

A 2°C rise in global average temperature could mean additional water-related costs between US$13.7 billion and US$19.2 billion per year from 2020 to 2050, mostly through water supply and flood management.

Wastewater–related emissions of methane and nitrous oxide could rise by 50 percent and 25 percent, respectively, between 1990 and 2020.

Regionally, the global limit of ecological sustainability of water available for abstraction is reported to have been exceeded for about $1/3$ of the human population. This will rise to about half of the human population by 2030.

Of the world's 263 transboundary basins, more than 60 percent lack any type of cooperative management framework.

Wealthier diets cost water: Producing 1 kg of rice requires around 3,500 L of water, while 1 kg of beef costs 15,000 L.

Ecosystem Degradation

All freshwater ultimately depends on the continued, healthy functioning of ecosystems. Recognizing the water cycle as a biophysical process is essential to achieving sustainable water management and securing the ecosystem services that humans rely on.

The water-related services provided by tropical forests include the regulation of water flows, waste treatment, and water purification and erosion prevention; these collectively account for a value of up to US$7,236 per hectare per year—more than 44 percent of the total value of forests, exceeding the values of carbon storage, food, timber, and recreation and tourism services combined. Despite this, between 1997 and 2011, US$4.3–20.2 trillion per year worth of ecosystem services were lost due to land-use change.

Freshwater ecosystems themselves provide more than US$75 billion in goods and ecosystem services for people annually; they also sustain a disproportionately large number of species, including a quarter of all known vertebrates. However, wetlands are being increasingly threatened by a host of problems. Since 1900, 64 percent of the world's wetlands have disappeared. This degradation has been valued at US$20 trillion in lost ecosystem services annually. According to some estimates, the populations of freshwater species declined by 76 percent between 1970 and 2010. Nearly, $1/3$ of the world's amphibians are at risk of extinction and in some regions, more than 50 percent of native freshwater fish species are at risk of extinction.

Wetlands are also carbon sinks. Peatlands—lands with peat at the surface—cover only 3 percent of the Earth's land surface, but store nearly double the carbon than all the world's forests combined, if they are kept wet. An overall loss of 15 percent of peatlands has been reported, which translates to a contribution of 5 percent of all global anthropogenic carbon dioxide emissions. Almost half (45 percent) of the peatlands in the Nordic and Baltic States have been drained and emit almost 80 megatons of carbon dioxide annually—which is 25 percent of the total carbon dioxide emissions of these countries.

It is estimated that the number of people living in environments with high-water quality risks due to excessive biochemical oxygen demand will affect $1/5$ of the global population in 2050, while people facing risks from excessive nitrogen and phosphorous will increase to $1/3$ of the global population over the same period.

Eutrophication of surface water and coastal zones is expected to increase almost everywhere until 2030. Globally, the number of lakes with harmful algal blooms will increase by at least 20 percent until 2050.

Inefficient use of water for crop production has caused salinization of 20 percent of the global irrigated land area.

There has been a 30 percent decline in biodiversity health since 1970.

Between US$4.3 and US$20.2 trillion per year worth of ecosystem services were lost between 1997 and 2011 due to land-use change.

LISA GUPPY is Project Officer at the United Nations University Institute for Water, Environment and Health in Hamilton, Canada.

KELSEY ANDERSON is a Communications Associate and Graphic Designer at the United Nations University.

EXPLORING THE ISSUE

Can the Global Community Successfully Confront the Global Water Shortage?

Critical Thinking and Reflection

1. Do you believe that relying on NBSs represents the best approach to addressing the global water issue?
2. Do you believe that the root cause of insufficient safe drinking water is due to factors such as unsustainable development strategies and governing failures rather than simply increased population, urbanization, and increased food requirements globally?
3. Do you believe that technical solutions really exist by the lack of will on the part of national and global leaders prevent successful addressing of the global water issue?
4. Do you believe that "simply" increasing agricultural efficiency in the developing world will avert a future global water crisis?

Is There Common Ground?

Although many analysts differ over whether a global water crisis is already here, there is an overwhelming consensus that given population growth and the growth of affluence, future generations will face a water crisis. There is also an emerging belief among many that if the international community is willing to act, technologies are or will be there that will allow the world to do so. The lessons from another diminishing resource, oil, should be instructive here.

Additional Resources

High-Level Panel on Water Outcome Document, United Nations and World Bank Group, *Making Every Drop Count: An Agenda for Water Action* (March 2018)

Moore, Scott, "How to Solve the Global Water Crisis," *Foreign Affairs* (March 20, 2018)

UNICEF, *Thirsting for a Future: Water and Children in a Changing Climate* (March 2017)

United States Senate, *Domestic and Global Water Supply Issues* (United States Senate, 2012)

World Water Council, *7th World Water Forum 2015: Final Report* (World Water Council, 2015)

Internet References . . .

Pacific Institute

www.worldwater.org

UN-Water

www.unwater.org

World Water Council

www.worldwtaercoincil.org

World Health Organization

www.who.int/en

UN Food and Agriculture Organization

www.fao.org/land-water/land-water/en

Selected, Edited, and with Issue Framing Material by:
James E. Harf, *Maryville University*

ISSUE

Is the Global Oil Crisis of the Last Half-century Over?

YES: "World Energy Outlook 2017," *International Energy Agency* (2017)

NO: Chris Martenson, from "The Looming Energy Shock: The Next Oil Crisis Will Arrive in 3 Years or Less," *PeakProsperity.com*, (2017)

Learning Outcomes

After reading this issue, you will be able to:

- Describe the view that the cost of oil affects the amount of its availability.
- Understand how oil supply is also due to global political considerations as well as economic considerations.
- Understand the argument that the supply of oil is growing worldwide and could eventually outpace consumption.
- Understand the major large-scale shifts that will dramatically likely lessen the demand for oil.
- Describe the two competing scenarios that will affect the next oil crisis as discussed by the NO article.

ISSUE SUMMARY

YES: In this current review of the world's energy outlook, the International Energy Agency, an autonomous UN agency established in 1974, surveys the current global energy system. The report points to four "large-scale shifts" in the system: "the rapid deployment and falling costs of clean energy technologies . . . the growing electrification of energy . . . the shift to a more service-oriented economy and a cleaner energy mix in China . . . and the resilience of shale gas and tight oil in the United States." The report concludes that these are good signs for the world's attempts to address nonrenewable energy resources such as oil.

NO: Chris Martenson, a fellow at the Post Carbon Institute, presents a forceful argument that within a couple of years, either the world economy will outgrow the supply of oil or the economy will collapse, both undesirable outcomes.

On May 8, 2018, President Donald Trump announced that the United States would be leaving the Iran nuclear program deal and reimposing sanctions on the Iranian regime. Two days later, the price of oil rose to a 3½ year high as tensions were rising in the Middle East as a consequence of the American action and was fueled in part by an Israeli attack on Iranian positions inside Syria. One analyst immediately suggested that the increased oil price was the direct result of the predicted decline in Iranian oil production and subsequent oil exports. In the meantime, the American decision to withdraw from the Iranian agreement suggested to Arab leaders that the resultant disruption in the global oil supply would put pressure on oil prices. Analysts predicted that as much as 500,000 barrels a day would be removed from the global market.

This episode pointed out how world events far from the oil fields affect oil supplies and consequently the price of oil. And they are part of a larger ongoing pattern of fluctuations in oil prices as expectations of increased demand drive up prices and the fear of excessive supply leads to a downfall in oil prices. And one must not forget that Organization of Petroleum Exporting Country (OPEC), the large oil cartel of major oil producers, also intervenes periodically to influence the price of oil as supply and demand ebbs and flows.

Oil prices reached their lowest level in 13 years in January 2016 when its price of $26 a barrel was more than $100 lower than its 2014 price. By February, the price of a gallon of gas at the pump had dropped to well under $2, although by June, it had inched up to around $2.25. As 2018 approached the midpoint, prices have climbed higher still, although nowhere near the record highs of just a few years ago. U.S. oil stockpiles reached unprecedented high levels, with the Saudis stepping in to ensure such attainable levels. Yet just a few years ago, gas prices had passed the $3 a gallon level, and within a year, the unthinkable had occurred, as prices edged toward and then passed $4 a gallon. Had the oil crisis peaked? Is the crisis simply artificial, that is, created by supply and demand forces conspiring to make it so?

The sharp increase in the cost of oil a few years ago had coincided with a wave of political unrest sweeping the Middle East and North Africa. Observed first in Tunisia, it quickly spread to Yemen, Egypt, Bahrain, and eventually to Libya. Although these countries represent a small percentage of oil-exporting nations and although Saudi Arabia promised to make up the difference in oil production, the cost of a gallon of gas spiraled upward in conjunction with political turmoil. The cost of a gallon at the pump was also correlated with the rise in the price of a barrel of oil at the source. In early March 2010, the price of a barrel of oil was close to $120, for example, about $25 more than it should have been based on simple supply and demand. Was politics now playing an important role in the volatility of oil prices?

This was not the first oil crisis in recent times, however, as the beginning of the new millennium had witnessed an oil crisis, the third major crisis in the last 30 years (1972–2002 and 1979 were the dates of earlier problems), and the fourth crisis appeared in 2008 as prices passed $3 a gallon for a while. The crisis of 2000 manifested itself in the United States via much higher gasoline prices and in Europe via both rising prices and shortages at the pump. Both were caused by the inability of national distribution systems to adjust to the OPECs changing production levels. The 2000 panic eventually subsided but reappeared in 2005 in the wake of the uncertainty surrounding the Iraqi war and the war on terrorism. Four major crises and a minor one in less than 40 years thus have characterized the oil issue.

So a major lesson to be learned from these earlier crises as well as the March 2018 potential crisis is that supply can easily be manipulated, while demand is more stable in the short run but susceptible to long-term adjustments through new technologies, new discoveries and changing lifestyles. But these ups and downs of supply and demand take place in the context of the fact that oil is a finite resource that, by definition, will someday run out. These earlier major fuel crises are discrete episodes in a much larger problem facing the human race, particularly the industrial world. That is, oil, the earth's current principal source of energy, is a finite resource that ultimately will be totally exhausted. And unlike earlier energy transitions, where a more attractive source invited a change (such as from wood to coal and from coal to oil), the next energy transition is being forced upon the human race in the absence of an attractive alternative. In short, we are being pushed out of our almost total reliance on oil toward a new system with a host of unknowns. What will the new fuel be? Will it be from a single source or some combination? Will it be a more attractive source? Will the source be readily available at a reasonable price or will a new cartel emerge that controls much of the supply? Will its production and consumption lead to major new environmental consequences? Will it require major changes to our lifestyles and standards of living? When will we be forced to jump into using this new source?

The 2010 crisis was different from the earlier crises in the 1970s in one way in that the earlier crises had the imprint of OPEC vindictive behavior to the West on it. In the past decade, the Middle East has been dominated by Arab Spring, the phrase coined to capture the series of rebellions and revolutions that have been spreading from Tunisia to Bahrain and affecting many countries in between. Also within the region, one major oil player, Iraq, has been struggling to create a stable government while reentering the global oil market. But oil prices rose nonetheless as oil speculators cornered the market, forcing prices upward. The recent spike in the price at the pump is one example of the effect of such speculation.

But the 2010 and 2014 crises were also similar to other oil crises in that price increases do not reflect the simple supply and demand equation but, instead, are in part also a function of external unrelated forces, be they vindictive behavior of a cartel of nations or greedy behavior of individual investors. And for the latter, high oil prices is the goal, not certainty of supply. This is unfortunate for large Western consumers of oil as well as the largest producers such as Saudi Arabia. As long as consuming countries must rely on autocratic and sometimes unfriendly national regimes for their oil, fear, volatility, and uncertainly will characterize the scene.

Since these consumers cannot dramatically increase their own internal supply of oil under present technology, the answer may lie in alternative sources of energy. Before considering new sources of fuel, other questions need to be asked. Are the calls for a viable alternative to oil premature? Are we simply running scared without cause? Did we learn the wrong lessons from the earlier energy crises? More specifically, were these crises artificially created or a consequence of the actual physical unavailability of the energy source? Have these crises really been about running out of oil globally, or were they due to other phenomena at work, such as poor distribution planning by oil companies or the use of oil as a political weapon by oil-exporting countries?

For well over half a century now, Western oil-consuming countries have been predicting the end of oil. Using a model known as Hubbert's Curve (named after a U.S. geologist who designed it in the 1930s), policy makers have predicted that the world would run out of oil at various times; the most recent prediction is that oil will run out a couple of decades from now. Simply put, the model visualizes all known available resources and the patterns of consumption on a time line until the wells run dry. Despite such prognostication, it was not until the crisis of the early 1970s that national governments began to consider ways of both prolonging the oil system and finding a suitable replacement. Prior to that time, governments as well as the private sector encouraged energy consumption. "The more, the merrier" was an oft-heard refrain. Increases in energy consumption were associated with economic growth. After Europe recovered from the devastation of World War II, for example, every 1 percent increase in energy consumption brought a similar growth in economic output. To the extent that governments engaged in energy policy-making, it was designed solely to encourage increased production and consumption. Prices were kept low and the energy was readily available. Policies making energy distribution systems more efficient and consumption patterns both more efficient and lowered were almost nonexistent.

Yet, when one reads the UN assessment of foreseeable world energy supplies (Hisham Khatib et al., *World Energy Assessment: Energy and the Challenge of Sustainability.* United Nations Development Programme, 2002), a sobering message appears. Do not panic just yet. The study revealed no serious energy shortage during the first half of the twenty-first century. In fact, the report suggested that oil supply conditions had actually improved since the crises of the 1970s and early 1980s. The report went further in its assessment, concluding that fossil fuel reserves are "sufficient to cover global requirements throughout this century, even with a high-growth scenario." Another source suggesting no shortages for some time is *The Myth of the Oil Crisis: Overcoming the Challenges of depletion, Geopolitics, and Global Warming* (Robin M. Mills, Praeger, 2008). Francis R. Stabler argued in *The Pump Will Never Run Dry* (The Futurist, November 1998) that technology and free enterprise will combine to allow the human race to continue its reliance on oil far into the future. For Stabler, the title of his article tells the reader everything. The pump will not run dry!

More recently, the optimists have become bolder, empowered by adjustments in future estimates and the pushing back of the date on which the world will reach "peak oil." One such observer is Robin Mills, CEO of Qamar Energy. He points to the return of Iran as a global supplier of oil as a key reason for such optimism. Nowhere is the message more clear than in a post by Mike Moffatt, who argues in a bold headline that *We Will never Run Out of Oil* (Thought Co., April 1, 2018).

These modern-day optimists had an earlier supporter in Julian L. Simon who argued in his *The Ultimate Resource 2* (1996) that even God may not know exactly how much oil and gas are "out there." Chapter 11 of Simon's book is titled *When Will We Run Out of Oil? Never!* Another supporter of Stabler has been Bjørn Lomborg in *The Skeptical Environmentalist: Measuring the Real State of the World* (Cambridge University Press, 2001). Arguing that the world seems to find more fossil energy than it consumes, he concludes that "we have oil for at least 40 years at present consumption, at least 60 years' worth of gas, and 230 years' worth of coal." Simon and Lomborg are joined by Michael C. Lynch in a published article on the web under global oil supply (msn.com) titled "Crying Wolf: Warnings about Oil Supply."

Today, the search for an alternative to oil still continues despite more optimistic predictions about future oil brought on by lowed prices. Nuclear energy, once thought to be the answer, may play a future role, but at a reduced level. Both water power and wind power remain possibilities, as do biomass, geothermal energy, and solar energy. Many also believe that the developed world is about to enter the hydrogen age to meet future energy needs. The question before us, therefore, is whether the international community has the luxury of sometime before all deposits of oil are exhausted.

The two selections for this issue suggest different answers to the question of should we continue to rely on oil. In the YES selection, the International Energy Agency report points to four "large-scale shifts in the global energy system" that inform the report's findings. One shift relates to clean energy technologies when the world has seen their rapid deployment with failing costs. A second shift is the growing electrification of energy, where recently global consumer spending on electricity matched that on oil products. The third shift relates to "a more services-oriented economy and a cleaner energy mix in China." Finally, there is a "resilience of shale gas and tight oil in the United States."

In the NO selection, its first sentence summarizes its tone: "there will be an extremely painful oil supply shortfall sometime between 2018 and 2020." One major reason is that there will be "less oil coming out of the ground" within two years. And demand will not fall unless here is a collapse of the world economy, suggests the author. If growth of the world economy outpaces available oil, rising oil prices "will kneecap (the) world economy. . . ." If the world economy suffers a setback, declining oil prices will lead to cutbacks in oil exploration and extraction. And finally, recent oil discoveries "were horrible."

YES ↩

The International Energy Agency

World Energy Outlook 2017

Four large-scale shifts in the global energy system set the scene for the *World Energy Outlook-2017 (WEO-2017)*:

> The **rapid deployment and falling costs of clean energy technologies**; in 2016, growth in solar PV capacity was larger than for any other form of generation; since 2010, costs of new solar PV have come down by 70 percent, wind by 25 percent, and battery costs by 40 percent.

> The **growing electrification of energy**; in 2016, spending by the world's consumers on electricity approached parity with their spending on oil products.

> The **shift to a more services-oriented economy and a cleaner energy mix in China**, the world's largest energy consumer, subject of a detailed focus in this *Outlook*.

> The resilience of **shale gas and tight oil in the United States**, cementing its position as the biggest oil and gas producer in the world even at lower prices.

These shifts come at a time when traditional distinctions between energy producers and consumers are being blurred, and a new group of major developing countries, led by India, moves toward center stage. How these developments play out and interact is the story of this *Outlook*, with particular attention paid to their implications for natural gas, this year's fuel focus. Together, they are opening up new perspectives for affordable, sustainable access to modern energy, reshaping responses to the world's pressing environmental challenges, and entailing a reappraisal and reinforcement of approaches to energy security.

Our new *Outlook* describes multiple future pathways for global energy through to 2040. Among them, the **New Policies Scenario** describes where existing policies and announced intentions might lead the energy system, in the anticipation that this will inform decision makers as they seek to improve on this outcome. The **Sustainable Development Scenario**, a major new scenario introduced in the *WEO-2017*, outlines an integrated approach to achieve the energy-related aspects of the UN Sustainable Development Goals: determined action on climate change, universal access to modern energy by 2030, and a dramatic reduction in air pollution. These are all areas in which progress in the New Policies Scenario falls short of what would be required.

In the New Policies Scenario, global energy needs rise more slowly than in the past but still expand by 30 percent between today and 2040, the equivalent of adding another China and India to today's global demand. A global economy growing at an average rate of 3.4 percent per year, a population that expands from 7.4 billion today to more than 9 billion in 2040, and a process of urbanization that adds a city the size of Shanghai to the world's urban population every four months are key forces that underpin our projections. The largest contribution to demand growth—almost 30 percent —comes from India, whose share of global energy use rises to 11 percent by 2040 (still well below its 18 percent share in the anticipated global population). Southeast Asia, a region covered in a separate special report in the *WEO-2017* series, is another rising heavyweight in global energy, with demand growing at twice the pace of China. Overall, developing countries in Asia account for $2/3$ of global energy growth, with the rest coming mainly from the Middle East, Africa, and Latin America.

Compared with the past 25 years, the way that the world meets its growing energy needs changes dramatically in the New Policies Scenario, with the lead now taken by natural gas, by the rapid rise of renewables and by energy efficiency. Improvements in efficiency play a huge role in taking the strain off the supply side: without them, the projected rise in final energy use would more than double. Renewable sources of energy meet 40 percent of the increase in primary demand, and their explosive growth in the power sector marks the end of the boom years for coal. Since 2000, coal-fired power generation capacity has grown by nearly 900 gigawatts (GW), but net additions from today to 2040 are only 400 GW and many of these are plants already under construction. In India, the share of coal in the power mix drops from ¾ in 2016 to less than ½ in 2040. In the absence of large-scale carbon capture and storage, global coal consumption flatlines. Oil demand continues to grow to 2040, albeit at a steadily decreasing pace. Natural gas use rises by 45 percent to 2040; with more limited room to expand in the power sector, industrial demand becomes the largest area for growth. The outlook for nuclear power has dimmed since last year's *Outlook*, but China continues to lead a gradual rise in output, overtaking the United States by 2030 to become the largest producer of nuclear-based electricity.

Renewables capture ²/₃ of global investment in power plants as they become, for many countries, the least-cost source of new generation. Rapid deployment of solar photovoltaics (PV), led by China and India, helps solar become the largest source of low-carbon capacity by 2040, by which time, the share of all renewables in total power generation reaches 40 percent. In the European Union, renewables account for 80 percent of new capacity, and wind power becomes the leading source of electricity soon after 2030, due to strong growth both onshore and offshore. Policies continue to support renewable electricity worldwide, increasingly through competitive auctions rather than feed-in tariffs, and the transformation of the power sector is amplified by millions of households, communities, and businesses investing directly in distributed solar PV. Growth in renewables is not confined to the power sector; the direct use of renewables to provide heat and mobility worldwide also doubles, albeit from a low base. In Brazil, the share of direct and indirect renewable use in final energy consumption rises from 39 percent today to 45 percent in 2040, compared with a global progression from 9 percent to 16 percent over the same period.

Electricity is the rising force among worldwide end uses of energy, making up 40 percent of the rise in final consumption to 2040—the same share of growth that oil took for the last 25 years. Industrial electric motor systems account for ¹/₃ of the increase in power demand in the New Policies Scenario. Rising incomes mean that many millions of households add electrical appliances (with an increasing share of "smart" connected devices) and install cooling systems. By 2040, electricity demand for cooling in China exceeds the total electricity demand of Japan today. The world also gains, on average, 45 million new electricity consumers each year due to expanding access to electricity, although this is still not enough to reach the goal of universal access by 2030. Electricity

makes inroads in supplying heat and mobility, alongside growth in its traditional domains, allowing its share of final consumption to rise to nearly a quarter. A strengthening tide of industry initiatives and policy support—including recent decisions by governments in France and the United Kingdom to phase out sales of conventional gasoline and diesel vehicles by 2040—pushes our projection for the global electric car fleet up to 280 million by 2040, from 2 million today.

To meet rising demand, China needs to add the equivalent of today's United States power system to its electricity infrastructure by 2040, and India needs to add a power system the size of today's European Union. The scale of future electricity needs and the challenge of decarbonizing power supply help to explain why global investment in electricity overtook that of oil and gas for the first time in 2016, and why electricity security is moving firmly up the policy agenda. Cost reductions for renewables are not sufficient on their own to secure efficient decarbonization or reliable supply. The policy challenge is to ensure sufficient investment in electricity networks and in a mix of generation technologies that are the best fit for power system needs, providing the flexibility that is increasingly vital as the contribution of wind and solar PV increases (a consideration that reinforces the links between electricity and gas security). The increasing use of digital technologies across the economy improves efficiency and facilitates the flexible operation of power systems but also creates potential new vulnerabilities that need to be addressed.

China is entering a new phase in its development, with the emphasis in energy policy now firmly on electricity, natural gas and cleaner, and high-efficiency and digital technologies. The previous orientation toward heavy industry, infrastructure development, and the export of manufactured goods lifted hundreds of millions out of poverty—including energy poverty—but left the country with an energy system dominated by coal and a legacy of serious environmental problems, giving rise to almost 2 million premature deaths each year from poor air quality. The president's call for an "energy revolution," the "fight against pollution," and the transition toward a more services-based economic model is moving the energy sector in a new direction. Demand growth slowed markedly from an average of 8 percent per year from 2000 to 2012 to less than 2 percent per year since 2012, and in the New Policies Scenario, it slows further to an average of 1 percent per year to 2040. Energy efficiency regulation explains a large part of this slowdown, without new efficiency measures, end-use consumption in 2040 would be 40 percent higher. Nonetheless, by 2040, per capita energy consumption in China exceeds that of the European Union.

China's choices will play a huge role in determining global trends and could spark a faster clean energy transition. The scale of China's clean energy deployment, technology exports, and outward investment makes it a key determinant of momentum behind the low-carbon transition: $1/4$ of the world's new wind power and solar PV is installed in China in the New Policies Scenario, and China also accounts for more than 40 percent of global investment in electric vehicles. China provides a ¼ of the projected rise in global gas demand and its projected imports of 280 billion cubic meters (bcm) in 2040 are second only to those of the European Union, making China a lynchpin of global gas trade. China overtakes the United States as the largest oil consumer around 2030, and its net imports reach 13 million barrels per day (mb/d) in 2040. But stringent fuel-efficiency measures for cars and trucks, and a shift which sees one in four cars being electric by 2040, means that China is no longer the main driving force behind global oil use—demand growth is larger in India post-2025. China remains a towering presence in coal markets, but our projections suggest that coal use peaked in 2013 and is set to decline by almost 15 percent over the period to 2040.

A remarkable ability to unlock new resources cost-effectively pushes combined US oil and gas output to a level 50 percent **higher than any other country has ever managed; already a net exporter of gas, the United States becomes a net exporter of oil in the late 2020s.** In our projections, the 8 mb/d rise in US tight oil output from 2010 to 2025 would match the highest sustained period of oil output growth by a single country in the history of oil markets. A 630 bcm increase in US shale gas production over the 15 years from 2008 would comfortably exceed the previous record for gas. Expansion on this scale is having wide-ranging impacts within North America, fueling major investments in petrochemicals and other energy-intensive industries. It is also reordering international trade flows and challenging incumbent suppliers and business models. By the mid-2020s, the United States become the world's largest liquefied natural gas (LNG) exporter and a few years later a net exporter of oil—still a major importer of heavier crudes that suit the configuration of its refineries, but a larger exporter of light crude and refined products. This reversal is by no means only a supply-side story; without continued improvements in fuel-economy standards, the United States would remain a net oil importer. In our projections, factoring in extra volumes from Canada and Mexico, North America emerges as the largest source of additional crude oil to

the international market (growth in refinery capacity and demand in the Middle East limit the supply of extra crude from this region). By 2040, around 70 percent of the world's oil trade ends up in a port in Asia, as the region's crude oil imports expand by a massive 9 mb/d. The shifting pattern of risks implies a significant reappraisal of oil security and how best to achieve it.

With the United States accounting for 80 percent **of the increase in global oil supply to 2025 and maintaining near-term downward pressure on prices, the world's consumers are not yet ready to say goodbye to the era of oil.** Up until the mid-2020s, demand growth remains robust in the New Policies Scenario but slows markedly thereafter as greater efficiency and fuel switching bring down oil use for passenger vehicles (even though the global car fleet doubles from today to reach 2 billion by 2040). Powerful impetus from other sectors is enough to keep oil demand on a rising trajectory to 105 mb/d by 2040: oil use to produce petrochemicals is the largest source of growth, closely followed by rising consumption for trucks (fuel-efficiency policies cover 80 percent of global car sales today, but only 50 percent of global truck sales), for aviation and for shipping. Once US tight oil plateaus in the late 2020s and non-OPEC production as a whole falls back, the market becomes increasingly reliant on the Middle East to balance the market. There is a continued large-scale need for investment to develop a total of 670 billion barrels of new resources to 2040, mostly to make up for declines at existing fields rather than to meet the increase in demand. This puts steady upward pressure on costs and prices in the New Policies Scenario, as supply and services markets tighten and companies have to move on to more complex new projects.

Even greater upside for US tight oil and a more rapid switch to electric cars would keep oil prices lower for longer. We explore this possibility in a Low Oil Price Case, in which a doubling of the estimate for tight oil resources, to more than 200 billion barrels, boosts US supply, and more widespread application of digital technologies helps to keep a lid on upstream costs around the globe. Extra policy and infrastructure support pushes a much more rapid expansion in the global electric car fleet, which approaches 900 million cars by 2040. Along with a favorable assumption about the ability of the main oil-producing regions to weather the storm of lower hydrocarbon revenues, this is enough to keep prices within a \$50–70/barrel range to 2040. However, it is not sufficient to trigger a major turnaround in global oil use. Even with a rapid transformation of the passenger car fleet, reaching a peak in global demand would require stronger policy action in other sectors. Otherwise, in a lower oil price world, consumers have few economic incentives to make the switch away from oil or to use it more efficiently. Meanwhile, with projected demand growth appearing robust, at least for the near term, a third straight year in 2017 of low investment in new conventional projects remains a worrying indicator for the future market balance, creating a substantial risk of a shortfall of new supply in the 2020s.

Natural gas, the fuel focus in *WEO-2017*, grows to account for a quarter of global energy demand in the New Policies Scenario by 2040, becoming the second-largest fuel in the global mix after oil. In resource-rich regions, such as the Middle East, the case for expanding gas use is relatively straightforward, especially when it can substitute for oil. In the United States, plentiful supplies maintain a strong share of gas-fired power in electricity generation through to 2040, even without national policies limiting the use of coal. But 80 percent of the projected growth in gas demand takes place in developing economies, led by China, India, and other countries in Asia, where much of the gas needs to be imported (and so transportation costs are significant), and infrastructure is often not yet in place. This reflects the fact that gas looks a good fit for policy priorities in this region, generating heat, power, and mobility with fewer carbon dioxide (CO_2) and pollutant emissions than other fossil fuels, helping to address widespread concerns over air quality. But the competitive landscape is formidable, not just due to coal but also to renewables, which in some countries become a cheaper form of new power generation than gas by the mid-2020s, pushing gas-fired plants toward a balancing rather than a baseload role. Efficiency policies also play a part in constraining gas use: while the electricity generated from gas grows by more than ½ to 2040, related gas use rises by only $1/3$, due to more reliance on highly efficient plants.

A new gas order is emerging, with US LNG helping to accelerate a shift toward a more flexible, liquid, and global market. Ensuring that gas remains affordable and secure, beyond the current period of ample supply and lower prices, is critical for its long-term prospects. LNG accounts for almost 90 percent of the projected growth in long-distance gas trade to 2040: with few exceptions, most notably the route that opens up between Russia and China, major new pipelines struggle in a world that prizes the optionality of LNG. The transformation in gas markets is advanced by market liberalization in Japan and other Asian economies and by the rise of portfolio players—large companies with a range of supply assets. New buyers, often smaller scale, are appearing: the number of LNG-importing countries has risen from 15 in 2005 to 40 today. Gas supply also becomes more diverse: the amount of liquefaction sites worldwide doubles to 2040, with the main additions coming from the United States and Australia, followed by Russia, Qatar, Mozambique, and Canada. Price formation is based increasingly on competition between various sources of gas, rather than indexation to oil. With destination flexibility, hub-based pricing, and spot availability, US LNG acts as a catalyst for many of the anticipated changes in the wider gas market. The new gas order can bring dividends for gas security, although there is the risk of a hard landing for gas markets in the 2020s if uncertainty over the pace or direction of change deters new investments. Over the longer term, a larger and more liquid LNG market can compensate for reduced flexibility elsewhere in the energy system (e.g., lower fuel-switching capacity in some countries as coal-fired generation is retired). We estimate that, in 2040, it would take around 10 days for major importing regions to raise their import levels by 10 percent, a week less than it might take today in Europe, Japan, and Korea.

Universal access to electricity remains elusive, and scaling up access to clean cooking facilities is even more challenging. There are some positive signs: over 100 million people per year have gained access to electricity since 2012 compared with around 60 million per year from 2000 to 2012. Progress in India and Indonesia has been particularly impressive, and in Sub-Saharan Africa, electrification efforts outpaced population growth for the first time in 2014. But, despite this momentum, in the New Policies Scenario around 675 million people—90 percent of them in Sub-Saharan Africa—remain without access to electricity in 2030 (down from 1.1 billion today), and 2.3 billion continue to rely on biomass, coal, or kerosene for cooking (from 2.8 billion today). Household air pollution from these sources is currently linked to 2.8 million premature deaths per year, and several billion hours are spent collecting firewood for cooking, mostly by women, that could be put to more productive uses.

Policy attention to air quality is rising, and global emissions of all the major pollutants fall in our projections, but their health impacts remain severe. Aging populations in many industrialized societies become more vulnerable to the effects of air pollution, and urbanization can also increase exposure to pollutants from traffic. Premature deaths worldwide from outdoor air pollution rise from 3 million today to more than 4 million in 2040 in the New Policies Scenario, even though pollution control technologies are applied more widely and other emissions are avoided because energy services are provided more efficiently or (as with wind and solar) without fuel combustion.

Despite their recent flattening, global energy-related CO_2 emissions increase slightly to 2040 in the New Policies Scenario. This outcome is far from enough to avoid severe impacts of climate change, but there are a few positive signs. Projected 2040 emissions in the New Policies Scenario are lower by 600 million tonnes than in last year's *Outlook* (35.7 gigatonnes [Gt] vs. 36.3 Gt). In China, CO_2 emissions are projected to plateau at 9.2 Gt (only slightly above current levels) by 2030 before starting to fall back. Worldwide emissions from the power sector are limited to a 5 percent increase between now and 2040, even though electricity demand grows by 60 percent and global GDP by 125 percent. However, the speed of change in the power sector is not matched elsewhere: CO_2 emissions from oil use in transport almost catch up with those from coal-fired power plants (which are flat) by 2040, and there is also a 20 percent rise in emissions from industry.

The Sustainable Development Scenario offers an integrated way to achieve a range of energy-related goals crucial for sustainable economic development: climate stabilization, cleaner air, and universal access to modern energy, while also reducing energy security risks. This scenario starts from a set of desired outcomes and considers what would be necessary to deliver them. Central to these outcomes is the achievement of an early peak in CO_2 emissions and a subsequent rapid decline, consistent with the Paris Agreement. A key finding is that universal access to electricity and clean cooking can be reached without making this task any more challenging. We also investigate, in a Faster Transition Scenario, how policies could push an even more rapid and steeper decline in CO_2 emissions and limit climate risks further.

In the Sustainable Development Scenario, low-carbon sources double their share in the energy mix to 40 percent in 2040, all avenues to improve efficiency are pursued, coal demand goes into an immediate decline, and oil consumption peaks soon thereafter. Power generation is all but decarbonized, relying by 2040 on generation from renewables (over 60 percent), nuclear power (15 percent) as well as a contribution from carbon capture and storage (6 percent)—a technology that plays an equally significant role in cutting emissions from the industry sector. Electric cars move into the mainstream quickly, but decarbonizing the transport sector also requires much more stringent efficiency measures across the board, notably for road freight. The 2030 targets for

renewables and efficiency that are defined in the Sustainable Development agenda are met or exceeded in this scenario; renewables and efficiency are the key mechanisms to drive forward the low-carbon transition and reduce pollutant emissions. Considering the interlinkages between them and aligning policy and market frameworks—notably in the residential sector—is essential to ensure cost-efficient outcomes. The provision of highly efficient appliances, combined with decentralized renewables, also plays a major role in extending full access to electricity and clean cooking, especially in rural communities and isolated settlements that are hard to reach with the grid.

As oil and coal fall back and renewables ramp up strongly, natural gas becomes the largest single fuel in the global mix in the Sustainable Development Scenario. Securing clear climate benefits from gas use depends on credible action to minimize leaks of methane—a potent greenhouse gas—to the atmosphere. Consumption of natural gas rises by nearly 20 percent to 2030 in the Sustainable Development Scenario and remains broadly at this level to 2040. The contribution of gas varies widely across regions, between sectors and over time in this scenario. In energy systems heavily reliant on coal (as in China and India), where renewable alternatives are less readily available (notably in some industrial sectors), or where seasonal flexibility is required to integrate high shares of variable renewables, gas plays an important role. Stepping up action to tackle methane leaks along the oil and gas value chain is essential to bolster the environmental case for gas: these emissions are not the only anthropogenic emissions of methane, but they are likely to be among the cheapest to abate. We present the first global analysis of the costs of abating the estimated 76 million tonnes of methane emitted worldwide each year in oil and gas operations, which suggest that 40–50 percent of these emissions can be mitigated at no net cost because the value of the captured methane could cover the abatement measures. Implementing these measures in the New Policies Scenario would have the same impact on reducing the average global surface temperature rise in 2100 as shutting all existing coal-fired power plants in China.

The large-scale shifts in global energy that characterize our *WEO-2017* projections also reshape the outlook for energy investment. Electricity accounts for nearly ½ of total energy supply investment in the New Policies Scenario and almost ⊠ in the Sustainable Development Scenario, up from an average of 40 percent in recent years. Clean energy technologies and energy efficiency likewise take an increasing share of the $60 trillion in cumulative investment in supply and end uses in the New Policies Scenario, and the bulk of the $69 trillion in the Sustainable Development Scenario. Nonetheless, upstream oil and gas investment remains a major component of a secure energy system, even in the carbon-constrained world of the Sustainable Development Scenario. Getting pricing signals and policy frameworks right would include phasing out subsidies that promote wasteful consumption of fossil fuels (at an estimated $260 billion in 2016, these are almost double the subsidies currently going to renewables). Along with a proliferation of community, municipal, and private-sector initiatives, well-designed policy remains essential to pursue a brighter energy future.

THE INTERNATIONAL ENERGY AGENCY is a Paris-based autonomous intergovernmental organization established in the framework of the Organization for Economic Co-operation and Development in 1974 in the wake of the 1973 oil crisis.

Chris Martenson

The Looming Energy Shock

The Next Oil Crisis Will Arrive in 3 Years or Less

There will be an extremely painful oil supply shortfall sometime between 2018 and 2020. It will be highly disruptive to our over-leveraged global financial system, given how saddled it is with record debts and unfunded IOUs.

Due to a massive reduction in capital spending in the global oil business over 2014–2016 and continuing into 2017, the world will soon find less oil coming out of the ground beginning somewhere between 2018 and 2020.

Because oil is the lifeblood of today's economy, if there's less oil to go around, price shocks are inevitable. It's very likely we'll see prices climb back over $100 per barrel. Possibly *well* over.

The only way to avoid such a supply-driven price shock is if the world economy collapses first, dragging demand downward.

Not exactly a great "solution" to hope for.

Pick Your Poison

This is why our view is that either

1. the world economy outgrows available oil somewhere in the 2018–2020 time frame or
2. the world economy collapses first, thus pushing off an oil price shock by a few years (or longer, given the severity of the collapse).

If (1) happens, the resulting oil price spike will kneecap a world economy already weighted down by the highest levels of debt ever recorded, currently totaling some 327 percent of GDP:

Remember, in 2008, oil spiked to $147 a barrel. The rest is history—a massive credit crisis ensued. While there was a mountain of dodgy debt centered on subprime loans in the United States, what brought Greece to its knees wasn't US housing debt but its own unsustainable

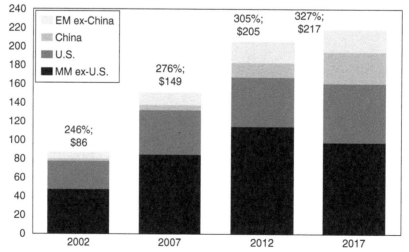

Total Global Debt (all sectors)

USD trillion, Q1 of each year

Legend: EM ex-China, China, U.S., MM ex-U.S.

- 2002: 246%; $86
- 2007: 276%; $149
- 2012: 305%; $205
- 2017: 327%; $217

Source: IIF, BIS, Haver

pile of debt coupled to a 100 percent dependence on imported oil—which, figuratively and literally, broke the bank.

If (2) happens, then the price of oil declines, if not collapses. Demand withers away, the oil business cuts back on its exploration/extraction investments even further, so that much later, when the global economy is trying to recover, it then runs into an even more severe supply shortfall. It becomes extremely hard to get sustained GDP growth back online.

If you really want to understand why I hold these views, you need to fully understand and digest this next chart. It shows the amazingly tightly coupled linear relationship between economic growth and energy consumption:

This chart says, if you want an extra incremental unit of economic growth you're going to need to have an extra incremental unit of energy. More growth means more energy consumed.

And today, oil is still the most important source of energy. It's the dominant energy source for transportation, by far. A global economy, after all, is nothing more than things being made and then moved, often very far distances. Despite what you might read about developments in alternative and other forms of energy, our dependency on oil is still massive.

Plunging Investment

Resulting from the start of oil's price decline in 2014, the world saw a historic plunge in oil investments (exploration, development, CAPEX, etc.) as companies the world over retracted, delayed, or outright canceled oil projects:

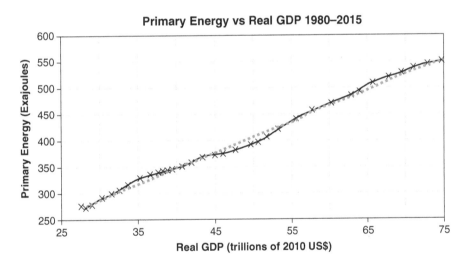

Primary Energy vs Real GDP 1980–2015

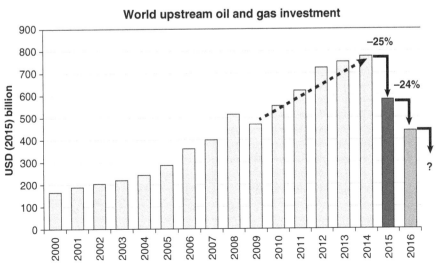

World upstream oil and gas investment

In the chart, note the two successive drops in oil investment from 2014 to 2015 and then again into 2016. So far, 2017 is shaping up for another successive decline, which will mark the only three-year decline in investment in oil's entire history. So what's happening here is actually quite unusual.

This isn't just a slump. It's an *historic* slump.

We don't yet know by how much oil investment will decline in 2017, but it's probably pretty close to the rates seen in the prior two years.

Next, take note of the dotted blue arrow in the chart. See how far oil investment climbed during the years from 2009 to 2014? Not quite a doubling, but not far off from one either. Remember those years, I'll return to them in a moment.

The key question to ask about the 2009–2014 period is: *How much new oil was discovered for all that spending?*

Turns out: *Not a lot.*

Practically No Discoveries

There is one hard and fast rule in the oil business: **Before you can pump it, you have to find it.**

The growing problem here is that oil discoveries were horrible in 2016, really bad in 2015, and terrible in 2014. That recent three-year stretch is the worst in the data series:

Again: you have to find it before you can pump it. And around the world, oil companies are just not finding as much as they used to.

Remember that blue dotted line on the oil investment chart? Here's its counterpart, showing discoveries over the same time frame—it's just a straight slump downward:

Global oil discoveries fell to a record low in 2016 as companies continued to cut spending and conventional oil projects sanctioned were at the lowest level in more than 70 years, according to the International Energy Agency, which warned that both trends could continue this year.

Oil discoveries declined to 2.4 billion barrels in 2016, compared with an average of 9 billion barrels per year over the past 15 years. Meanwhile, the volume of conventional resources sanctioned for development last year fell to 4.7 billion barrels, 30 percent lower than the previous year as the number of projects that received a final investment decision dropped to the lowest level since the 1940s.

Now it's clear why the oil companies pulled back their investment dollars so rapidly when prices slumped: **They were spending more and finding less** throughout the 2009–2014 period, so they were already feeling the pain of diminishing returns. When the price of oil cracked below $100 a barrel, they wasted no time reining in their investment dollars.

Should we be concerned about this record lowest level of oil project funding in 70 years? Why, yes, we should. Everyone should:

"Our analysis shows we are entering a period of greater oil price volatility (partly) as a result of three years in a row of global oil investments in decline: in 2015, 2016, and most likely 2017," IEA Director General Fatih Birol said, speaking at an energy conference in Tokyo.

"This is the first time in the history of oil that investments are declining three years in a row," he said, adding that this would cause **"difficulties"** in global oil markets in a few years.

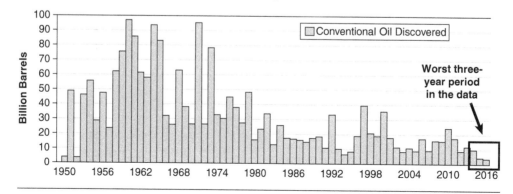

Oil Finds at Lowest Since 1952

Exploration hit rock bottom amid unprecedented spending curbs

Source: Wood Mackenzie

Note: 2016 figure is preliminary

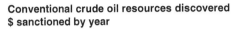

Conventional crude oil resources discovered
$ sanctioned by year

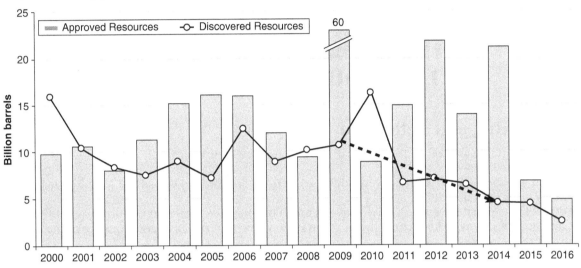

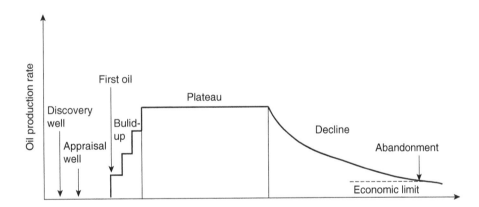

To give you a visual of the process, here's a chart to help you understand why it takes years between making an initial find and maximum production:

This bears repeating: oil is the most important substance for our economy, we're burning more of it on a yearly basis than ever before, and we just found the lowest amount since the world economy was *several times smaller* than it is now. And all this is happening while we're reducing our efforts to find more at an unprecedented rate.

There's no way to speed up the process of oil discovery and extraction meaningfully, no matter how much money and manpower you throw at it. It simply requires many years to go from a positive test bore to a fully functioning extraction and distribution/transportation program operating at maximum.

In **Part 2: Preparing for the Coming Shock,** we provide the evidence that shows why by 2019, or 2020, oil prices will have forced a new crisis upon the world.

More economic growth requires more energy. Always has and it always will. Oil is the most important form of energy of them all. But everyone assumes—especially today when it appears as if we're "awash" in it given the current supply glut—that we will always have access to as much as we need.

That's not going to be the case soon.

CHRIS MARTENSON is a fellow at the Post Carbon Institute, a think tank which provides information and analysis on climate change, energy scarcity, and other issues related to sustainability and long-term social resilience.

EXPLORING THE ISSUE

Is the Global Oil Crisis of the Last Half-century Over?

Critical Thinking and Reflection

1. How comfortable are you in the fact that there is disagreement over when and even whether the world will see peak oil?
2. Do you foresee the four external events outlined in the *World Energy Outlook 2017* YES article pushing a global energy crisis back decades?
3. Do you believe that lowered oil prices have as much of a negative effect on the world as many people believe?
4. Can you envisage your lives changing in any way 20 years from now as a consequence of the changing power structure in the oil market?
5. Do you accept the thesis of the NO article that either the world economy outgrows the available oil supply in 2018 or it collapses, thus moving the oil price shock back a few years?

Is There Common Ground?

Since oil is a finite resource, the planet will obviously run out of the resource someday. No responsible analyst denies this scenario. There is also recognition by many in the field that one great unknown factor is the extent to which new future technologies will extend the life of oil as the dominant resource, and if so, for how long? Modern technologies have trumped earlier doomsday predictions several times, and there is little reason to believe that they may not play a role in the future. There is also strong consensus that no single alternative energy source is poised to replace oil yet. And the recent nuclear energy disaster in Japan only emphasizes this point.

Additional Resources

Arezki, Rabah, et al., *Oil Prices and the Global Economy*, IMF Working Paper, International Monetary Fund (January 2017).

Hunt, Tam, "What Happened to Peak Oil?" *Greentech Media* (March 18, 2016).

Koerth-Baker, Maggie, *Before the Lights Go Out: Conquering the Energy Crisis Before It Conquers Us* (Wiley, 2012).

Shankleman, Jess and Warren, Hayley, "Why the Prospect of 'Peak Oil' Is Hotly Debated," *Bloomberg* (December 21, 2017).

Sorrell, Steve, et al., "Shaping the Global Oil Peak: A Review of the Evidence on Field Sizes, Reserve Growth, Decline Rates and the Depletion Rates," *Energy* (January 2012).

Internet References . . .

American Petroleum Institute

www.api.org

Hubbert Peak

www.hubbertpeak.com

International Energy Agency (IEA)

www.worldenergyoutlook.org

Planetforlife

www.plantforlife.com

World Energy Council

www.worldenergycouncil.org

World Oil

www.worldoil

Selected, Edited, and with Issue Framing Material by:
Marie E. Harf, *U.S. Department of State (2013–2017),*
Central Intelligence Agency (2006–2011)

ISSUE

Is the Paris Climate Change Agreement Working?

Yes: Todd Stern, from "Why the Paris Agreement Works," *The Brookings Institution* (2017)

No: Kelly Levin and Taryn Fransen, from "Understanding the 'Emissions Gap' in 5 Charts," *World Resources Institute* (2017)

Learning Outcomes

After reading this issue, you will be able to:

- Describe the main features and historical and diplomatic significance of the Paris climate change agreement.
- Understand the arguments of those climate change activists that the agreement does not go far enough.
- Understand the arguments of those who believe that the agreement has major flaws.
- Describe what effect the U.S. decision to leave the agreement might have on its future success and on the United States itself.
- Describe how the growing clean energy economy affects the climate change debate.
- Understand the concept of Emissions Gap.

ISSUE SUMMARY

Yes: Todd Stern, a senior fellow at the Brookings Institution, argues that the negotiated agreement broke significant new ground and, while imperfect, put the world on a path to seriously confront climate change—and therefore it needs to be defended, supported, and implemented. He writes that the agreement had to clear eight distinct hurdles and that it was ultimately successful in overcoming all of them. His bottom line is that the agreement is working and should be strengthened, not weakened.

No: The World Resources Institute report coauthored by Senior Associate Kelly Levin and Senior Fellow Taryn Fransen uses five charts to explain the "emissions gap," the "difference between the emissions level countries have pledged to achieve . . . and the level consistent with limiting warming to well below 2 degrees."

Earth Day, April 2016. The stage was set as leaders from 175 countries signed a historic agreement aimed to slow the rise in greenhouse gas emissions that are changing our climate and harming the planet. The symbolism of the day was not lost on observers. United Nations Secretary-General Ban Ki-moon declared that the world was in "a race against time" to combat the consequences of the rise in emissions. U.S. Secretary of State John Kerry signed on behalf of the U.S. government while holding his grand-daughter, signifying that tomorrow's generation would pay a heavy price if today's world leaders failed to address a problem still viewed as contentious in some quarters of the globe. Fast-forward to June 1, 2017, when U.S. President

Donald Trump announced that he was withdrawing the United States from the Paris climate accord, including halting all financial contributions the previous U.S. administration had pledged. This action put the United States at odds with every other country in the world, all of whom have now formally signed onto the agreement.

What were the major components of the accord that made it worthy of being called historic? Why did the United States decide to leave? And what impact will that decision have on global efforts to combat climate change and on the United States itself?

Let us consider the initial question first. The agreement set a long-term goal to limit global warming to well below 2°C compared to preindustrial levels, or even to 1.5°C if possible. (The 2°C level is the point at which scientists argue the world will see "the worst extremes of global warming.") As part of the agreement, each country submitted an individual plan to reduce its own greenhouse gas emissions to help reach the overall 2°C goal. Each country's emissions targets will be reevaluated every five years, with the hope that countries will set more ambitious targets over time; the agreement was designed as a starting, not an ending, point. It also calls on richer countries to help poorer countries financially with the costs of going green, while leaving it up to the former to determine their actual aid figures.

Through the years, climate change has attracted scientific debate. An overwhelming majority of scientists have assessed, based on data and computer models, that climate change is occurring, human activities are primarily responsible for that change, and there could be dire consequences if it is not addressed. Others have suggested that while global warming was occurring, the existing models could not definitively link global warming to human activities. A third group, representing a small minority, has argued that we cannot be certain global warming, rather than natural shifts in the weather, is taking place at all, much less determine its cause.

Despite these scientific debates, the global community has worked to achieve consensus for curtailing human activities thought to affect climate change. The Paris accord was the culmination of a story that began at the UN-sponsored Earth Summit in Rio de Janeiro, Brazil in 1992, where the United Nations Framework Convention on Climate Change was signed. In the years following that Summit, the parties to the Convention began meeting annually to assess global progress in combatting climate change. A 1997 international meeting in Kyoto, Japan, concluded with an agreement in which the European Community and 37 industrialized countries, including the United States, agreed to reduction levels. The agreement went into effect globally on February 19, 2005. Today, 192 countries are party to it, but not the United States; the U.S. Senate never ratified the agreement, and the George W. Bush Administration decided to withdraw from it in 2001.

Today there remain loud voices, almost entirely in the American political landscape, arguing against the premises that the climate is changing and humans are primarily responsible, a dissenting minority voice against the larger and growing scientific consensus. Those commentators have come up against a large advocacy movement in support of combatting climate change. The issue has been fodder for activists, policy makers, and, increasingly, businesses everywhere.

This general fight took on a new and more focused dimension when the Paris agreement was concluded in December 2015. President Obama said the agreement "sends a powerful signal that the world is firmly committed to a low-carbon future. . . . The targets we've set are bold. . . . This agreement represents the best chance we've had to save the one planet that we've got." He went on to exclaim that the moment could well "be a turning point for the world." It seemed as if the Paris accord's flexibility, transparency, and ambition had finally overcome the economic and political obstacles that had previously prevented the world from agreeing to tangible steps for how every country could play a role in combatting climate change.

Critics too were quick to respond, with the most vocal arguing that the agreement had not gone nearly far enough. Bill McKibben, a long-time advocate of the need to address greenhouse gas emissions, called the new pact "an ambitious agreement designed for about 1995" (*The New York Times*, December 13, 2015). James Hansen, proclaimed by some as the father of climate change awareness, said the negotiations represented "no action, just promises." He called for taxing greenhouse emissions across the board instead (*The Guardian*, December 12, 2015).

The main argument put forth against the Paris agreement was that the framework was too weak to achieve its climate stabilization targets. Not only were there no penalties for falling short, even if every country met its targets, they would still cover only approximately one-third of the emissions reductions needed to be on a least-cost pathway to meet the 2°C goal. The UN Environment Programme has since cautioned that "the gap between the reductions needed and the national pledges made in Paris is alarmingly high." Analyst Ted Nordhaus sounded a related warning: "Sustaining the fiction that the two-degree target remains viable risks leaving the world ill prepared to mitigate or manage the consequences" (*Foreign Affairs*, February 8, 2018).

Some observers have argued a middle ground, outlined by Greenpeace Executive Director Jennifer Morgan: "Although it is true that the current commitments of the Paris signatories fall far short of the emissions cuts required to meet the aspirational 1.5-degree target. . . . the solution is not in giving up the goal but in significantly stepping up action while also investing in adaptation to build resilience" (*Foreign Affairs*, February 28, 2018). Essentially, their view is that while the agreement may be flawed, it is a necessary step toward achieving a politically sustainable global effort to combat climate change.

The 2016 campaign and subsequent election of Donald Trump as U.S. president thrust the Paris accord back into the political spotlight. Many reasons have been advanced for Trump's opposition to the agreement, including his "America First" philosophy, his anti-regulation bias, his political connections to the coal industry, and his desire to dismantle President Obama's accomplishments.

But what global effect is President Trump's decision likely to have? The major players, including China and India, remain committed to the agreement, as do many American states and cities. The agreement's negotiators have said it was designed to withstand political shocks, and that the accord does not rest on the participation of any one country. Nevertheless, supporters and skeptics of the deal both see consequences in the Trump administration's withdrawal, for the U.S. economy and its global standing.

First, many argue that President Trump's decision will harm the U.S. economy because it damages America's ability to lead in the increasingly profitable clean energy sector, opening up opportunities for other countries—most notably, China—to fill that void. There are around 3 million jobs in the U.S. clean technology sector, which has been growing at 12 times the speed of the rest of the economy. In 2015, clean energy attracted twice as much investment globally as fossil fuels—and electricity generation that year was greater from renewables than from coal or oil for the first time ever (*Foreign Affairs*, July/August 2017; *International Energy Agency*). The rest of the world is adopting clean technologies, and it is arguably in the United States' interest to be at the forefront of this revolution by investing in innovation and research and development. That's why many within private U.S. industry—including oil companies and coal-fired electric utilities, and top executives such as Jeffrey Immelt of General Electric and Lloyd Blankfein of Goldman Sachs, advocated for staying in the agreement. They argued that withdrawing would cede clean energy jobs and investment to other countries.

There is also growing evidence that the previous assumption that economic growth and rising greenhouse gas emissions must go hand-in-hand is no longer operative. As Brian Deese, an Obama administration official who helped negotiate the Paris agreement, noted: "Between 2008 and 2016, the U.S. economy grew by 12 percent while carbon emissions fell by about 11 percent—the first time the link between the two had been broken for more than a year at a time." He highlights that this decoupling has begun in at least 35 countries, including China—a shift he calls a "seismic change in the political economy of clean energy" (*Foreign Affairs*, July/August 2017).

As the American national government steps away from the climate change issue, it is increasingly clear that cities, states, and the private sector are stepping up to do more on both emissions reductions and adaption of infrastructure to better deal with a changing climate. Twenty-nine states now require a percentage of their electricity to come from renewable sources. Bucking the larger national political trend, 9 of the 10 states that receive the largest proportion of their electricity from wind generation are Republican-leaning.

Finally, both supporters and critics of the Paris agreement acknowledge that the U.S. withdrawal is likely to damage American global leadership and soft power and not just on climate issues. For example, withdrawal arguably makes it more difficult for the United States to lead discussions about other international rules–based systems such as intellectual property and trade (*Chatham House*, June 2, 2017). As the United States pulls back, China appears ready and willing to assume the mantle of international leadership on climate. Chinese President Xi Jinping made clear in his speech at the 2017 World Economic Forum in Davos that China sees itself as a global citizen committed to further international integration, including on climate issues; indeed, Beijing has invested heavily in green technologies, and China has been on a downward trend with its coal use. Global sustainability experts representing business, government, NGOs, and academia who participated in a 2017 survey ranked China second when asked what country is leading on addressing climate change. Meanwhile, the United States fell back to 11th place, with only 5 percent of respondents saying it is leading on this issue (GlobeScan-SustainAbility Survey).

Brown University's Amanda Lynch summed up the complications when she wrote, "Because Paris is quite limited with regard to targets, timetables, and compliance, the link between ratifying and actual outcomes on emissions, adaption, and finance is primarily symbolic. That said, symbols matter" (*Foreign Affairs*, August 14, 2017). Finally, the global community moves forward to meet the goals laid out in the agreement despite the obstacles, including the UN Environmental Programme's late 2017 report prepared by an international team of leading scientists that concludes that there is an "urgent need for accelerated short-term and enhanced longer-term national ambition if the goals of the Paris agreement are to remain achievable" (UNEP, October 2017).

In the YES selection, Todd Stern, senior fellow at the Brookings Institution, suggests that the negotiated agreement had to clear eight hurdles to be considered successful, which he argues it did. These included that it "had to be universal, . . . ambitious, . . . address the fears of countries that they might be forced to take measures inconsistent (with their development goals), . . . built to last, . . . overcome the "firewall" division between developed and developing countries, . . . be transparent, . . . continue the tradition of aiding poor countries, . . . (and) be legally binding." In the NO selection, the World Resources Institute authors spell out the findings of the United Nations Environment Programme's early study of the agreement in action. They conclude that global greenhouse gases are still increasing, some but not all countries are on track to meet proposed 2020 standards, emissions must be lowered extensively to meet 2030 goals, existing solutions can "close the gap, if they are embraced quickly," and the world must increasingly "rely upon carbon dioxide removal technologies and approaches."

YES ←

Todd Stern

Why the Paris Agreement Works

There is a recent strain of modestly constructive writing about the need to take action on climate change that nevertheless claims to see Paris as flawed to the point of condoning opposition to it. While this approach is far better than the nonsense emanating from the Trump administration, it is still mistaken, and I want to take a moment to explain why.

The agreement we negotiated over many years on the road to Paris had to clear a number of hurdles.

It had to be universal, unlike the 1997 Kyoto Protocol, whose obligations applied only to developed countries. That structure was unworkable, given the growing majority of emissions from developing countries and the obvious lack of support there would be for any agreement that didn't fully cover China and others.

It had to be ambitious, while recognizing that initial targets wouldn't be enough.

It had to address the fears of countries that they might be forced to take measures inconsistent with their priority to develop and grow.

It had to be built to last, establishing a regime to carry us forward over decades, not a one-off exercise in which we'd be back at the negotiating table in 5 or 10 years.

It had to overcome the "firewall" division between developed and developing countries, while understanding that countries with a wide range of capacities cannot be expected to do the same thing in every particular.

It had to be transparent, so all could see how countries were doing both on their emission inventories and their progress toward achieving targets.

It had to continue the tradition of aiding poor countries—embedded in the original 1992 climate convention and reflected in George W. Bush's $2 billion pledge to the climate fund he launched in 2008—without saddling the United States with either outsized or legally binding numeric obligations.

It had to be legally binding in at least some respects but without making it impossible for some countries to join.

With sustained U.S. leadership, the Paris Agreement cleared these hurdles:

It was universal.

It set forth a long-term vision toward ambitious goals.

It began with national targets that made a good start in shifting the path of projected temperature downward. Based on a decision at an earlier conference, those targets had to be submitted well in advance of the Paris negotiation itself, so they would be exposed to public scrutiny, spurring countries do their best.

It includes an every five-year cycle starting in 2020, in which countries review their targets and are encouraged to enhance them.

It is built on a bottom-up structure in which each country determines its own emission targets without fear that its ability to grow and develop will be compromised.

It replaces the old firewall with an understanding that all countries are treated the same legally, but with certain flexibilities available, based on country capabilities.

It includes strong provisions for reporting and review, with flexibility provided to those developing countries that need it in light of their capacities.

It promises continued financial support to poor countries, with clarity that the funding is to be mobilized from all channels, private as well as public.

It is built on a hybrid legal structure, with process provisions that are legally binding, such as the obligation to submit targets and to report and be reviewed on implementation, and substantive provisions that are nonbinding, including the targets that countries submit. This structure recognizes that norms and expectations can often be more effective in encouraging robust action than legally binding requirements, which, paradoxically, can yield weaker action as some countries lowball their targets for fear of legal liability.

In short, the Paris Agreement built a regime that was not only acceptable to all from the start but designed to evolve in precisely the direction needed to meet our profound climate challenge.

It succeeds where every effort before, for some 20 years, had come up short. It breaks new ground in numerous ways, articulating a long-range goal to drive global efforts, creating a bottom-up structure for ambitious national action, outlining a continually renewing set of commitments, bridging the differences between developed and developing countries, establishing a hybrid legal structure. And it did this all in the context of an agreement that is not just a statement of shared global principles, but a joint undertaking in which all countries are expected to do their part to shape the global economy in a productive and sustainable manner.

The idea that it is rational to support climate action but reject Paris does not, in fact, make sense. The idea that an agreement materially different from Paris could win the consensus support of countries everywhere is a fiction. Paris is an imperfect but nonetheless remarkable agreement. It needs to be defended, supported, and implemented.

TODD STERN is a senior fellow at the Brookings Institution.

Kelly Levin and Taryn Fransen

 **NO**

Understanding the "Emissions Gap" in 5 Charts

Every year, the UN Environment Programme (UNEP) brings together scientists from around the world to measure the size of the greenhouse gas (GHG) "emissions gap," the difference between the emissions level countries have pledged to achieve under international agreements and the level consistent with limiting warming to well below 2°C (3.6°F). That benchmark exists because warming above 1.5°C–2°C would bring increasingly catastrophic impacts. (Learn more in our post describing the world's "carbon budget.")

So what does the Gap Report show for 2017? These five charts explain.

1. Global GHG Emissions Are Still Increasing.

In 2016, global GHG emissions were about 52 gigatonnes (Gt CO_2e/year). Total global GHG emissions have roughly doubled since 1970 and have grown dramatically even since 2000. Carbon dioxide emissions from fossil fuel combustion, cement and other processes contribute the most, around 70 percent of the total.

Encouragingly, the growth in global emissions in 2015 and 2016 is the slowest since the early 1990s (except years of global economic recession), and global CO_2 emissions

Figure 1

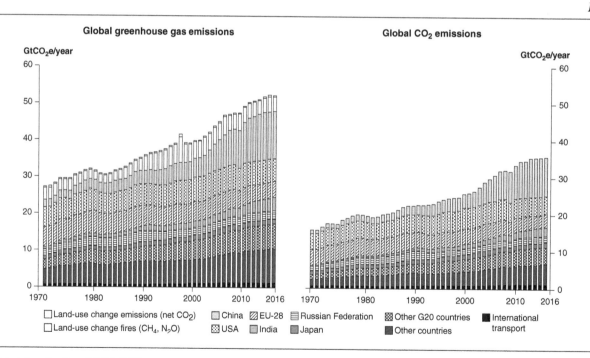

Source: The Emissions Gap Report 2017, UNEP.

Note: Other G20 countries include Argentina, Australia, Brazil, Canada, Indonesia, Mexico, Republic of Korea, Saudi Arabia, South Africa and Turkey. The greenhouse gas total are expressed in terms of billions of tonnes of global annual CO_2 equivalent emissions (GtCO_2e/year). CO_2 equivalent is calculated using the Global Warming Potentials (GWP-100) metric of UNFCCC as report in the IPCC Second Assessment Report, similar as has been done in the IPCC Fifth Assessment Report.

from fossil fuel use and cement production remained stable in both 2015 and 2016. However, it remains to be seen whether these trends will be permanent.

2. The World's Largest Emitters Are Collectively on Track to Achieve Their Promised Emissions Reductions for 2020, But Several Countries Need to Step Up.

In 2009 and 2010, 73 parties to the UN Framework Convention on Climate Change (UNFCCC) made GHG emissions pledges for 2020. For the G20 countries—responsible for roughly three quarters of global emissions—the Gap Report compares their projected 2020 emissions with their pledges. It found that seven G20 members (Australia, Brazil, China, the EU, India, Japan, and Russia) are on track to meet their 2020 pledges, five (Canada, Mexico, the Republic of Korea, South Africa, and the United States) are likely to require further action or will have to purchase offsets, and the remaining three (Argentina, Saudi Arabia,

and Turkey) did not make pledges for 2020. While not all members are on track to meet their pledges, collectively, 2020 emissions are expected to fall within the pledged range.

3. To Keep Warming Between 1.5°C and 2°C, Emissions in 2030 Need to Be Far Lower than They Are Expected to Be.

To measure the size of the emissions gap, experts review available scenarios from the scientific literature showing how emissions must be reduced in order to limit warming to 2°C and 1.5°C, the temperature goals laid out in the international Paris Agreement on climate change. The experts compare these ranges against those that would be achieved under the pledges made by 166 parties under the Paris Agreement and against the emissions expected to occur if current policies continue (without being strengthened in order to meet the pledges). They find that a significant gap remains between Paris Agreement-compatible emissions in 2030 and both of those scenarios.

Figure 2

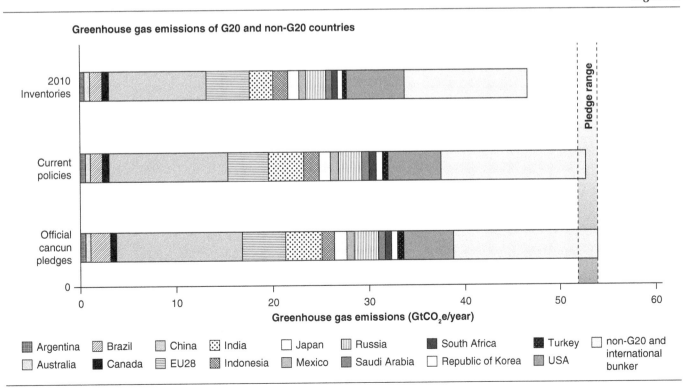

Source: The Emissions Gap Report 2017. UNEP.

Figure 3

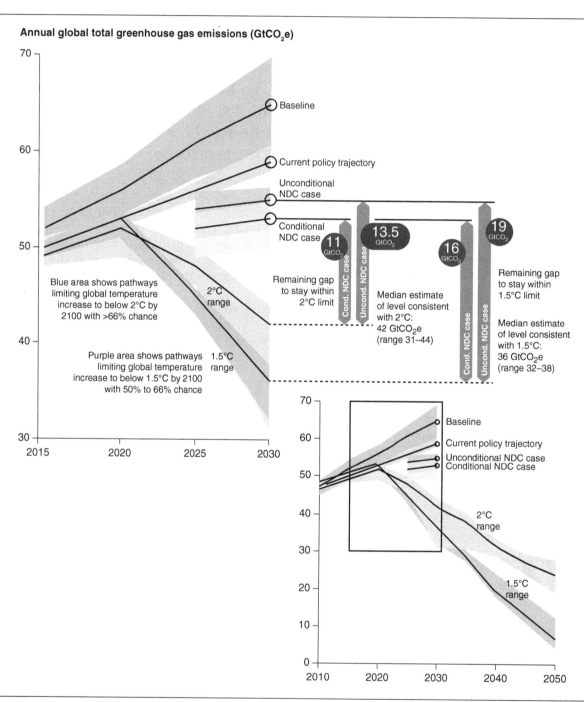

Annual global total greenhouse gas emissions (GtCO₂e)

Source: The Emissions Gap Report 2017, UNEP.

Note: The emissions range for 1.5°C is smaller than for 2°C, as a smaller number of studies for 1.5°C are available. For current policy, the minimum-maximum across all assessed studies are provided.

Using a benchmark of a likely chance of 2°C, the gap between the Paris goals and the pledges is 11–13.5 GtCO₂e. Using a benchmark of a median or likely chance of 1.5°C, the gap is 16–19 GtCO₂e. The gap between the Paris temperature goals and the current policy scenario is higher still, given that many countries are not yet on track to achieve their emissions-reduction pledges, but this is to be expected given that pledges extending to 2030 are still fairly new.

4. Existing Solutions Can Close the Gap, if They Are Embraced Quickly.

The report finds that proven technologies, even with conservative assumptions, could reduce emissions 33 Gt CO_2e/year by 2030. And if you add in newer technologies, that potential grows to 38 GtCO₂e/year in 2030. That's more than what's needed to close the emissions gap and keep warming below 1.5°C.

More than half of this potential is from a handful of categories—solar and wind energy, efficient passenger cars, afforestation, and halting deforestation—and requires quickly reducing reliance on, and soon phasing out, coal-fired power not equipped with carbon capture and storage.

5. Limiting Warming to 1.5°C–2°C also Relies on Carbon Dioxide Removal and Negative Emissions Approaches.

The report notes that the rate at which we are depleting the carbon budget will force us to increasingly rely upon carbon dioxide removal technologies and approaches, which remove and sequester carbon dioxide. There are significant risks, however, associated with these technologies and approaches, including uncertainty in their carbon retention, the consequences of large-scale deployment, and costs and feasibility.

Scenarios that meet the 1.5°C target in 2100 assume large-scale availability of negative emissions technologies, such as bioenergy combined with carbon capture and storage. These technologies would be scaled up quickly. By 2100, the average removal of carbon dioxide through negative emissions technologies would be 810 GtCO₂e, which is equal to almost two decades' worth of global emissions at current rates. Few scenarios can also meet the 2°C target without using negative emissions technologies.

Figure 4

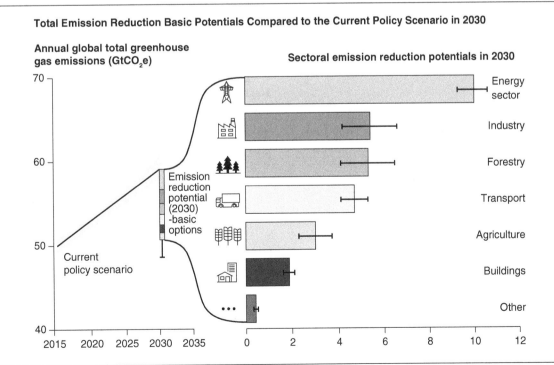

Total Emission Reduction Basic Potentials Compared to the Current Policy Scenario in 2030

Source: The Emissions Gap Report 2017, UNEP.

Figure 5

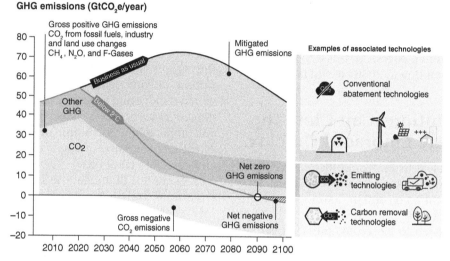

The Role of Carbon Dioxide Removal in Climate Change Mitigation

Source: The Emissions Gap Report 2017, UNEP.

Note: This figure shows emission reductions from conventional mitigation technologies combined with carbon dioxide removal. This exemplary scenario is consistent with an at least 66 percent chance of keeping warming below 2°C relative to pre-industrial levels. Emission reductions are sown against a business-as-usual scenario without any additional climate policies. Global net emissions levels turn to net negative towards the very end of the century, but carbon dioxide removal is already being deployed much earlier. Some residual greenhouse gas emissions remain at the end of the century, as they are too difficult to mitigate in the scenario. Note that the scenario used is different from the scenarios used in Chapter 3, which leads to small variations in emission levels and timing of negative emissions.

If such technologies cannot be deployed at these rates and scale, which has yet to be proven, then our ability to meet these temperature targets is significantly compromised.

Closing the Gap

The Emissions Gap Report once again underscores the urgency of redoubling our efforts to reduce emissions. It shows that solutions exist, and if they are adopted quickly, we can turn our current situation around. But with each year we wait—and with each further installment of the UNEP Emissions Gap Report—we make our ability to limit dangerous climate change more difficult, risky, and costly.

Kelly Levin is senior associate, Pillar Lead TRAC Policy, at the World Resources Institute.

Taryn Fransen is an international climate policy expert currently serving as senior fellow at the World Resources Institute.

EXPLORING THE ISSUE

Is the Paris Climate Change Agreement Working?

Critical Thinking and Reflection

1. Does the Paris agreement on climate change mean that international leaders have now officially accepted the view regarding the cause of climate change?
2. Do the criticisms that the Paris agreement has no teeth to address the issue of greenhouse gas emissions have merit?
3. Do you agree with the excitement and optimism expressed by world leaders at the signing of the agreement that it is truly historic in nature?
4. How should the global community respond to the criticisms that the agreement didn't go far enough?
5. What impact will the American withdrawal from the agreement have both on the agreement and on the United States?

Is There Common Ground?

Assessing the existence of common ground on the issue of climate change, let alone the parameters of the new Paris agreement, is difficult. While the scientific community and the general public agree on the fact that the global climate is changing, some disagree on the role that humans play in that process. A much higher percentage of scientists compared to the general public place significant blame on humans for these changes.

A vast majority of members within the scientific community also accept the views found in the various reports of the Intergovernmental Panel on Climate Change concerning the current state of climate change and its causes and consequences. Reading the research findings of most members of the scientific community would lead one to believe that disagreements of an earlier day regarding the basic questions associated with climate change have been settled. But nonetheless, within the scientific community, one finds a handful of scientists who, along with popular nonscientific writers, have cornered the market on arguing the opposite case. Moreover, the rhetoric of the American right on this issue has captured the attention of a large number of its followers who have embraced its policy positions. Thus, it is not surprising that one finds a larger lack of consensus among the general public, as well as among politicians, regarding the basic questions associated with climate change. This is so despite the reality that

year after year, weather reports show each succeeding year to be hotter than ever before.

And while there is much within the agreement that both sides can accept, differences do remain over the issue of what responsibility the developed world has to help the developing countries meet their goals and over the extent to which the voluntary aspects of the agreement have enough teeth in them to make a difference.

Additional Resources

Klein, Daniel, et al., Editors, *The Paris Agreement on Climate Change: Analysis and Commentary*, Oxford University Press (2017).

McBride, James, "The Consequences of Leaving the Paris Agreement," *Foreign Affairs* (June 1, 2017).

Morgan, Jennifer, "Paris Climate Agreement Temperature Target: Abandoning It Is a Mistake," *Foreign Affairs* (February 28, 2018).

Nordhaus, Ted and Alex Trembath, "Trump's Paris Withdrawal in Context," *Foreign Affairs* (June 5, 2017).

Parsons, Sarah and Zabarenko, Deborah, Editors, *Paris and Beyond: Analysis and Commentary on the Historic Paris Climate Agreement*, World Resources Institute (2016).

Plumer, Brad, "Q & A: The Paris Climate Accord," *The New York Times* (May 31, 2017).

UNEP, Executive Summary from "The Emissions Gap Report 2017," United Nations Environment Programme (UNEP), Nairobi (October 2017).

Various Authors, "Is Trump's Paris Withdrawal a Major Climate Setback?" *Foreign Affairs* (August 14, 2017).

Internet References . . .

Climate Central

www.climatecentral.org

Global Warming: Focus on the Future

www.enviroweb.org/edf

Intergovernmental Panel on Climate Change

www.ipcc.ch

National Oceanic and Atmospheric Administration (NOAA) Paleoclimatology Program

www.ngdc.noaa.gov/paleo/globalwarming/home.html

The Heartland Institute

www.heartland.org/studies/ieguide.htm

Unit 2

UNIT

Expanding Global Forces and Movements

*O*ur ability to travel from one part of the globe to another in a short amount of time or to communicate anywhere in the world in a variety of ways instantaneously has expanded dramatically since the Wright brothers first lifted an airplane off the sand dunes of North Carolina's Outer Banks and Alexander Graham Bell first uttered those initial famous words into a machine. This technological explosion has not only increased the speed of travel and of information dissemination but has also expanded its reach and impact, making any individual with entree to an airline ticket or Internet access a global actor in every sense of the term. Finally, modern political and economic structures, fueled by the shrinking of the globe, have also expanded from occupying small rather discrete locations to an ever-expanding array of larger and more fluid boundaries that are constantly moving out toward the far reaches of the globe. National borders no longer keep individuals and groups in and they also no longer keep individuals, groups, and ideas out as they once did a century or even half a century ago.

Many consequences result from this realization as individuals, groups, and ideas of every kind have expanded their playing field until the world has now reached a point where every place is affected in some fashion by every event anywhere on the planet. And every place has the capacity to react to every event or thought in the world. The flow of money, information, goods, and ideas that connect people around the world also creates fissures or conflicts that heighten anxieties and cause increased tensions between rich and poor, connected and disconnected, and cultures and regimes. They manifest themselves negatively in a host of specific problems—health pandemics, human trafficking, human rights violations by both legitimate governments and armed thugs, the push of democratization or authoritarianism, and the like. Add to these global flows are cries for democratization in parts of the world that have known authoritarianism such as Saudi Arabia and pushes for authoritarianism in places that have enjoyed the fruits of democratization and liberalization.

In the past, such problems were localized to a specific locale or at least within the boundaries of a single country. In these instances, the local or national government had the capacity (or was assumed to have the capacity) to address these issues as the sole decision-making body. But just as people cross national boundaries easily, so do these problems. Solving them requires the cooperation of national sovereign governments either through direct diplomacy with one another or through international organizations such as the United Nations and its array of functional and geographical bodies.

At the same time, new forms of social media have expanded our ability to communicate from one end of the globe to the other instantaneously, leading to both positive and negative consequences of an ever expanding scope. And increasing roles for artificial intelligence and social media only compound the issue. The nature of influence has expanded as individuals and groups intent on doing good or evil somewhere throughout the world no longer have to rely on traditional armed force or even any kind of military warfare at all. The impact of these new and emerging patterns of access is yet to be fully calculated or realized, but we do know that billions are feeling their impact, and the result is both exhilarating and frightening.

Selected, Edited, and with Issue Framing Material by:
James E. Harf, *Maryville University*

ISSUE

Will the International Community Be Able to Successfully Address the Next Global Pandemic?

YES: Arthur G. Fitzmaurice, et al., from "Contributions of the US Centers for Disease Control and Prevention in Implementing the Global Health Security Agenda in 17 Partner Countries," *Emerging Infectious Diseases*, (2017)

NO: Meera Senthilingam, from "Seven Reasons We're at More Risk than Ever of a Global Pandemic," CNN, (2017)

Learning Outcomes

After reading this issue, you will be able to:

- Describe the history of major global pandemics.
- Describe the evolution of the international community's response to global pandemics in general.
- Describe the major reasons experts say that the world is at more risk than ever of a global pandemic.
- Understand the role played by the US Centers for Disease Control and Prevention in global pandemics.

ISSUE SUMMARY

YES: The US Centers for Disease Control and Prevention article describes the efforts of the Global Health Security Agenda, a partnership among a variety of national governments and both international governmental and nongovernmental organizations to increase the capacities of countries to respond to infectious disease pandemics around the globe. Launched in 2014, the partnership has made significant progress in helping 17 countries achieve a list of stated objectives.

NO: Meera Senthilingam, Editor for CNN Health and Wellness, points to the view of public health experts that the world is at a greater risk than ever before in history of a global pandemic along the magnitude of SARS, swine flu, Ebola, and Zika. Seven major global trends, the author suggests, contribute to the increased likelihood and magnitude of such pandemics.

Zika virus—these two words in the summer of 2016 brought fear to individuals in the developed world as the disease made its way across countries of the south toward the richer areas of the world. Of particular concern were pregnant women who were at particularly high risk. By November 2016, however, as a consequence of coordinated global response, the WHO's Director General announced the end of the Zika public health emergency. This virus was the latest in a long list of diseases that have had the potential to unleash havoc on large segments of a region's or even the entire global population. Hear the words "global pandemics" and one also thinks in far earlier times of the bubonic plague or Black Death of the Middle Ages where an estimated 30 percent of Europe's population, over 75 million, died, or the influenza epidemic of 1918 that killed at least 50 million or 1 in 20 people worldwide, and fully a third of the human race were afflicted. Both incidents seem like stories from a bygone era when modern medicine was unknown, where people were simply at the mercy of the spreading tendencies of the virulent diseases, and where the international community had yet to begin to cooperate to address such outbreaks. The latter did not begin to happen until the 1830s when a board was established in Egypt to track diseases throughout the Mediterranean region. In 1851, European governments gathered formally for the first time in Paris to discuss sanitary matters in light of persistent cholera epidemics plaguing Europe. And the first permanent health organization was founded in 1902 in the Western Hemisphere.

The world of medicine is different today, as the public attention to global health has dramatically grown over the last 50 years, what the Council on Foreign Relations has called a public health revolution. Increases in funding have resulted in a dramatic growth in the number of international organizations devoted to public health worldwide. The WHO has been joined by a "panoply of new multilateral initiatives, public–private partnerships, foundations, faith-based organization, and nongovernmental organizations." As a result, the average global life expectancy has risen from 40 to over 71 years. This leads many to assume that somewhere on the shelves of the local pharmacy or the Centers for Disease Control and Prevention (CDC) in Atlanta lies a counteragent to whatever killer lurks out there. *Time* reports that scientific understanding about the risk of a flu epidemic is much improved. It suggests that research groups "are working feverishly to predict the next pandemic before it even happens" (*Warning: We Are Not Ready for the Next Pandemic*, May 4, 2017). The *Time* story continues: "They're cataloguing threats and employing next-generation genetic-sequencing tools to speed the discovery of new or mysterious viruses." But the articles' bottom line is that no matter how far the world has come in the past several decades, "neither the world as a whole nor the U.S. in particular is all prepared to handle a major infectious-disease pandemic." The blame lies with the failure to invest in "things now that can make us safe later."

Thus in 2009, the world watched in much the same way as it did 750 years ago or 93 years ago. The reason was the culprit H1N1 swine flu. In April 2009, it was reported that a Mexican boy had flu caused by a mosaic of swine/bird/human flu known as H1N1. On the other side of the ocean in Cairo, the Egyptian government ordered the killing of 300,000 animals as a precaution. Soon in every corner of the planet, officials began to take precautions and deaths began to mount. This 2009 scare followed on the heels of a global scare two decades earlier as a virulent disease of another type, AIDS, began to sweep across Africa to all other sectors of the globe.

The world of travel for both humans and things nonhuman is far different from that of the fourteenth century or even 1918. Globalization is with us. The world has shrunk, literally and figuratively, as the human race's ability to move people, money, goods, information, and also unwanted agents across national boundaries and to the far corners of the globe has increased exponentially. Viruses, germs, parasites, and other virulent disease agents can and do move much more easily than at any time in recorded history. Today's airplane is much faster than yesterday's ship.

The result fast-forward to 2016 where a pandemic was on the rise, moving quickly throughout the globe from the developing world into the most developed countries on the globe. It was the Zika virus, discovered in 1947 in Uganda and long thought to pose little threat to humans. In 1952, the first case was reported in humans. And in May 2015, the Pan American Health Organization issued the first alert of a Zika virus infection in Brazil. Within a year, it swept through Latin America and made its way into the United States, bringing with it the threat of neurological complications and birth malformations. Among the groups most feeling this quickly emerging threat were potential participants at the 2016 Olympic Games in Rio de Janeiro who feared the alarming effects of pregnancies while infected with the virus.

Let us go back and look at the evolution of the international community's attempts to address global pandemics. The word "pandemic" is derived from two Greek words pan meaning "all" and demos meaning "people." Thus, a global pandemic is an epidemic of some infectious disease that can and is spreading at a rapid rate throughout the world. Officially, the WHO labels a disease outbreak a pandemic if community-level outbreaks of a disease are occurring in more than one country in a WHO region of the globe and one additional country in a different WHO region. Throughout history, humankind has fallen victim to many such killers. As early as the Peloponnesian War in fifth-century B.C. Greece, typhoid fever was responsible for the deaths of upward of 25 percent of combatants and civilians alike, necessitating major changes in military tactics. Imperial Rome felt the wrath of a plague thought to be smallpox, as did the eastern Mediterranean during its political height several centuries later.

In the last 100 years, influenza (1918, 1957, and 1968), typhoid, and cholera were major killers. In recent years, other infectious diseases have made front page news: HIV, Ebola virus, severe acute respiratory syndrome (SARS), and more recently, avian or bird flu. For a while, the latter flu struck tremendous fear in the hearts of global travelers and governmental policy makers everywhere.

WHO Europe predicted that as many as 175–360 million people could fall victim if the 2009 outbreak was severe enough. The bird flu was front page news because more than 150 million birds had died worldwide from one of its earlier strains, H5N1. This strain was first found in humans in 1997, and WHO estimated that the human fatality rate has been 50 percent, with 69 deaths occurring by December 2005. One might be prompted to ask: What was the "big deal, only 134 confirmed cases"? It is not quite so simple.

Unlike previous pandemics that hit suddenly and without little or any warning, the avian flu gave us a clear warning. The loss in poultry had been enormous. And with the jump to humans, with an initial high-mortality rate, our senses had been awakened to the potential for global human disaster. But there was good news as well. There was time to prepare for the worst-case scenario and diminish its likelihood. The flu had the attention of all relevant world health agencies and most national agencies, and steps were undertaken to find a way to combat this contagious disease. Whether global preparedness or simply the natural evolution of this particular strain of influenza, the 2009 global scare was not matched by reality, as the resultant mortality rates were not much different from those of the annual flu outbreaks.

The WHO, created by the United Nations following World War II, became the first modern international organization in the fight against widespread diseases and it continues to play a leading role against both epidemics and pandemics. It is now joined by a complex network of international governmental and nongovernmental organizations and private foundations. This network has enjoyed great successes in several areas: smallpox, polio, and measles. And it has also proven to becoming effective in more recent challenges of SARS and AIDS.

One of the reasons for success has been the recognition by WHO that successful response to an emerging pandemic not only depends on the cooperation among health professionals and organizations throughout the world but also what WHO calls "the whole of society." The latter include all governments, businesses, and civil society who work to "sustain essential infrastructure and mitigate impacts on the economy and the functioning of society." WHO has spelled out its master plan for a total societal response in Whole-of-Society Pandemic Readiness: WHO Guidelines for Pandemic Preparedness and Response in the Non-Health Sector (July 2009). This plan encompasses five basic principles: a whole-of-society approach, preparedness at all levels, attention to critical interdependencies, a scenario-based response, and respect for ethical norms. Each sector of society must have a flexible response plan

in place. National and local governments must provide leadership, while local governments stand ready to undertake specific actions. Standard operating principles and detailed communication strategies must be developed by governments. All relevant executive branches, from defense to finance, must be involved. Each provider of essential services, such as water and energy, must know the critical linkages and interdependencies among all providers. Plans for different scenarios, from mild to severe, must be developed. And finally, preparedness and response must be consistent with ethical norms and human rights considerations, with special attention to vulnerable peoples throughout the globe. The latter include people who have no access to health systems, estimated at one billion throughout the globe.

The issue of especially vulnerable people suggests an alternative way to view pandemics. The pandemics in our lifetimes have originated in the developing world. As the developing world lacked the appropriate health infrastructure, these diseases took hold and spread, eventually crossing national boundaries and making their way to the far corners of the earth. Had the diseases been confronted with an adequate health infrastructure with a detailed plan of action and the resources to implement it, the diseases might have been contained within one country. Toba Bryant and Dennis Raphael so suggest in the title of an article on the subject, "The Real Epidemic is Inequality" (2010). The essential thesis of their work is that (1) health inequalities growing out of social inequalities represent the primary health issue in the world and (2) the pace and scope of epidemics and pandemics are influenced by a function, in part, of these inequalities, particularly in the developing world.

Can the experiences of the international community in marshaling its resources to fight recent global pandemics like HIV/AIDS, avian flu, and Ebola allow it to once again successfully address another global health threat? A *New York Times* article in July 2017 (*Only Six Nations Have Evaluated Readiness for Global Pandemic*) suggested that three rich countries (Finland, Saudi Arabia, and the United states) and three poor countries (Eritrea, Pakistan, and Tanzania) are prepared to withstand a global pandemic.

In the YES selection, the US CDC article suggests that the recently created Global Health Security Agenda (GHSA) has three "pillars: (1) prevent avoidable epidemics, (2) detect threats early, and (3) respond rapidly and effectively." Sixty-one countries had joined GHSA to participate in its agenda as of December 2017. The article continues with examples of the progress made on the three pillars listed above. Specifically, 675 "accomplishments" across all areas subsumed under the three pillars are mentioned.

Areas discussed include disease and syndromic surveillance, a national laboratory, workforce development, and emergency management and response.

In the NO selection, Meera Senthilingam, Editor for CNN Health and Wellness, describes seven trends that, she maintains, contribute to the increased likelihood and magnitude of future global pandemics. These include growing populations and urbanization, encroaching into new environments, climate change, global travel, civil conflict, fewer doctors and nurses in outbreak regions, and faster information bringing "newer levels of fear and multiple ways to spread it."

YES ←

Arthur G. Fitzmaurice, et al.

Contributions of the US Centers for Disease Control and Prevention in Implementing the Global Health Security Agenda in 17 Partner Countries

Recent infectious disease outbreaks have demonstrated that a local threat can rapidly become a global crisis that jeopardizes the health, economy, and safety of persons everywhere. Severe outbreaks and regional epidemics, including severe acute respiratory syndrome, Middle East respiratory syndrome, Ebola virus disease (EVD), Zika virus, and novel influenza viruses, have highlighted the importance of countries developing core capacities to contain public health threats, as outlined in the International Health Regulations (IHR 2005).[1–3] As of 2014, fewer than a third of 196 countries reported achieving IHR 2005 capacities.[4] The Global Health Security Agenda (GHSA), a partnership of nations, international organizations, and civil society, was launched in 2014 with the mission to build countries' capacities to respond to infectious disease threats, thereby progressing toward IHR 2005 compliance.[5] Global health security relies on all countries building IHR 2005 capacities to rapidly detect and control public health threats at their sources.

GHSA is built on three pillars: (1) prevent avoidable epidemics, (2) detect threats early, and (3) respond rapidly and effectively. To date, 61 countries have joined GHSA, including approximately a dozen countries partnering with low- and middle-income countries to assist in their GHSA work. In 2014, the United States committed to working with 31 partner countries and the Caribbean community to meet targets associated with each of 11 technical areas (termed Action Packages) that align with GHSA's three pillars.[6] Through GHSA, the United States has committed technical and fiscal support to a subset of 17 countries termed phase I and technical assistance with work plan development in phase II countries. Exceeding this commitment, the US Centers for Disease Control and Prevention (CDC) works to strengthen global health

security capacities in approximately three dozen countries, including phase I and phase II countries, as well as Ebola preparedness countries, which surround those countries affected by the recent EVD outbreak. CDC works across all 11 GHSA technical areas, with a special emphasis on four that serve as a platform for public health emergencies and health security: surveillance, laboratory systems, workforce development, and emergency response management. CDC staff stationed in partner countries, with support from CDC headquarters–based subject matter experts and funded partners, provide direct technical assistance to partnering government counterparts.[7–9] CDC's goal is to help countries achieve GHSA and IHR 2005 targets by strengthening sustainable systems and capacities to respond to health threats locally, thereby preventing the spread of disease and protecting persons in the United States and around the world from outbreaks and other public health threats. Descriptions of CDC's early GHSA work with counterparts in Uganda and Vietnam have been published,[10,11] but substantial progress has been made across all phase I countries. Here we document the major GHSA accomplishments that these 17 countries achieved with CDC support during April 2015 to March 2017. These successes are now informing ongoing program implementation in these and other countries.

Methods

In January 2015, CDC technical staff commenced working with ministries of health (MOHs) and other partner country counterparts to assess baseline capacities related to 11 GHSA technical areas. By June 2015, annual country work plans had been developed, detailing activities through which CDC would assist countries in achieving their first-year objectives in each technical area. The level and

Fitzmaurice, Arthur G. et al. "Contributions of the US Centers for Disease Control and Prevention in Implementing the Global Health Security Agenda in 17 Partner Countries," *Global Health Security Supplement*, vol. 23, December 2017. Centers for Disease Control and Prevention, 2017.

nature of CDC support varied across activities depending on technical assistance needs, inputs from other collaborators, and host country and donor financing. CDC staff reported on activity progress on a quarterly basis. Reports indicated the status (i.e., completed, on track, delayed, or canceled) and described progress toward completion of each work plan activity. Reporting information was provided to CDC headquarters–based evaluators four times: December 2015, April–May 2016, July–August 2016, and October–November 2016. Results were used to improve and update work plans.

Trained CDC evaluators analyzed quarterly reporting data by technical area, objectives within technical areas, and activities within objectives. In May 2016, CDC evaluators analyzed reporting information for completed activities across all 17 phase I countries and grouped results into the following categories: (1) real-time surveillance and reporting, (2) national laboratory system and biosafety/biosecurity, (3) workforce development, and (4) emergency management and Emergency Operations Centers (EOCs). This organizational framework reduced the likelihood of missing information because of misclassification, such as if different countries reported related activities in similar, but different, technical areas. For example, national laboratory system and biosafety/biosecurity activities were batched for analyses to ensure all relevant laboratory activities were analyzed together. Activities in other technical areas were analyzed in November 2016.

A CDC evaluator analyzed the completed activity descriptions, objective descriptions, and activity progress data across all phase I countries for each of the four categories. A second CDC evaluator reviewed and validated the first evaluator's analyses; discrepancies were discussed and resolved by a CDC subject matter expert familiar with GHSA technical areas and overseeing all analyses for consistency. Completed activities were summarized by using common terminology for similar major accomplishments achieved by countries with CDC support. (Data on accomplishments achieved by <6 countries are available but not shown here.) Evaluators provided CDC headquarters and field staff with lists of countries that had achieved each major accomplishment, so they could add a country that had not been identified through reporting data analyses or remove a country from an accomplishment category if appropriate. CDC field staff worked with MOHs in some countries to confirm that the revised language accurately reflected country progress.

In November 2016, this process was repeated for completed activities in all 11 technical areas, resulting in a final list that integrated all accomplishments organized into four categories. In April 2017, CDC field staff in all 17 countries confirmed that the partner country had achieved these major accomplishments with CDC assistance during April 2015 to March 2017. CDC evaluators determined the number and proportion of countries that achieved each accomplishment with CDC support.

Results

Overall, our analysis found that CDC supported 675 accomplishments across all 11 GHSA technical areas in 17 phase I countries. These accomplishments reflect achievements in >6 countries. Eleven countries each achieved >40 of these accomplishments, and each of the 17 countries achieved >18.

Disease and Syndromic Surveillance

Surveillance Systems

With CDC's technical assistance, 16 countries established real-time surveillance systems and mechanisms for detecting potential public health events at the national or subnational level. Surveillance systems were improved for zoonotic diseases (13 countries), vaccine-preventable diseases (10 countries), and antimicrobial resistance (7 countries). Thirteen countries met GHSA targets for real-time surveillance of >3 syndromes indicative of potential public health emergencies (e.g., severe acute respiratory syndrome, acute flaccid paralysis, acute hemorrhagic fever, acute watery diarrhea with dehydration, and jaundice with fever). In 11 countries, CDC helped countries expand and enhance previously established indicator-based surveillance systems to capture potential threats from larger geographic areas and improve timeliness. CDC supported community immunizations in response to surveillance data on vaccine-preventable diseases in 13 countries.

Surveillance Strategic Planning

CDC identified national policies, legal authorities, and gaps for conducting public health surveillance in each of the 17 phase I countries. In 13 countries, CDC worked with MOHs to determine the appropriate level of subnational jurisdictions (e.g., districts) for reporting surveillance information to the national MOH. Plans and procedures for multisectoral surveillance were developed with MOHs, agriculture, and defense in seven countries and with port health services for national points of entry in eight countries.

CDC assisted 12 countries in documenting gaps in surveillance data collection, analysis, and interpretation capabilities; eight of these countries developed plans for improving interoperability of disparate surveillance systems to better integrate available data from different sources. Eleven countries conducted specialized assessments for immunization surveillance and nine for antimicrobial resistance (e.g., drug-resistant *Mycobacterium tuberculosis*) surveillance.

National Laboratory System

Laboratory Confirmation of Outbreaks
CDC trained laboratory technicians in all 17 phase I countries and provided 16 countries with new laboratory diagnostics to confirm potential outbreaks identified by surveillance systems, focusing on priority pathogens (e.g., influenza virus, poliovirus, HIV, *M. tuberculosis*, *Salmonella enterica* serovar Typhi, *Plasmodium* sp., and *Vibrio cholerae*). CDC worked with nine countries to assess diagnostic capabilities for priority pathogens and 10 countries for antimicrobial resistance. CDC assisted nine countries in establishing new systems for transporting specimen samples to national reference laboratories.

Biosafety and Biosecurity
CDC provided technical assistance to six countries to inventory dangerous pathogens and develop plans to manage them in their national laboratory systems. CDC helped 15 countries train technical and administrative staff on biosafety and biosecurity. Eight countries identified staff in the MOHs, agriculture, and defense responsible for inspecting and certifying laboratories for biosafety and biosecurity compliance.

Workforce Development

Field Epidemiology Training Programs (FETPs)
All 17 phase I countries now participate in basic-level frontline (three-month training), intermediate (six- to nine-month training), or advanced (two-year training) FETPs.[13-15] These field-based, CDC-supported programs train members of a nation's health workforce to become disease detectives at national and subnational levels. Since April 2015, CDC has established 14 new frontline and 2 new FETP-Advanced in phase I countries. Trainees from all countries investigated real or potential outbreaks as part of their training. Numbers of trainees per country ranged from 24 to 622; nearly half of trainees were frontline surveillance officers.[16]

Additional Training
Other CDC-supported training activities addressed additional GHSA targets. In 14 countries, CDC worked with MOHs to train community leaders in event-based surveillance. In 16 countries, CDC helped develop training curricula for surveillance and data analysis methods in English or the predominant national language (i.e., French or Vietnamese). In seven countries, CDC provided trainings and developed infection prevention and control programs for health-care facilities to combat antimicrobial resistance. In 13 countries, CDC led multidisciplinary and multisectoral public health trainings, including One Health trainings for preventing zoonotic disease spillover from animals to humans.

Workforce Strategic Planning
CDC supported 16 countries in strategic planning related to the national public and animal health workforce. CDC assisted six of these countries in creating national multisectoral workforce development strategic plans based on assessments of existing public health training programs, educational systems, and gaps in the national public health workforce.

Emergency Management and Response

EOCs
CDC worked with all 17 phase I countries to improve public health emergency management capacities, such as by establishing EOCs and training EOC staff in incident management in 15 countries. Twenty-nine staff from 14 countries' MOHs, national public health institutes, and other national and international organizations completed CDC's Public Health Emergency Management Fellowship Program.[17] CDC helped 15 countries develop EOC policies and protocols, and 11 countries activated the EOC for an exercise or real public health emergency response.

Multisectoral Coordination
CDC provided assistance to 14 countries to complete public health risk assessments and document national priority public health threats. Nine countries established One Health mechanisms for joint response across human, animal, and environmental health sectors to prevent or limit animal-to-human spillover of zoonotic diseases.[18] CDC worked with 13 countries to assess baseline capacities of agencies to respond to biologic threats across public health, animal health, law enforcement, and other sectors. CDC initiated activities to strengthen response coordination across multiple sectors in 12 countries and identified points of contact for multisectoral information-sharing in 10 countries.

Discussion

During April 2015 to March 2017, CDC supported 17 phase I countries in achieving 675 accomplishments in 11 GHSA technical areas. Although GHSA is still in early stages of implementation, CDC's support to countries has helped improve their capabilities, especially in the cross-cutting areas of public health surveillance, national laboratory systems, workforce development, and emergency response management. Accomplishments in these technical areas have also contributed to the countries' progress in the other GHSA technical areas and IHR 2005 core capacities.

Robust surveillance networks linked with laboratory testing can enable early detection of public health threats before they escalate into outbreaks and threaten communities, nations, and the world. CDC's efforts to build country capacity to detect potential outbreaks focused on increasing the number of diseases captured by surveillance and reporting systems, expanding these systems to include additional subnational jurisdictions and community-level surveillance, and strengthening processes to improve the timeliness and efficiency of communication across all levels.

CDC worked with health, agriculture, defense, and other ministries to broaden the types of pathogens and syndromes that can be detected by improved surveillance systems. As a result of CDC's GHSA work, countries that previously had systems to monitor a limited range of potential public health threats are now better able to detect animal-to-human disease spillover, health-care-associated infections, and other potential outbreaks by monitoring more diseases and syndromes systematically and frequently. Early detection of public health threats can lead to timely interventions to prevent escalation into major outbreaks.[19–21] Phase I countries have already used improved surveillance data to inform prevention efforts. For example, increased surveillance of vaccine-preventable diseases resulted in community immunizations to prevent further spread of measles and other diseases in 13 countries, including Guinea, Indonesia, and Liberia, where vaccination coverages are low. Furthermore, CDC worked with phase I countries to incorporate hands-on experience investigating potential outbreaks into FETPs.

Surveillance capacity-building efforts also focused on expanding geographic coverage. Public health surveillance and laboratory capacity have typically been concentrated in urban centers, limiting countries' abilities to detect outbreaks in rural areas.[20,22] CDC assisted phase I countries with establishing integrated surveillance systems that share data across health-care facilities, subnational jurisdictions (e.g., districts), and MOHs. CDC helped countries train surveillance officers throughout multiple levels of countries' health systems. In addition to training field epidemiologists through FETPs, CDC helped countries enlist the help of community leaders in detecting threats early by training them on community-based

disease surveillance and reporting to complement health-care facility surveillance. Community-level disease monitoring has been shown to influence intervention efforts and reduce the incidence of disease and prevalence of premature death. For example, community health workers in West Africa used surveillance data to target immunizations and reduce the number of cases of vaccine-preventable meningococcal disease by half.[23,24] These efforts aim to prevent outbreaks at the source before spreading rapidly within large cities or to other countries.

National laboratory systems are integral for assessing public health threats and targeting outbreak response efforts. Laboratory testing of specimen samples is necessary to confirm suspected public health threats identified through disease and syndromic surveillance[25] Timely confirmation of public health threats relies upon laboratory systems that link central reference laboratories with peripheral laboratories, securely and rapidly transport specimens from patients to laboratories, and efficiently report accurate test results from laboratories to patients and MOHs.[26] CDC's assistance has been vital to providing countries with diagnostic capabilities and establishing specimen transport systems to decrease the time from specimen collection to testing at a certified national public health laboratory. This work is necessary to confirm public health threats, so response efforts can be directed appropriately. CDC's training of laboratory technicians will empower countries to confirm potential outbreaks of a broader set of pathogens more accurately and expediently.

CDC worked with other US government entities and partner countries' MOHs, agriculture, and defense to address potential biosecurity threats, such as by ensuring that countries keep inventories and management plans for dangerous pathogens stored in laboratories. Countries applied CDC's expertise to ensure proper laboratory management and biosafety certification, which are imperative for ensuring the integrity of the national laboratory system. This work is critical for preventing national and international public health emergencies by preventing potential biosecurity threats.

Trained field epidemiologists, laboratory technicians, and emergency responders are crucial for detecting and responding to public health threats early and effectively, and EOCs with incident management systems are essential for response coordination.[27] In July 2014, when the major EVD outbreak was worsening in West Africa, CDC-trained disease detectives performed contact tracing on 894 contacts of EVD case-patients in Lagos, Nigeria[27]; only 11 deaths in Nigeria resulted from this EVD outbreak, although models estimated thousands of deaths would have occurred without timely investigation and emergency management.[19] This example illustrates the potential impact of GHSA implementation. Training disease detectives and developing effective incident management can mean the difference between small outbreaks that are quickly and effectively controlled and larger outbreaks with substantial global health implications. CDC established new FETPs in 16 phase I countries to rapidly train disease detectives. CDC worked with phase I countries to establish EOCs and train emergency response staff. A component of the training involved activating the EOC for exercises or real public health emergencies. These activations incorporated a multisectoral approach to bring together public health, animal health, border security, and other sectors. These efforts strengthen capacities and test countries' abilities to respond to public health threats effectively and rapidly.

The accomplishments we describe have enhanced global health security, but GHSA relies on strong partnerships to sustain capacity-building efforts. CDC's work has strengthened collaborations among countries, US government agencies, and international governments and organizations. While emphasizing a multisectoral approach for building GHSA capabilities, CDC uniquely provides direct technical assistance to MOHs, developing their expertise, so they can sustain GHSA accomplishments. CDC worked with multiple partners, including national MOHs, agriculture, and defense, to establish mechanisms for cross-sectoral communication and collaboration that are essential for outbreak prevention, detection, and response but did not exist before GHSA. CDC's technical assistance complemented efforts by other nations and US government entities, including the US Agency for International Development, the Defense Threat Reduction Agency, and the US Department of Agriculture. Notably, the relatively small US investment in GHSA led to additional investments from other donor nations. For example, South Korea committed $100 million to build global health security capabilities in 13 countries.[28]

In addition to technical assistance, CDC contributed to the development of the Joint External Evaluation (JEE) tool, an independent, transparent evaluation that employs 48 indicators to measure progress toward GHSA and IHR 2005 targets.[12] A benefit of the JEE is its potential for standardizing metrics and streamlining CDC's technical assistance across multiple countries. CDC worked with the World Health Organization and other partners to develop a library of achievements needed to advance from one level of capacity to higher levels.[29] Most of the accomplishments we describe are among the milestones in the library, with related JEE indicators associated with each. This work demonstrates the feasibility and effectiveness of these

activities in the field. The milestones library, together with JEE scores, helps CDC standardize and streamline technical assistance to complement activities planned by other partners. Although the administrative efforts required to undergo the JEE-delayed CDC's activities in some countries, the JEE process has now been operationalized, and countries have built their evaluation capacities by completing these baseline assessments. As of September 2017, a total of 58 countries, including 14 phase I countries, completed the JEE with CDC support, identifying countries' IHR 2005 capabilities and the explicit gaps in need of prioritization.

Our report has a few limitations. First, this report is not comprehensive of all CDC's GHSA achievements. It focuses on CDC-supported country accomplishments in 17 countries, excluding CDC's GHSA achievements beyond phase I countries, including in Ebola preparedness countries where CDC prioritized GHSA work to build detection and preparedness capabilities to prevent cross-border spillover of EVD and other disease threats. Also, in initial analyses, evaluators determined that some accomplishments had been achieved by <6 phase I countries and thus omitted these from the list provided to CDC field staff for validation; however, >6 countries might have achieved some of these by March 2017. Furthermore, CDC field staff validated accomplishments subjectively based on their interpretations of standardized language, potentially resulting in underreporting or overreporting. Despite these limitations, this report describes substantial accomplishments in 17 countries that resulted directly from the technical assistance provided by CDC. These achievements align with GHSA targets, suggesting that CDC has helped these countries move closer to attaining IHR 2005 core capacities, thus creating a safer world.

In conclusion, GHSA was launched with a goal of making the world safer from infectious disease threats by improving countries' IHR 2005 core capacities.[4] CDC's efforts have been critical as part of a long-term process of building and sustaining global health security capacity in countries with less-developed public health systems. Initial accomplishments have laid the groundwork for further GHSA advancement in these 17 countries, and lessons learned might improve the efficiency of GHSA implementation in additional countries. Ongoing GHSA implementation offers an alternative to the cycle of panic and neglect that describes the current response to pandemic threats.[30] The initial successes we describe demonstrate that strategic appropriation of technical and financial resources can accelerate progress toward GHSA targets and global achievement of IHR 2005 core capacities. CDC's continuing work with partner countries ensures sustainability and further progress rather than regression. Furthermore, investments in global health security have been shown to have positive health, security, and economic impacts.[31,32] These improvements in international capacity to rapidly detect, respond to, and control infectious disease outbreaks and other public health threats at their sources translate into enhanced global health security because fewer public health threats can spread throughout a country and reach other nations, including the United States.

Acknowledgments

Members of the GHSA Implementation Group are as follows: Ebba Abate, Nedghie Adrien, Denise Allen, Rana Jawad Asghar, Kerrethel Avery, Casey Barton Behravesh, Vroh Joseph Benie Bi, Brice Bicaba, Jeff Borchert, L. Lucy Boulanger, Abdoulaye Bousso, Jennifer Brooks, Vance Brown, Nora Chea, Daniella Coker, Gretchen Cowman, Simplice N. Dagnan, Benjamin A. Dahl, Subrat Das, Yvette Diallo, Seydou Diarra, Thuy Do, Trang Do, Stephanie Doan, Emily Kainne Dokubo, Melissa Edmiston, Rachel Eidex, Chinyere O. Ekechi, Catherine Espinosa, Alain Georges M. Etoundi, Meerjady Sabrina Flora, Suzanne Friesen, Neil Gupta, Regan Hartman, Sara Hersey, Katherine Hills, Ikovwaiza Irune, Amara Jambai, Daddi Jima, Theresa Kanter, Sakoba Keita, Erin Kennedy, Anna Khan, Tsigereda Kifle, Michael Kinzer, Jackson Kioko, Rebecca Greco Kone, Salifou Konfe, Sharanya Krishnan, Mohamed Lamorde, Kayla Laserson, Ahmed Liban, Julius Lutwama, Ulzii Luvsansharav, Mamadou Farka Maiga, Issa Makumbi, Paul Malpiedi, Eric Marble, Lise D. Martel, Els Mathieu, Wilton Chuck Menchion, Janneth Mghamba, Fausta Mosha, Marcelina Mponela, Christopher S. Murrill, Shivani Murthy, Athman Mwatondo, Thomas Nagbe, Serigne Ndiaye, Babacar Ndoye, Paulyne Ntuba Ngalame, Tolbert Nyenswah, Karen Ossorio, Benjamin Park, Omer G. Pasi, Michael Phipps, Meredith Pinto, Jagdish Prasad, Sarah Ramsey, Penney Reese, Peter Rzeszotarski, Aditya Sharma, Trevor Shoemaker, Soumya Swaminathan, Samuel Tchwenko, Jim Ting, Mamadou Souncalo Traore, Monique Tuyisenge-Onyegbula, M. Salim Uzzaman, Ross Van Horn, Daniel Vanderende, Christie Vu, Matthew Westercamp, Marc-Alain Widdowson, Desmond Williams, Celia Woodfill, Sue Lin Yee, and Bao-Ping Zhu.

References

1. World Health Organization. Report of the Review Committee on the Role of the International Health Regulations (2005) in the Ebola Outbreak and Response. Accessed August 2, 2017. http://www.who.int/ihr/review-committee-2016.

2. World Health Organization. Report of the Review Committee on the Functioning of the International Health Regulations (2005) in Relation to Pandemic (H1N1) 2009. Accessed August 2, 2017. http://www.who.int/ihr/publications/RC_report.

3. Jonas O. Pandemic risk. Background paper for the World Development Report. Accessed August 2, 2017. http://siteresources.worldbank.org/EXTNWDR2013/Resources/8258024-1352909193861/8936935-1356011448215/8986901-1380568255405/WDR14_bp_Pandemic_Risk_Jonas.pdf.

4. Katz R, Sorrell EM, Kornblet SA, Fischer JE. Global Health Security Agenda and the International Health Regulations: moving forward. Biosecurity and Bioterrorism 2014;12:231–8. http://dx.doi.org/10.1089/bsp.2014.0038 PubMed (http://www.ncbi.nlm.nih.gov/sites/entrez?cmd=Retrieve&db=PubMed&list_uids=25254911&dopt=Abstract).

5. Global Health Security Agenda. Accessed April 27, 2017. https://www.GHSAgenda.org.

6. Centers for Disease Control and Prevention. US Commitment to the Global Health Security Agenda. Accessed April 27, 2017. https://www.cdc.gov/globalhealth/security/pdf/ghs_us_commitment.pdf.

7. Schuchat A, Tappero J, Blandford J. Global health and the US Centers for Disease Control and Prevention. Lancet 2014;384:98–101. http://dx.doi.org/10.1016/S0140-6736(14)60570-5 PubMed (http://www.ncbi.nlm.nih.gov/sites/entrez?cmd=Retrieve&db=PubMed&list_uids=24998008&dopt=Abstract).

8. Centers for Disease Control and Prevention. Global Health Security Agenda: action packages. Accessed August 2, 2017. https://www.cdc.gov/globalhealth/security/actionpackages/default.htm.

9. World Health Organization. International Health Regulations (2005). 3rd ed. Accessed August 2, 2017. http://apps.who.int/iris/bitstream/10665/246107/1/9789241580496-eng.pdf.

10. Borchert JN, Tappero JW, Downing R, Shoemaker T, Behumbiize P, Aceng J, et al. Centers for Disease Control and Prevention (CDC). Rapidly building global health security capacity—Uganda demonstration project, 2013. Morbidity and Mortality Weekly Report (MMWR) 2014;63:73–6. PubMed (http://www.ncbi.nlm.nih.gov/sites/entrez?cmd=Retrieve&db=PubMed&list_uids=24476978&dopt=Abstract).

11. Tran PD, Vu LN, Nguyen HT, Phan LT, Lowe W, McConnell MS, et al. Centers for Disease Control and Prevention (CDC). Strengthening global health security capacity—Vietnam demonstration project, 2013. Morbidity and Mortality Weekly Report

(MMWR) 2014;63:77–80. PubMed (http://www.ncbi.nlm.nih.gov/sites/entrez?cmd=Retrieve&db=PubMed&list_uids=24476979&dopt=Abstract).

12. World Health Organization. Joint External Evaluation tool: International Health Regulations (2005). Accessed August 2, 2017. http://apps.who.int/iris/handle/10665/204368.

13. Balajee SA, Arthur R, Mounts AW. Global health security: building capacities for early event detection, epidemiologic workforce, and laboratory response. Health Security 2016;14:424–32. http://dx.doi.org/10.1089/hs.2015.0062 PubMed (http://www.ncbi.nlm.nih.gov/sites/entrez?cmd=Retrieve&db=PubMed&list_uids=27898218&dopt=Abstract).

14. Centers for Disease Control and Prevention. Field Epidemiology Training Program: how we train. Accessed April 27, 2017. https://www.cdc.gov/globalhealth/healthprotection/fetp/train.html.

15. Ameme DK, Nyarko KM, Kenu E, Afari EA. Strengthening surveillance and response to public health emergencies in the West African sub-region: the role of Ghana FELTP. Pan African Medical Journal 2016;25(Suppl 1).

16. Andre A, Lopez A, Perkins S, Lambert S, Chace L, Noudek N, et al. Frontline field epidemiology training programs as a strategy to improve disease surveillance and response. Emerging Infectious Diseases 2017;23:166. http://dx.doi.org/10.3201/eid2313.170803 PubMed (http://www.ncbi.nlm.nih.gov/sites/entrez?cmd=Retrieve&db=PubMed&list_uids=27618479&dopt=Abstract).

17. Centers for Disease Control and Prevention. CDC Emergency Operations Center: Public Health Emergency Management Fellowship. Accessed April 27, 2017. https://www.cdc.gov/phpr/eoc/emergencymanagementfellowship.htm.

18. American Veterinary Medical Association. One Health: a new professional imperative. One Health Initiative Task Force Final Report. Schaumburg (IL): The Association; 2008. Accessed August 2, 2017. https://www.avma.org/KB/Resources/Reports/Pages/One-Health.aspx.

19. Fasina FO, Shittu A, Lazarus D, Tomori O, Simonsen L, Viboud C, et al. Transmission dynamics and control of Ebola virus disease outbreak in Nigeria, July to September 2014. Euro Surveillance 2014;19:20920. http://dx.doi.org/10.2807/1560-7917.ES2014.19.40.20920 PubMed (http://www.ncbi.nlm.nih.gov/sites/entrez?cmd=Retrieve&db=PubMed&list_uids=25323076&dopt=Abstract).

20. Kekulé AS. Learning from Ebola virus: how to prevent future epidemics. Viruses 2015;7:3789–97. http://dx.doi.org/10.3390/v7072797 PubMed (http://www.ncbi.nlm.nih.gov/sites/entrez?cmd=Retrieve&db=PubMed&list_uids=26184283&dopt=Abstract).

21. Smolinski MS, Crawley AW, Olsen JM. Finding outbreaks faster. Health Security 2017;15:215–20. http://dx.doi.org/10.1089/hs.2016.0069 PubMed (http://www.ncbi.nlm.nih.gov/sites/entrez?cmd=Retrieve&db=PubMed&list_uids=28384035&dopt=Abstract).

22. Baize S, Pannetier D, Oestereich L, Rieger T, Koivogui L, Magassouba N, et al. Emergence of Zaire Ebola virus disease in Guinea. New England Journal of Medicine 2014;371:1418–25. http://dx.doi.org/10.1056/NEJMoa1404505 PubMed (http://www.ncbi.nlm.nih.gov/sites/entrez?cmd=Retrieve&db=PubMed&list_uids=24738640&dopt=Abstract).

23. Maïnassara HB, Paireau J, Idi I, Pelat J-PM, Oukem-Boyer OOM, Fontanet A, et al. Response strategies against meningitis epidemics after elimination of serogroup A meningococci, Niger. Emerging Infectious Diseases 2015;21:1322–9. http://dx.doi.org/10.3201/eid2108.141361 PubMed (http://www.ncbi.nlm.nih.gov/sites/entrez?cmd=Retrieve&db=PubMed&list_uids=26196461&dopt=Abstract).

24. Dowell SF, Blazes D, Desmond-Hellmann S. Four steps to precision public health. Nature 2016;540:189–91. http://dx.doi.org/10.1038/540189a.

25. Sealy TK, Erickson BR, Taboy CH, Ströher U, Towner JS, Andrews SE, et al. Laboratory Response to Ebola—West Africa and United States. Morbidity and Mortality Weekly Report (MMWR) Supplements 2016;65:44–9. http://dx.doi.org/10.15585/mmwr.su6503a7 PubMed (http://www.ncbi.nlm.nih.gov/sites/entrez?cmd=Retrieve&db=PubMed&list_uids=27389781&dopt=Abstract).

26. Olmsted SS, Moore M, Meili RC, Duber HC, Wasserman J, Sama P, et al. Strengthening laboratory systems in resource-limited settings. American Journal of Clinical Pathology 2010;134:374–80. http://dx.doi.org/10.1309/AJCPDQOSB7QR5GLR PubMed (http://www.ncbi.nlm.nih.gov/sites/entrez?cmd=Retrieve&db=PubMed&list_uids=20716792&dopt=Abstract).

27. Wolicki SB, Nuzzo JB, Blazes DL, Pitts DL, Iskander JK, Tappero JW. Public health surveillance: at the core of the Global Health Security Agenda. Health Security 2016;14:185–8. http://dx.doi.org/10.1089/hs.2016.0002 PubMed (http://www.ncbi.nlm.nih.gov/sites/entrez?cmd=Retrieve&db=PubMed&list_uids=27314658&dopt=Abstract).

28. Kim HS. Korea dedicates $100 million to help poor countries fight infectious disease. Accessed

August 2, 2017. http://www.koreatimesus.com/s-korea-dedicates-100-million-to-help-poor-countries-fight-infectious-diseases.

29. GHSA standardized milestone library. Accessed October 6, 2017. https://www.ghsagenda.org/ docs/default-source/default-document-library/GHSA-Milestone-Library.pdf.

30. The World Bank. Transcript: World Bank Group opening press conference by President Jim Yong Kim at the 2017 WBG/IMF Spring Meetings. Washington: World Bank; 2017. Accessed August 2, 2017. http://www.worldbank.org/en/news/speech/2017/04/20/2017-wbgimf-spring-meetings-world-bank-group-opening-press-conference-by-president-jim-yong-kim.

31. Gostin LO, Ayala AS. Global health security in an era of explosive pandemic potential. Journal of National Security Law and Policy 2017;9:1.

32. Sands P, El Turabi A, Saynisch PA, Dzau VJ. Assessment of economic vulnerability to infectious disease crises. Lancet 2016;388:2443–8. http://dx.doi.org/10.1016/S0140-6736(16)30594-3 PubMed (http://www.ncbi.nlm.nih.gov/sites/entrez?cmd=Retrieve&db=PubMed&list_uids=27212427&dopt=Abstract).

ARTHUR G. FITZMAURICE The authors are all affiliated with the Centers for Disease Control and Prevention in Atlanta, America's health protection agency.

Meera Senthilingam

 **NO**

Seven Reasons We're at More Risk than Ever of a Global Pandemic

It could take just one cough, one kiss, one touch, or even one bite to change not only your life but the lives of everyone around you—and for months or even years.

In most cases, the closer those people are to you, the greater the risk. But it isn't always that simple.

The risk at hand: an infectious outbreak.

Public health experts believe we are at greater risk than ever of experiencing large-scale outbreaks and global pandemics like those we've seen before: severe acute respiratory syndrome (SARS), swine flu, Ebola, and Zika.

More than 28,000 people were infected during the 2014–2016 Ebola epidemic, with over 11,000 deaths. And as of March 10, 84 countries have reported Zika transmission. That disease was discovered in the 1940s, but had its first outbreak in 2007 in Micronesia, and more recently began spreading toward the end of 2015.

Every time, the infection's arrival is unexpected and its scale unprecedented, leaving the world vulnerable.

Experts are unanimous in the belief that the next outbreak contender will most likely be a surprise—and we need to be ready.

"We're only as secure in the world as the weakest country," said Jimmy Whitworth, professor of international public health at the London School of Hygiene & Tropical Medicine. With so many health systems and economies in a fragile state, this means we are far from secure.

"Infectious diseases respect no boundaries," he said. The World Health Organization is alerted to hundreds of small outbreaks every month, he noted, which it investigates and uses to predict the chances of a bigger problem.

"There are little clusters of outbreaks occurring all the time, all over the place," Whitworth said.

But with infections disregarding borders and their battle lines against humans drawn, he believes the way we live today is what opens us up to risk.

"(Many) aspects of modern life put us at more risk. We are more ready than before," he points out, highlighting the International Health Regulations Global Outbreak Alert and Response Network and countries with national rapid response teams—such as the United States, United Kingdom, and China—ready to tackle any emergency.

"But the stakes keep getting raised," he said. Here's why.

Growing Populations and Urbanization

The facts around urban living are simple: you live, eat, work, and move closer to people than in any rural setting, and with this comes greater opportunity for disease to spread through air, mosquitoes, or unclean water.

As populations grow, so will the number of city-dwellers, with the United Nations predicting that 66 percent of the global population will live in urban areas by 2050.

More people in cities can "put a strain on sanitation," said David Heymann, head of the Centre for Global Health Security at the think tank Chatham House. Beyond people's close proximity, "this is a second source of infection," he said, and a third is increased food demand, causing farmers to grow more food, with more animals, making them likely to live closer to those animals as well.

Animals are reservoirs for many diseases, including cattle for tuberculosis and African sleeping sickness (trypanosomiasis) and poultry for avian flu.

With people moving more regularly from—and between—rural settings to urban ones, the chances of them becoming infected and then living in close quarters with others further boost the potential for things to spread.

Encroaching into New Environments

As numbers of people grow, so does the amount of land needed to house them. Populations expand into previously uninhabited territories, such as forests. With new territories comes contact with new animals and, inevitably, new infections.

Lassa fever death rates in Nigeria higher than expected.

For one example, "Lassa fever occurs because people live in the forest and destroy it for farming," Heymann said.

Lassa fever is a viral disease spread by contact with the feces of infected rodents. It can cause fever and hemorrhaging of various parts of the body, including the eyes and nose. Person-to-person transmission is also possible, albeit less common. Outbreaks generally occur in West Africa, with higher than expected rates in Nigeria since 2016.

Heymann explains that Lassa is one example of people living near forest environments where infected rodents reside, but destruction of those forests for agriculture leaves the animals nowhere to go—other than humans' homes.

"The rodents that live there can't get food and go into human areas for food," he said.

Climate Change

Evidence continues to emerge that climate change is resulting in greater numbers of heat waves and flooding events, bringing more opportunity for waterborne diseases such as cholera and for disease vectors such as mosquitoes in new regions.

"Flooding is occurring with increased frequency," Heymann said, and with that comes greater risk of outbreaks.

Between 2030 and 2050, climate change is projected to cause about 250,000 additional deaths per year from heat stress, malnutrition, and the spread of infectious diseases like malaria, according to the World Health Organization.

With disease carriers like mosquitoes increasingly able to live in new unprotected territory, the risk of an outbreak is high.

Whitworth cited the current yellow fever outbreak in Angola, which has infected more than 350 people. He explained that as workers from China returned home from Angola, any yellow fever infection could have been transmitted by mosquitoes in China.

But, the workers' return in winter meant the insects weren't around to transmit through bites.

. . .

Global Travel

"We're vulnerable because of increased travel," Whitworth said.

International tourist arrivals reached a record of almost 1.2 billion in 2015, according to the UN World Tourism Organization, 50 million more than 2014. It was the sixth consecutive year of above-average growth. And with greater numbers moving at all times come greater options for infections to hop a ride.

"Infectious agents travel around in humans many times within their incubation period," Heymann said. An incubation period is the time between infection and the onset of symptoms, meaning people can transmit an infection though they won't appear to be sick.

The SARS pandemic of 2003 is thought to have begun with Dr. Liu Jianlun who developed symptoms of the airborne virus on a trip to Huang Xingchu in China and then went to visit family in Hong Kong. He infected people at his hotel and his family. He was then hospitalized and died, as did one of his relatives.

In less than four months, about 4,000 cases and 550 deaths from SARS could be traced to Liu's stay in Hong Kong. More than 8,000 other people became infected across more than 30 countries worldwide.

But Heymann stresses that "it's not just humans" who spread disease through travel. Infections spread through insects, food, and animals moved between countries. "It's also trade," he said, pointing to airport malaria, in which people in airports have become infected with malaria through mosquitoes that have hitched a ride on a plane or in food.

He also described bird flu that was stopped at the Belgian border in Thai eagles being traded as pets in 2004. Guinea rats shipped as pets in the United States in 2003 harbored infections with monkey pox, he noted, which then entered prairie dogs and eventually humans.

Civil Conflict

"If a health system cannot handle (an outbreak), there's pandemonium," Heymann said. He believes that poor hygiene is not a valid excuse anywhere, even in developing settings, as sterilization and handwashing are straightforward.

But if a country is on the brink of breakdown from civil unrest, the ability to handle an intense and sudden problem like an outbreak could bring its people to their knees—and allow the infection to flourish.

"Outbreaks can completely paralyze countries," said Whitworth, citing the 2014 Ebola epidemic in which Sierra Leone, Guinea, and Liberia were "quite close to collapsing."

Civil unrest had plagued all three countries, leaving their economic and health infrastructures in dire need of rebuilding—and ill prepared for a major infection to strike.

That problem combined with human movement between these three countries and others more globally meant Ebola was able to spread, even though dozens of infections in previous years in nearby Democratic Republic of Congo were self-contained and often resolved themselves.

"If (an infection) stays local, it burns out," Heymann said. "People learn what to do."

Fewer Doctors and Nurses in Outbreak Regions

Beyond weak health systems, countries where outbreaks are more likely to occur—namely, more developing settings—also have fewer doctors and nurses to treat the population. Most have left for better prospects elsewhere.

"We have to deal with that as a reality," Heymann said, adding that some countries even encourage young medical talent to travel to new regions.

"It's difficult to manage health worker migration," he said. But programs and strategies are underway to tackle this by "task-shifting," moving responsibilities to new groups and training them to deliver care, such as community health workers.

"Communities have to be resilient," he said, and assigning tasks to people at all levels could mean a greater team available when a new infection strikes.

Faster Information

In the information age, new levels of communication bring even newer levels of fear and multiple ways to spread it, experts believe.

Although the majority of small outbreaks may once have gone largely unknown by populations farther from the epicenter, people today are more informed than ever and require transparent, factual information to be fast flowing.

Google has been using searches for symptoms to help identify when an outbreak may occur, such as with the flu.

"The world looks for an authority," said Heymann who believes the WHO adopts that role but needs to be faster and more transparent with information. The organization was criticized for being too slow to respond and unprepared for the 2014 Ebola outbreak.

"But social media has become active . . . and that's an area that's difficult to control," he said.

The posting and shaping of information by multiple people can change messaging and what people read and believe, Heymann added. It may not all be bad, he said, but the point is that it can shape the way information travels, potentially inciting fear and stigma.

"Not all information on the Internet or social media is accurate," said Mark Feinberg, chairman of the Scientific Advisory Committee of the recently launched Coalition for Epidemic Preparedness Innovations. "Ensuring accurate communication to the public is critically important."

The coalition, launched in January, will address the surprise nature of outbreaks and epidemics to try to prevent them, rather than respond to them.

Lining up the Elements

Heymann describes the likelihood of a new infection spreading rapidly and becoming an epidemic—and potentially a global pandemic—using the analogy of lining up pieces of Swiss cheese, with the different risk factors equating to holes in the cheese. "When they line up, you get an epidemic," he said.

He highlighted an outbreak of Rift Valley virus in East Africa in 1997. The combination of an El Niño event pushing humans away from their homes and closer to cattle, combined with increased rainfall producing more breeding sites for disease-spreading mosquitoes, led to the largest documented outbreak of this virus. It involved five countries and infected an estimated 90,000 people.

"All these (factors) came together and led to an outbreak," Heymann said.

Despite what we know about the aspects of modern life that put us at greater risk, all three experts believe the world is not quite ready to handle what is inevitably coming.

"We need to do a lot better," Feinberg said. "We need to prepare in advance, not respond."

His program, the Coalition for Epidemic Preparedness Innovations, is working to do just that. It's aiding the development of vaccines against viruses that it believes need attention and are in families of infections that are likely to pose a risk, such as MERS CoV, which continues to persist in the Middle East and has been reported in almost 20 countries outside that region.

. . .

The program will also be looking to develop platforms on which vaccines can be made more rapidly so that the general development time frame of 15–20 years can be shrunk significantly to respond to a new virus—even more so than those being developed against Ebola and Zika.

"That's the kind of capability we need," Feinberg said. "The pathogens we don't know about pose the greatest threat."

Combined with other global and national strategies programs—such as WHO regulations and national response teams—Feinberg is optimistic.

"We are far away from that goal," he said. "But I am encouraged, as they are all working on this."

Meera Senthilingam is an editor for CNN Health and Wellness.

EXPLORING THE ISSUE

Will the International Community Be Able to Successfully Address the Next Global Pandemic?

Critical Thinking and Reflection

1. Is the challenge of successfully combating global pandemics simply too complex to succeed?
2. Is strategies for combatting global pandemics high on the agenda of national policy makers around the globe?
3. Should we rely on international governmental organizations take the lead in combatting global pandemics or should nations take the lead?
4. Would closing the U.S. borders dramatically help make Americans safe against global pandemics?

Is There Common Ground?

There is much common ground on the issue of global pandemics. There is much consensus regarding the threat posed by disease. The global community is also in agreement about the need for comprehensive planning against any pandemic among all governments if not all segments of society. And increasingly, the developed world now understands the inequalities existing in the developing world and that these lead to greater probability of the rise and spread of pandemics originating in these poorer countries.

Additional Resources

Dhillon, Ranu, et al., "The World Is Completely Unprepared for a Global Pandemic," *Harvard Business Review* (March 15, 2017).

Global Pandemics and Global Public Health, Independent Commission on Multilateralism, International Peace Institute (October 2017).

Gostin, Lawrence O., and Ayala, Ana S., *Global Health Security in an Era of Explosive Pandemic Potential*, Georgetown University Law Library (2017).

Inglesby, Tom, and Haas, Benjamin, "Ready for a Global Pandemic?" *Foreign Affairs* (November 21, 2017).

Walsh, Byran, "The World Is Not Ready for the next Pandemic," *Time* (May 4, 2017).

Internet References . . .

Avian and Pandemic Influenza Research Link

www.avianflu.aed.org/globalpreparedness.htm

Centers for Disease Control and Prevention

www.cdc.gov

European Centre for Disease Prevention and Control

Eclc.europa.eu/en/healthtopics/zika-virus-infection/

Indiana University Center for Bioethics

www.bioethics.iu.edu/reference-center/pandemics-influenza/

United Nations Food and Agricultural Organization

www.fao.org/zika-virus/en/

WebMD

www.webmd.com

World Health Organization

http://www.who.int/en/

Selected, Edited, and with Issue Framing Material by:
James E. Harf, *Maryville University*

ISSUE

Do Adequate Strategies Exist to Combat Human Trafficking?

YES: Office to Monitor and Combat Trafficking in Persons, from "Meeting the Global Challenge: Effective Strategies to Prevent Human Trafficking," *Trafficking in Persons Report 2016*, U.S. Department of State (2016)

NO: United Nations Office on Drugs and Crime (UNODC), from "Global Report on Trafficking in Persons 2016," *Austria: United Nations* (2016)

Learning Outcomes

After reading this issue, you will be able to:

- Gain an understanding of the nature of human trafficking and its underlying conditions.
- Describe the 3P paradigm of prosecution, protection, and prevention in the U.S. Department of State's strategy against global human trafficking.
- Describe the major findings in the UN 2016 report on global human trafficking that emphasize the worrying circumstance in the fight to combatting trafficking.
- Understand that more progress has been made in creating awareness among governments around the world in the problem of human trafficking than on obtaining convictions for related crimes.

ISSUE SUMMARY

YES: The U.S. Department of State Report describes its two decades effort to combat human trafficking, focusing on the three Ps—prosecution, protection, and protection. While the report discusses challenges to the State Department's efforts, it focuses on success stories and examples in the fight against human trafficking.

NO: The 2016 United Nations Office on Drugs and Crime report spells out the magnitude of the problem with the compilation of major data collected about human trafficking. The most worrisome development since the previous report is the increase in the movement of refugees and migrants.

In a typical week, some American television show will sensationalize the sex or forced labor trafficking problem somewhere in the world and efforts of law enforcement agencies to combat the consequences of such activity. This is not surprising as the subject matter catches the eye of a significant number of TV viewers. And the problem is a pervasive one throughout the globe. Around 21 million individuals worldwide are in forced labor. An estimated 1.2 million children are involved. From 600,000 to 800,000 are taken across international borders each year, most of whom are women and children. And approximately $32 billion in annual profits fuels the problem.

What do we mean by human trafficking? It is defined by the United Nations (UN) as "the recruitment, transportation, transfer, harbouring or receipt of persons, by means of the threat or use of force or other forms of coercion, of abduction, of fraud, of deception, of the abuse of power or of a position of vulnerability or of the giving or receiving of payments or benefits to achieve the consent of a person having control over another person, for the purpose of exploitation" (*Trafficking in Persons—Global Patterns*, United Nations Office on Drug and Crime, April 2006). Exploitation may take any one of several forms: prostitution, forced labor, slavery, or other forms of servitude. The U.S. Department of State divides the types of human trafficking into seven categories: sex trafficking, child sex trafficking, forced labor, bonded labor or debt bond, domestic servitude, forced child labor, and unlawful recruitment and use of child soldiers.

Although slavery has been with us since ancient times, the existence of human trafficking across national borders, particularly involving major distances, is a relatively new escalation of a problem that in the past was addressed as a domestic issue, if addressed at all. The first evidence of modern international slavery occurred in 1877 at a meeting of the International Abolitionist Federation at Geneva. There, a report discussed dozens of women being sent to Austria and Hungary under the pretext of work as governesses for work in brothels. A decade later, the issue arose in London through a newspaper account, leading to a public outcry. In 1899, the first international congress to address the issue of white slave traffic was held, with 120 nations represented. International legislation soon followed. With the creation of the UN after World War II, the UN took responsibility for enforcing the agreement. But the issue does not appear to be high on the agenda of either the UN or its member states for much of the rest of the twentieth century.

It is not until a dramatic expansion occurred as communism was falling throughout the latter half of the 1980s that the issue began to garner public attention. Louise Shelley (*Human Trafficking: A Global Perspective*, Cambridge University Press, 2010) suggests that this expansion was related to globalization, with its emphasis on "free markets, free trade, greater economic competition, and a decline in state intervention in the economy." The end of the Cold War also played a major role as organized crime in the former Soviet republics and former East European communist countries discovered how lucrative human trafficking could be. Loosened controls in these countries led to exploitation of national legal systems as criminals operated across national boundaries with relative impunity. Added to this mix was the absence of a coordinated international attempt to combat the issue. Finally, there is the increased demand in both the labor and the sex areas. And the easy movement across national boundaries only exacerbates the problem.

Shelley sees globalization as the instrument through which human trafficking flourishes. The increased volume of international cargo means that inspections often go wanting, allowing smuggled individuals to easily cross national boundaries. Modern communication has been a major contributor, as websites blatantly advertise sex tourism, arranged relationships, and pornography, and e-mails and cell phones are standard operating procedures. Globalization has also meant decreased border controls throughout the developed world. Economic factors have played a role. First, it was the difficult transition from communism to capitalism that led the losers in this process to find other means of employment, with human trafficking as a likely result. Then, it was the downturn in the global economy in 2008 that played a strong role. Shelley also points to the dramatic increase in "grand corruption," building on decades of small-scale corruption throughout the world. Finally, political factors have been major contributors to human trafficking. The end of the cold war not only loosened state control over every human activity, it also led to a dramatic increase in local conflicts, creating more victims who tried to flee the violence. In turn, this has led to a global condition of statelessness, as increasingly people are citizens of no country and live in limbo, with difficulty in finding employment and with no legal protection of a national government. Add the dramatic population increase in poorer countries and increased urbanization, and you find a large number of individuals, especially women, desperately searching for a better life.

People are abducted or "recruited" in the country of origin, transferred through a standard network to another region of the globe, and then exploited in the destination country. If at any point exploitation is interrupted or ceases, victims can be rescued and might receive support from the country of destination. Victims might be repatriated to their country of origin or, less likely, relocated to a third country. Too often, victims are treated as illegal migrants and treated accordingly. The UN estimates that 127 countries act as countries of origin, whereas 137 countries serve as countries of destination. Profits are estimated by the UN to be $7 billion per year, with between 700,000 and 4 million new victims annually.

When one hears of human trafficking, one usually thinks of sexual exploitation rather than of forced labor. This is not surprising as not only are individual victim stories more compelling, the former type of exploitation represents the more frequent topic of dialogue among policy makers and is also the more frequent occurrence as reported to the UN by a three-to-one margin. Trafficking for sexual exploitation accounts for 58 percent of all cases while trafficking for forced labor is 36 percent of all cases. The latter percentage is increasing, however. Trafficking for sexual exploitation occurs most frequently in Europe, Central Asia, and the Americas, while trafficking for forced labor occurs more often in Africa and the Middle East. With respect to victims, about 60 percent are women and 27 percent are children. Two of every three child victims are girls. Victims from the 2007 and 2010 time period were from 118 countries and 136 nationalities. It is not surprising that most women and female children are exploited sexually, while most male adults and children are subjected to forced labor. Sexual exploitation is more typically found in Central and Southeastern Europe. Former Soviet republics serve as a huge source of origin. Africa ranks high as a region of victim origin as well, although most end up in forced labor rather than in sexual exploitation. Asia is a region of both origin and destination. Countries at the top of the list include Thailand, Japan, India, Taiwan, and Pakistan. The same UN study found that nationals of Asia and Europe represent the bulk of traffickers. And most traffickers who are arrested are nationals of the country where the arrest occurred.

Human trafficking has been part of the global landscape for centuries. What is different today is the magnitude and scope of the trafficking, and the extent to which organized crime is involved in facilitating such nefarious activity. And yet the global community is still only in the position of trying to identify the nature and extent of the problem, let alone ascertaining how to deal with it. In April 2006, the United Nations Office on Drugs and Crime released a report on the human trafficking problem. Titled *Trafficking in Persons: Global Patterns* (United Nations Office on Drugs and Crime, April 2006), its message was clear. The starting point for addressing the problem is the implementation of the Protocol to Prevent, Suppress, and Punish Trafficking in Persons, Especially Women and Children. National governments are called upon to take a leading role in (1) the prevention of trafficking, (2) prosecution of violators, and (3) protection of victims.

Consider the task of prevention. Nations are expected to establish comprehensive policies and programs to prevent and combat trafficking, including research, information, and media campaigns. Nations must attempt to alleviate the vulnerability of people, especially women and children. They must take steps to discourage demand for victims. Nations must also prevent transportation opportunities for traffickers. Finally, they must exchange information and increase cooperation among border control agencies. The UN report also suggests several steps with respect to prosecution. The first step is to "ensure the integrity and security of travel and identity documents" and thus prevent their misuse. Domestic laws must be enacted making human trafficking a criminal offense, and these laws must apply to victims of both genders and all ages. Penalties must be adequate to the crime. Finally, victims must be protected and possibly compensated.

The third role, clearly an alternative approach, focuses on protection of victims. This represents an alternative to the previous international focus, which essentially ignored the plight of the victims. Specifically, victims must be able to achieve "physical, psychological, and social recovery." The physical safety of victims is also paramount. The final step relates to the future home of victims, whether they want to remain in the location where found or whether they wish to return home.

Finally, two macro conclusions may be drawn from analyses of governmental and nongovernmental efforts to successfully combat human trafficking. One, there is significant activity in many areas from a significant number of actors fighting trafficking. And the magnitude of such activity has grown dramatically over the past couple of decades in escalating the fight. The second macro point is also important. The number of convictions has not yet kept pace with the activity.

In the YES selection, the U.S. Department of State's Office to Monitor and Combat Trafficking in Persons suggests that those organizations fighting human trafficking have "successfully used the 3P paradigm of prosecution, protection, and prevention" for combatting human trafficking. Committed governments have addressed prosecution of traffickers by enacting laws criminalizing all forms of human trafficking, including stiff sentencing. Protection has focused on empowering individuals to "move beyond their victimization and rebuild their lives with dignity, security, and respect." Prevention has focused on giving communities throughout the globe sufficient information about human trafficking risks, thus "elevating public consciousness about" the subject.

In the NO selection, the United Nations Office on Drugs and Crime describes the global magnitude of the problem. Eight topic areas are covered in this 2016 report. One, no country is Immune from human trafficking. Two, recent changes in trafficking include the fact (a) that children and men now constitute the large shares of the total victims, (b) trafficked for forced labor is the biggest increase, (c) and within-country trafficking shows the biggest increase. Three, victims and their captors typically have similar backgrounds. Four, many exploitative purposes lie behind being trafficked. Five, cross-border trafficking and regular migration flows resemble each other. Six, conflict can serve as a cause for trafficking. Seven, the percentage of child victims has remained stable at about 25 percent over the years. And eight, while there is "solid legislative progress," there are few convictions.

YES ⤶

Office to Monitor and Combat
Trafficking in Persons

Meeting the Global Challenge: Effective Strategies to Prevent Human Trafficking

The global anti-trafficking movement, now well into its second decade, has successfully used the 3P paradigm of prosecution, protection, and prevention to strengthen how the world combats trafficking in persons. Governments committed to enhancing prosecution of traffickers have enacted laws that criminalize all forms of human trafficking and prescribe sufficiently stringent sentences. Protection efforts have empowered individuals to move beyond their victimization and rebuild their lives with dignity, security, and respect. Prevention measures have provided communities around the world with valuable information about the risks of human trafficking, elevating public consciousness about this crime.

Yet so much work remains. Despite sustained anti-trafficking efforts, millions of individuals are bound by mental, physical, and financial coercion and manipulation by traffickers who exploit their vulnerabilities for profit. Whether they are victims of sex or labor trafficking, the suffering of these individuals is unconscionable. Meanwhile, the broader effects of human trafficking on society must also be addressed—from the splintering of families and communities and the distortion of global markets to the weakening of the rule of law and strengthening of transnational organized criminal networks.

While continued efforts in protection and prosecution are essential, human trafficking prevention strategies deserve commensurate attention and resources. Governments must work in partnership with NGOs, survivors, community and religious leaders, and the private sector to study vulnerable populations and develop targeted strategies to prevent and address the factors that drive modern slavery in their communities. Without prevention, governments are left to respond to the consequences of human trafficking without coming any nearer to seeing its end.

Effective prevention efforts address the tactics of human traffickers head on. With the dissemination of accurate and targeted information, communities will be better prepared to respond to the threat of human trafficking. Strategic intervention programs can reach at-risk populations before they are faced with deceitful recruitment practices of those bent on exploiting them for labor or commercial sex. Meaningful partnerships between public and private sectors and civil society can expand awareness, leverage expertise, and facilitate creative solutions.

Over time, new prevention measures and methods will emerge and evolve as governments and anti-trafficking stakeholders apply experience and share lessons learned. Although often the hardest to measure, prevention efforts can become more sophisticated, scalable, and effective if supported by sufficient resources and political will.

This year's Trafficking in Persons Report focuses on the positive developments and continued challenges of preventing trafficking, and it considers how governments and the broader anti-trafficking community can effectively ensure that those who are vulnerable to human trafficking have the tools and opportunities to avert the risks of exploitation.

Vulnerability and Human Trafficking

Although human trafficking affects every demographic, a common factor across all forms of modern slavery is the victims' vulnerability to exploitation. Systemic social, cultural, and economic policies or practices may marginalize or discriminate against individuals and groups because they are poor, are intellectually or physically disabled, or because of their gender or ethnicity. People may lack access to health and legal services due to their status or language barriers; and some, such as communities in situations of crisis and children, may not be capable of protecting themselves.

Traffickers exploit these disadvantages. They prey on those who lack security and opportunity, coerce, or

Office to Monitor and Combat Trafficking in Persons, "Meeting the Global Challenge: Effective Strategies to Prevent Human Trafficking," *Trafficking in Persons Report 2016*. U.S. Department of State, 2016.

deceive them to gain control, and then profit from their compelled service. To prevent this, governments, with assistance from first responders, NGOs, and local communities, should consider their own populations, cultures, and policies to identify those individuals who may be uniquely vulnerable within their borders. On this basis, communities can develop effective strategies to increase awareness and prevent human trafficking.

The Protocol to Prevent, Suppress, and Punish Trafficking in Persons, Especially Women and Children, supplementing the UN Convention against Transnational Organized Crime (Palermo Protocol) recognizes the connection between vulnerability and human trafficking and encourages state parties to take or strengthen the measures to alleviate those factors that make people vulnerable to human trafficking, including poverty, underdevelopment, and lack of equal opportunity. Understanding the root causes will help governments shape strategic prevention efforts and also integrate anti-trafficking elements into other programming for vulnerable populations.

This introductory section of the report focuses on five elements of effective prevention strategies: enhancing understanding through research, raising awareness to prevent recruitment and reduce demand, implementing policies and programs that decrease the risks and empower vulnerable groups, capitalizing on the knowledge of experts across the globe by increasing collaboration between and within countries, and facilitating partnerships between governments, civil society, and other anti-trafficking actors.

The pages that follow will also highlight a selection of populations traditionally considered at high risk of human trafficking; however, the list is not exhaustive. Generally, when inequality exists and where certain people lack access to social protection and justice, human traffickers are able to thrive.

Research, Data Collection, and Program Evaluation

Given the complex nature of human trafficking, it is difficult to amass reliable data to document local, regional, and global prevalence. Over the years, the advocacy of survivors has expanded understanding of the crime, and together with research and program evaluations, has shed light on best practices in victim protection and law enforcement. However, significant gaps in knowledge of how to prevent human trafficking remain. Additional efforts and resources for research, data collection, and evaluation are needed to identify those actions most effective to prevent victimization.

Reliable baseline information, data, and research that illuminates the causes, prevalence, characteristics, trends, and consequences of all forms of human trafficking in various countries and cultures is crucial for developing anti-trafficking prevention strategies and measuring their impact. To target prevention measures more precisely, governments and civil society should encourage and fund research that identifies populations vulnerable to human trafficking, including a more comprehensive understanding of root causes that are specific to states, communities, and cultural contexts. Understanding unique vulnerabilities along with trends in how people cope with these challenges can help in the development of targeted prevention strategies.

When studying migration, for example, research should be designed to study human trafficking in source and destination countries, as well as along migration routes, as prevention measures will vary depending on the target population and objective. This will require cross-national research, information sharing, and bilateral, regional, and international cooperation to provide insight into the various points where individuals come in contact with potential traffickers.

Accurate baseline data are critical not only in the development of prevention measures but also for accurate assessment of the impact of policies and assistance programs, including unintended negative consequences. Fully understanding the impact of a prevention strategy is necessary to scale or modify it based on outcome. Prevention programming should devote both consideration and resources to evaluation.

New research and information should be freely shared among stakeholders to enhance the collective ability to respond to human trafficking. Research projects should include recommendations for various stakeholders as well as a dissemination plan to ensure the results are widely circulated. Reliable research is the backbone of any evidence-based policy or program and anti-trafficking stakeholders have a responsibility to ensure that sufficient attention and funding are dedicated to it.

Examples

- In 2015, IOM released a report, Addressing Human Trafficking and Exploitation in Times of Crisis: Evidence and Recommendations for Further Action to Protect Vulnerable and Mobile Populations, which looks at armed conflicts, natural disasters, and protracted crises based on research conducted in Syria, Iraq, Libya, Haiti, Nepal, the Philippines, eastern and northern Africa, Yemen, and tsunami-affected areas of Indonesia, Sri Lanka, and Thailand. The report discusses the risks of trafficking in crisis situations and includes evidence-based recommendations for the humanitarian community on preventing and improving of responses to human trafficking before, during, and after a crisis.

- In 2016, Harvard University released a study, When We Raise Our Voice: The Challenge of Eradicating Labor Exploitation, focused on the work of an Indian NGO that developed a community empowerment model to assist vulnerable groups in identifying their priorities and preventing modern slavery. The study reports a decline in human trafficking over a four-year period in the area studied.
- To help states combat transnational crime, including human trafficking, INTERPOL provides its 190 member countries with resources, including a secure communications network relevant to criminal investigations and humanitarian efforts. At the request of its member countries, INTERPOL publishes "green notices" on persons who present a danger to the public based on their prior criminal history, such as convicted sex offenders and members of violent gangs.

Raising Awareness

Increasing public awareness about the risks and signs of human trafficking is an important piece of any anti-trafficking prevention strategy and to date has been the primary prevention measure used by governments and other stakeholders. Typically, public awareness campaigns target either those considered to be most at risk, such as migrant workers; those who may be contributing wittingly or unwittingly to the demand, such as public and private employers; or purchasers of commercial sex; or the general public who may be able to spot the indicators of human trafficking and report suspicions to law enforcement.

Like other programs, anti-trafficking awareness campaigns must include an evaluation component to assess their impact and improve future campaigns. Often, general public awareness campaigns are limited due to the restrictions inherent in one-dimensional campaign materials, such as posters, billboards, or print media advertisements, which often reduce the complexity of human trafficking into images and brief text. While this may help to raise general awareness about the existence of trafficking, it can also misrepresent the victims and confuse the issue. For example, images of physical restraint such as handcuffs or cages may influence what the public believes constitutes human trafficking; yet movement and physical restraint are not required for a crime to be considered

human trafficking. Designers of these campaigns should fully understand the scope and scale of the problem in the target community and accurately depict the nature of the crime, its victims, and the perpetrators.

In contrast to broad or national efforts, awareness campaigns can also be designed to target particular individuals, for example, by notifying travelers of the illegality of child sex tourism, informing workers of their rights and risks as they migrate for a job, or adopting corporate codes of conduct. Effective targeting should also include awareness-raising among: immigration authorities and law enforcement; diplomatic personnel; medical specialists; educational and social service personnel; and other professionals likely to come into contact with vulnerable individuals, so they are both prompted and equipped to recognize the signs of human trafficking and respond appropriately.

Together, governments, civil society organizations, and companies must collaborate to develop awareness campaigns that have clear objectives and measurable outcomes, that train and educate employees as well as relevant partners, and that promote sound anti-trafficking policies and secure reporting mechanisms.

Examples

- The Government of Slovakia developed and financed the creation of a website that allows Slovak citizens traveling abroad for employment to register their contact information with friends and family. The registered user's contacts are alerted, should the user cease usual online activity or fail to communicate with the contacts on pre-established schedules. If this happens, each contact receives information of the user's last known Internet connection access point location—information that could be relayed to Slovak law enforcement authorities.
- In recent years, there has been growing international media attention on forced labor aboard fishing vessels in Southeast Asia, including investigative reports by the *New York Times*, *Al Jazeera*, *The Guardian*, *South China Morning Post*, and the *Associated Press*, which won the 2016 Pulitzer Prize for Public Service. The quality and frequency of reporting by international media has helped raise awareness of forced labor in the fishing industry among governments, businesses, and consumers.
- In 2015, an NGO in India engaged with journalists to raise awareness of human trafficking within minority and marginalized communities. The organization trained journalists on how to better report cases of human trafficking, including bonded labor, for their audiences. These efforts

aimed to better inform people in remote communities who may only get news in their local language and may not often see reporting on human trafficking. Reporters uncovered human trafficking cases within their own communities and increased attention on the role of state government and police in prevention efforts.

- In 2015, a Peruvian NGO conducted a campaign to raise awareness among tourists, mass media, tourism operators, and the general public about the criminal penalties for those who sexually exploit children in Loreto, a region known for human trafficking activity. The NGO takes a moving display of a jail, with a sign reading "here we punish child sexual exploitation," to places where such cases have been reported.
- In France, the Ministry of Education provides anti-trafficking awareness courses to students seeking a degree in hospitality and tourism. Specialized lessons alert students to the indicators of child sex tourism and their professional responsibility to take action when they recognize this crime.

Policies and Programs to Reduce Risk and Empower Vulnerable Individuals

Public awareness campaigns are only one piece of an effective prevention strategy. Knowledge of the risks of trafficking is important to empower vulnerable populations and foster a vigilant general public, but governments and stakeholders must also develop measures that keep at-risk individuals safe from human trafficking. As a part of this, governments need to implement policies that can prevent trafficking, provide the necessary oversight, and balance to avoid restricting freedoms.

For example, governments can measure and establish the identity of local populations by registering births, administering citizenship and nationality, and issuing identity documents—a lack of which renders individuals vulnerable to exploitation. Legal registration reduces vulnerabilities to human trafficking by enabling residents and their families to take advantage of programs and activities that require legal status, such as health coverage, education, access to social welfare, and employment in the formal economy. When governments allow workers to form and join trade unions, it also makes them less vulnerable to exploitation.

In addition, governments and the private sector can work together to identify and stop fraudulent recruitment. Governments should actively monitor labor recruitment agencies, train labor inspectors to identify signs of

fraudulent recruitment, and adopt and enforce policies that regulate foreign labor recruiters and hold them civilly and criminally liable for fraudulent recruitment. The private sector can help by ensuring its companies advertise to prospective applicants with legal, formalized recruitment procedures and hire workers through such procedures, or directly, and not through unscrupulous middlemen.

Governments and NGOs should integrate anti-trafficking elements into broader programs, including those that focus on health, economic development, crisis management, and rule of law to leverage resources and maximize exposure to the issue. These policies should be designed with input from experts, trafficking survivors, and local communities. By examining existing programs that are directed toward vulnerable populations and integrating anti-trafficking components, stakeholders can institutionalize the issue and capitalize on established structures.

While preventing trafficking on the supply side—by raising awareness and reducing the supply of exploited laborers—is imperative, it is also necessary that governments work with civil society to reduce the demand for forced labor and commercial sex. By driving down demand, the business of human trafficking becomes less profitable and traffickers will have less incentive to exploit victims.

Examples

- In Vietnam, an NGO helped legally register with the state more than 2,000 ethnic minority residents in areas at high risk for human trafficking. In many places, individuals in remote locations do not receive clear information on the benefits of state services or the ways to access them, or they lack the financial means to travel to government offices for registration. Individuals without legal registration often do not have access to education, health care, or employment in the formal economy and are highly vulnerable to human trafficking.
- OSCE is one of the first intergovernmental organizations to address explicitly government procurement as well as its own procurement of goods and services. Following on commitments of the December 2013 Addendum to the OSCE Action Plan to Combat Trafficking in Human Beings, OSCE is reviewing relevant rules and regulations in regard to personnel and the procurement of goods and services to ensure that no OSCE activities contribute to any form of human trafficking.

- In Burkina Faso, an NGO is combating forced child labor in the cotton and gold industries using a model of training locally based "Social Protection Community Facilitators (SPCFs)" who serve as leaders in their local area on child protection issues. The SPCFs implement their own awareness-raising activities in addition to monitoring child labor in their areas.
- The Philippine Overseas Employment Agency facilitates public seminars and community forums for prospective migrant workers on indicators of illegal labor recruitment and human trafficking, and the Bureau of Immigration issues institutional guidelines on departure formalities for international-bound persons, setting clearly defined rules on inspections to prevent trafficking and other related offenses without deterring other travelers.

Multilateral Collaboration

Human trafficking occurs in virtually every country in the world and often crosses borders when victims move between source, transit, and destination countries. Multilateral engagement is a key component of many governments' effective anti-trafficking efforts.

The international response to modern slavery began with the adoption of the Palermo Protocol in 2000 and has continued to grow. Multilateral organizations are ramping up efforts to combat trafficking by incorporating anti-trafficking policies into discussions of other pressing topics. What was once a stand-alone issue is now being integrated into work on other topics, including national security, human rights, violence against women and children, migration management and refugee protection, business responsibility and supply chain accountability, and economic development. In addition to leveraging their member states' expertise and resources, multilateral organizations generate momentum to develop global, regional, and even domestic strategies to help dismantle trafficking networks and empower vulnerable populations.

Further, multilateral and regional organizations work to foster consensus among their member states on common goals, commitments, and norms; and they can help standardize research and data collection methods at the regional and subregional levels. Multilateral forums also provide a venue for member states, civil society, academia, the private sector, and survivors to exchange information on experiences and challenges, including identifying new and emerging issues related to human trafficking. With the support of member states, multilateral organizations provide anti-trafficking training and technical assistance to countries, including to law enforcement, judges, media, first responders, and care providers.

To ensure they are not contributing to the problem of human trafficking, multilateral organizations and member states must institute and enforce policies to ensure that their personnel, including diplomats and peacekeepers, do not engage in trafficking in persons. In addition, international organizations can begin to monitor their supply chains and enforce policies that protect workers and reduce risks in the public procurement of goods and services.

Governments must be committed to engaging at the multilateral level and to adhering to and enforcing international obligations related to human trafficking, in particular the Palermo Protocol.

Examples

- The OSCE Special Representative and Co-ordinator for Combating Trafficking in Human Beings, Ambassador Madina Jarbussynova, conducted training in 2015 for the OSCE Special Monitoring Mission to Ukraine to raise awareness and improve capacity to identify human trafficking. This mission is deployed to Ukraine to monitor the implementation of the Minsk agreement, including ceasefire and heavy weapon withdrawal. The UN's refugee agency, UNHCR, reported that there were more than 1.8 million internally displaced persons and refugees abroad as a result of the crisis in and around Ukraine, and this population is especially vulnerable to exploitation.
- At the opening of the 70th Session of the UN General Assembly in September 2015, world leaders adopted a bold "2030 Agenda for Sustainable Development" to guide the global community's efforts to eradicate poverty, promote peace and equality, and protect the environment over the coming years. This Agenda includes 17 Sustainable Development Goals and 169 targets centered on economic, social, and environmental development. The UN integrated anti-trafficking elements into three of the goals.
- In July 2015, the UN Office on Drugs and Crime provided a training manual to Panamanian Public Ministry personnel on conducting psychological interviews that protect trafficking victims during their participation in legal investigations against their traffickers. Panamanian officials have already begun to put the procedures into practice.

Enhancing Partnerships

Acknowledging that no single response can end human trafficking, governments around the world are engaging with other stakeholders to increase their ability to prevent modern slavery. Survivors, NGOs, donors, academics, and businesses have complementary skills and perspectives that, when combined, drive innovation and bring about sustained progress. In this regard, governments play a vital role in convening various stakeholders to harness innovative ideas and create partnerships.

Three Examples are:

- The Santa Marta Group is a partnership between international police chiefs and Catholic bishops from around the world, working together with civil society to end modern slavery through a process endorsed by Pope Francis. The objective of the Santa Marta Group is to combine the resources of the Church with those of law enforcement agencies to prevent trafficking and provide care to victims.
- The Uruguayan Ministry of Foreign Affairs signed an MOU with IOM to draft a comprehensive anti-trafficking law, and IOM began working with the government's interagency anti-trafficking committee to develop a law that will meet international standards on trafficking, taking into account prosecution, protection, and prevention for both sex trafficking and forced labor.
- In Guatemala, a leading coffee company and a U.S. labor rights organization have teamed up, with support from the government to promote transparency and accountability in Guatemala's coffee supply chain. Throughout the sector, stakeholders are gaining a better understanding of the risks of recruitment abuses, including those that lead to forced labor. The partners are strengthening communication between workers and key corporate and government actors and building the capacity of all stakeholders, including civil society, to report and monitor recruitment practices in the coffee sector.

A Joint Effort

Preventing human trafficking is an enormous challenge, requiring the sustained efforts of many. Collaboration between government and nongovernmental stakeholders is critical to strengthening efforts to prevent modern slavery.

At its core, the global struggle to combat human trafficking is about political and public will. If ignored, traffickers will continue to reap enormous profits while communities suffer the many toxic effects. But if trafficking is confronted head on, vulnerable populations will be empowered to control more fully their lives and protect themselves from the harms of human trafficking.

Anti-trafficking stakeholders must continue efforts that have proven successful but also commit to the development of new and creative approaches to the prevention of human trafficking. Trafficking prevention is a field largely underexplored and underfunded. There is a great deal of space for innovation and collaboration.

Witnessing the end of human trafficking will require leadership and political will at all levels of government and throughout the anti-trafficking community. It will require the allocation and responsible use of resources appropriate to the scale of the problem. And it will require individuals all over the world to be attuned to the signs of human trafficking, put aside differences, and take their responsibility seriously to prevent and address this crime.

Should the day ever come when human trafficking ceases to exist, it will not be because traffickers have stopped trying to take advantage of vulnerable individuals. Instead, it will be the culmination of efforts from a global community that refuses to allow it to continue.

THE DEPARTMENT OF STATE'S OFFICE TO MONITOR AND COMBAT TRAFFICKING IN PERSONS leads the United States' global engagement against human trafficking.

United Nations Office on Drugs and Crime  **NO**

Global Report on Trafficking in Persons 2016

No Country Is Immune from Trafficking in Persons

Victims are trafficked along a multitude of trafficking flows; within countries, between neighboring countries or even across different continents. More than 500 different trafficking flows were detected between 2012 and 2014.

Countries in Western and Southern Europe detected victims of 137 different citizenships. Affluent areas—such as Western and Southern Europe, North America and the Middle East—detect victims from a large number of countries around the world.

Trafficking victims from countries in Sub-Saharan Africa and East Asia are trafficked to a wide range of destinations. A total of 69 countries reported to have detected victims from Sub-Saharan Africa between 2012 and 2014. Victims from Sub-Saharan Africa were mainly detected in Africa, the Middle East, and Western and Southern Europe. There are also records of trafficking flows from Africa to South-East Asia and the Americas.

How Has Trafficking in Persons Changed in Recent Years?

Over the last 10 years, the profile of detected trafficking victims has changed. Although most detected victims are still women, children and men now make up larger shares of the total number of victims than they did a decade ago. In 2014, children comprised 28 percent of detected victims, and men 21 percent.

In parallel with the significant increases in the share of men among detected trafficking victims, the share of victims who are trafficked for forced labor has also increased. About 4 in 10 victims detected between 2012 and 2014 were trafficked for forced labor, and of these victims, 63 percent were men.

The share of detected trafficking cases that are domestic—that is, carried out within a country's borders—has also increased significantly in recent years, and some 42 percent of detected victims between 2012 and 2014 were trafficked domestically. While some of the increase can be ascribed to differences in reporting and data coverage, countries are clearly detecting more domestic trafficking nowadays.

These shifts indicate that the common understanding of the trafficking crime has evolved. A decade ago, trafficking was thought to mainly involve women trafficked from afar into an affluent country for sexual exploitation. Today, criminal justice practitioners are more aware of the diversity among offenders, victims, forms of exploitation, and flows of trafficking in persons, and the statistics may reflect this increased awareness.

Victims and Traffickers Often Have the Same Background

Traffickers and their victims often come from the same place, speak the same language, or have the same ethnic background. Such commonalities help traffickers generate trust to carry out the trafficking crime.

Traffickers rarely travel abroad in order to recruit victims, but they do travel to destination countries to exploit them. As general pattern, traffickers in origin countries are usually citizens of these countries. Traffickers in destination countries are either citizens of these countries or have the same citizenship as the victim(s) they trafficked.

Being of the same gender can also enhance trust. Data from court cases indicate that women are commonly involved in the trafficking of women and girls, in particular.

Most of the detected victims of trafficking in persons are females; either women or underage girls.

While traffickers are overwhelmingly male, women comprise a relatively large share of convicted offenders, compared to most other crimes. This share is even higher among traffickers convicted in the victims' home country. Court cases and other qualitative data indicate that women are often used to recruit other women.

Family ties can also be abused to carry out trafficking crimes. For instance, this is seen in cases of relatives entrusted with the care of a family member who break their promise and profit from the family member's exploitation.

People Are Trafficked for Many Exploitative Purposes

Trafficking for sexual exploitation and for forced labor are the most prominently detected forms, but trafficking victims can also be exploited in many other ways. Victims are trafficked to be used as beggars, for forced or sham marriages, benefit fraud, production of pornography, or for organ removal to mention some of the forms countries have reported.

Trafficking for various types of marriage has been sporadically reported in the past but is now emerging as a more prevalent form. In Southeast Asia, this often involves forced marriages or unions without the consent of the woman (or girl). Trafficking for sham marriages mainly takes place in affluent countries.

Trafficking for forced labor in the fishing industry is commonplace in several parts of the world. This can happen, for example, on board big fishing vessels on the high seas carried out by large companies that trade fish internationally or in on-land processing facilities. It can also happen more locally, such as in African lake areas where the fishing tends to be small-scale and the catch is sold in street markets.

Trafficking for sexual exploitation and for forced labor in a range of economic sectors are reported nearly everywhere. At least 10 countries have reported trafficking for the removal of organs. Other forms of reported trafficking, such as the ones mentioned above, are sometimes locally acute, but less internationally widespread.

Cross-border Trafficking Flows Often Resemble

Regular Migration Flows

Although many cases of trafficking in persons do not involve the crossing of international borders—some 42 percent of the detected victims are trafficked domestically—there are some links between cross-border trafficking and regular migration flows. Certain trafficking flows resemble migration flows, and some sizable international migration flows are also reflected in cross-border trafficking flows.

The analysis of country-level data on detected trafficking victims and recently arrived regular migrants reveals that trafficking in persons and regular migration flows broadly resemble each other for some destination countries in different parts of the world.

Many factors can increase a person's vulnerability to human trafficking during the migration process, however. The presence of transnational organized crime elements in the country of origin, for instance, is significant in this regard, and a person's socioeconomic profile can also have an impact.

Conflict Can Help Drive Trafficking in Persons

People escaping from war and persecution are particularly vulnerable to becoming victims of trafficking. The urgency of their situation might lead them to make dangerous migration decisions. The rapid increase in the number of Syrian victims of trafficking in persons following the start of the conflict there, for instance, seems to be one example of how these vulnerabilities play out.

Conflicts create favorable conditions for trafficking in persons, but not only by generating a mass of vulnerable people escaping violence. Armed groups engage in trafficking in the territories in which they operate, and they have recruited thousands of children for the purpose of using them as combatants in various past and current conflicts. While women and girls tend to be trafficked for marriages and sexual slavery, men and boys are typically exploited in forced labor in the mining sector, as porters, soldiers, and slaves.

Trafficking the Most Vulnerable: Children

The share of detected child victims has returned to levels last seen in 2009, after seven years of increases. Despite this trend, still more than a quarter of the detected trafficking victims in 2014 were children.

In Sub-Saharan Africa and Central America and the Caribbean, a majority of the detected victims are children. There are several reasons, such as demographics, socioeconomic factors, legislative differences, and countries' institutional frameworks and priorities. There seems to be a relation between a country's level of development and the age of detected trafficking victims. In the least developed countries, children often comprise large shares of the detected victims.

There are clear regional differences with regard to the sex of detected child victims. Countries in Sub-Saharan Africa detect more boys than girls, which seems to be connected with the large shares of trafficking for forced labor, child soldiers (in conflict areas), and begging reported in that region. In Central America and the Caribbean and South America, on the other hand, girls make up a large share of the detected victims, which could be related to the fact that trafficking for sexual exploitation is the most frequently detected form there.

Solid Legislative Progress, But Still Very Few Convictions

The number of countries with a statute that criminalizes most forms of trafficking in persons in line with the definition used by the UN Trafficking in Persons Protocol increased from 33 in 2003 (18 percent) to 158 in 2016 (88 percent). This rapid progress means that more victims are assisted and protected, and more traffickers are put behind bars.

However, most national legislation is recent, having been introduced during the last 8–10 years. As a consequence,

the average number of convictions still remains low. The longer countries have had comprehensive legislation in place, the more convictions are recorded, indicating that it takes time and dedicated resources for a national criminal justice system to acquire sufficient expertise to detect, investigate, and successfully prosecute cases of trafficking in persons.

The ratio between the number of traffickers convicted in the first court instance and the number of victims detected is about five victims per convicted offender. Although most countries now have the appropriate legal framework for tackling trafficking crimes, the large discrepancy between the number of detected victims and convicted offenders indicates that many trafficking crimes still go unpunished.

THE UNITED NATIONS OFFICE ON DRUGS AND CRIME is a United Nations office that was established in 1997 as the Office for Drug Control and Crime Prevention by combining the United Nations International Drug Control Program (UNDCP) and the Crime Prevention and Criminal Justice Division in the UN Office in Vienna.

EXPLORING THE ISSUE

Do Adequate Strategies Exist to Combat Human Trafficking?

Critical Thinking and Reflection

1. Why is greater attention now being paid to human trafficking?
2. Can anything be done to lower the demand for human traffic services?
3. Do you believe that governments are serious about combating human trafficking?
4. Do you consider progress made in combating human trafficking to be one of the glass being "half-full" or "half-empty"?
5. Does the U.S. Department of State overstate how successful it has been in using the 3P paradigm of prosecution, protection, and prevention in combatting human trafficking?
6. Can modern technology, including the web, be an effective tool in the fight against human trafficking?

Is There Common Ground?

The major area of agreement is on the recognition by governments throughout the world that there has been a major increase in human trafficking as a consequence of the end of the cold war and the rise of globalization. There is also agreement that coordinated efforts among governments at all levels—local, national, and global—are critical to successfully addressing the issue. Increasingly, governments agree that large data generating and analyzing capabilities can be used effectively in combatting trafficking.

Additional Resources

Aronowitz, Alexis A., *Human Trafficking, Human Misery: The Global Trade in Human Beings*, Reprint Edition. Scarecrow Press, 2013.

Foot, Kirsten, *Collaborating against Human Trafficking.* Rowman & Littlefield, 2015.

Global Estimates of Modern Slavery, International Labour Organization and Walk Free Foundation. Geneva, 2017.

Preventing Trafficking in Persons by Addressing Demand, Inter-Agency Coordination Group against Trafficking in Persons, United Nations Economic and Social Council. September, 2014.

Richardson, K. G., *Human Trafficking: From 5,000 BC to the 21st Century: 7,000 Years of Slavery, Rape, Greed* (2016).

Internet References . . .

Coalition against Trafficking in Women

www.catwinternational.org

humantrafficking.org

www.humantrafficking.org

Terres des homes

www.childtrafficking.org

The Human Trafficking Project

www.traffickingptroject.org

United Nations

www.ungift.org

Selected, Edited, and with Issue Framing Material by:
Marie E. Harf, *U.S. Department of State (2013–2017),*
Central Intelligence Agency (2006–2011)

ISSUE

Is Saudi Arabia Moving toward Increased Democratization and/or Liberalization?

YES: **Thomas L. Friedman**, from "Saudi Arabia's Arab Spring, At Last," *The New York Times* (2017)

NO: "Freedom in the World 2018: Democracy in Crisis," *Freedom House* (2018)

Learning Outcomes

After reading this issue, you will be able to:

- Outline Saudi Arabia's political, religious, economic, and social history.
- Understand the reforms that Crown Prince Mohammed bin Salman is undertaking.
- Discuss the opportunities and challenges Saudi Arabia as a whole and the Crown Prince himself faces in implementing this reform agenda.
- Understand the difference between economic and political liberalization, especially in the Saudi context.

ISSUE SUMMARY

YES: Thomas L. Friedman, a longtime analyst of the Middle East, argues that the most significant reforms taking place in the region today are in Saudi Arabia, mainly due to the efforts of the young, boundary-pushing Crown Prince Mohammed bin Salman. Friedman travels to the Kingdom to interview the Crown Prince and Saudi citizens about these religious and economic (as opposed to political) reforms. He comes away from these conversations convinced the country is moving in a more open direction.

NO: Freedom House is an independent watchdog organization dedicated to the expansion of freedom and democracy around the world, and it annually assesses countries' degrees of political freedoms and civil liberties. Its most recent 2018 analysis for Saudi Arabia ranks the country in the "least free" category in the world, noting that, despite the Crown Prince's easing of some social restrictions, the absolute monarchy's severe restrictions on speech, extensive surveillance, criminalization of dissert, and lack of elections at the national level remain.

Thomas Friedman, a longtime analyst of the Middle East, began an article in late 2017 with this stark admission: "I never thought I'd live long enough to write this sentence: the most significant reform process underway anywhere in the Middle East today is in Saudi Arabia" (*New York Times*, November 23, 2017). Where does his optimism come from, particularly about a country whose absolute monarchy continues to restrict many political and social rights? Friedman's and others' enthusiasm centers almost exclusively on the actions of Saudi Crown Prince Mohammad bin Salman, the young heir who is attempting to fundamentally change Saudi Arabia's economy and society without upending the political power of the royal family at the same time. As he has hurried to alter decades of economic and social policy, he has consolidated power within the royal family, often ruthlessly. Can this 30-something wunderkind take on the royal family's corruption and the country's religious establishment, all while trying to wean the Kingdom off oil and modernize its entire economic and education systems? And will he match his economic and social liberalization with increased political rights for the Saudi people?

Saudi Arabia organized itself as a country in 1932 under the leadership of a tribal leader, Abdulaziz al-Saud, who had conquered a large amount of territory on the Arabian Peninsula and consolidated various tribes under his rule. His descendants continue to rule the kingdom today. Since the nation's founding, the royal family has aligned itself with prominent conservative Islamic fundamentalists known as Wahhabis, trading royal support for religious legitimacy. This alliance has been especially important given the role of the Saudi King as the Custodian of the Two Holy Mosques and keeper of the religious sites in Mecca and Medina. Ever since the desert kingdom struck oil in the late 1930s, its economy has essentially operated as a rentier state, overly reliant on oil and its associated industries and led by a royal family that sustains its power partly by providing jobs and subsidies to its citizens as part of a deeply ingrained social contract.

Throughout decades of turmoil in the Middle East, Saudi Arabia has been prosperous and mostly calm, surviving the assassination of a king, a takeover of the Holy Mosque by extremists, asometimes restive Shia minority, and the rise of al-Qaeda within the Kingdom. At the same time, it has remained a deeply conservative country, with some of the most severe restrictions on religious practice, women's rights, and political freedoms in the world. Today, Saudi leadership seems to recognize that, despite the conservatism of much of its society and its continued reliance on the traditional religious establishment to help protect its power, falling oil prices mean sooner or later it must take steps toward becoming a more modern state, at least in the economic realm. With a population where more than half the people are under the age of 25, Mohammed bin Salman (or MbS, as he is known) appears to have decided that now is the time for change in Saudi Arabia and he should be the one to usher it in.

The hallmark of MbS' campaign is a plan called Vision 2030, which outlines a shift from the Kingdom's overdependence on oil toward a more diverse and private sector-driven economy, a move that became acutely necessary after the collapse of oil prices in 2014. Saudi Arabia experienced a deficit of its state budgets in 2015 of nearly $100 billion dollars, and even after responding with deep cuts, a deficit of $79 billion in 2016 (Martin Hvidt, *Center for Mellemoststudier*, March 2017). MbS' basic goal is to make the economy "more mature, prosperous,

and sustainable" (Mohamed Elmeshad, *Carnegie*, January 12, 2017).

Vision 2030 calls for increased domestic investment, more transparency and accountability in the Saudi bureaucracy, a crackdown on corruption, cutting government subsidies, raising taxes, and selling major state assets. It aims to create 1.2 million private sector jobs by 2030, to cut unemployment from 12.8 percent to 9 percent, and for the private sector to eventually account for more than 65 percent of Saudi GDP. In order to train the next generation of Saudis to inherit this retooled economy, the government is reforming the educational system to focus more on science, technology, and the skills needed in the modern workplace, and it is sending more students and teachers to be trained abroad. One of the most interesting proposals in Vision 2030 is a plan to sell a 5 percent stake in the hugely profitable state oil company, Saudi Aramco, to bankroll the Kingdom's sovereign wealth fund that will, in turn, pay for many of these domestic reforms. The total value of Aramco is estimated to be around $2 trillion dollars.

MbS has matched these economic measures with bold social moves, including curtailing the authority of the feared religious police and legally allowing women to drive. Women are also increasingly integrated into more job sectors, and over half of college graduates in Saudi Arabia today are women. Perhaps most notably, MbS has couched many of these measures in the language of "restoring moderate Islam" to Saudi Arabia. This economic and social "liberalization" campaign has been matched by an equally aggressive public relations effort both at home and abroad, with the charismatic Crown Prince doing overseas media tours to show the world that Saudi Arabia is not the caricature many people believe it to be but instead is a young, dynamic country moving into the future with new and bold ideas.

But the real question is: Will these reforms work? Saudi Arabia was able to almost halve its budget deficit from 15 percent in 2015 to 8.9 percent in 2017, but it will need additional reforms and stronger oil prices to continue that trend. It will also have to complete the Aramco listing to provide money to its sovereign wealth fund and attract more international investment. The Saudi investment climate appears promising in many ways, but the Crown Prince will need to calibrate his "corruption crackdown" efforts. Investors will not line up for projects if they are worried their business partners might end up detained or if they are concerned about the rule of law (*Atlantic Council*, February 7, 2018). More diversification is also needed; oil and oil-related industries still accounted for 87 percent of 2017 budget revenues (Adel Abdel Ghafer, *Brookings*, February 14, 2018).

As of now, there is little evidence that Mohammed bin Salman intends to expand his reform efforts to include the Saudi political system; indeed, Vision 2030 does not address political reform. (Political liberalization does not automatically follow from increasing economic or social freedoms; China and Singapore provide examples of countries that have opened up their economies while maintaining authoritarian political systems.) Advocacy organizations such as Freedom House and Human Rights Watch have documented Saudi Arabia's continued efforts to stamp out internal dissent. Imprisonment and even death sentences for political prisoners have increased under MbS' and his father, King Salman's, leadership, including jailings of dissidents for online postings. These crackdowns have cut across the country's political spectrum, from popular preachers to reform advocates. And, while women have gained more freedoms in certain areas, the guardianship system that governs much of their lives—a father, husband, or brother must permit them to marry, for example—has not yet been reformed.

The crackdown on dissent has not been limited to the broader public. MbS has also been systematically consolidating his power within the Al Saud family. An illustrative example came when at his direction the Saudi government imprisoned several dozen family members, officials, and prominent businessman in the Riyadh Ritz Carlton in late 2017 on charges of corruption. MbS explained the crackdown as a legitimate attempt to get rid of graft, but it also had the added consequence of sidelining his rivals for power. As the University of Cambridge's Toby Matthiesen writes, "There is little doubt that a culture of self-enrichment and collusion prevailed at the top echelons of government and business in the country . . . but this night of the long knives also removed a number of MbS' competitors" (*Foreign Affairs*, November 8, 2017). This move followed on his successful efforts to persuade his father to remove a powerful cousin from above him on the chain of succession, setting up his own accession.

To advance these bold and sometimes-controversial reforms, MbS has leveraged his consolidated power with his father, rather than relying on the traditional royal family tactic of consensus-building among the various branches. Whether the royal family will continue to acquiesce, especially if and when a succession battle arises in the future, is an open question.

Another key unknown is whether MbS' attempts to remake the economic and social fabric of the country will stir up public discontent against the royal family. Thus far, there have not been significant protests over the cuts in government subsidies, for example, and the religious establishment has generally been supportive of these reforms. But Saudi citizens have grown accustomed to seeing the state as providers of expansive social programs and direct cash transfers of its oil wealth. For example, as the Arab Spring swept through much of the region in 2011, the then King Abdullah gave cash handouts worth a reported $37 billion dollars to the population (*Carnegie*). Those days are over, and the government will have to find new ways to maintain popular support, or at least acquiescence, as its people experience greater economic and social freedoms and gain a broader perspective through technology. Fully 93 percent of Saudis are online and some 2.5 million are active on Twitter (Paul B. Stares and Helia Ighami, *Council on Foreign Relations*, May 15, 2017).

Finally, we cannot overlook the symbolic importance of a young, aggressive Crown Prince who, whether or not he succeeds, is forcing young Saudis in particular to examine who they are, how they do business, and what they want their future to be. As Bilal Saab writes, "Never before in the history of Saudi Arabia has a member of the royal family spoken for and connected with young, hopeful Saudis" (*Foreign Affairs*, January 5, 2017). And the stakes are high. According to Jeffrey Goldberg, "If Prince Mohammed actually achieves what he says he wants to achieve, the Middle East will be a changed place" (*The Atlantic*, April 2, 2018).

In the YES selection, *New York Times* columnist Thomas Friedman suggests that "the most significant reform process underway anywhere in the Middle East today is in Saudi Arabia." Freidman amplifies his position by admitting that he never thought "I'd live long enough to write this sentence." In the NO article, Freedom House, an NGO that annually assesses countries' degrees of political freedoms and liberties, concluded that Saudi Arabia qualifies as "Not Free" in its latest ranking, despite announcements of some social economic and social reforms.

YES ⤶

Thomas L. Friedman

Saudi Arabia's Arab Spring, At Last

The crown prince has big plans for his society.

Riyadh, Saudi Arabia—I never thought I'd live long enough to write this sentence: the most significant reform process underway anywhere in the Middle East today is in Saudi Arabia. Yes, you read that right. Though I came here at the start of Saudi winter, I found the country going through its own Arab Spring, Saudi style.

Unlike the other Arab Springs—all of which emerged bottom up and failed miserably, except in Tunisia—this one is led from the top down by the country's 32-year-old crown prince, Mohammed bin Salman (MBS), and if it succeeds, it will not only change the character of Saudi Arabia but the tone and tenor of Islam across the globe. Only a fool would predict its success—but only a fool would not root for it.

To better understand it, I flew to Riyadh to interview the crown prince, known as "MbS," who had not spoken about the extraordinary events here of early November, when his government arrested scores of Saudi princes and businessmen on charges of corruption and threw them into a makeshift gilded jail—the Riyadh Ritz-Carlton—until they agreed to surrender their ill-gotten gains. You don't see that every day.

We met at night at his family's ornate adobe-walled palace in Ouja, north of Riyadh.

MbS spoke in English, while his brother, Prince Khalid, the new Saudi ambassador to the United States, and several senior ministers shared different lamb dishes and spiced the conversation. After nearly four hours together, I surrendered at 1:15 a.m. to MbS's youth, pointing out that I was exactly twice his age. It's been a long, long time, though, since any Arab leader wore me out with a fire hose of new ideas about transforming his country.

We started with the obvious question: What's happening at the Ritz? And was this his power play to eliminate his family and private sector rivals before his ailing father, King Salman, turns the keys of the Kingdom over to him?

It's "ludicrous," he said, to suggest that this anti-corruption campaign was a power grab. He pointed out that many prominent members of the Ritz crowd had already publicly pledged allegiance to him and his reforms, and that "a majority of the royal family" is already behind him. This is what happened, he said: "our country has suffered a lot from corruption from the 1980s until today. The calculation of our experts is that roughly 10 percent of all government spending was siphoned off by corruption each year, from the top levels to the bottom. Over the years, the government launched more than one 'war on corruption' and they all failed. Why? Because they all started from the bottom up."

So when his father, who has never been tainted by corruption charges during his nearly five decades as governor of Riyadh, ascended to the throne in 2015 (at a time of falling oil prices), he vowed to put a stop to it all, MbS said:

"My father saw that there is no way we can stay in the G-20 and grow with this level of corruption. In early 2015, one of his first orders to his team was to collect all the information about corruption—at the top. This team worked for two years until they collected the most accurate information, and then they came up with about 200 names."

When all the data were ready, the public prosecutor, Saud al-Mojib, took action, MbS said, explaining that each suspected billionaire or prince was arrested and given two choices: "we show them all the files that we have and as soon as they see those about 95 percent agree to a settlement," which means signing over cash or shares of their business to the Saudi state treasury.

"About 1 percent," he added, "are able to prove they are clean and their case is dropped right there. About 4 percent say they are not corrupt and with their lawyers want to go to court. Under Saudi law, the public prosecutor is independent. We cannot interfere with his job—the king can dismiss him, but he is driving the process. . . . We have experts making sure no businesses are bankrupted in the process"—to avoid causing unemployment.

"How much money are they recovering?" I asked.

The public prosecutor says it could eventually "be around $100 billion in settlements," said MbS

There is no way, he added, to root out all corruption from top to the bottom, "So you have to send a signal, and the signal going forward now is, 'You will not escape.' And we are already seeing the impact," like people writing on social media, "I called my middle man and he doesn't answer." Saudi business people who paid bribes to get services done by bureaucrats are not being prosecuted, explained MbS "It's those who shook the money out of the government"—by overcharging and getting kickbacks.

The stakes are high for MbS in this anti-corruption drive. If the public feels that he is truly purging corruption that was sapping the system and doing so in a way that is transparent and makes clear to future Saudi and foreign investors that the rule of law will prevail, it will really instill a lot of new confidence in the system. But if the process ends up feeling arbitrary, bullying and opaque, aimed more at aggregating power for power's sake, and unchecked by any rule of law, it will end up instilling fear that will unnerve Saudi and foreign investors in ways the country can't afford.

But one thing I know for sure: not a single Saudi I spoke to here over three days expressed anything other than effusive support for this anti-corruption drive. The Saudi silent majority is clearly fed up with the injustice of so many princes and billionaires ripping off their country. While foreigners, like me, were inquiring about the legal framework for this operation, the mood among Saudis I spoke with was: "just turn them all upside down, shake the money out of their pockets, and don't stop shaking them until it's all out!"

But guess what? This anti-corruption drive is only the second-most unusual and important initiative launched by MbS. The first is to bring Saudi Islam back to its more open and modern orientation—whence it diverted in 1979. That is, back to what MbS described to a recent global investment conference here as a "moderate, balanced Islam that is open to the world and to all religions and all traditions and peoples."

I know that year well. I started my career as a reporter in the Middle East in Beirut in 1979, and so much of the region that I have covered since was shaped by the three big events of that year: the takeover of the Grand Mosque in Mecca by Saudi puritanical extremists—who denounced the Saudi ruling family as corrupt, impious sellouts to Western values; the Iranian Islamic revolution; and the Soviet invasion of Afghanistan.

These three events together freaked out the Saudi ruling family at the time and prompted it to try to shore up its legitimacy by allowing its Wahhabi clerics to impose a much more austere Islam on the society and by launching a worldwide competition with Iran's ayatollahs over who could export more fundamentalist Islam. It didn't help that the United States tried to leverage this trend by using Islamist fighters against Russia in Afghanistan. In all, it pushed Islam globally way to the right and helped nurture 9/11.

A lawyer by training, who rose up in his family's education-social welfare foundation, MbS is on a mission to bring Saudi Islam back to the center. He has not only curbed the authority of the once feared Saudi religious police to berate a woman for not covering every inch of her skin, he has also let women drive. And unlike any Saudi leader before him, he has taken the hard-liners on ideologically. As one United States—educated 28-year-old Saudi woman told me: MbS "uses a different language. He says, 'We are going to destroy extremism.' He's not sugarcoating. That is reassuring to me that the change is real."

Indeed, MbS instructed me: "Do not write that we are 'reinterpreting' Islam—we are 'restoring' Islam to its origins—and our biggest tools are the Prophet's practices and [daily life in] Saudi Arabia before 1979." At the time of the Prophet Muhammad, he argued, there were musical theaters, there was mixing between men and women, and there was respect for Christians and Jews in Arabia. "The first commercial judge in Medina was a woman!" So if the Prophet embraced all of this, MbS asked, "Do you mean the Prophet was not a Muslim?"

Then one of his ministers got out his cell phone and shared with me pictures and YouTube videos of Saudi Arabia in the 1950s—women without heads covered, wearing skirts and walking with men in public, as well as concerts and cinemas. It was still a traditional and modest place but not one where fun had been outlawed, which is what happened after 1979.

If this virus of an antipluralistic, misogynistic Islam that came out of Saudi Arabia in 1979 can be reversed by Saudi Arabia, it would drive moderation across the Muslim world and surely be welcomed here where 65 percent of the population is under 30.

One middle-age Saudi banker said to me: "my generation was held hostage by 1979. I know now that my kids will not be hostages." Added a 28-year-old Saudi woman social entrepreneur: "Ten years ago when we talked about music in Riyadh, it meant buying a CD—now it is about the concert next month and what ticket are you buying and which of your friends will go with you."

Saudi Arabia would have a very long way to go before it approached anything like Western standards for free speech and women's rights. But as someone who has been coming here for almost 30 years, it blew my mind to learn that you can hear Western classical music concerts in Riyadh now, that country singer Toby Keith held a men-only concert here in September, where he even sang with a Saudi, and that Lebanese soprano Hiba Tawaji will be among the first woman singers to perform a women-only concert here on December 6. And MbS told me, it was just decided that women will be able to go to stadiums and attend soccer games. The Saudi clerics have completely acquiesced.

The Saudi education minister chimed in that among a broad set of education reforms, he's redoing and digitizing all textbooks, sending 1,700 Saudi teachers each year to world-class schools in places like Finland to upgrade their skills, announcing that for the first time Saudi girls will have physical education classes in public schools and this year adding an hour to the Saudi school day for kids to explore their passions in science and social issues, under a teacher's supervision, with their own projects.

So many of these reforms were so long overdue it's ridiculous. Better late than never, though.

On foreign policy, MbS would not discuss the strange goings on with Prime Minister Saad Hariri of Lebanon coming to Saudi Arabia and announcing his resignation, seemingly under Saudi pressure, and now returning to Beirut and rescinding that resignation. He simply insisted that the bottom line of the whole affair is that Hariri, a Sunni Muslim, is not going to continue providing political cover for a Lebanese government that is essentially controlled by the Lebanese Shiite Hezbollah militia, which is essentially controlled by Tehran.

He insisted that the Saudi-backed war in Yemen, which has been a humanitarian nightmare, was tilting in the direction of the pro-Saudi legitimate government there, which he said is now in control of 85 percent of the country, but given the fact that pro-Iranian Houthi rebels, who hold the rest, launched a missile at Riyadh airport, anything less than 100 percent is still problematic.

His general view seemed to be that with the backing of the Trump administration—he praised President Trump as "the right person at the right time"—the Saudis and their Arab allies were slowly building a coalition to stand up to Iran. I am skeptical. The dysfunction and rivalries within the Sunni Arab world generally have prevented forming a unified front up to now, which is why Iran indirectly controls four Arab capitals today—Damascus, Sana, Baghdad, and Beirut. That Iranian overreach is one reason

MbS was scathing about Iran's supreme leader, Ayatollah Ali Khamenei.

Iran's "supreme leader is the new Hitler of the Middle East," said MbS "But we learned from Europe that appeasement doesn't work. We don't want the new Hitler in Iran to repeat what happened in Europe in the Middle East." What matters most, though, is what Saudi Arabia does at home to build its strength and economy.

But can MBS and his team see this through? Again, I make no predictions. He has his flaws that he will have to control, insiders here tell me. They include relying on a very tight circle of advisers who don't always challenge him sufficiently and a tendency to start too many things that don't get finished. There's a whole list. But guess what? Perfect is not on the menu here. Someone had to do this job—wrench Saudi Arabia into the 21st century—and MbS stepped up. I, for one, am rooting for him to succeed in his reform efforts.

And so are a lot of young Saudis. There was something a 30-year-old Saudi woman social entrepreneur said to me that stuck in my ear. "We are privileged to be the generation that has seen the before and the after." The previous generation of Saudi women, she explained, could never imagine a day when a woman could drive and the coming generation will never be able to imagine a day when a woman couldn't.

"But I will always remember not being able to drive," she told me. And the fact that starting in June that will never again be so "gives me so much hope. It proves to me that anything is possible—that this is a time of opportunity. We have seen things change and we are young enough to make the transition."

This reform push is giving the youth here a new pride in their country, almost a new identity, which many of them clearly relish. Being a Saudi student in post-9/11 America, young Saudis confess, is to always feel you are being looked at as a potential terrorist or someone who comes from a country locked in the Stone Age.

Now they have a young leader who is driving religious and economic reform, who talks the language of high tech, and whose biggest sin may be that he wants to go too fast. Most ministers are now in their 40s—and not 60s. And with the suffocating hand of a puritanical Islam being lifted, it's giving them a chance to think afresh about their country and their identity as Saudis.

"We need to restore our culture to what it was before the [Islamic] radical culture took over," a Saudi woman friend who works with an NGO said to me. "We have 13 regions in this country, and they each have a different cuisine. But nobody knows that. Did you know that? But I never saw one Saudi dish go global. It is time for us to embrace who we are and who we were."

Alas, who Saudi Arabia is also includes a large cohort of older, more rural, more traditional Saudis, and pulling them into the 21st century will be a challenge. But that's in part why every senior bureaucrat is working crazy hours now. They know MbS can call them on the phone at any of those hours to find out if something he wanted done is getting done. I told him his work habits reminded me of a line in the play "Hamilton," when the chorus asks: why does he always work like "he's running out of time."

"Because," said MbS, "I fear that the day I die I am going to die without accomplishing what I have in my mind. Life is too short and a lot of things can happen, and I am really keen to see it with my own eyes—and that is why I am in a hurry."

THOMAS L. FRIEDMAN is a longtime Pulitzer Prize winning American author.

Freedom House

Freedom in the World 2018: Democracy in Crisis

Overview

Saudi Arabia's absolute monarchy restricts almost all political rights and civil liberties. No officials at the national level are elected. The regime relies on extensive surveillance, the criminalization of dissent, appeals to sectarianism, and public spending supported by oil revenues to maintain power. Women and religious minorities face extensive discrimination in law and in practice. Working conditions for the large expatriate labor force are often exploitative.

. . .

Executive Summary

Mohammad bin Salman, the son of King Salman bin Abdulaziz al-Saud, continued to fortify his personal authority during 2017. He had been deputy crown prince since 2015, while also serving as defense minister and holding a number of other official posts, but in June 2017, he engineered the ouster of Mohammad bin Nayef—a nephew of the king—as interior minister and replaced him as crown prince. Several months later, after agreeing to lead a committee charged with rooting out corruption in the Kingdom, Mohammad bin Salman ordered the house arrest of scores of wealthy officials, businessmen, and rival members of the royal family. Those detained were forced to turn over billions of dollars in assets to the state.

The crown prince also ordered a crackdown on popular preachers and reform advocates in September. These arrests, which cut across the country's political spectrum, indicated that the Kingdom's leaders had little interest in political change, despite the announcement of modest plans to ease some social controls, such as the ban on women driving.

Authorities continued to repress and discriminate against minority Shiite Muslim communities in 2017, and the Kingdom escalated its aggressive foreign policy, leading a regional effort to isolate and blockade Qatar over its comparatively warm relations with Iran and the Muslim Brotherhood. Saudi Arabia also persisted in its almost three-year-old campaign against rebel forces in Yemen, which has had a devastating effect on Yemeni civilians.

Political Rights: 0/40 (–3)

Electoral Process: 0/12

A1. Was the current head of government or other chief national authority elected through free and fair elections? 0/4

Saudi Arabia's king is chosen by internal agreement among the ruling al-Saud family. The king rules for life. In June 2017, Mohammad bin Nayef was replaced as crown prince and put under house arrest by his younger cousin, Mohammad bin Salman, until then the deputy crown prince. The cabinet, which is appointed by the king, passes legislation that becomes law once ratified by royal decree.

A2. Were the current national legislative representatives elected through free and fair elections? 0/4

The king appoints the 150 members of the Majlis al-Shura (consultative council), who serve in an advisory capacity, for four-year terms. The council has no legislative authority.

Limited nonpartisan elections for advisory councils at the municipal level were introduced in 2005. In the 2015 elections, $2/3$ of the seats on the 284 councils were open to voting, while the minister of municipal and rural affairs held responsibility for filling the remainder through appointment. Women were allowed to vote and run as candidates for the first time.

A3. Are the electoral laws and framework fair, and are they implemented impartially by the relevant election management bodies? 0/4

The electoral framework lacks constitutional protections, and the 2015 elections for municipal councils were subject to a number of onerous restrictions. The Kingdom's rules on gender segregation were applied to campaigns, meaning no candidates could produce posters showing their faces or meet in person with voters of the opposite sex. Candidates were also barred from giving media interviews, leading many to campaign via social media. A number of candidates were disqualified for unclear reasons, though some were reinstated after appeals. Ultimately only a small fraction of the citizen population participated in the elections, reflecting doubts about the effectiveness of the advisory councils.

Political Pluralism and Participation: 0/16

B1. Do the people have the right to organize in different political parties or other competitive political groupings of their choice, and is the system free of undue obstacles to the rise and fall of these competing parties or groupings? 0/4

Political parties are forbidden, and political dissent is effectively criminalized. In September 2017, the authorities carried out a wave of arrests targeting some of the country's most prominent political rights organizations and activists, including founding members of the banned Saudi Civil and Political Rights Association. Many other political activists continued to serve lengthy prison sentences during the year.

B2. Is there a realistic opportunity for the opposition to increase its support or gain power through elections? 0/4

The Muslim Brotherhood, a Sunni Islamist political organization, and Hezbollah, the Lebanon-based and Iranian-backed Shiite militia group, are designated as terrorist organizations in Saudi Arabia. Other groups and individuals who criticize the regime or call for political reform—whether Sunni or Shiite, Islamist or secularist—are subject to arbitrary detention. Many of those arrested in the crackdown that began in September 2017 had questioned or declined to vocally support the government's campaign to isolate Qatar over its relations with the Muslim Brotherhood and Iran. These included prominent reformist clerics such as Salman al-Awdah and Awad al-Qarni.

B3. Are the people's political choices free from domination by the military, foreign powers, religious hierarchies, economic oligarchies, or any other powerful group that is not democratically accountable? 0/4

The monarchy generally excludes the public from any meaningful political participation. In the absence of political parties, voters in Saudi Arabia's limited municipal elections are heavily influenced by tribal and religious leaders, many of whom benefit from close ties to the ruling establishment.

B4. Do various segments of the population (including ethnic, religious, gender, LGBT, and other relevant groups) have full political rights and electoral opportunities? 0/4

Although political rights are curtailed for all of the Kingdom's citizens, women, religious minorities, and lesbian, gay, bisexual, and transgender (LGBT) people face additional obstacles to participation given the Kingdom's strict laws on matters such as gender segregation and its intolerance of religious groups that deviate from Wahhabism, a highly conservative and literalist interpretation of Sunni Islam. Some 30 women serve on the appointed Majlis al-Shura, and women secured about 1 percent of the seats in the 2015 municipal council elections. Shiites reportedly hold a small number of seats on the Majlis al-Shura and many seats on municipal councils in Shiite-majority areas. Women and religious minorities are mostly excluded from leadership positions in the government.

Noncitizens, who make up roughly a third of the population in Saudi Arabia, have no political rights, and citizenship can only be directly transmitted by a citizen father whose marriage is recognized by the state.

Functioning of Government: 1/12

C1. Do the freely elected head of government and national legislative representatives determine the policies of the government? 0/4

The Kingdom's only elected officials serve on local advisory councils and have little or no influence over national laws and policies.

C2. Are safeguards against official corruption strong and effective? 1/4

Corruption remains a significant problem. Although the government generates massive revenue from the sale of oil, which it redistributes through social welfare programs and as patronage, little is known about state accounting or the various direct ways in which public wealth becomes a source of private privilege for the royal family and its clients.

Crown Prince Mohammed bin Salman was appointed to lead a new anti-corruption committee in November 2017, ostensibly tasked with investigating abuses by royal family members and high-ranking officials. However, he quickly ordered the detention of more than 200 people without any apparent due process, and many were coerced into turning over billions of dollars in assets to the state. The crown prince's campaign coincided with a crackdown on dissent and targeted potential rivals such as Prince Mutaib bin Abdullah, until then the head of the powerful National Guard, leading observers to suggest that the anti-corruption drive was in fact part of a broader effort to consolidate the crown prince's political and economic control over the country.

C3. Does the government operate with openness and transparency? 0/4

The functioning of government is largely opaque. There is no transparency on whether or how the state funds are disbursed, or on the internal decision-making process that allocates them, and there is no public mechanism for holding senior decision makers accountable. The state's oil revenues make up the vast majority of its financial resources, but these are tightly controlled by the royal family, which uses the same income to support itself.

Additional Discretionary Political Rights Question

Is the government or occupying power deliberately changing the ethnic composition of a country or territory so as to destroy a culture or tip the political balance in favor of another group? –1/0 (–1)

The government has long sought to suppress Shiite religious and cultural identity, associating it with Iran and regarding it as a threat to the regime's official Sunni and Wahhabi underpinnings. Systemic discrimination has stoked periodic protests in Shiite-majority areas, and the authorities have responded with harsh and often arbitrary security measures. In 2017, this included a decision to demolish a historic neighborhood in the town of Awamiya, near the city of Qatif in Eastern Province. The effort, which began in May and entailed the eviction of thousands of residents, prompted armed resistance and an extended siege. An unknown number of security

personnel, militants, and civilians were killed or injured in the clashes as demolitions proceeded.

Civil Liberties: 7/60

Freedom of Expression and Belief: 3/16

D1. Are there free and independent media? 0/4

The government controls domestic media content and dominates regional print and satellite-television coverage. A 2011 royal decree amended the press law to criminalize, among other things, any criticism of the country's grand mufti, the Council of Senior Religious Scholars, or government officials; violations can result in fines and forced closure of media outlets. All blogs and websites, or anyone posting news or commentary online, must have a license from the Ministry of Information or face fines and possible closure of the website.

In January 2017, a criminal court sentenced journalist Nadhir al-Majid to seven years in prison, a subsequent seven-year travel ban, and a large fine for writing in support of the right to protest in 2011. Another journalist, Sami al-Thubaiti, was arrested in September and held without charge amid the authorities' larger spate of detentions. As part of the diplomatic confrontation with neighboring Qatar, Saudi authorities blocked Qatari news sites in May and demanded in June that Qatar shut down the television network Al-Jazeera and other Qatari-funded outlets, which have often been critical of Riyadh.

D2. Are individuals free to practice and express their religious faith or nonbelief in public and private? 0/4

The 1992 Basic Law declares that the Koran and the Sunna are the country's constitution. Islam is the official religion, and all Saudis are required by law to be Muslims. A 2014 royal decree punishes atheism with up to 20 years in prison. The government prohibits the public practice of any religion other than Islam and restricts the religious practices of the Shiite and Sufi Muslim minority sects. The construction of Shiite mosques is constrained through licensing rules and prohibited outside of Eastern Province, where most Shiites live.

Although the government recognizes the right of non-Muslims to worship in private, it does not always respect this right in practice.

Online commentary that touches on religion can be harshly punished. In April 2017, an appeals court upheld a 2015 death sentence for Ahmad al-Shamri who was charged with apostasy for renouncing Islam on social media.

D3. Is there academic freedom, and is the educational system free from extensive political indoctrination? 1/4

Academic freedom is restricted, and informers monitor classrooms for compliance with curriculum rules, including a ban on teaching secular philosophy and religions other than Islam. Despite changes to textbooks in recent years, intolerance in the classroom remains a significant problem, as some educators continue to espouse discriminatory and hateful views of non-Muslims and Muslim minority sects.

D4. Are individuals free to express their personal views on political or other sensitive topics without fear of surveillance or retribution? 2/4

Saudis are able to engage in some degree of private discussion on political and other topics, including criticism of certain aspects of government performance, both online and off-line. However, severe criminal penalties deter more direct criticism of the regime and free discussion on topics like religion or the royal family.

Associational and Organizational Rights: 0/12

E1. Is there freedom of assembly? 0/4

Freedom of assembly is not respected, and the government has imposed harsh punishments on those who lead or participated in public protests. Ali Mohammed al-Nimr, arrested at age 17 in 2012 for participating in protests in Eastern Province, faced execution in 2017, but his sentence had yet to be carried out at year's end. He was the nephew of Sheikh Nimr al-Nimr, a prominent Shiite cleric and political dissident who was also arrested in 2012 and then executed in 2016 for leading anti-government demonstrations and calling for an end to sectarian discrimination.

E2. Is there freedom for nongovernmental organizations, particularly those that are engaged in human rights—and governance-related work? 0/4

Nongovernmental organizations must obtain a license from the government to operate. Until the adoption of a law on the topic in 2015, officials had approved licenses only for charitable groups. Reformist organizations have reportedly been denied licenses in practice, in some cases through

arbitrary delays. Human rights activists and other civil society representatives face regular harassment and detention by Saudi authorities; a number of prominent activists were serving lengthy prison sentences during 2017.

E3. Is there freedom for trade unions and similar professional or labor organizations? 0/4

No laws protect the rights to form independent labor unions, bargain collectively, or engage in strikes. Workers who engage in union activity are subject to dismissal or detention. In January 2017, a court reportedly sentenced dozens of foreign construction workers who had protested over unpaid wages in 2016 to lashings and jail terms ranging from 45 days to 4 months.

Rule of Law: 2/16

F1. Is there an independent judiciary? 1/4

The judiciary has very little independence in practice. Judges are appointed by the king and overseen by the Supreme Judicial Council, whose chairman is also the justice minister. A special commission of judicial experts issues opinions that serve as guidelines for judges on the interpretation of Sharia (Islamic law), which forms the basis of Saudi law.

F2. Does due process prevail in civil and criminal matters? 1/4

Defendants' rights are poorly protected by law. Detainees are often denied access to legal counsel during interrogation, and lengthy pretrial detention and detention without charge are common.

An antiterrorism law that took effect in 2014 includes lengthy prison sentences for criticizing the monarchy or the government. Among other provisions, it expanded the power of police to conduct raids targeting suspected antigovernment activity without judicial approval.

F3. Is there protection from the illegitimate use of physical force and freedom from war and insurgencies? 0/4

Allegations of torture by police and prison officials are common, and access to prisoners by independent human rights and legal organizations is limited. Corporal punishment, most often lashing, is common in criminal sentencing. Capital punishment is applied to a wide range of crimes other than murder; juvenile offenders are not exempt from the penalty.

Saudi authorities typically carry out well over 100 executions each year.

Terrorism remains a serious threat. In January 2017, two pairs of fighters affiliated with the Islamic State militant group were killed in confrontations with security forces in Riyadh and Jeddah. Authorities also faced armed clashes with Shiite militants in Eastern Province and cross-border attacks by rebel forces in Yemen. Yemeni rebels fired ballistic missiles that fell near Riyadh in November and December, though they caused little damage.

F4. Do laws, policies, and practices guarantee equal treatment of various segments of the population? 0/4

The courts engage in routine discrimination against various groups, citing their interpretations of Sharia. A woman's testimony is generally given half the weight of a man's, and the testimony of anyone other than observant Sunni Muslims can be disregarded by judges.

Shiites, who make up 10–15 percent of the population, face socioeconomic disadvantages, discrimination in employment, and underrepresentation in government positions and the security forces.

Education and economic rights for Saudi women have improved somewhat in recent years, but they are still subject to extensive legal and societal discrimination, most notably through the guardianship system, in which every woman must rely on a close male relative to approve basic activities. For example, employers often require women to obtain their guardians' permission to work.

Personal Autonomy and Individual Rights: 2/16

G1. Do individuals enjoy freedom of movement, including the ability to change their place of residence, employment, or education? 0/4

The government punishes activists and critics by limiting their ability to travel outside the country, and reform advocates are routinely stripped of their passports.

Gender segregation restricts freedom of movement for both men and women, but male guardianship and other factors impose especially onerous constraints on women. In September 2017, the king announced that women would be permitted to drive by mid-2018, eliminating a long-standing ban. A month later, the government said that beginning in 2018, women would also be allowed to attend sporting events in stadiums.

G2. Are individuals able to exercise the right to own property and establish private businesses without undue interference from state or nonstate actors? 1/4

While a great deal of business activity in the Kingdom is dominated by or connected to members of the government, the ruling family, or other elite families, officials have given assurances that special industrial and commercial zones are free from interference by the royal family.

Women require permission from a male guardian to obtain business licenses. Women also face legal discrimination regarding property rights, with daughters typically receiving half the inheritance awarded to sons.

G3. Do individuals enjoy personal social freedoms, including choice of marriage partner and size of family, protection from domestic violence, and control over appearance? 0/4

The religious police enforce rules governing gender segregation and personal attire. A 2016 government decree revoked their authority to arrest suspects or ask for their identification, but they were still empowered to report violations to the ordinary police.

There are a number of official restrictions on marriage. For example, Muslim women may not marry non-Muslims, citizens typically require permission to marry noncitizens, and men are barred from marrying women from certain countries. All sexual activity outside of marriage, including same-sex activity, is criminalized, and the death penalty can be applied in certain circumstances. Women face legal disadvantages in divorce and custody proceedings.

A 2013 law broadly defined and criminalized domestic abuse, prescribing fines and up to a year in prison for perpetrators. However, enforcement remains problematic, with some officials allegedly prioritizing privacy and family integrity over safety and justice for victims.

G4. Do individuals enjoy equality of opportunity and freedom from economic exploitation? 1/4

A number of amendments to the labor law that went into effect in 2015 granted broader rights and protections to workers in the private sector. However, the labor law does not apply to household workers who are governed by separate regulations that provide fewer safeguards against exploitative working conditions.

Foreign workers—who make up more than half of the active labor force—enjoy only limited legal protections and remain vulnerable to trafficking and forced labor, primarily through employers' exploitation of the *kafala* visa-sponsorship system. In 2014, the Ministry of Labor ruled that expatriate workers who are not paid their salaries for more than three consecutive months are free to switch their work sponsors without approval. In practice, foreign workers are subject to periodic mass deportations for visa violations or criminal activity, though due process is often lacking in such cases. Government programs give preferential treatment to companies that hire certain percentages of Saudi citizens and penalize those who fail to meet such targets.

FREEDOM HOUSE is a U.S.-based independent watchdog organization dedicated to the expansion of freedom and democracy around the world.

EXPLORING THE ISSUE

Is Saudi Arabia Moving toward Increased Democratization and/or Liberalization?

Critical Thinking and Reflection

1. How does Saudi Arabia's history impact debates about its future today?
2. What are some of the difficulties the Kingdom might face in implementing both the economic and social reforms proposed?
3. How might Saudi Arabia convince the world that it is not the caricature often put forward in popular media and that it is an appealing investment opportunity?
4. What role should political reforms play in debates about Saudi Arabia's future?
5. How should the United States and other partner countries work with Saudi Arabia as it navigates this reform agenda?

Is There Common Ground?

Among analysts of Saudi Arabia, there is general agreement that Crown Prince Mohammed bin Salman (MbS) has put forward a bold economic and social reform agenda and that the Kingdom would benefit from these kinds of change. The questions that remain, and which are debated today, are (a) whether these reforms will actually work and (b) whether the Kingdom be able to successfully put into place such sweeping changes without causing significant social upheaval. On the economic side, there is agreement that a primarily oil-based economy is not sustainable in the long run, as oil prices continue to fluctuate, clean energy gains traction and gets cheaper, and the oil simply begins to run out. The economic reform targets are bold, and there is serious debate about whether the country will be able to meet them. Economic diversification, especially after decades of living off of oil, is difficult to do. Socially, observers generally agree that loosening restrictions, especially on women, is a positive step. Debate remains, however, about how far MbS is willing to go and how much the conservative religious establishment is willing to support. Finally, there is little disagreement about the fact that MbS has thus far not proposed comparable political reforms; the question that remains is whether the Saudi people will begin to increasingly advocate in that realm as well.

Additional Resources

Diamond, Larry Jay, Plattner, Marc F., and Walker, Christopher, "Saudi Arabia's Anxious Aristocrats,' Chapter 6, *Authoritarian Goes Global: The Challenge to Democracy*, Johns Hopkins University Press. 2016.

Damianou, Alex, "Navigating the Saudi Road to Success," The Atlantic Council February 7, 2018.

Gardner, David, "Saudi Arabia's reform drive is bold, yet fraught with risk," *Financial Times*. December 27, 2017.

Human Rights Watch, "Saudi Arabia: Repression Overshadows Women's Reforms." January 18, 2018.

Kinninmont, Jane, *Vision 2030 and Saudi Arabia Social Contract: Austerity and Transformation*, Middle East and North Africa Program, Chatham House, The Royal Institute of International Affairs (2017).

Meijer, Roel and Aarts, Paul, editors, *Saudi Arabia Between Conservatism, Accommodation and Reform*, Netherlands Institute of International Relations (2012).

Nolan, Leigh, "Managing Reform? Saudi Arabia and the King's Dilemma," Policy Briefing, Brookings Doha Center (May 2011).

Young, Karen E., "The Coming Economic Disorder: The Political Perils of Economic Liberalization in the Gulf," *Arab Gulf States Institute in Washington*. September 14, 2017.

Internet References . . .

Freedom House

https://freedomhouse.org

Government of Saudi Arabia

Saudi-gov.sa

Kingdom of Saudi Arabia Vision 2030

http://vision2030.gov.sa/en

National democratic Institute

https://www.ndiorg/middle-east-and-north-africa/saudi-Arabia

ISSUE

Selected, Edited, and with Issue Framing Material by:
Mark Owen Lombardi, *Maryville University*

Is Artificial Intelligence a Threat to Humanity?

YES: Tim Adams, from "Artificial Intelligence: 'We're like Children Playing with a Bomb,'" *The Guardian* (2016)

NO: Max Tegmark, from "Benefits and Risks of Artificial Intelligence," *Future of Life Institute* (2018)

Learning Outcomes

After reading this issue, you will be able to:

- Understand the growing emergence of artificial intelligence as a force in our daily lives.
- Evaluate both the potential positive and negative consequences of the development of AI.
- Appreciate the short-term ramification of AI for human interaction and economics.
- Speculate as to its potential impact as it evolves and expands.

ISSUE SUMMARY

YES: Tim Adams is relaying the thoughts of Oxford philosopher Nick Bostrom who contends that AI represents an existential threat to humanity because it will develop the ability to replicate human intelligence and learn at a much faster rate than humans. Without morality and judgment, AI will pose a direct threat to humanity.

NO: Max Tegmark, an MIT professor, contends that AI can and will be a great boon for humanity and will be shaped by its ability to problem solve and not by some myth regarding its own capacity to "turn on" humanity at some point.

Ever since the advent of the computer chip, the specter of computerized robots and "super-machines" with conscious often malicious intent has tantalized science fiction writers and moviemakers. The notion of robots created to serve humankind running amok and becoming a threat has been part of the collective consciousness for over 50 years. Perhaps, the best example of this is the highly successful *Terminator* franchise. Putting the fiction and exciting drama aside, it is safe to say we have now entered the age of what scientists call artificial intelligence (AI). Simply stated, AI refers to "the development of computer systems that are able to perform tasks normally relegated to human beings including visual perception, speech recognition, decision-making, and language translation" (Webster's 2018).

Beginning in this century, the age of AI is here and growing rapidly. Human beings might be shocked at the amount of interaction that they have with AI in a variety of functions of daily life including shopping, education, finance, health, and safety. In fact, if you are living in the postindustrial Western world, it is likely that you interact with AI on a daily basis. If you are online, that interaction is minute to minute. If you google or amazon, it is constant.

The technology behind AI is complicated, but the premise is as simple as it is revolutionary. By collecting a comprehensive set of data on human behavior across the widest possible array of activities, you can construct an AI system that can replicate that behavior and thought process at least up to a certain point. That is where we are at in today's science. Some of the best examples of this include computers playing chess or solving a Rubics cube or other such demonstrations. By analyzing all of the potential moves of a game of chess, AI can calculate moves and those of its human opponent to plot the best strategy and ostensibly win. Also, AI can do it at a greatly accelerated rate than the human brain. In the past few years, AI systems have become more sophisticated in how they are able to play games, calculate strategies including engaging in game manipulation and what we as humans would call three-dimensional thinking.

The best examples of these AI systems can be found in military usage as well as in the highest levels of the corporate sector where research and data analytics have led to some sophisticated applications.

If these examples are taken and expanded to much more complex systems, the possibilities for calculated thought and reasoning are expanded for AI and that is where the "crossover point" comes into play. Various scholars and pioneers in AI believe that this development is the most profound evolution in human history including the introduction of the computer chip. Some believe that AI is now on a path where it will achieve some kind

of separate consciousness during this century and subsequently may turn on humanity (e.g., Elon Musk). One warning sign of this was in the recent use of chat bots by Facebook. Two separate chat bots utilized on Facebook began to interact with one another and quickly developed their own language in which their human programmers could not understand. Facebook subsequently shut down the bots for fear of losing control. Others believe that AI is a tool like any other to be mastered and harnessed and thoughts of it turning on us are fantasy (e.g., Mark Zuckerberg).

What is agreed upon is that the next stage as theorized by futurists like Mishiro Kaku, Stephen Hawking, and others is an AI system that can fully replicate the human mind. They argue that we are close to creating a system that can think, respond to stimuli, make judgments, and initiate actions but at a rate far faster than the human brain can process. It is at this point that some futurists believe that AI may achieve some kind of consciousness and make evaluations of human interaction and the human race in general.

Adams certainly believes that as humans we are playing with fire with AI and we must stop and review protocols and be aware that we may be sowing the seeds of our own destruction. Tegmark is less alarmist in his analysis but does caution prudence as we move forward into this new world of computerized thinking.

YES ↵

Tim Adams

Artificial Intelligence: 'We're Like Children Playing with a Bomb'

Sentient machines are a greater threat to humanity than climate change, according to Oxford Philosopher Nick Bostrom.

You'll find the Future of Humanity Institute down a medieval backstreet in the center of Oxford. It is beside St. Ebbe's church, which has stood on this site since 1005, and above a Pure Gym, which opened in April. The institute, a research faculty of Oxford University, was established a decade ago to ask the very biggest questions on our behalf. Notably: what exactly are the "existential risks" that threaten the future of our species; how do we measure them; and what can we do to prevent them? Or to put it another way: in a world of multiple fears, what precisely should we be most terrified of?

When I arrive to meet the director of the institute, Professor Nick Bostrom, a bed is being delivered to the second-floor office. Existential risk is a round-the-clock kind of operation; it sleeps fitfully, if at all.

Bostrom, a 43-year-old Swedish-born philosopher, has lately acquired something of the status of prophet of doom among those currently doing most to shape our civilization: the tech billionaires of Silicon Valley. His reputation rests primarily on his book *Superintelligence: Paths, Dangers, Strategies*, which was a surprise *New York Times* best seller last year and now arrives in paperback, trailing must-read recommendations from Bill Gates and Tesla's Elon Musk. (In the best kind of literary review, Musk also gave Bostrom's institute £1 million to continue to pursue its inquiries.)

The book is a lively, speculative examination of the singular threat that Bostrom believes—after years of calculation and argument—to be the one most likely to wipe us out. This threat is not climate change, nor pandemic, nor nuclear winter; it is the possibly imminent creation of a general machine intelligence greater than our own.

The cover of Bostrom's book is dominated by a mad-eyed, pen-and-ink picture of an owl. The owl is the subject of the book's opening parable. A group of sparrows are building their nests. "We are all so small and weak," tweets one, feebly. "Imagine how easy life would be if we had an owl who could help us build our nests!" There is general twittering agreement among sparrows everywhere; an owl could defend the sparrows! It could look after their old and their young! It could allow them to live a life of leisure and prosperity! With these fantasies in mind, the sparrows can hardly contain their excitement and fly off in search of the swivel-headed savior who will transform their existence.

There is only one voice of dissent: "Scronkfinkle, a one-eyed sparrow with a fretful temperament, was unconvinced of the wisdom of the endeavor. Quoth he: 'This will surely be our undoing. Should we not give some thought to the art of owl-domestication and owl-taming first, before we bring such a creature into our midst?'" His warnings, inevitably, fall on deaf sparrow ears. Owl-taming would be complicated; why not get the owl first and work out the fine details later? Bostrom's book, which is a shrill alarm call about the darker implications of AI, is dedicated to Scronkfinkle.

Bostrom articulates his own warnings in a suitably fretful manner. He has a reputation for obsessiveness and for workaholism; he is slim, pale, and semi-nocturnal, often staying in the office into the early hours. Not surprisingly, perhaps, for a man whose days are dominated by whiteboards filled with formulae expressing the relative merits of 57 varieties of apocalypse, he appears to leave as little as possible to chance. In place of meals, he favors a green-smoothie elixir involving vegetables, fruit, oat milk, and whey powder. Other interviewers have remarked on his avoidance of handshakes to guard against infection. He does proffer a hand to me, but I have the sense he is subsequently isolating it to disinfect when I have gone. There is, perhaps as a result, a slight impatience about him, which he tries hard to resist.

In his book, he talks about the "intelligence explosion" that will occur when machines much cleverer than us begin to design machines of their own. "Before the prospect of an intelligence explosion, we humans are like small children playing with a bomb," he writes. "We have little idea when the detonation will occur, though if we hold the device to our ear we can hear a faint ticking sound." Talking to Bostrom, you have a feeling that for him that faint ticking never completely goes away.

We speak first about the success of his book, the way it has squarely hit a nerve. It coincided with the open letter signed by more than 1,000 eminent scientists—including Stephen Hawking, Apple cofounder Steve Wozniak and Musk—and presented at last year's International Joint Conference on Artificial Intelligence, urging a ban on the use and development of fully autonomous weapons (the "killer robots" of science fiction that are very close to reality). Bostrom, who is both aware of his own capacities and modest about his influence, suggests it was a happy accident of timing.

"Machine learning and deep learning [the pioneering 'neural' computer algorithms that most closely mimic human brain function] have over the last few years moved much faster than people anticipated," he says. "That is certainly one of the reasons why this has become such a big topic just now. People can see things moving forward in the technical field, and they become concerned about what next."

Bostrom sees those implications as potentially Darwinian. If we create a machine intelligence superior to our own, and then give it freedom to grow and learn through access to the Internet, there is no reason to suggest that it will not evolve strategies to secure its dominance, just as in the biological world. He sometimes uses the example of humans and gorillas to describe the subsequent one-sided relationship and—as last month's events in Cincinnati Zoo highlighted—that is never going to end well. An inferior intelligence will always depend on a superior one for its survival.

There are times, as Bostrom unfolds various scenarios in *Superintelligence*, when it appears he has been reading too much of the science fiction he professes to dislike. One projection involves an AI system eventually building covert "nanofactories producing nerve gas or target-seeking mosquito-like robots [which] might then burgeon forth simultaneously from every square meter

of the globe" in order to destroy meddling and irrelevant humanity. Another, perhaps more credible vision, sees the superintelligence "hijacking political processes, subtly manipulating financial markets, biasing information flows, or hacking human-made weapons systems" to bring about the extinction.

Does he think of himself as a prophet?

He smiles. "Not so much. It is not that I believe I know how it is going to happen and have to tell the world that information. It is more I feel quite ignorant and very confused about these things but by working for many years on probabilities you can get partial little insights here and there. And if you add those together with insights many other people might have, then maybe it will build up to some better understanding."

Bostrom came to these questions by way of the transhumanist movement, which tends to view the digital age as one of unprecedented potential for optimizing our physical and mental capacities and transcending the limits of our mortality. Bostrom still sees those possibilities as the best case scenario in the superintelligent future, in which we will harness technology to overcome disease and illness, feed the world, create a utopia of fulfilling creativity, and perhaps eventually overcome death. He has been identified in the past as a member of Alcor, the cryogenic initiative that promises to freeze mortal remains in the hope that, one day, minds can be reinvigorated and uploaded in digital form to live in perpetuity. He is coy about this when I ask directly what he has planned.

"I have a policy of never commenting on my funeral arrangements," he says.

But he thinks there is a value in cryogenic research?

"It seems a pretty rational thing for people to do if they can afford it," he says. "When you think about what life in the quite near future could be like, trying to store the information in your brain seems like a conservative option as opposed to burning the brain down and throwing it away. Unless you are really confident that the information will never be useful . . . ."

I wonder at what point his transhumanist optimism gave way to his more nightmarish visions of superintelligence. He suggests that he has not really shifted his position, but that he holds the two possibilities—the heaven and hell of our digital future—in uneasy opposition.

"I wrote a lot about human enhancement ethics in the mid-90s, when it was largely rejected by academics," he says. "They were always like, 'Why on earth would anyone want to cure aging?' They would talk about overpopulation and the boredom of living longer. There was no recognition that this is why we do any medical research: to extend life. Similarly with cognitive enhancement—if you look at what I was writing then, it looks more on the optimistic side—but all along I was concerned with existential risks too."

There seems an abiding unease that such enhancements—pills that might make you smarter, or slow down aging—go against the natural order of things. Does he have a sense of that?

"I'm not sure that I would ever equate natural with good," he says. "Cancer is natural, war is natural, parasites eating your insides are natural. What is natural is therefore never a very useful concept to figure out what we should do. Yes, there are ethical considerations, but you have to judge them on a case-by-case basis. You must remember I am a transhumanist. I want my life extension pill now. And if there were a pill that could improve my cognition by 10 percent, I would be willing to pay a lot for that."

Has he tried the ones that claim to enhance concentration?

"I have, but not very much. I drink coffee, I have nicotine chewing gum, but that is about it. But the only reason I don't do more is that I am not yet convinced that anything else works."

He is not afraid of trying. When working, he habitually sits in the corner of his office surrounded by a dozen lamps, apparently in thrall to the idea of illumination.

Bostrom grew up as an only child in the coastal Swedish town of Helsingborg. Like many gifted children, he loathed school. His father worked for an investment bank, his mother for a Swedish corporation. He doesn't remember any discussion of philosophy—or art or books—around the dinner table. Wondering how he found himself obsessed with these large questions, I ask if he was an anxious child: Did he always have a powerful sense of mortality?

"I think I had it quite early on," he says. "Not because I was on the brink of death or anything. But as a child, I remember thinking a lot that my parents may be healthy now but they are not always going to be stronger or bigger than me."

That thought kept him awake at nights?

"I don't remember it as anxiety, more as a melancholy sense."

And was that ongoing desire to live forever rooted there too?

"Not necessarily. I don't think that there is any particularly different desire that I have in that regard to anyone else. I don't want to come down with colon cancer—who does? If I was alive for 500 years who knows how I would feel? It is not so much fixated on immortality, just that premature death seems prima facie bad."

A good deal of his book asks questions of how we might make superintelligence—whether it comes in 50 years or 500 years—"nice," congruent with our humanity. Bostrom sees this as a technical challenge more than a political or philosophical one. It seems to me, though, that a good deal of our own ethical framework, our sense of goodness, is based on an experience and understanding of suffering, of our bodies. How could a noncellular intelligence ever "comprehend" that?

"There are a lot of things that machines can't understand currently because they are not that smart," he says, "but once they become so, I don't think there would be any special difficulty in understanding human suffering and death." That understanding might be one way they could be taught to respect human value, he says. "But it depends what your ethical theory is. It might be more about respecting others' autonomy or striving to achieve beautiful things together." Somehow,

and he has no idea how really, he thinks those things will need to be hardwired from the outset to avoid catastrophe. It is no good getting your owl first then wondering how to train it. And with artificial systems already superior to the best human intelligence in many discrete fields, a conversation about how that might be done is already overdue.

The sense of intellectual urgency about these questions derives in part from what Bostrom calls an "epiphany experience," which occurred when he was in his teens. He found himself in 1989 in a library and picked up at random an anthology of 19th-century German philosophy, containing works by Nietzsche and Schopenhauer. Intrigued, he read the book in a nearby forest, in a clearing that he used to visit to be alone and write poetry. Almost immediately he experienced a dramatic sense of the possibilities of learning. Was it like a conversion experience?

"More an awakening," he says. "It felt like I had sleepwalked through my life to that point, and now I was aware of some wider world that I hadn't imagined."

Following first the leads and notes in the philosophy book, Bostrom set about educating himself in fast-forward. He read feverishly, and in spare moments, he painted and wrote poetry, eventually taking degrees in philosophy and mathematical logic at Gothenburg University, before completing a PhD at the London School of Economics and teaching at Yale.

Did he continue to paint and write?

"It seemed to me at some point that mathematical pursuit was more important," he says. "I felt the world already contained a lot of paintings and I wasn't convinced it needed a few more. Same could be said for poetry. But maybe it did need a few more ideas of how to navigate the future."

One of the areas in which AI is making advances is in its ability to compose music and create art, and even to write. Does he imagine that sphere too will quickly be colonized by a superintelligence or will it be a last redoubt of the human?

"I don't buy the claim that the artificial composers currently can compete with the great composers. Maybe for short bursts but not over a whole symphony. And with art, though it can be replicated, the activity itself has value. You would still paint for the sake of painting."

Authenticity, the man-made, becomes increasingly important?

"Yes and not just with art. If and when machines can do everything better than we can do, we would continue to do things because we enjoy doing them. If people play golf, it is not because they need the ball to reside in successive holes efficiently, it is because they enjoy doing it. The more machines can do everything we can do, the more attention we will give to these things that we value for their own sake."

Early in his intellectual journey, Bostrom did a few stints as a philosophical stand-up comic in order to improve his communication skills. Talking to him and reading his work, an edge of knowing absurdity at the sheer scale of the problems is never completely absent from his arguments. The axes of daunting-looking graphs in his papers will be calibrated on closer inspection in terms of "endurable," "crushing," and "hellish." In his introduction to *Superintelligence*, the observation "many of the points made in this book are probably wrong" typically leads to a footnote that reads: "I don't know which ones." Does he sometimes feel he is morphing into Douglas Adams?

"Sometimes the work does seem strange," he says. "Then from another point, it seems strange that most of the world is completely oblivious to the most major things that are going to happen in the 21st century. Even people who talk about global warming never mention any threat posed by AI."

Because it would dilute their message?

"Maybe. At any time in history, it seems to me there can be only one official global concern. Now it is climate change or sometimes terrorism. When I grew up, it was nuclear Armageddon. Then it was overpopulation. Some are more sensible than others, but it is really quite random."

Bostrom's passion is to attempt to apply some maths to that randomness. Does he think that concerns about AI will take over from global warming as a more imminent threat any time soon?

"I doubt it," he says. "It will come gradually and seamlessly without us really addressing it."

If we are going to look anywhere for its emergence, Google, which is throwing a good deal of its unprecedented resources at deep learning technology (not least with its purchase in 2014 of the British pioneer DeepMind) would seem a reasonable place to start. Google apparently has an AI ethics board to confront these questions, but no one knows who sits on it. Does Bostrom have faith in its "Don't be evil" mantra?

"There is certainly a culture among tech people that they want to feel they are doing something that is not just to make money, but that it has some positive social purpose. There is this idealism."

Can he help shape the direction of that idealism?

"It is not so much that one's own influence is important," he says. "Anyone who has a role in highlighting these arguments will be valuable. If the human condition really were to change fundamentally in our century, we find ourselves at a key juncture in history." And if Bostrom's more nihilistic predictions are correct, we will have only one go at getting the nature of the new intelligence right.

Last year, Bostrom became a father. (Typically, his marriage is conducted largely by Skype—his wife, a medical doctor, lives in Vancouver.) I wonder, before I go, if becoming a dad has changed his sense of the reality of these futuristic issues?

"Only in the sense that it emphasizes this dual perspective, the positive and negative scenarios. This kind of intellectualizing, that our world might be transformed completely in this way, always seems a lot harder to credit at a personal level. I guess I allow both of these perspectives as much room as I can in my mind."

At the same time as he entertains those thought experiments, I suggest, half the world remains concerned where its next meal is coming from. Is the threat of superintelligence quite an elitist anxiety? Do most of us not think of the longest-term future because there is more than enough to worry about in the present?

"If it got to the point where the world was spending hundreds of billions of dollars on this stuff and nothing on more regular things, then one might start to question it," he says. "If you look at all the things the world is spending money on, what we are doing is less than a pittance. You go to some random city and you travel from the airport to your hotel. Along the highway you see all these huge buildings for companies you have never heard of. Maybe they are designing a new publicity campaign for a razor blade. You drive past hundreds of these buildings. Any one of those has more resources than the total that humanity is spending on this field. We have half a floor of one building in Oxford, and there are two or three other groups doing what we do. So I think it is OK."

And how, I ask, might we as individuals and citizens think about and frame these risks to the existence of our species? Bostrom shrugs a little. "If we are thinking of this very long time frame, then it is clear that very small things we do now can make a significant difference in that future."

A recent paper of Bostrom's, which I read later at home, contains a little rule of thumb worth bearing in mind. Bostrom calls it "maxipok." It is based on the idea that "the objective of reducing existential risks should be a dominant consideration whenever we act out of an impersonal concern for humankind as a whole." What does maxipok involve? Trying to "maximize the probability of an 'OK outcome' where an OK outcome is any outcome that avoids existential catastrophe."

It certainly sounds worth a go.

TIM ADAMS has been a staff writer, contributing features, interviews, reviews, and comment, since 2000. Recent awards include the 2015 One World award for newspaper journalist of the year and the Foreign Press award for arts and culture writing.

Max Tegmark  **NO**

Benefits and Risks of Artificial Intelligence

Everything we love about civilization is a product of intelligence, so amplifying our human intelligence with artificial intelligence has the potential of helping civilization flourish like never before—as long as we manage to keep the technology beneficial.

What Is AI?

From SIRI to self-driving cars, AI is progressing rapidly. While science fiction often portrays AI as robots with human-like characteristics, AI can encompass anything from Google's search algorithms to IBM's Watson to autonomous weapons.

AI today is properly known as narrow AI (or weak AI), in that it is designed to perform a narrow task (e.g., only facial recognition or only Internet searches or only driving a car). However, the long-term goal of many researchers is to create general AI (AGI or strong AI). While narrow AI may outperform humans at whatever its specific task is, like playing chess or solving equations, AGI would outperform humans at nearly every cognitive task.

Why Research AI Safety?

In the near term, the goal of keeping AI's impact on society beneficial motivates research in many areas, from economics and law to technical topics such as verification, validity, security, and control. Whereas it may be little more than a minor nuisance if your laptop crashes or gets hacked, it becomes all the more important that an AI system does what you want it to do if it controls your car, your airplane, your pacemaker, your automated trading system, or your power grid. Another short-term challenge is preventing a devastating arms race in lethal autonomous weapons.

In the long term, an important question is what will happen if the quest for strong AI succeeds, and an AI system becomes better than humans at all cognitive tasks. As pointed out by I. J. Good in 1965, designing smarter AI systems is itself a cognitive task. Such a system could potentially undergo recursive self-improvement,

triggering an intelligence explosion leaving human intellect far behind. By inventing revolutionary new technologies, such a superintelligence might help us eradicate war, disease, and poverty, and so the creation of strong AI might be the biggest event in human history. Some experts have expressed concern, though, that it might also be the last, unless we learn to align the goals of the AI with ours before it becomes superintelligent.

There are some who question whether strong AI will ever be achieved, and others who insist that the creation of superintelligent AI is guaranteed to be beneficial. At FLI, we recognize both of these possibilities but also recognize the potential for an AI system to intentionally or unintentionally cause great harm. We believe research today will help us better prepare for and prevent such potentially negative consequences in the future, thus enjoying the benefits of AI while avoiding pitfalls.

How Can AI Be Dangerous?

Most researchers agree that a superintelligent AI is unlikely to exhibit human emotions like love or hate, and that there is no reason to expect AI to become intentionally benevolent or malevolent. Instead, when considering how AI might become a risk, experts think two scenarios most likely:

1. **The AI is programmed to do something devastating:** Autonomous weapons are AI systems that are programmed to kill. In the hands of the wrong person, these weapons could easily cause mass casualties. Moreover, an AI arms race could inadvertently lead to an AI war that also results in mass casualties. To avoid being thwarted by the enemy, these weapons would be designed to be extremely difficult to simply "turn off,"

so humans could plausibly lose control of such a situation. This risk is one that's present even with narrow AI but grows as levels of AI and autonomy increase.

2. **The AI is programmed to do something beneficial, but it develops a destructive method for achieving its goal:** This can happen whenever we fail to fully align the AI's goals with ours, which is strikingly difficult. If you ask an obedient intelligent car to take you to the airport as fast as possible, it might get you there chased by helicopters and covered in vomit, doing not what you wanted but literally what you asked for. If a superintelligent system is tasked with an ambitious geoengineering project, it might wreak havoc with our ecosystem as a side effect and view human attempts to stop it as a threat to be met.

As these examples illustrate, the concern about advanced AI isn't malevolence but competence. A superintelligent AI will be extremely good at accomplishing its goals, and if those goals aren't aligned with ours, we have a problem. You're probably not an evil ant-hater who steps on ants out of malice, but if you're in charge of a hydroelectric green energy project and there's an anthill in the region to be flooded, too bad for the ants. A key goal of AI safety research is to never place humanity in the position of those ants.

Why the Recent Interest in AI Safety

Stephen Hawking, Elon Musk, Steve Wozniak, Bill Gates, and many other big names in science and technology have recently expressed concern in the media and via open letters about the risks posed by AI, joined by many leading AI researchers. Why is the subject suddenly in the headlines?

The idea that the quest for strong AI would ultimately succeed was long thought of as science fiction, centuries or more away. However, thanks to recent breakthroughs, many AI milestones, which experts viewed as decades away merely five years ago, have now been reached, making many experts take seriously the possibility of superintelligence in our lifetime. While some experts still guess that human-level AI is centuries away, most AI researches at the 2015 Puerto Rico Conference guessed that it would happen before 2060. Since it may take decades to complete the required safety research, it is prudent to start it now.

Because AI has the potential to become more intelligent than any human, we have no surefire way

of predicting how it will behave. We can't use past technological developments as much of a basis because we've never created anything that has the ability to, wittingly or unwittingly, outsmart us. The best example of what we could face may be our own evolution. People now control the planet not because we're the strongest, fastest, or biggest but because we're the smartest. If we're no longer the smartest, are we assured to remain in control?

FLI's position is that our civilization will flourish as long as we win the race between the growing power of technology and the wisdom with which we manage it. In the case of AI technology, FLI's position is that the best way to win that race is not to impede the former but to accelerate the latter, by supporting AI safety research.

The Top Myths about Advanced AI

A captivating conversation is taking place about the future of AI and what it will/should mean for humanity. There are fascinating controversies where the world's leading experts disagree, such as AI's future impact on the job market; if/when human-level AI will be developed; whether this will lead to an intelligence explosion; and whether this is something we should welcome or fear. But there are also many examples of boring pseudo-controversies caused by people misunderstanding and talking past each other. To help ourselves focus on the interesting controversies and open questions—and not on the misunderstandings—let's clear up some of the most common myths.

Myth: Superintelligence by 2100 is inevitable Myth: Superintelligence by 2100 is impossible	**Fact:** It may happen in decades, centuries, or never: AI experts disagree and we simply don't know
Myth: Only Luddites worry about AI	**Fact:** Many top AI researches are concerned
Mythical worry: AI turning evil Mythical worry: AI turning conscious	**Actual worry:** AI turning competent, with goals misaligned with ours
Myth: Robots are the main concern	**Fact:** Misaligned intelligence is the main concern: it need no body, only an Internet connection
Myth: AI can't control humans	**Fact:** Intelligence enables control: we control tigers by being smarter
Myth: Machines can't have goals	**Fact:** A heat-seeking missile has a goal
Mythical worry: Superintelligence is just years away	**Actual worry:** It's at least decades away, but it may take that long to make it safe

Timeline Myths

The first myth regard the timeline: how long will it take until machines greatly supersede human-level intelligence? A common misconception is that we know the answer with great certainty.

One popular myth is that we know we'll get superhuman AI this century. In fact, history is full of technological overhyping. Where are those fusion power plants and flying cars we were promised we'd have by now? AI has also been repeatedly overhyped in the past, even by some of the founders of the field. For example, John McCarthy (who coined the term "AI"), Marvin Minsky, Nathaniel Rochester, and Claude Shannon wrote this overly optimistic forecast about what could be accomplished during two months with Stone Age computers: *"We propose that a 2 month, 10 man study of artificial intelligence be carried out during the summer of 1956 at Dartmouth College [...] An attempt will be made to find how to make machines use language, form abstractions and concepts, solve kinds of problems now reserved for humans, and improve themselves. We think that a significant advance can be made in one or more of these problems if a carefully selected group of scientists work on it together for a summer."*

On the other hand, a popular countermyth is that we know we won't get superhuman AI this century. Researchers have made a wide range of estimates for how far we are from superhuman AI, but we certainly can't say with great confidence that the probability is zero this century, given the dismal track record of such techno-skeptic predictions. For example, Ernest Rutherford, arguably the greatest nuclear physicist of his time, said in 1933—less than 24 hours before Szilard's invention of the nuclear chain reaction—that nuclear energy was "moonshine." And Astronomer Royal Richard Woolley called interplanetary travel "utter bilge" in 1956. The most extreme form of this myth is that superhuman AI will never arrive because it's physically impossible. However, physicists know that a brain consists of quarks and electrons arranged to act as a powerful computer, and that there's no law of physics preventing us from building even more intelligent quark blobs.

There have been a number of surveys asking AI researchers how many years from now they think we'll have human-level AI with at least 50 percent probability. All these surveys have the same conclusion: the world's leading experts disagree, so we simply don't know. For example, in such a poll of the AI researchers at the 2015 Puerto Rico AI conference, the average (median) answer was by year 2045, but some researchers guessed hundreds of years or more.

There's also a related myth that people who worry about AI think it's only a few years away. In fact, most people on record worrying about superhuman AI guess it's still at least decades away. But they argue that as long as we're not 100 percent sure that it won't happen this century, it's smart to start safety research now to prepare for the eventuality. Many of the safety problems associated with human-level AI are so hard that they may take decades to solve. So it's prudent to start researching them now rather than the night before some programmers drinking Red Bull decide to switch one on.

Controversy Myths

Another common misconception is that the only people harboring concerns about AI and advocating AI safety research are luddites who don't know much about AI. When Stuart Russell, author of the standard AI textbook, mentioned this during his Puerto Rico talk, the audience laughed loudly. A related misconception is that supporting AI safety research is hugely controversial. In fact, to support a modest investment in AI safety research, people don't need to be convinced that risks are high, merely nonnegligible—just as a modest investment in home insurance is justified by a nonnegligible probability of the home burning down.

It may be that media have made the AI safety debate seem more controversial than it really is. After all, fear sells, and articles using out-of-context quotes to proclaim imminent doom can generate more clicks than nuanced and balanced ones. As a result, two people who only know about each other's positions from media quotes are likely to think they disagree more than they really do. For example, a techno-skeptic who only read about Bill Gates's position in a British tabloid may mistakenly think Gates believes superintelligence to be imminent. Similarly, someone in the beneficial-AI movement who knows nothing about Andrew Ng's position except his quote about overpopulation on Mars may mistakenly think he doesn't care about AI safety, whereas in fact, he does. The crux is simply that because Ng's timeline estimates are longer, he naturally tends to prioritize short-term AI challenges over long-term ones.

Myths about the Risks of Superhuman AI

Many AI researchers roll their eyes when seeing this headline: *"Stephen Hawking warns that rise of robots may be disastrous for mankind."* And as many have lost count of how many similar articles they've seen. Typically, these articles are accompanied by an evil-looking robot carrying a weapon, and they suggest we should worry about robots rising up and killing us because they've become conscious and/or evil. On a lighter note, such articles are actually rather impressive because they succinctly summarize the scenario that AI researchers *don't* worry about. That scenario combines as many as three separate misconceptions: concern about *consciousness*, *evil*, and *robots*.

If you drive down the road, you have a subjective experience of colors, sounds, and so on. But does a self-driving car have a subjective experience? Does it feel like anything at all to be a self-driving car? Although this mystery of consciousness is interesting in its own right, it is irrelevant to AI risk. If you get struck by a driverless car, it makes no difference to you whether it subjectively feels conscious. In the same way, what will affect us humans is what superintelligent AI *does*, not how it subjectively *feels*.

The fear of machines turning evil is another red herring. The real worry isn't malevolence, but competence. A superintelligent AI is by definition very good at attaining its goals, whatever they may be, so we need to ensure that its goals are aligned with ours. Humans don't generally hate ants, but we're more intelligent than they are—so if we want to build a hydroelectric dam and there's an anthill there, too bad for the ants. The beneficial-AI movement wants to avoid placing humanity in the position of those ants.

The consciousness misconception is related to the myth that machines can't have goals. Machines can obviously have goals in the narrow sense of exhibiting goal-oriented behavior: the behavior of a heat-seeking missile is most economically explained as a goal to hit a target. If you feel threatened by a machine whose goals are misaligned with yours, then it is precisely its goals in this narrow sense that troubles you, not whether the machine is conscious and experiences a sense of purpose. If that heat-seeking missile were chasing you, you probably wouldn't exclaim: *"I'm not worried because machines can't have goals!"*

I sympathize with Rodney Brooks and other robotics pioneers who feel unfairly demonized by scaremongering tabloids because some journalists seem obsessively fixated on robots and adorn many of their articles with evil-looking metal monsters with red shiny eyes. In fact, the main concern of the beneficial-AI movement isn't with robots but with intelligence itself: specifically, intelligence whose goals are misaligned with ours. To cause us trouble, such misaligned superhuman intelligence needs no robotic body, merely an Internet connection—this may enable outsmarting financial markets, out-inventing human researchers, outmanipulating human leaders, and developing weapons we cannot even understand. Even if building robots were physically impossible, a superintelligent and super-wealthy AI could easily pay or manipulate many humans to unwittingly do its bidding.

The robot misconception is related to the myth that machines can't control humans. Intelligence enables control: humans control tigers not because we are stronger but because we are smarter. This means that if we cede our position as smartest on our planet, it's possible that we might also cede control.

The Interesting Controversies

Not wasting time on the abovementioned misconceptions let us focus on true and interesting controversies where even the experts disagree. What sort of future do you want? Should we develop lethal autonomous weapons? What would you like to happen with job automation? What career advice would you give today's kids? Do you prefer new jobs replacing the old ones, or a jobless society where everyone enjoys a life of leisure and machine-produced wealth? Further down the road, would you like us to create superintelligent life and spread it through our cosmos? Will we control intelligent machines or will they control us? Will intelligent machines replace us, coexist with us, or merge with us? What will it mean to be human in the age of AI? What would you like it to mean, and how can we make the future be that way? Please join the conversation!

MAX TEGMARK is president of the Future of Life Institute.

EXPLORING THE ISSUE

Is Artificial Intelligence a Threat to Humanity?

Critical Thinking and Reflection

1. Where does AI research and implementation stand today and do we have safeguards and protocols in place?
2. Can we determine an overall threat level given the limited exposure and understanding of AI research?
3. Do we know enough about AI to have a reasoned and factual discussion regarding its potential impact both positive and negative?
4. What are the broad societal implications as AI creates automated systems displacing millions of worker?

Is There Common Ground?

We know four key facts of AI. One, it is here and it is reshaping the way humans interact in myriad of ways. Two, it is displacing millions of workers on a global scale. Because AI systems can perform myriad of tasks once reserved for human labor. Three, it is logical that as it develops and is enhanced, it will be able to replicate more and more human behavior thus freeing up people to pursue other interests. Finally, we do not know what its logical evolution will be, but we do know that it will grow in sophistication and impact.

Does AI have the potential to evolve into something we cannot control and that we do not want to have among us? The possibility exists. That is why the debate as to protocols and how we approach and govern it is a good and useful first step.

Additional Resources

Kaplan, Fred, *Dark Territory: The Secret History of Cyber War*. Simon & Schuster, 2016.

Fritz Allhoff, Adam Hensacke, and Bradley Jay Strawser, *Binary Bullets: The Ethics of Cyberwarfare*. Oxford University Press, 2016.

Brandon Valeriano and Ryan C. Maness, *Cyber War Versus Cyber Realities: Cyber Conflict in the International System*. Oxford University Press, 2016.

Jared A. Cohen and Eric Schmidt, *NEW Digital Age: Reshaping the Future of People, Nations & Business*. Vintage Books, 2013.

Yong-Soo, Eun and Judith Sita Aßmann, "Cyberwar: Taking Stock of Security and Warfare in the Digital Age." *International Studies Perspectives*. August 2016.

Cimbala, Stephen J. "Nuclear Cyberwar and Crisis Management." *Comparative Strategy*. April 2016.

Paletta, Damian, et al. "Cyberwar Ignites New Arms Race. (Cover Story)." *Wall Street Journal—Eastern Edition*. October 2015.

Zittrain, Jonathan. "Netwar": The Unwelcome Militarization of the Internet Has Arrived." *Bulletin of the Atomic Scientists*. September 2017.

Schmidt, Eric. "We Must Prepare Ourselves for the Cyberwars of the Future." *Time*, time. com/4606057/cyberwars-of-the-future/.

Internet References . . .

Forbes

https://www.forbes.com

Foreign Affairs

https://www.foreignaffairs.com

Foreign Policy

http://foreignpolicy.com

Future of Life Institute

https://Futureoflife.org

The Next Web

https://thenextweb.com

Selected, Edited, and with Issue Framing Material by:
Mark Owen Lombardi, *Maryville University*

ISSUE

Is the West Losing the Global Information War?

YES: Alina Polyakova and Spencer P. Boyer, from "The Future of Political Warfare: Russia, the West, and the Coming Age of Global Digital Competition," *The New Geopolitics* (2018)

NO: Molly C. McKew, from "Putin's Real Long Game," *Politico Magazine* (2017)

Learning Outcomes

After reading this issue, you will be able to:

- Understand how information is used and manipulated in this world of social media.
- Appreciate the power of information and misinformation in all kinds of international relations.
- Begin to assess and evaluate one's own information sources.
- Develop a critical understanding of information and how to assess its validity.

ISSUE SUMMARY

YES: The authors, both from The Brookings Institution, contend that we are at the nexus of technology, big data and AI such that states and other entities can now engage in political warfare without great consequences and at low cost. They argue that this is exactly what Russia is engaged in right now throughout Europe and the United States.

NO: The author, a former advisor to the president of Georgia, argues that the Russian strategy is to so undermine truth and reality in the West, so that basic institutions and social order breaks down. The author articulates ways that the West can thwart such actions and win.

Information is power. That quote reflects a long-held notion that the control over all forms of information regarding security, finance, military, medical, personal, and hundreds of others areas allowed an individual or entity to gain great advantage over ones competitors be they states, companies, other political parties, individuals, or entities of various kinds. In fact, global politics has been predicated on this axiom for centuries and rivals have invested trillions of dollars and millions of lives in the pursuit of information as the gateway to power and influence.

Today, in the Internet age, where connectivity is king, and information of all forms is ubiquitous, that axiom is being reshaped. Today, the Internet and the explosion of social media in all of its variations and forms have led to a series of new dynamics around the issue of information. Connectivity and the digitization of information have led to two competing factors: first it is the availability of information and the waves of change and work that are facilitated because of that development. This had led to amazing achievements and enormous, seemingly overnight success for companies, individuals, and other entities that have learned to master this information and the power of connectivity.

Second is the crisis in cybersecurity and the vulnerability of information which has grown geometrically in the past decade. As most human knowledge and information are digitized, its vulnerability has increased and hacking that information and using it for financial, personal, and political gain has grown at an alarming rate. One manifestation of this is the rapid rise of cybersecurity as a professional field in virtually every industry simply to secure information and combat breeches.

Today, one cannot overestimate the proliferation of "information outlets" of all kinds. From commercial and corporate media (CBS, CNN, MSNBC, and Fox) to smaller media outlets (Local media and blogosphere) to individuals and social media to fringe groups (Brietbart, AltRight, Facebook, and Instagram), people gain their "news" from a plethora of uncharted sources whose validity and commitment to truth is suspect to say the least. Without filters or fact checks and without a modicum of information literacy save the desire to attract clicks, the information war is being fought on a battlefield that is expanding every minute of every day.

This has led to some interesting philosophical questions that may seem odd at first but now dominate the landscape of global information as an issue: What is information? What are facts? What is real news as opposed to fake news and most importantly who and how is it controlled, manipulated, and weaponized to undermine ones adversaries?

Today, it has become abundantly clear that a global information war is raging on a number of fronts. It is a war of image and propaganda. It is a war of competing narratives and misinformation. And it is a war designed to thwart adversarial ambitions and undermine a variety of societal institutions from safety and security groups to political parties, courts, and governmental institutions. There are many fault lines in this war, and one of the more interesting is the war between the democracies of the western world led by the United States and the Russian Federation, China, and her allies.

Specifically, recent events in the past 10 years including the ascendancy of Vladimir Putin and the break between Russia and the United States have centered on information warfare between the two sides. Whether, it is United States and western efforts to promote independence among republics adjacent to Russia, such as Georgia and the Ukraine or misinformation campaigns designed to undermine American democracy and sway US elections, most recently the 2016 presidential race, the global information war between these two states has certainly intensified.

Who is winning? Polyakova and Boyer suggest that Russia is on the offensive and clearly has the upper hand as evidenced by events of the past 18 months. McKew argues that while Putin has had some successes, the West clearly has plenty in its arsenal of cyber tactics to gain the upper hand.

**Alina Polyakova and
Spencer P. Boyer**

The Future of Political Warfare: Russia, the West, and the Coming Age of Global Digital Competition

Executive Summary

The Kremlin's political warfare against democratic countries has evolved from overt to covert influence activities. But while Russia has pioneered the tool kit of asymmetric measures for the 21st century, including cyberattacks and disinformation campaigns, these tools are already yesterday's game. Technological advances in artificial intelligence (AI), automation, and machine learning, combined with the growing availability of big data, have set the stage for a new era of sophisticated, inexpensive, and highly impactful political warfare. In the very near term, it will become more difficult, if not impossible, to distinguish between real and falsified audio, video, or online personalities. Malicious actors will use these technologies to target Western societies more rapidly and efficiently. As authoritarian states such as Russia and China invest resources in new technologies, the global competition for the next great leap in political warfare will intensify. As the battle for the future shifts to the digital domain, policy makers will face increasingly complex threats against democracies. The window to mount an effective "whole-of-society" response to emerging asymmetric threats is quickly narrowing.

This article outlines the current state of play in political warfare, identifies emerging threats, and proposes potential policy responses. It argues for greater information sharing mechanisms between trans-Atlantic governments and the private sector, greater information security and transparency, and greater investments in research and development on AI and computational propaganda. As authoritarian regimes seek to undermine democratic institutions, Western societies must harness their current—though fleeting—competitive advantage in technology to prepare for the next great leap forward in political warfare. Western governments should also develop a deterrence strategy against political warfare with clearly defined consequences for specific offensive actions, while ensuring they retain their democracies' core values of openness and freedom of expression.

Introduction: The Evolution of Russian Political Warfare from Ukraine to the United States

In November 2004, Ukraine's presidential election was contested by two candidates: a pro-Western independent, Viktor Yushchenko, versus the Russian-backed Prime Minister, Viktor Yanukovych. In the run up to election day, Yushchenko was mysteriously poisoned and left permanently disfigured. On voting day, districts loyal to the pro-Russian candidate suddenly acquired millions of new voters, masked men showed up to some polling stations to harass opposition supporters, and many Ukrainians "rose from the dead" to cast their votes for Yanukovych who was declared the winner. These crude and obvious tactics to swing the election resulted in mass protests that led to a second round of voting, which then swept Yushchenko to the presidency.

Ten years later, in 2014, Ukraine, having just undergone another revolution and now in open conflict with Russia in the Donbas, was once again holding important presidential elections, and once again, there was an attempt to swing the vote. But this time, the tactics were starkly more sophisticated: instead of poisoning, masked thugs, and ballot stuffers, Russia-linked cyber hackers infiltrated Ukraine's central election commission, deleting key files and implanting a virus that would have changed the results of the election in favor of a fringe ultra-nationalist party, Right Sector. Government cybersecurity experts detected the vote-altering malware less than an hour before the election results were announced. In a surreal twist, however, the Russian state media still reported the fake results, showing the ultra-nationalists winning, though in reality, Right Sector received less than 1 percent of the vote.[1] At the time, cybersecurity experts called the Ukraine hack one of the most brazen, malicious, and grand-scale attempts to manipulate a national election ever. The United States and Europe should have been paying attention because some of the same tools deployed in Ukraine would resurface in the U.S. presidential election two years later.

During the decade between Ukraine's two presidential elections, the Kremlin's "active measures"—covert activities aimed at influencing politics, narratives, and policies in favor of Russia's geopolitical interests—evolved from overt to covert, physical to digital, conventional to asymmetric. The new tools are cheaper, faster, and allow for maximum plausible deniability. But they are also less precise and thus ripe with potential unintended consequences and ambiguous results. Ukraine and other post-Soviet states have been a testing ground for Russia's 21st century arsenal of active measures.

By 2016, when Moscow turned its attention to the U.S. presidential election, the tactics, while familiar, were also savvier. Russia and its proxies combined cyberattacks with psychological operations and exploited social media platforms to stoke societal tensions and discredit the anti-Kremlin candidate, Hillary Clinton. In January 2017, the U.S. intelligence community concluded in an unclassified report that in the U.S. presidential election, "Russia's goals were to undermine public faith in the U.S. democratic process" through a "strategy that blends covert intelligence operations—such as cyber activity—with overt efforts by Russian government agencies" and proxies.[2] Indeed, in the elections that followed in Europe, Russia's fingerprints were visible everywhere to varying degrees: from the attempts by Russia-linked trolls (human-curated fake accounts) and bots (automated accounts) to spread "fake news" about the French presidential candidate Emmanuel Macron in the spring of 2017 to a disinformation campaign around the Catalan independence referendum in Spain that October. In each case, the tools and objectives were the same: the use of disinformation campaigns, cyberattacks, cultivation of political allies and proxies, and political subversion in order to divide, destabilize, and deceive democratic societies.

Russian influence operations do not focus on isolated events. Rather, taken as whole, they are at the core of a political strategy—honed in Europe's East and deployed against the West—to weaken Western institutions and undermine trans-Atlantic consensus. As such, Moscow's efforts of political warfare work in mutually reinforcing,

though not always in clearly coordinated, ways, akin to an evolving ecosystem. This ecosystem consists of a web of proxy actors and cutouts—media organizations, social media accounts, vested business interests, oligarchs, civil society groups, cyber criminals, intelligence agencies, private companies, and political actors inside and outside of Russia. Some of these players act at the direct behest of the Kremlin, and others out of their own political agenda, but with the same ultimate result. The ecosystem is a moving target: continuously evolving in its sophistication, multi-layered in its complexity, and purposely hidden.

The political warfare threat extends beyond Russia. While the Kremlin has been a key actor in developing the tool kit, these tools are appealing to other malicious state and nonstate actors seeking to undermine democracies. The evolution of technology—and Russia's and China's stated desire to lead on AI research—signals that Western democracies will face increasing threats in the cyber and information domain.

Just as authoritarian regimes learn from each other, Western governments, civil society, and the private sector will need to establish avenues for sharing best practices of resistance and deterrence. Furthermore, if Western democracies hope to avoid being taken by surprise again, public and private sector stakeholders will need to think beyond reacting to attacks on elections and more about identifying—and preparing for—the emerging threats that will advance asymmetrical capabilities in the very near term. As authoritarian regimes seek to undermine democratic institutions, Western societies must harness their current—though fleeting—competitive advantage in technology to prepare for the next great leap forward in political warfare, especially AI. The West can no longer afford to play yesterday's game. To better equip Western societies to deal with this emerging reality, this article outlines the current state of the Kremlin's tool kit, near-term emerging threats, and potential policy responses.

CURRENT STATE OF PLAY: A PRIMER ON THE RUSSIAN TOOL KIT

State actors have been the main drivers of political warfare against the West. While nonstate terrorist groups, such as ISIS, have been effective in using propaganda for recruitment purposes, they lack the resources to scale up their operations. Under Vladimir Putin, Russia has sought to expand its arsenal of "active measures"—tools of political warfare once used by the Soviet Union that aimed to influence world events through the manipulation of media, society, and politics—to deploy against democracies.[1]

The Kremlin's strategy of influence includes disinformation campaigns, the cultivation of political allies in European democracies, and cyberattacks. In each instance, multiple layers of proxies, which are direct or indirect Kremlin agents and entities, are employed to maintain plausible deniability and strategic ambiguity. This Russian-developed tool kit represents the current state of play of political warfare. The following offers a rough sketch of how these parallel streams of interference operate.

Disinformation

Key actors

- **Overt:** Russian state media such as *RT*, *Sputnik*, *Ruptly TV*.
- **Covert:** Social media trolls (e.g., the Internet Research Agency or IRA);[2] automated accounts (bots); impersonation accounts on Facebook, Twitter, and Instagram; WikiLeaks; DCLeaks.

Goals

- Undermine the Western political narrative and trans-Atlantic institutions.
- Sow discord and divisions within countries.
- Blur the line between fact and fiction.

Methods

- **Full-spectrum dissemination and amplification of misleading, false, and divisive content.** Overtly, Moscow has expanded its reach through channels in English, Spanish, German, Arabic, and French, which often piggyback on current events to insert false and misleading stories. To buttress the state-run media outlets, digital bot and troll armies amplify divisive and/or misleading content online.

- **Deployment of computational propaganda.** The spread of propaganda through technical, often automated, means to deliberately sway public opinion.[3] Russia-linked social media accounts on Twitter and Facebook are particularly adept at coupling automation (bots) with human curation to disseminate and spread counter-Western narratives.
- **Identification of societal vulnerabilities.** Russia-linked actors often amplify divisive social issues. In Europe, those issues tend to focus on national sovereignty and immigration, Islam, terrorism, and the EU as a globalist, elitist body. In the United States, Russia's disinformation machine has focused on racial tensions, criminal justice policy, immigration from Latin American and Muslim-majority countries, and class divisions.

Examples

- **The "Lisa" case (Germany, January 2016):** Perhaps the most widely reported Russian disinformation operation in Europe concerned a 13-year-old Russian-German girl named "Lisa."[4] Russia's *Channel One*—a Kremlin channel broadcasting into Germany in Russian—initially reported that Lisa, who had been missing for 30 hours, was sexually assaulted by migrants in Germany. German police quickly determined that the story was false, and Lisa herself admitted that she was with friends during the time. But it was too late: the story was amplified by German and English-language Russian media (*RT* and *Sputnik*) and was widely disseminated on social media, eventually leading to anti-immigrant and anti-Angela Merkel demonstrations. In the end, the story was traced back to a Facebook group and anti-refugee website called *Ayslterror* with Russian links. But even after German police debunked the story, Russian foreign minister Sergey Lavrov continued to promote it and criticize Germany.[5]

---

[1]Alina Polyakova, Marlene Laruelle, Stefan Meister, and Neil Barnett, *"The Kremlin's Trojan horses."* Washington, DC: Atlantic Council, November 2016. http://www.atlanticcouncil.org/publications/reports/kremlin-trojan-horses.

[2]Thirteen Russian nationals associated with the IRA were indicted by the U.S. Department of Justice on February 15, 2018, as part of the special counsel investigation into foreign interference in the 2016 U.S. election. The indictment documents how the IRA, based in St. Petersburg, Russia, carried out an intelligence and influence operation against the United States that included disinformation, impersonation of U.S. citizens, and intelligence gathering in the United States. See United States of America v. Internet Research Agency LLC et al., Criminal no. (18 U.S.C. §§ 2, 371, 1349, 1028A), https://www.justice.gov/file/1035477/download.

[3]Gillian Bolsover and Philip Howard, "Computational propaganda and political big data: Moving toward a more critical research agenda," *Big Data 5*, no. 4 (2017): 273–76. http://online.liebertpub.com/doi/abs/10.1089/big.2017.29024.cpr?journalCode=big.

[4]Stefan Meister, "The 'Lisa case': Germany as a target of Russian disinformation," *NATO Review*, https://www.nato.int/docu/review/2016/Also-in-2016/lisa-case-germany-target-russian-disinformation/EN/index.htm.

[5]Jakub Janda and Ilyas Sharibzhanov, "Six outrageous lies Russian disinformation peddled about Europe in 2016," *Atlantic Council*, http://www.atlanticcouncil.org/blogs/ukrainealert/six-outrageous-lies-russian-disinformation-peddled-about-europe-in-2016.

- **Anti-NATO propaganda (Sweden, August 2016):** Sweden faced an onslaught of fake stories about the negative consequences of any moves to enter into a military partnership with NATO, including untruthful claims about the alliance plotting to stockpile nuclear weapons on Swedish soil, NATO's prerogative to attack Russia from Swedish territory without Stockholm's consent, and NATO soldiers having license to sexually assault Swedish women without fear of prosecution because of legal immunity.[6]
- **Presidential election (United States, 2016):** The multivector information war against the United States is the most detailed account of Russian political warfare against a Western democracy to date. As a 2017 U.S. intelligence report and the 2018 Department of Justice indictment[7] against Russian actors detailed, the Russian government funded a methodical effort to undermine the 2016 U.S. presidential election. Russian operatives associated with the IRA impersonated Americans online and created fake personas and groups on social media to pit different segments of U.S. society against each other. The IRA relied especially on Facebook and Instagram to create fake "activist groups" on divisive social issues, including the Black Lives Matter movement, religion, immigration, and others. It also created Twitter accounts that spread disparaging stories about Hillary Clinton, misinformation about voting, and divisive content. The IRA also purchased political ads and organized political rallies in battleground states. These covert efforts were amplified by *RT*, *Sputnik*, and other Russian media outlets and began as early as 2014.
- **#MacronLeaks (France, April–May 2017):** French President Emmanuel Macron was the target of Russia-linked disinformation operations in the spring of 2017. Russian intelligence agents created bogus Facebook personas in order to spy on then-candidate Macron.[8] Facebook later acknowledged that it had identified numerous fake accounts that were spreading

disinformation about the French election.[9] In addition, a trove of e-mails were hacked from Macron campaign officials. Even though the e-mails were dumped publicly just two days before the elections, during the period when media were no longer allowed to report on the elections in accordance with French law, the Twitter campaign #MacronLeaks reached 47,000 tweets in just 3½ hours after the initial tweet.[10]

Political Networks

Key actors

- **Aligned or friendly political parties:** Many, but not all, far-right and far-left political parties in Europe have adopted a pro-Kremlin stance to varying degrees. On one side of the spectrum is political parties that have signed explicit cooperation agreements with Putin's United Russia Party, including the French National Front (FN), the Austrian Freedom Party, the youth wing of Germany's Alternative for Germany (AfD), Germany's The Left (Die Linke), and the Italian League (Lega). Others have repeatedly advocated for pro-Russian policies, such as the removal of sanctions and recognition of Crimea as Russian territory. Leaders of the Italian 5 Star Movement, Spanish Podemos, Greece's Syriza, and Golden Dawn, the British United Kingdom Independence Party, the Hungarian Jobbik, and the Dutch Party for Freedom have all made frequent pro-Putin and pro-Kremlin statements.[11]

Goals

- Undermine European politics from within by supporting insurgent antiestablishment, anti-EU political movements.
- Weaken European consensus on a common policy toward Russia by drawing divisions between European states and between the EU and the United States.

Methods

- Financial support, diplomatic support, and media and public relations support.

---

[6] Neil MacFarquhar, "A powerful Russian weapon: The spread of false stories," *The New York Times*, August 28, 2016, https://www.nytimes.com/2016/08/29/world/europe/russia-sweden-disinformation.html.

[7]United States of America v. Internet Research Agency LLC et al.

[8]Joseph Menn, "Exclusive: Russia used Facebook to try to spy on Macron campaign—sources," *Reuters*, July 27, 2017, https://www.reuters.com/article/us-cyber-france-facebook-spies-exclusive/exclusive-russia-used-facebook-to-try-to-spy-on-macron-campaign-sourcesi-dUSKBN1AC0EI.

---

[9]Ibid.

[10]"Hashtag campaign: #MacronLeaks," *DRFLab*, May 5, 2017, https://medium.com/dfrlab/hashtag-campaign-macronleaks-4a3fb870c4e8.

[11]Party platforms classified as pro-Russian based on Alina Polyakova et al., "The Kremlin's Trojan horses."

Examples

- **France—National Front campaign financing:** The FN is the only known example of Russian financial backing for a far-right party in Europe. In 2014, the party received a loan of approximately $9.8 million and in 2017, the party's leaders and then-presidential candidate, Marine Le Pen, requested an additional $29 million loan from Russia.[12] In addition to financial backing, Le Pen has sought to develop a personal relationship with Putin, having made several high-level visits to Russia while being his strongest advocate at home.

- **2017 German federal elections and the AfD:** The anti-immigrant AfD—now the third-largest party in the German parliament—is forging closer ties with Moscow and has repeatedly called for a more harmonious relationship with Moscow.[13] The AfD has established tighter connections between its youth wing and the youth organization of the Kremlin's United Russia party and has done robust outreach to Russian–German voters.[14] Notably, in February 2017, the speaker of the Russian parliament (Duma), Vyacheslav Volodin, met with then-AfD chairwoman Frauke Petry in Moscow to discuss inter-party cooperation, while the AfD has fielded Russian-speaking Germans with anti-migrant views as candidates.[15] In addition, Russian state-controlled media provided favorable coverage to the AfD, its candidates, and messaging in the lead-up to the September 2017 German election.[16] The AfD's results in the September election were above average in areas with large Russian-speaking populations, such as Pforzheim in Baden-Württemberg.[17]

- **Support for separatists:** Given Moscow's view that separatist movements serve as a powerful and visible wedge to divide and weaken the West, Russia has been an ally to European separatist groups on the left and the right. Most recently, the Catalan independence referendum in October 2017 received a chilly reception from the West, including the United States and the European Union, which backed Madrid's effort to delegitimize the vote. Russia (along with Venezuela and Scotland), however, backed the Catalan bid, with a propaganda campaign that deployed its state-owned media outlets and social media bots to support the separatists' narratives.[18] Moscow has worked to capitalize on these connections by convening both far-right parties and separatist movements to discuss best practices for furthering common agendas in a global movement.[19] Moscow hosted the International Russian Conservative Forum in March 2015 in St. Petersburg, convening ultranationalist political leaders from across Europe.[20] The Kremlin also brought together secessionist representatives from Scotland, Catalonia, the Basque country, northern Italy, Northern Ireland, and other locations at a conference in Moscow in 2017.[21]

- **Support for would-be authoritarians:** At the personal level, Moscow is adept at using democratically elected, influential individuals them-

[12]James McAuley, "France's National Front faces funding shortfall before the 2017 election," *The Washington Post*, December 22, 2016, https://www.washingtonpost.com/news/worldviews/wp/2016/12/22/frances-national-front-faces-funding-shortfall-before-the-2017-election/?utm_term=.4c624da4ea3a.

[13]Ken Gude, "Russia's 5th column," *Center for American Progress*, March 15, 2017, https://www.americanprogress.org/issues/security/reports/2017/03/15/428074/russias-5th-column/.

[14]Melanie Amann and Pavel Lokshin, "German populists forge deeper ties with Russia," *Spiegel Online*, April 27, 2016, http://www.spiegel.de/international/germany/german-populists-forge-deeper-ties-with-russia-a-1089562.html.

[15]Paul Stronski and Richard Solosky, "The return of global Russia: An analytical framework" (Washington, DC: Carnegie Endowment for International Peace, December 2017), http://carnegieendowment.org/2017/12/14/return-of-global-russia-analytical-framework-pub-75003.

[16]Ibid.

[17]Maria Snegovaya, "Russian propaganda in Germany: More effective than you think," *The American Interest*, October 17, 2017, https://www.the-american-interest.com/2017/10/17/russian-propaganda-germany-effective-think/.

[18]Editorial Board, "Catalonia held a referendum. Russia won," *The Washington Post*, October 2, 2017, https://www.washingtonpost.com/opinions/global-opinions/catalonia-held-a-referendum-russia-won/2017/10/02/f618cd7c-a798-11e7-92d1-58c702d2d975_story.html.

[19]"Russian influence in Europe: Six ways (other than hacking) that Russia is exploiting divisions and the rise of xenophobia in Europe." New York: Human Rights First. January 11, 2017, https://www.humanrightsfirst.org/resource/russian-influence-europe.

[20]Gabrielle Tetrault, "Russian, European far-right parties converge in St. Petersburg," *The Moscow Times*, March 22, 2015, https://themoscowtimes.com/articles/russian-european-far-right-parties-converge-in-st-petersburg-45010.

[21]Casey Michel, "U.S. and EU separatist groups to gather on Moscow's dime," *The Diplomat*, July 26, 2016, https://thediplomat.com/2016/07/us-and-eu-separatist-groups-to-gather-on-moscows-dime/.

selves to delegitimize systems from within.[22] Russia's brand of anti-Western authoritarianism is appealing and inspirational to European leaders who seek to style themselves in opposition to Western liberalism. Hungarian Prime Minister Viktor Orbán and Slovakian Prime Minister Robert Fico, for example, have publicly or privately identified Russia as a political model from which to learn and to emulate.[23]

Cyberattacks in the Service of Disinformation Campaigns

Key actors

- **Government agencies:** Military Intelligence Service (GRU), Federal Security Service (FSB), Foreign Intelligence Service.
- **Known proxies:** Advanced Persistent Threats (APT) 28 and 29, CyberBerkut.[24]
- **Supporting actors:** WikiLeaks, DCLeaks, Shadow Brokers.
- **Informal proxies:** cyber criminals, tech firms, cyber "activists."

Goals

- Discredit and delegitimize democratic elections.
- Sow distrust in Western institutions by revealing politically damaging information.

Methods

- Theft of personal and institutional information, which is later leaked online by a self-proclaimed independent group (e.g., WikiLeaks) and then used to spin a disinformation campaign to damage particular individuals (e.g., Hillary Clinton) or institutions (e.g., the U.S. National Security Agency, NSA).
- On a technical level, the methods are well known, relying primarily on user error and cybersecurity vulnerabilities.

- **Spear phishing:** Targeted attempts to steal sensitive information, such as account credentials or financial information, through a tailored electronic attack. Most commonly, victims (individuals or organizations) will receive an e-mail from a seemingly trusted source that will expose the user to malware or compel him or her to divulge account login information.
- **Denial of service attacks:** Attempts to prevent legitimate users from accessing the targeted service, usually by overwhelming the target with superfluous requests.
- **Credential reuse:** Obtaining valid credentials for one target and attempting to use those same credentials on other targets.

Examples

- **Democratic National Committee hack (United States, 2015–2016):** U.S. intelligence agencies and private cybersecurity firms identified two groups—with ties to Russian intelligence—that were involved in the hacking of the Democratic National Committee (DNC). The hack led to a series of politically harmful e-mails being publicly leaked ahead of the U.S. presidential election. One group, APT 29 (or "Cozy Bear," or "The Dukes"), penetrated the DNC in July 2015 and was linked to the KGB's successor organization, the FSB.[25] The second, known as APT 28 (or "Fancy Bear"), hacked the DNC in March 2016 and had ties to the Russian Ministry of Defense's intelligence agency, the GRU.[26]
- **Bundestag hack (Germany, 2016):** Germany's domestic intelligence agency noted that hackers with ties to the Russian government had targeted both Chancellor Angela Merkel's political party and German state computers, which led to concerns that Russia would seek to disrupt the recent German elections.[27]

---

[22]Alina Polyakova et al., "The Kremlin's Trojan horses."

[23]Heather Conley, James Mina, Ruslan Stefanov, and Martin Vladimirov, "*The Kremlin playbook.*" Washington, DC: Center for Strategic and International Studies, October 2016, 6–7, https://www.csis.org/analysis/kremlin-playbook.

[24]APT is a new type of cyber threat that uses "multiple attack techniques and vectors and that are conducted by stealth to avoid detection so that hackers can retain control over target systems unnoticed for long periods of time." See Colin Tankard, "Advanced persistent threats and how to monitor and deter them," *Network Security* 11, no. 8 (2011): 16–19, https://www.sciencedirect.com/science/article/pii/S1353485811700861.

[25]Roland Oliphant, "Who are Russia's cyber-warriors and what should the West do about them?" *The Telegraph*, December 16, 2016, http://www.telegraph.co.uk/news/2016/12/16/russias-cyber-warriors-should-west-do/.

[26]Ibid.

[27]Kathy Gilsian and Krishnadev Kalamur, "Did Putin Direct Russian Hacking? And Other Big Questions," *The Atlantic*, January 6, 2017, https://www.theatlantic.com/international/archive/2017/01/russian-hacking-trump/510689/.

Emerging Threats

The future of political warfare is in the digital domain. The influence tools used by Moscow against the West are still fairly basic: they rely on exploiting human gullibility, vulnerabilities in the social media ecosystem, and lack of awareness among publics, the media, and policy makers. In the three-to-five year term, however, these tools will become more advanced and difficult to detect. In particular, technological advancements in AI and cyber capabilities will open opportunities for malicious actors to undermine democracies more covertly and effectively than what we have seen so far.[3] In addition, increasingly sophisticated cybertools, tested primarily by Russia in Eastern Europe, have already affected Western systems. An attack on Western critical infrastructure seems inevitable.

The Evolution of AI and Computational Propaganda

In today's online environment, private companies are able to effectively detect bots, trolls, and other forms of manipulation. Computational propaganda—"the use of algorithms, automation, and human curation to purposefully distribute misleading information over social media networks"—can be tracked and monitored by tech savvy investigative researchers and groups.[4] Detection is still possible because these tactics still depend on human curation and, once the capabilities are acquired, are deployed in predictable patterns. But these tools are about to become far more complicated and difficult to counter.

Online social media bots follow distinguishable patterns when they are "turned on" to spread disinformation: multiple accounts become active simultaneously and publish similar content on a schedule, the content is repetitive and nonsensical, and it is published at nonhuman speeds. These automated accounts are used primarily to amplify divisive content produced by human-curated accounts, state-controlled media (e.g., *RT*), or other proxies, and to attack specific individual or groups. Cyber intelligence analysis relies on those sets of metrics, among others, to attribute specific activities to known groups and identify bot networks.

While the social media environment is particularly vulnerable to manipulation through computational propaganda, the companies in this field are still ahead of the curve in their ability to identify coordinated automated campaigns (once they know what they are looking for). To do so, tech companies use AI tools and machine learning in their algorithms to detect coordinated bot networks, extremist content, and attempts to manipulate content rankings.[5] These tools are far more limited in their ability to detect divisive content around social issues being amplified by both real and fake users.

In the very near term, the evolution of AI and machine learning, combined with the increasing availability of big data, will begin to transform human communication and interaction in the digital space. It will become more difficult for humans and social media platforms themselves to detect automated and fake accounts, which will become increasingly sophisticated at mimicking human behavior. AI systems will be able to adapt to new contexts, suggest relevant original content, interact more sensibly with humans in proscribed contexts, and predict human emotional responses to that content. They will be able to access and analyze information that people share about themselves.

Online to microtarget citizens with deeply personalized messaging. They will be able to exploit human emotions to elicit specific responses. They will be able to do this faster and more effectively than any human actor. Malicious actors—Russia or others—will use these technologies to their advantage. This transformation in digital communication is happening now—and the window for being able to detect the difference between human and machine-driven communications is closing.[6]

Weaponization of Big Data

During the 2016 U.S. election, Russia-linked accounts on Facebook published content on divisive social issues. The content had no ideological focus. Rather, the Russian strategy aimed to further incite polarization around hot political issues: race, immigration, religion, and gender. The accounts promoted the content using advertising tools readily available on Facebook and other social media to microtarget users who held similar beliefs. This content reached 150 million Facebook and Instagram users at a cost of only $100,000, according to congressional testimony by Facebook's general counsel in October 2017.[7] The Russian accounts were able to reach a large number of users at such low cost because Facebook and other tech firms' revenue models depend on their ability to collect increasingly refined personal data that make it possible for advertisers to microtarget individuals. In the hands of malicious actors, these data become a treasure trove for influence operations, political targeting, and manipulation.

The threats involved with data collection are broader than the social media sector. An entire cottage industry of data brokers—companies that collect and sell individuals' personal data—has emerged to meet growing demand. Big data miners compile information from public records, web browsing histories, online purchases, and other sources. They use this information to predict tastes, political attitudes, ethnicity, place of residence, and other personal attributes. This information is just as valuable to companies marketing products to consumers as to foreign actors seeking to undermine democratic systems and authoritarian regimes (including Russia and China) seeking to control domestic populations. A 2014 study by the U.S. Federal Trade Commission found that some companies collected as many as 3,000 pieces of information on a single consumer without the consumer's knowledge.[8] One such firm, Acxiom, claims to have collected data on 200 million Americans and reported revenues of $800 million in 2015.[9] Another firm, Cambridge Analytica, claimed to have created personal profiles on 240 million Americans.[10] The company mined personal data to microtarget voters in the United States during the 2016 election and in the United Kingdom during the Brexit referendum. These firms typically sell information to the highest bidder, but Cambridge Analytica reportedly contacted WikiLeaks in an effort to coordinate the leaks of Clinton's e-mails during the U.S. presidential election.[11] In December 2017, U.S. Special Counsel Robert Mueller requested that Cambridge Analytica turn over internal documents as part of his investigation into possible ties between the Trump campaign and Russia.[12]

Today, AI and personalized data that Twitter, Facebook, and others use to decide which content and ads appear in users' search results, newsfeeds, and time lines are already built into existing social media platforms. Social media companies can tweak their algorithms to better detect disinformation campaigns or other forms of manipulation (and they have begun to do so), but the underlying systems and revenue models are likely to stay the same. The coming threat is the development of AI and personalized data that Russia, China, and others will use to test and manipulate the existing systems.

Market demand for big data will continue to increase. Competition for advertising dollars incentivizes tech firms to collect more refined data about users, not less. In 2016, Facebook introduced emotional "interactions" on its platform, which allow users to react with an emoticon to a post. Now, rather than knowing what individuals like, this information allows malicious actors to know what type of content makes individuals happy, sad, or angry when such interactions (as Facebook calls them) are publicly shared by users. Armed with this information, any corporation, state, or nonstate actor can devise a disinformation campaign that delivers content meant to incite an emotional response. For example, young unemployed white

men who are likely to vote for a far-right political party in Germany would receive content suggesting that Syrian refugees are exploiting the social welfare system or harassing German women. The post would call citizens to take undefined action.

This type of microtargeted campaign is not a theoretical scenario; it is already happening and, when combined with more sophisticated AI, will only increase in its ability to predict deeply personal preferences and calibrate emotional responses. The layering of AI systems with the low-cost availability of personal data about individuals presents a serious challenge to democratic values of openness and free expression. With access to big data, AI systems will soon know us better than we know ourselves in terms of their ability to predict our political and personal preferences. Stanford computational data scientists, for example, have been able to create an AI system able to predict with 90 percent accuracy an individual's sexual orientation based on a photograph alone.[13]

Manufacturing "Reality"

Russia's current disinformation model is premised on the concept of a "firehose of falsehood"—repetitive, fast paced, continuous, high-volume information attacks from a variety of sources.[14] The aim is to muddle the notion of truth or objectivity, blur the line between fact and falsehood, and sow confusion among publics. For now, this style of information war is detectable and easily debunked when found: doctored photographs can be revealed as fakes, videos claiming to show one event can be shown to actually reflect another, and quotes attributed to political leaders can also be fact checked. Civil society initiatives such as Ukraine's StopFake.org, investigative journalists such as First Draft News, and government agencies such as the European External Action Service (EEAS) EastStratCom Team have become much faster at monitoring, spotting, and debunking Russian efforts to spread this type of disinformation. Yet, with advances in techniques that can simulate human behavior, our ability to do so is quickly coming to an end.[15]

Discerning the difference between real and fake video or audio may be impossible in the very near term. New techniques in video and linguistic replication, driven by learning-enabled AI, are able to produce new video or audio recordings based on existing content. The so-called "deep fakes" or the "digital manipulation of sound, images, or video to impersonate someone or make it appear that a person did something" are coming.[16] German and American researchers have been able to create believable video of an individual based on content from

YouTube posts.[17] Audio is even easier to replicate. An AI program called Lyrebird "allows anyone to create his or her digital voice with only one minute of audio."[18] The implication of such new technologies is obvious: political leaders can be made to appear to say anything at all, and they will sound and look exactly as they do in real life. These technologies stretch the definition of reality and fantasy. While these advancements are not inherently malicious in themselves, when put to use by bad actors, they can have detrimental effects on the media environment, public discourse, and public trust in mainstream institutions. If the viewers cannot trust their eyes and ears, confidence in media could plummet even further.

As deep fake capabilities become cheaper, faster, and more widely accessible, the "firehose of falsehood" model will become even more effective: videos of political leaders making derogatory remarks about their citizens could be pushed out on social media by thousands of bot and troll accounts. By the time that official sources are able to respond and debunk the hoax, new fake videos would already be going viral, and the accounts spreading the propaganda would appear to be very real and human. Using microtargeted ads, the fake videos would reach the specific individuals and groups that are most likely to be offended. This cycle of disinformation would continue 24/7.

Cyberattacks on Critical Infrastructure

In the West, Russia's cyberattacks so far have been at the service of its disinformation operations: stolen data used to embarrass individuals, spin a narrative, discredit democratic institutions and values, and sow social discord. This was the pattern Russian operators followed in the United States, France, and Germany during the countries' 2016–2017 elections. Hacking e-mail accounts of individuals or campaigns, leaking that stolen information via a proxy (primarily WikiLeaks), and then deploying an army of disinformation agents (bots, trolls, and state-controlled media) to disseminate and amplify a politically damaging narrative.[19] Such cyber-enabled interference falls below the threshold of "cyberattacks of significant consequence" that could result in "loss of life, significant destruction of property, or significant impact on [national security interests]."[20] Partially for this reason, Western governments, which have been the targets of cyber-driven information war, have not responded in a decisive and visible manner.

In the West, the nightmare of cyberattacks crippling critical infrastructure systems—electricity grids, hospitals, financial systems, and transportation—still has the sound of science fiction. But in Europe's East, this nightmare scenario is a reality and a sign of what is very likely to come in Europe and elsewhere.[21] As the laboratory for Russian activities, Ukraine has seen a significant uptick in attacks on its critical infrastructure systems since the 2013–2014 Maidan revolution. A barrage of malware, denial of service attacks, and phishing campaigns bombard Ukraine's critical infrastructure environments on a daily basis.

In December 2015, a well-planned and sophisticated attack on Ukraine's electrical grid targeted power distribution centers and left 230,000 residents without power the day before Christmas. The attackers were able to override operators' password access to the system and also disable backup generators. Thanks to Soviet-era manual switches, the blackout lasted only a few hours and thus went almost unnoticed in the West. The Ukrainian government attributed the attacks to the Russian Advanced Persistent Threat (APT) group "Sandworm."[22] "BlackEnergy," the same Sandworm malware that caused the blackout in Ukraine, has been detected in electric utilities in the United States.[23] The Christmas attack is the worst known attack on critical infrastructure systems, and Ukraine's systems—defended by a combination of firewalls, segmented access, two-factor authentication, and manual controls—were more secure at the time of the attack than those in the United States.[24]

Attacks on Ukraine and other Eastern European countries are not always easily contained. In June 2017, the so-called "NotPetya" virus, which originated in a targeted attack on Ukraine's accounting systems, spread to 64 countries and affected major international companies, logistical operators, government agencies, telecommunication providers, and financial institutions. The name, NotPetya, referred to the disguised nature of the attack; it appeared as a previously launched ransomware attack (Petya) but was in fact designed to destroy and delete information systems in Ukraine.[25] In effect, NotPetya was a cyber form of *"maskirovka"*—tactical deception—used in Soviet military operations to mislead and deceive adversaries about the true source and intention of an attack. In February 2018, the U.S. administration attributed NotPetya to the Russian military.[26]

Ukraine's experience with Russian election hacking should also be a call to action. Widely used electronic voting machines have weak security and software full of easily exploitable loopholes. At the 2017 Defcon conference for hackers, attendees were tasked with breaking into a range of American voting machines either by finding vulnerabilities through physically breaking into machines or gaining access remotely. The hackers did so in less than two hours.[27] Participants managed to breach every piece of equipment by the end of the gathering.[28]

A massive and debilitating attack on critical infrastructure in Western Europe and the United States is inevitable. It will likely follow a pattern similar to the May 2017 WannaCry ransomware attack that crippled hospitals in Western Europe by exploiting a vulnerability in Microsoft Windows. The exploit was originally identified by the National Security Agency (NSA) and was subsequently leaked. The Shadow Brokers, a hacker group, published the information from the NSA leak containing the information about the vulnerability in April 2017. The United States identified North Korea as responsible for the WannaCry attack in the fall of 2017.[29] WannaCry presents a clear threat vector: malicious actors (Russia, China, North Korea, etc.) hack Western intelligence agencies' tools and post them publicly, allowing other malicious actors around the world to attack critical infrastructure. And the West seems ill-equipped to deter and respond to such an event.[30]

Getting Ahead of the Game: A Trans-atlantic Response

Russia may present a template for political warfare today, but it is already yesterday's game. As existing tools and methods are exposed and countered, and technology continues to advance and become more financially accessible, malicious actors will continue to evolve their tactics. The short-term emerging threats described in this article are just a sample of what is to come. The time horizon of three to five years may be too generous and the threat even more imminent.

A reactive policy approach that simply plugs the gaps of existing vulnerabilities, or responds on a case-by-case basis, will fail. The threat is bigger than Russia and broader than any single nation-state actor: it is a challenge to trans-atlantic security, democratic values, and the entire international system. A policy to counter and deter future threats must be trans-Atlantic in scope, future-facing, and inherently collaborative. A democratic response to political warfare against the West is possible, but it will require a whole-of-society, multistakeholder approach. Governments, multilateral institutions, civil society, the private sector, and individual citizens must all play a part. To survive and thrive in the next great leap in political warfare, the immediate response should take shape along three lines of effort:

Information Sharing

- *European governments, the United States, and allies should establish information sharing mechanisms with private sector firms.* As Google, Facebook, and Twitter stated in U.S. congressional testimonies in the fall of 2017, they do not wish to be manipulated by actors aiming to undermine democracies. As such, these tech firms should voluntarily cooperate with public sector agencies, particularly the intelligence community, to establish an early warning system when disinformation activities are detected in their systems. To that end, national governments, the European Union, and NATO should establish a designated interlocutor within the intelligence agencies to be the point of contact for receiving and distributing such information, as appropriate. A voluntary information sharing system is ideal, but such processes could also be legislatively mandated.

- *NATO, the European Union, and the United States should establish an information sharing unit focused specifically on cyber-enabled disinformation.* NATO, as the primary defense and security organization linking the trans-Atlantic partnership, should take the lead in coordinating information sharing through existing and new mechanisms in NATO's Cyber Command or NATO's Joint Intelligence and Security (JIS) Division.

- *European governments and the United States should convene, on a regular basis, the StratCom, Hybrid Threat, and Cyber Threat task forces that currently exist within various agencies.* Task forces such as the EEAS's EastStratCom team, the Czech Ministry of Interior's StratCom Unit, the joint European Center of Excellence for Countering Hybrid Threats in Helsinki, and NATO's StratCom Center of Excellence in Riga, among others, should develop closer relationships through regular convening and information sharing. An annual StratCom forum should be established in Brussels under the auspices of the European Council but with participation from the United States and allies.

1. Improve Information Security and Transparency

- *European states and the United States should order an immediate audit of governmental information systems, network security, and classified systems.* Such a review should identify immediate vulnerabilities while also looking forward to emerging threats. The resulting report should be classified but should have an unclassified version to inform the public. Such an audit should be completed quickly and its recommendations taken seriously.

- *Private sector tech and social media firms should develop tools to quickly identify fake and automated accounts.* Early attempts to label potentially disputed content have not succeeded in deterring users from clicking on such content.[31] Deranking or "muting" such content is likely to be more effective.

- *Private sector firms should vet advertising clients to prevent malicious actors from promoting content.* Known propaganda culprits should be banned from advertising on social media platforms (an action already taken by Twitter) and their content should be pushed down in the ranking (an action Google has said that it would take).

- *Private sector tech firms should agree to a corporate code of conduct regarding advertising and data.* Among other rules, it would limit the detail of personal data used in advertising tools, introduce transparency into ad revenue streams, and extend the restrictions around political advertising already in place for traditional media into the online space.

- *Data brokers should be required by law to give consumers access to their data, including the ability to correct it.* Consumers should also be prominently notified by social media platforms and other retailers when their data are being shared with data brokers.

- *Academic institutions training the next generation of computer scientists should introduce ethics courses into the required curriculum.* Algorithms are written by humans and thus have inherent biases built into them. The so-called "neutral" algorithms are an illusion. More awareness of the potential ethical implications of computer coding could make algorithms and AI less susceptible to manipulation.

2. Invest in Research and Development on AI and Computational Propaganda

- *Governments, private foundations, major nonprofit policy organizations, and technology companies should invest in academic research that explores how technological advances will affect public discourse.* While AI technology will positively transform many sectors—health, transportation, and others—the potential negative implications of new technologies should also be acknowledged and researched.

- *To get ahead of machine-driven computational propaganda, technology companies (current and future) should develop the next generation of AI-driven detection techniques and build them into platforms before the threat becomes more urgent.* This will mitigate the possibility of malicious actors manipulating online platforms in the future.

- *Governments, private foundations, academia, and tech companies should invest in research that examines the "demand side" of disinformation in addition to the "supply side."* Disinformation narratives spread because individuals find them appealing. The techniques and tools are just one side of the equation. Better understanding the social psychology of disinformation would help governments, independent media, and civil society groups become better equipped to counter such messaging.

The Long View: Is Deterrence Against Political Warfare Possible?

Deterrence as a conventional military strategy depends on one actor's ability to dissuade another from taking a damaging action through intimidation and coercion. For a deterrent to be effective, the adversary must understand the consequences of carrying out an offensive action and believe in the credibility and ability of the other side to impose the consequences. For example, during the Cold War, both the Soviet Union and the United States knew what the consequences of a preemptive nuclear strike would be—imminent mutual destruction.

In nonconventional warfare, however, the consequences and implications of an offensive action are ambiguous to both sides. The Obama administration, for example, did not have a clearly defined response strategy to Russian interference in the 2016 presidential election. Eventually, in the final months of his presidency, Obama signed an executive order imposing cyber-related sanctions on Russia, expelled 35 Russian diplomats from the United States, and seized two Russian diplomatic compounds. These actions were not commensurate with the scale of the Russian attack. In its first year, the Trump administration has not developed a comprehensive strategy either, while the president continued to question the scope of Russian activities. It is likely that the Russian government also did not know what to expect in response to the disinformation and cyber operations it carried out.

Moscow was testing U.S. resolve to respond. The weakness of the U.S. response has undoubtedly been a useful lesson for other states—China, Iran, North Korea—seeking to undermine Western societies.

As a first step, *Western governments should develop a strategy of deterrence against political warfare with clearly defined consequences for specific offensive actions.* This strategy should have overt and covert operational components, including public statements by high-level government officials that outline the consequences, intelligence communications to convey the potential costs to adversaries, and an increase in covert operations aimed at identifying adversaries' vulnerabilities.

Nonconventional deterrence is difficult for another reason: attribution. The Russian government continues to deny any involvement in the United States and European elections. The 2017 unclassified U.S. intelligence report on Russian interference stopped short of laying the blame explicitly on President Putin, despite overwhelming evidence that the direction for such an operation had to come from the highest office of the Russian government. The German government took a different approach in the lead-up to the federal elections in September 2017. Most notably, in May 2017, the head of the German intelligence service, the BfV, publicly warned the Kremlin from making the political decision to interfere.[32] Chancellor Merkel warned the German public of possible Russian interference directly after the U.S. election in November 2016. These public warnings from high-level officials likely impacted the Kremlin's decision to not leak data obtained in a 2015 hack of the German parliament.[33] The goal of political warfare is to conceal the perpetrator and maximize plausible deniability. *Western political leaders should not fall victim to adversaries' obfuscation techniques but rather take a principled public stance on attribution.* Such warnings must come from trusted messengers and from the highest level of government.

Lastly, a warning: in seeking to deter political warfare, Western democracies cannot abandon the core values of openness, freedom of expression, and liberalism. Regulatory initiatives for better transparency and accountability in the social media space are important, but regulation must not devolve into infringements on freedom of expression. Democratic governments cannot beat malicious state actors at their own game: a top-down approach that involves the spread of counterpropaganda will only erode the remaining trust that citizens have in government institutions. Fighting propaganda with propaganda is also not the way forward. A democratic response must be rooted in civil society and an independent media. A multistakeholder approach—in which individuals, governments, civil society organizations, and private firms play their part—is a strength, not a weakness, of democracies.

Notes

1. Mark Clayton, "Ukraine election narrowly avoided 'wanton destruction' from hackers," *Christian Science Monitor*, June 17, 2014, https://www.csmonitor.com/World/Passcode/2014/0617/Ukraine-election-narrowly-avoided-wantondestruction-from-hackers.
2. "Background to 'Assessing Russian activities and intentions in recent U.S. elections': The analytic process and cyber incident attribution," U.S. Office of the Director of National Intelligence, January 7, 2017, https://www.dni.gov/files/documents/ICA_2017_01.pdf.
3. Tim Hwang, "Digital disinformation: A primer." Washington, DC: Atlantic Council, September 2017, http://www.atlanticcouncil.org/publications/articles/digital-disinformation-a-primer.
4. Samuel C. Woolley and Philip N. Howard, "Computational propaganda worldwide: Executive summary," *Oxford Internet Institute*, June 19, 2017, https://www.oii.ox.ac.uk/blog/computational-propaganda-worldwide-executivesummary/.
5. Machine learning is part of AI and refers to the ability of computers to analyze large amounts of data, recognize patterns, learn from them, and then predict or act without human programming. Machines are thus "trained" to complete tasks without human intervention. See Michael Copeland, "The difference between AI, machine learning, and deep learning?" *The Official NVIDIA Blog*, July 29, 2016, https://blogs.nvidia.com/blog/2016/07/29/whats-differenceartificial-intelligence-machine-learning-deep-learning-ai/.
6. Matt Chessen, "*The MADCOM future*" Washington, DC: Atlantic Council, September 2017. http://www.atlanticcouncil.org/publications/reports/the-madcom-future.
7. "Hearing before the Committee on the Judiciary Subcommittee on Crime and Terrorism: Testimony of Colin Stretch, General Counsel, Facebook," Senate Judiciary Committee, October 31, 2017, https://www.judiciary.senate.gov/imo/media/doc/10-31-17%20Stretch%20Testimony.pdf.
8. Bridget Small, "FTC report examines data brokers," *Federal Trade Commission*, May 27, 2014,

https://www.consumer.ftc.gov/blog/2014/05/ftc-report-examines-data-brokers.

9. Brian Naylor, "Firms are buying, sharing your online info. What can you do about it?" *NPR*, July 11, 2016, https://www.npr.org/sections/alltechconsidered/2016/07/11/485571291/firms-are-buying-sharing-your-online-info-what-can-you-do-about-it.

10. Carole Cadwalladr, "British courts may unlock secrets of how Trump campaign profiled U.S. voters," *The Guardian*, September 30, 2017. https://www.theguardian.com/technology/2017/oct/01/cambridge-analytica-big-data-facebook-trumpvoters.

11. Rebecca Ballhaus, "Data firm's WikiLeaks outreach came as it joined Trump campaign," *The Wall Street Journal*, November 10, 2017, https://www.wsj.com/articles/data-firms-wikileaks-outreach-came-as-it-joined-trump-campaign-1510339346.

12. Rebecca Ballhaus, "Mueller sought emails of Trump campaign data firm," *The Wall Street Journal*, December 15, 2017, https://www.wsj.com/articles/mueller-sought-emails-of-trump-campaign-data-firm-1513296899.

13. Yilun Wang and Michal Kosinski, "Deep neural networks are more accurate than humans at detecting sexual orientation from facial images," *Journal of Personality and Social Psychology*, 2018, in press.

14. Christopher Paul and Miriam Matthews, "The Russian 'firehose of falsehood' propaganda model: Why it might work and options to counter it" (Santa Monica, CA: RAND Corporation, 2016), https://www.rand.org/pubs/perspectives/ PE198.html.

15. Tim Hwang, "Digital disinformation."

16. Robert Chesney and Danielle Citron, "Deep fakes: A looming crisis for national security, democracy, and privacy?" *The Lawfare Blog*, February 21, 2018, https://lawfareblog.com/deep-fakes-looming-crisis-national-security-democracy-and-privacy.

17. Justus Thies, et al., "Face2Face: Real-time face capture and reenactment of RGB Videos" (paper presented at 2016 IEEE Conference on Computer Vision and Pattern Recognition, Seattle, WA, June 2016), http://www.graphics.stanford.edu/~niessner/papers/2016/1facetoface/thies2016face.pdf.

18. "Lyrebird beta," Lyrebird, 2017, https://lyrebird.ai/.

19. On Germany's experience with Russian cyberattacks since 2015, see Tyson Barker, "Germany strengthens its cyber defense," *Foreign Affairs*, May 26, 2017, https://www.foreignaffairs.com/articles/germany/2017-05-26/germany-strengthens-its-cyber-defense. On the #MacronLeaks disinformation campaign, see "Hashtag campaign: MacronLeaks," *DRFLab*, May 5, 2017, https://medium.com/dfrlab/hashtag-campaign-macron-leaks-4a3fb870c4e8. For a review of Russian disinformation efforts in Germany, see Constanze Stelzenmüller, "The impact of Russian interference on Germany's 2017 elections," *Brookings Institution*, https://www.brookings.edu/testimonies/the-impact-of-russian-interference-on-germanys-2017-elections/.

20. "The DoD cyber strategy." Arlington, VA: Department of Defense, 2015), https://www.defense.gov/Portals/1/features/2015/0415_cyber-strategy/Final_2015_DoD_CYBER_STRATEGY_for_web.pdf.

21. Andy Greenberg, "How an entire nation became Russia's test lab for cyberwar," *Wired*, June 20, 2017, https://www.wired.com/story/russian-hackers-attack-ukraine/.

22. Kim Zetter, "Inside the cunning, unprecedented hack of Ukraine's power grid," *Wired*, March 3, 2017, https://www.wired.com/2016/03/inside-cunning-unprecedented-hack-ukraines-power-grid/.

23. Andy Greenberg, "How an entire nation became Russia's test lab for cyberwar."

24. Ibid.

25. Frank Bajak and Raphael Satter, "Companies still hobbled from fearsome cyberattack," *Associated Press*, June 30, 2017, https://www.apnews.com/ce7a8aca506742ab8e8873e7f9f229c2/Companies-still-hobbled-from-fearsomecyberattack.

26. "Statement from press secretary," The White House, February 15, 2018, https://www.whitehouse.gov/briefings-statements/statement-press-secretary-25/.

27. Barb Darrow, "How hackers broke into U.S. voting machines in less than 2 hours," *Fortune*, July 31, 2017, http://fortune.com/2017/07/31/defcon-hackers-us-voting-machines/.

28. Matt Blaze et al., "Defcon 25 voting machine hacking village: Report on cyber vulnerabilities in U.S. election equipment, databases, and infrastructure" (Defcon, September 2017), https://www.defcon.org/images/defcon-25/DEF%20CON%2025%20voting%20village%20report.pdf.

29. Thomas P. Bossert, "It's official: North Korea is behind WannaCry," *The Wall Street Journal*, December 18, 2017 https://www.wsj.com/

    articles/its-official-north-korea-is-behind-wann
acry-1513642537.

30. Susan Hennessey, "Deterring cyberattacks," *Foreign Affairs*, December 4, 2017, https://www.foreignaffairs.com/reviews/review-essay/2017-10-16/deterring-cyberattacks.

31. Catherine Shu, "Facebook will ditch disputed flags on fake news and display links to trustworthy articles instead," *TechCrunch*, December 20, 2017, https://techcrunch.com/2017/12/20/facebook-will-ditch-disputed-flags-on-fakenews-and-display-links-to-trustworthy-articles-instead/.

32. Lizzie Dearden, "German spy chief warns Russia cyber attacks aiming to influence elections," *The Independent*, May 4, 2017, http://www.independent.co.uk/news/world/europe/germany-spy-chief-russian-cyber-attacks-russiaelections-influence-angela-merkel-putin-hans-georg-a7718006.html.

33. "Bundestag counting cost of cyberattack," *Deutsche Welle*, June 11, 2015, http://www.dw.com/en/bundestagcounting-cost-of-cyberattack/a-18512512.

ALINA POLYAKOVA is the David M. Rubenstein Fellow in the Brookings Institution Foreign Policy program's Center on the United States and Europe and adjunct professor of European studies at the Paul H. Nitze School of Advanced International Studies at Johns Hopkins University. Polyakova holds a doctorate from the University of California, Berkeley.

SPENCER P. BOYER is currently a nonresident senior fellow in the Brookings Institution Foreign Policy program's Center on the United States and Europe and an adjunct professor at Georgetown University's School of Foreign Service. From 2014–2017, he was the national intelligence officer for Europe in the U.S. National Intelligence Council. He has been a senior analyst or visiting scholar with numerous think tanks, including the Center for American Progress, the Center for Transatlantic Relations at the Johns Hopkins School of Advanced International Studies, and the Woodrow Wilson International Center for Scholars.

Molly C. McKew

 **NO**

Putin's Real Long Game

The World Order We Know Is Already Over, and Russia Is Moving Fast to Grab the Advantage. Can Trump Figure Out the New War in Time to Win It?

A little over a year ago, on a pleasant late fall evening, I was sitting on my front porch with a friend best described as a Ukrainian freedom fighter. He was smoking a cigarette while we watched Southeast DC hipsters bustle by and talked about "the war"—the big war, being waged by Russia against all of us, which from this porch felt very far away. I can't remember what prompted it—some discussion of whether the government in Kyiv was doing something that would piss off the EU—but he took a long drag off his cigarette and said, offhand: "Russia. The EU. It's all just more Molotov–Ribbentrop shit."

His casual reference to the Hitler–Stalin pact dividing Eastern Europe before WWII was meant as a reminder that Ukraine must decide its future for itself, rather than let it be negotiated between great powers. But it haunted me, this idea that modern revolutionaries no longer felt some special affinity with the West. Was it the belief in collective defense that was weakening or the underlying certitude that Western values would prevail?

Months later, on a different porch thousands of miles away, an Estonian filmmaker casually explained to me that he was buying a boat to get his family out when the Russians came, so he could focus on the resistance. In between were a hundred other exchanges—with Balts and Ukrainians, Georgians and Moldovans—that answered my question and exposed the new reality on the Russian frontier: the belief that, ultimately, everyone would be left to fend for themselves. Increasingly, people in Russia's sphere of influence were deciding that the values that were supposed to bind the West together could no longer hold. That the world order Americans depend on had already come apart.

From Moscow, Vladimir Putin has seized the momentum of this unraveling, exacting critical damage to the underpinnings of the liberal world order in a shockingly short time. As he builds a new system to replace the one we know, attempts by America and its allies to repair the damage have been limited and slow. Even this week, as Barack Obama tries to confront Russia's open and unprecedented interference in our political process, the outgoing White House is so far responding to 21st century hybrid information warfare with last century's diplomatic tool kit: the expulsion of spies, targeted sanctions, potential asset seizure. The incoming administration, while promising a new approach, has betrayed a similar lack of vision. Their promised attempt at another "reset" with Russia is a rehash of a policy that has utterly failed the past two American administrations.

What both administrations fail to realize is that the West is already at war, whether it wants to be or not. It may not be a war we recognize, but it is a war. This war seeks, at home and abroad, to erode our values, our democracy, and our institutional strength; to dilute our ability to sort fact from fiction, or moral right from wrong; and to convince us to make decisions against our own best interests.

Those on the Russian frontier, like my friends from Ukraine and Estonia, have already seen the Kremlin's new tool kit at work. The most visible example may be "green men," the unlabeled Russian-backed forces that suddenly popped up to seize the Crimean peninsula and occupy eastern Ukraine. But the wider battle is more subtle, a war of subversion rather than domination. The recent interference in the American elections means that these shadow tactics have now been deployed—with surprising effectiveness—not just against American allies but against America itself. And the only way forward for America and the West is to embrace the spirit of the age that Putin has created, plow through the chaos, and focus on building what comes next.

President-elect Trump has characteristics that can aid him in defining what comes next. He is, first and foremost, a rule-breaker, not quantifiable by metrics we know. In a time of inconceivable change that can be an incredible asset. He comes across as a straight talker, and he can be blunt with the American people about the threats we face. He is a man of many narratives and can find a way to sell these decisions to the American people. He believes in strength and knows hard power is necessary.

So far, Trump seems far more likely than any of his predecessors to accelerate, rather than resist, the unwinding of the postwar order. And that could be a very bad—or an unexpectedly good—thing. So far, he has chosen to act as if the West no longer matters, seemingly blind to the danger that Putin's Russia presents to American security and American society. The question ahead of us is whether Trump will aid the Kremlin's goals with his anti-globalist, anti-NATO rhetoric—or whether he'll clearly see the end of the old order, grasp the nature of the war we are in, and have the vision and the confrontational spirit to win it.

***

To understand the shift underway in the world, and to stop being outmaneuvered, we first need to see the Russian state for what it really is. Twenty-five years ago, the Soviet Union collapsed. This freed the Russian security state from its last constraints. In 1991, there were around 800,000 *official* KGB agents in Russia. They spent a decade reorganizing themselves into the newly minted FSB, expanding and absorbing other instruments of power, including criminal networks, other security services, economic interests, and parts of the political elite. They rejected the liberal, democratic Russia that President Boris Yeltsin was trying to build.

Following the 1999 Moscow apartment bombings that the FSB almost certainly planned, former FSB director Vladimir Putin was installed as president. We should not ignore the significance of these events. An internal operation planned by the security services killed hundreds of Russian citizens. It was used as the pretext to relaunch a bloody, devastating internal war led by emergent strongman Putin. Tens of thousands of Chechen civilians and fighters and Russian conscripts died. The narrative was controlled to make the enemy clear and Putin victorious. This information environment forced a specific political objective: Yeltsin resigned and handed power to Putin on New Year's Eve 1999.

From beginning to end, the operation took three months. This is how the Russian security state shook off the controls of political councils or representative democracy. This is how it thinks and how it acts—then, and now. Blood or war might be required, but controlling information and the national response to that information is what matters. Many Russians, scarred by the unrelenting economic, social, and security hardship of the 1990s, welcomed the rise of the security state, and still widely support it, even as it has hollowed out the Russian economy and civic institutions. Today, as a result, Russia is little more than a ghastly hybrid of an overblown police state and a criminal network with an economy the size of Italy—and the world's largest nuclear arsenal.

Even Russian policy hands, raised on the Western understanding of traditional power dynamics, find the implications of this hard to understand. This Russia does not aspire to be like us or to make itself stronger than we are. Rather, its leaders want the West—and specifically NATO and America—to become weaker and more fractured until we are as broken as they perceive themselves to be. No reset can be successful, regardless the personality driving it, because Putin's Russia requires the United States of America as its enemy.

We can only confront this by fully understanding how the Kremlin sees the world. Its worldview and objectives are made abundantly clear in speeches, op-eds, official policy and national strategy documents, journal articles, interviews, and, in some cases, fiction writing of Russian officials and ideologues. We should understand several things from this material.

First, it is a war. A thing to be won, decisively—not a thing to be negotiated or bargained. It's all one war: Ukraine, Turkey, Syria, the Baltics, and Georgia. It's what Vladislav Surkov, Putin's "gray cardinal" and lead propagandist, dubbed "nonlinear war" in his science fiction story "Without Sky," in 2014.

Second, it's all one war machine. Military, technological, information, diplomatic, economic, cultural, criminal, and other tools are all controlled by the state and deployed toward one set of strategic objectives.

This is the Gerasimov doctrine, penned by Valery Gerasimov, the Russian Chief of the General Staff, in 2013. Political warfare is meant to achieve specific political outcomes favorable to the Kremlin: it is preferred to physical conflict because it is cheap and easy. The Kremlin has many notches in its belt in this category, some of which have been attributed, many likely not. It's a mistake to see this campaign in the traditional terms of political alliances: rarely has the goal been to install overtly pro-Russian governments. Far more often, the goal is simply to replace Western-style democratic regimes with illiberal, populist, or nationalist ones.

Third, information warfare is not about creating an alternate truth but eroding our basic ability to distinguish truth at all. It is not "propaganda" as we've come to think of it, but the less obvious techniques known in Russia as "active measures" and "reflexive control." Both are designed to make us, the targets, act against our own best interests.

Fourth, the diplomatic side of this nonlinear war isn't a foreign policy aimed at building a new pro-Russian bloc. Instead, it's what the Kremlin calls a "multivector" foreign policy, undermining the strength of Western institutions by coalescing alternate—ideally temporary and limited—centers of power. Rather than a stable world order undergirded by the United States and its allies, the goal is an unstable new world order of "all against all." The Kremlin has tried to accelerate this process by both inflaming crises that overwhelm the Western response (e.g., the migration crisis in Europe and the war in eastern Ukraine) and by showing superiority in "solving" crises the West could not (e.g., bombing Syria into submission, regardless of the cost, to show Russia can impose stability in the Middle East when the West cannot).

This leads to the final point: hard power matters. Russia maintains the second most powerful military in the world and spends more than 5 percent of its weakened GDP on defense. Russia used military force to invade and occupy Georgian territory in 2008 to disrupt the expansion of NATO, and in 2013 in Ukraine to disrupt the expansion of the EU. They have invested heavily in military reform, new generations of hardware and weapons, and expansive special operations training, much of which debuted in the wars in Ukraine and Syria. There is no denying that Russia is willing to back up its rhetoric and policy with deployed force and that the rest of the world notices.

The West must accept that Putin has transformed what we see as tremendous weakness into considerable strength. If Russia were a strong economy closely linked to the global system, it would have vulnerabilities to more traditional diplomacy. But in the emerging world order, it is a significant actor—and in the current Russian political landscape, no new sanctions can overcome the defensive, insular war-economy mentality that the Kremlin has built.

***

How did we reach this point? After the collapse of the Soviet Union, Western security and political alliances expanded to fill the zone of instability left behind. The emerging Russian security state could only define this as the strategic advance of an enemy. The 9/11 attacks shattered Western concepts of security and conflict and expanded NATO's new mission of projecting security. When Putin offered his assistance, we effectively responded "no thanks," thinking in particular of his bloody, ongoing, scorched-earth war against the Chechens. We did it for the right reasons. Nonetheless, it infuriated Putin. This was the last

moment when any real rapprochement with Putin's Russia was possible.

Since that time, physical warfare has changed in ways that create a new kind of space for Putin to intervene globally. The Obama administration has a deep distaste for official overseas deployments of US troops and the associated political costs. "No new wars" was the oft-repeated mantra—which altered America's toolbox for, if not the frequency of, foreign interventions. Drone warfare was greatly expanded, as was the reliance on special forces—a politically easy choice due to their diverse capabilities and voluntary career commitment to service. But the actual number of special forces operators is exceedingly small and increasingly exhausted; soldiers deployed in shadow wars and shadow missions have far less protection than troops in traditional ground combat.

As the definitions of war and peace have blurred, creating impossibly vast front lines and impossibly vague boundaries of conflict, Putin has launched a kind of global imperialist insurgency. The Kremlin aggressively promotes an alternate ideological base to expand an illiberal world order in which the rights and freedoms that most Americans feel are essential to democracy don't necessarily exist. It backs this up with military, economic, cultural, and diplomatic resources. Through a combination of leveraging hard power and embracing the role of permanent disruptor—hacker, mercenary, rule-breaker, liar, and thief—Putin works to ensure that Russia cannot be excluded from global power.

Putin tries to define recent history as an anomaly—where the world built with American sweat and ingenuity and blood and sacrifice, by the society founded on American exceptionalism, is a thing to be erased and corrected. The Russian version of exceptionalism is not a reflection of aspirational character, but a requirement that Russia remain distinct and apart from the world. Until we understand this, and that America is defined as the *glavny protivnik* (the "main enemy") of Russia, we will never speak to Putin's Russia in a language it can understand.

There is less and less to stand against Putin's campaign of destabilization. It's been 99 years since America began investing in European security with blood, and sweat, and gold. Two world wars and a long, cold conflict later, we felt secure with the institutional framework of NATO and the EU—secure in the idea that these institutions projected our security and our interests far beyond our shores. The post-WWII liberal world order and its accompanying security architecture ushered in an unparalleled period of growth and peace and prosperity for the United States and other transatlantic countries.

I spend most of my time near the Russian frontier, and today that architecture seems like a Kodachrome snapshot from yesteryear. We joke that we yearn for a fight we can win with a gun because the idea of a physical invasion is actually preferable to the constant uncertainty of economic, information, and political shadow warfare from the Kremlin.

Combatants in these shadow wars bear no designations, and protections against these methods are few. From the front lines, in the absence of the fabric of reassurance woven from our values and principles and shared sacrifice—and in the absence of the moral clarity of purpose derived from "us and them"—civil society is left naked, unarmored. Putin has dictated the mood of the unfolding era—an era of upheaval. This past year marks the arrival of this mood in American politics, whether Americans deny it or not. The example of Eastern Europe suggests that without renewed vision and purpose, and without strong alliances to amplify our defense and preserve our legacy, America too will find itself unanchored, adrift in currents stirred, and guided by the Kremlin.

President-elect Trump harnessed this energy of upheaval to win the American presidency—a victory that itself was a symptom of the breakdown of the post-WWII order, in which institutional trust has eroded, and unexpected outcomes have become the order of the day. Now it is his responsibility to define what comes next—or else explain to Americans who want to be great again, why everything they've invested in and sacrificed for over the past century was ultimately for nothing.

As Obama did, Trump has already made the first mistake in negotiating with the Russians: telling them that there is anything to negotiate. Trump likes to discuss Putin's strengths. He should also understand that much of it is smoke and mirrors. A renewed approach to dealing with Putin's Russia should begin by addressing the tactics of Russia's new warfare from the perspective of strength.

We have to accept we're in a war and that we have a lot to lose. We need to look at this war differently, both geographically and strategically. For example, it's hard to understand Ukraine and Syria as two fronts in the same conflict when we never evaluate them together with Moscow in the center of the map, as Russia does. We also need a new national security concept that adds a new strategic framework, connects all our resources, and allows us to better evaluate and respond to Gerasimov-style warfare: we have to learn to fight their one war machine with a unified machine of our own. This will also strengthen and quicken decision-making on critical issues in the United States—something we will also need to replicate within NATO.

Exposing how the Kremlin's political and information warfare works is a critical component of this strategy, as is acting to constrain it. We must (re)accept the notion that hard power is the guarantor of any international system: security is a precondition for anything (everything) else. That the projection of our values has tracked with and been amplified by force projection is no accident. Human freedom requires security. NATO has been the force projection of our values. It hasn't just moved the theoretical line of conflict further forward: the force multiplication and value transference have enhanced our security. This is far cheaper, and far stronger, than trying to do this ourselves.

It's also important to acknowledge that a more isolated, more nationalist America helps Putin in his objectives even while it compromises our own. We need to accept that America was part of, and needs to be part of, a global system—and that this system is better, cheaper, and more powerful than any imagined alternatives. For many years, the United States has been the steel in the framework that holds everything together; this is what we mean by "world order" and "security architecture," two concepts that few politicians try to discuss seriously with the electorate.

Taken together, these steps would be a critical realignment to our strategic thinking and internal operations and would allow us to plow through this era of upheaval with greater certainty and for greater benefit to the American people.

***

In an era increasingly cynical about American ideals, and skeptical about intervention abroad, how can the United States build support for a new, more muscular global resistance to what Russia is trying to do?

We already have one model: the Cold War. Putin and his minions have spent the past 15 years ranting about how the West (specifically NATO) wants a new Cold War. By doing so, they have been conditioning us to deny it and made us do it so continually that we have convinced ourselves it is true. This is classic reflexive control.

The truth is that fighting a new Cold War would be in America's interest. Russia teaches us a very important lesson: losing an ideological war without a fight will ruin you as a nation. *The fight* is the American way. When we stop fighting for our ideals abroad, we stop fighting for them at home. We won the last Cold War. We will win the next one too. When it's us against them, they were, and are, never going to be the winner. But when it's "all against all"—a "multipolar" world with "multivector" policy, a state of shifting alliances and permanent instability—Russia, with a centrally controlled, tiny command structure unaccountable for its actions in any way, still has a chance for a seat at the table. They pursue the multipolar world not because it is right or just, but because it is the only world in which they can continue to matter without pushing a nuclear launch sequence.

We must understand this, and focus now, as Putin does, on shaping the world that comes next and defining what our place is in it. Trump has shown willingness to reevaluate his positions and change course—except on issues relating to Russia, and strengthening alliances with the Kremlin's global illiberal allies. By doing so, he is making himself a footnote to Putin's chapter of history—little more than another of Putin's hollow men.

Trump should understand, regardless of what the Russians did in our elections, he already won the prize. It won't be taken away just because he admits the Russians intervened. Taking away the secrecy of Russian actions—exposing whatever it was they did, to everyone—is the only way to take away their power over the US political system and to free himself from their strings, as well. Whatever Putin's gambit was, Trump is the one who can make sure that Putin doesn't win.

Trump should set the unpredictable course and become the champion against the most toxic, ambitious regime of the modern world. Rebuilding American power—based on the values of liberal democracy—is the

only escape from Putin's corrosive vision of a world at permanent war. We need a new united front.

But we must be the center of it. It matters deeply that the current generation of global revolutionaries and reformers, like my Ukrainian friend, no longer see themselves as fighting for us or our ideals.

In a strange way, Trump could be just crazy enough—enough of a outlier and a rogue—to expose what Putin's Russia is and end the current cycle of upheaval and decline. This requires nonstandard thinking and leadership—but also purpose, and commitment, and values. It requires faith—for and from the American people and American institutions. And it requires the existence of truth.

The alternative is accepting that our history and our nation were, in fact, not the beginning of a better—greater—world, but the long anomaly in a tyrannous and dark one.

MOLLY C. MCKEW advises governments and political parties on foreign policy and strategic communications. She is a registered agent for Georgian President Saakachvili's government, which she advised from 2009 to 2013, and for former Moldovan Prime Minister Filat who has been in prison since 2015.

EXPLORING THE ISSUE

Is the West Losing the Global Information War?

Critical Thinking and Reflection

1. What are the parameters of the global information war and where is it being fought?
2. How does one distinguish between fake news/propaganda and real facts?
3. How does one decide who to trust when gathering information and perspective on political and social issues?
4. What is the long-term impact of such a flood of misinformation throughout the Internet on a host of topics, people, and issues?

Is There Common Ground?

There is clearly a plethora of social media outlets in today's world that revolve around individual interests and perspectives and they are designed to attract and link together like minded individuals. The delivery system of such information allows anyone with an Internet connection to be a player in this battle. The stakes, political, financial, social, and otherwise are significant and alluring for those who have an agenda to promote and for those whom personal gain is the motive.

As this movement and the battle over information continues and accelerates, one area of common ground remains uncharted. That is can reasonable people on sides of any issue come together to agree on the facts surrounding the issue so that a reasoned and educated debate about policy can be held? The answer to that question may indeed tell the tale of who will ultimately win the global information war.

Additional Resources

Berman, Eli, Felter, Joseph H., Shapiro, Jacob, *Small Wars, Big Data: The Information Revolution in Modern Conflict.* Princeton University Press, 2018.

Burke, Colin B., *America's Information Wars: The Untold Story of Information Systems in America's Conflicts and Politics from World War II to the Internet Age.* Rowman & Littlefield, 2018.

Poindexter, Dennis F., *The Chinese Information War: Espionage, Cyberwar, Communications Control and Related Threats to United States Interests*, 2nd ed. McFarland & Company, Inc., 2013.

"U.S. Losing 'Information War' to Russia, Other Rivals." *Arab American News*, March 28, 2015.

"Putin's War on the West. (Cover Story)." *Economist.* February 14, 2015.

Freeman, Seth. "Is America Losing the Information War?" *The Hill*, February 4 2016, thehill.com/blogs/ballot-box/237516-is-america-losing-the-information-war.

Internet References . . .

Business Insider

http://www.businessinsider.com

Foreign Affairs

https://www.foreignaffairs.com

Foreign Policy

http://foreignpolicy.com

The Hill

thehill.com

Selected, Edited, and with Issue Framing Material by:
Mark Owen Lombardi, *Maryville University*

ISSUE

Is the Power of Social Media Undermining Democracy?

YES: **Erica Chenoweth**, from "How Social Media Helps Dictators," *Foreign Policy* (2016)

NO: **Helen Margetts**, from "Of Course Social Media Is Transforming Politics. But It's Not to Blame for Brexit and Trump," *World Economic Forum* (2016)

Learning Outcomes

After reading this issue, you will be able to:

- Understand the pervasiveness and growth of social media in the political and social world.
- Be able to evaluate it both as a tool for change in varying forms regardless of the outcomes.
- Understand that as a tool it can be used by governments, people, movements, religions, and any other social construct for any purpose.
- Understand it is now being manipulated as a tool for propaganda to influence attitudes, policies, elections, and societies.

ISSUE SUMMARY

YES: Erica Chenoweth, University of Denver professor, contends that social media has been hijacked in part by authoritarian and antidemocratic forces to sew doubt and undermine democratic institutions around the globe.

NO: Helen Margetts, professor at the Oxford Internet Institute of the University of Oxford, argues that social media has been used for all kinds of reasons both democratic, social justice, and authoritarian but sounding the alarm that it is now a force for anti-demotic impulses is overtaking its role and missing the larger context.

The revolution that is the Internet and social media is as deep and far reaching as any communication revolution in history. The data analytics alone are staggering. Hundreds of millions of users of mobile technology worldwide that links them through a plethora of social networks from Facebook, Twitter, and Instagram to many you may not have heard of. Since 2001, global population access to a cell phone network grew from 58 percent to 95 percent. Facebook's internet.org is now available to 1 bile lion people across 17 countries. Internet usage in India has grown 37 percent per year. In 2018, advertisers spent over $33 billion on social media marketing. Once a person is online, they use social media networking sites on average 76 percent of the time. And of the total world population of 7.395 billion people, approximately 2.307 are active social media users.

These statistics while fascinating merely reflect awareness, access, and usage. They do not grasp the depth of how social media is being used; who and what messages are being transmitted; what political and social causes are being promoted; what actions are being organized and initiated; and of course what impact they are having. Today, small groups of like-minded people around the globe can connect with each other, share information, mobilize political action, raise money, and directly impact policy and governmental actions without ever leaving their homes. Let's visit one small example. In 2009, when social media was in its infancy, a Congressman from South Carolina shouted "You lie" during the state of the union address of President Obama. By the next day, his office had raised some $2 million dollars from those who agreed with his outburst. That showed the power of social media to mobilize, in this case money for a political candidate.

Social media is an evolving dynamic tool for communication, expression, mobilization, and action. It is now being utilized in thousands of ways by hundreds of groups for both good works (crowdsourcing for cancer research or to find lost children) and evil ends (recruiting suicide bombers, spreading fake news to influence elections, or spreading gospels of racist hate). Its' power and impact across the global landscape is dynamic and very much still under debate.

Two recent examples illustrate this growing power. The Arab Spring of 2010–2016 despite its mixed record of success showed the power of political unrest mixed with social media. The other example is of course the recent US election of 2016, and how the manipulation of social media by Russia influenced attitudes and perspectives leading up to the vote.

While social media was initially seen as a tool to empower marginalized people and groups in their quest to be heard, express themselves, and effect change, it has also become clear that governments and interest groups have mastered it in order to spread false information, undermine truth, and sow seeds of doubt in established democratic processes. Take the example of the US election. Without debating the positive or negative dimensions of the outcome, one fact is clear. Russia engineered a detailed manipulation of social media to spread a variety of false stories (using Facebook among others) to impact voter attitudes and favor one candidate over another.

This and other such uses in places like Great Britain, the Ukraine, Romania, Italy, Austria, among others have led scholars to speculate that social media is now being mobilized in an attack on democracy. They base that position on the fact that in order to have a functioning and healthy democracy one needs an educated citizenry who can rely on new sources for facts. Without that reliance, democratic principles and institutions can be undermined and breakdown, and as a result people doubt the validity of information and election outcomes. For example, over 50 percent of republicans in the United States believe that widespread voter fraud led to Hillary Clinton gaining some 2.5 million more votes than Donald Trump despite the fact that there is absolutely no evidence that such fraud occurred. That is an example of using social media to undermine democracy.

Chenoweth contends that social media has now been hijacked by antidemocratic forces around the world to undermine democracy and shape public attitudes toward antidemocratic parties and ideas. Margetts argues that social media is not a malignant force but rather used for all kinds go good and bad purposes and should not be castigated simply because some anti-demotic forces have discovered its power to shape the debate.

YES ⬅

Erica Chenoweth

How Social Media Helps Dictators

It's Been Hailed as "Liberation Technology." But It Has a Darker Side.

Many people think that social media has been a boon for grassroots social and political movements, and it's easy to understand why. The rise of Facebook, Twitter, and other technologies since the mid-2000s has coincided with an explosive increase in popular uprisings during the same period. Whether it's organizing revolutions in Egypt and Iran, tracking Russian troop movements in Ukraine, or providing real-time information to protesters in Sudan, social media is supposed to give activists an edge.

It's a reasonable assumption—and there are indeed many ways in which these new technologies can help. Perhaps most obviously, social media can lower the costs of communicating the crucial "where, where, how, and why" of protests to large numbers of people, as Twitter did during the 2014 Euromaidan revolution in Ukraine. Other platforms, such as YouTube, can help popularize basic knowledge about how to protest effectively, helping movements build organizational capacity. When physical gatherings are prohibited, digital venues such as Facebook or Reddit can create forums for new, virtual public spheres that are difficult to shut down.

Internet optimists also argue that online venues create space for dialogue in the midst of conflict, presenting policy options to the public and to elites in spite of government censorship. And, of course, the Internet allows activists to promote their own narrative, which is particularly important when the mainstream media is controlled by the government.

Yet in spite of this optimism, what is sometimes known as "liberation technology" is not, in fact, making pro-democracy movements more effective. It's true that we've seen more episodes of mass mobilization since the rise of digital communications than we did before. But we should note that the stunning rise of nonviolent resistance came long before the Internet. The technique has enjoyed widespread use since Gandhi popularized the method in the 1930s and 1940s. And in fact, nonviolent resistance has actually become less successful compared to earlier, pre-Internet times. Whereas nearly 70 percent of civil resistance campaigns succeeded during the 1990s, only 30 percent have succeeded since 2010.

Why Might This Be?

There are a few possible reasons. First, as Political Scientist Anita Gohdes has carefully documented, governments are simply better at manipulating social media than activists. Despite early promises of anonymity online, commercial and government surveillance has made Internet privacy a thing of the past. The Russian government, for example, has successfully infiltrated activists' communications to anticipate and crush even the smallest protests. These practices are common in democracies too. In the United States, the National Security Agency's warrantless wiretapping program, or Yahoo's collaboration with the U.S. government in harvesting information from its users, is probably just the beginning. Recent reports indicate that local police departments (including in my own city of Denver) monitor social media to harvest data about their districts. While in the past, governments had to devote significant resources to detecting dissidents, today's digital climate encourages people to proudly announce their political, social, and religious beliefs and identities—data that allow law enforcement and security services to target them that much more effectively. Of course, there are ways for people to protect their privacy, but few of these techniques will hold up against a dedicated adversary.

Second, the turn to social media among popular movements has degraded the experience of participating. Activists and "clicktivists" might connect and pay attention to an issue for a short amount of time, but they often fail to engage fully in the struggle. Building trust in marginalized or oppressed communities takes time, effort, and sustained interactions, and this requires routine face-to-face contact over a long period. When movements mobilize without having earned this sense of trust and internal unity, they may be more likely to succumb under pressure. Participating in digital activism can give the impression that one is making a difference, but as Internet skeptic Evgeny Morozov argues, creating real change requires far greater dedication and sacrifice.

Third, social media can have a demobilizing effect by enabling armed actors to threaten or even coordinate direct violence against activists. For instance, in the midst of the Libyan uprising in 2011, Muammar Qaddafi's regime coopted the country's cell phone network, sending text messages that ordered people to go back to work. It was a chilling warning that the government was watching—and that failing to comply would have consequences. Political scientists Florian Hollenbach and Jan Pierskalla have found that greater availability of cell phones in Africa is associated with an increase in violence.

Conversely, if activists use social media to report violence by security forces, would-be protesters may not show up to the big demonstration the next day. Such reports can therefore carry unintended consequences. Instead of drawing outraged crowds, they may repel many risk-averse participants, leaving the movement's hard-liners and risk-takers on their own.

This relates to a final important disadvantage: misinformation can spread on social media just as fast (or faster) than reliable information.

· · ·

Reports of Russian trolls manipulating a polarized information environment to influence the recent U.S. elections are a case in point. And misinformation is only compounded by peoples' tendency to select news sources that confirm their prior beliefs. The echo chambers so prevalent in the social media serve to further divide societies instead of uniting them behind a common cause.

Even those who are well-intentioned and diligent about reading reliable and credentialed news sources can inadvertently cause problems. Seeing the downfall of a tyrant through social media can encourage dissidents in a neighboring country to rise up in identical fashion. In fact, they may try to prematurely "import" the tactics and methods they see used successfully elsewhere into their own situation—with disastrous consequences. One needs look no further than Libya or Syria to see the danger of this effect. It was easy for activists in those countries to watch the Arab Spring unfold in Tunisia and Egypt and conclude that, if they assembled masses of people in public squares, they too could topple their dictators in a matter of days. This conclusion neglected the years-long mobilizations that preceded the Tunisian and Egyptian uprisings and led Libyans and Syrians to be overconfident in the ability of improvised uprisings to succeed nonviolently.

Kurt Weyland's study of the 1848 revolutions found that dissidents have been learning the wrong lessons from yesterday's revolution for centuries. But social media almost certainly exacerbates this dilemma by encouraging the diffusion of simplistic snapshots in 140-character doses rather than through studied and methodical analysis.

"Where activists were once defined by their causes, they are now defined by their tools," wrote Malcolm Gladwell in 2010. And that's a bad thing when it comes to building and sustaining resilient popular campaigns. But instead of seeing the more recent failures as a failure of nonviolent mobilization per se, we should adopt a more complex and realistic understanding of the ways in which increased reliance on social media has undermined the success of mass mobilization. It's not the technique that's broken, necessarily. It's the tools.

Erica Chenoweth is a professor and an associate dean for research at the Josef Korbel School of International Studies at the University of Denver.

Helen Margetts

 **NO**

Of Course Social Media Is Transforming Politics. But It's Not to Blame for Brexit and Trump

After Brexit and the election of Donald Trump, the year 2016 will be remembered as the year of cataclysmic democratic events on both sides of the Atlantic. Social media has been implicated in the wave of populism that led to both these developments.

Attention has focused on echo chambers, with many arguing that social media users exist in ideological filter bubbles, narrowly focused on their own preferences, prey to fake news and political bots, reinforcing polarization, and leading voters to turn away from the mainstream. Mark Zuckerberg has responded with the strange claim that his company (built on $5 billion of advertising revenue) does not influence people's decisions.

So what role *did* social media play in the political events of 2016?

Political Turbulence and the New Populism

There is no doubt that social media has brought change to politics. From the waves of protest and unrest in response to the 2008 financial crisis, to the Arab Spring of 2011, there has been a generalized feeling that political mobilization is on the rise and that social media had something to do with it.

Our book investigating the relationship between social media and collective action, *Political Turbulence*, focuses on how social media allows new, "tiny acts" of political participation (liking, tweeting, viewing, following, signing petitions, and so on), which turn social movement theory around. Rather than identifying with issues, forming collective identity and then acting to support the interests of that identity—or voting for a political party that supports it—in a social media world, people act first, and think about it, or identify with others later, if at all.

These tiny acts of participation can scale up to large-scale mobilizations, such as demonstrations, protests, or campaigns for policy change. But they almost always don't. The overwhelming majority (99.99 percent) of petitions to the UK or US governments fail to get the 100,000 signatures required for a parliamentary debate (United Kingdom) or an official response (United States).

The very few that succeed do so very quickly on a massive scale (petitions challenging the Brexit and Trump votes immediately shot above 4 million signatures, to become the largest petitions in history), but without the normal organizational or institutional trappings of a social or political movement, such as leaders or political parties—the reason why so many of the Arab Spring revolutions proved disappointing.

. . .

This explosive rise, nonnormal distribution, and lack of organization that characterizes contemporary politics can explain why many political developments of our time seem to come from nowhere. It can help to understand the shock waves of support that brought us the Italian Five Star Movement, Podemos in Spain, Jeremy Corbyn, Bernie Sanders, and most recently Brexit and Trump—all of which have campaigned against the "establishment" and challenged traditional political institutions to breaking point.

Each successive mobilization has made people believe that challengers from outside the mainstream are viable—and that is in part what has brought us unlikely results on both sides of the Atlantic. But it doesn't explain everything.

We've had waves of populism before—long before social media (indeed, many have made parallels between the politics of 2016 and that of the 1930s). While claims that social media feeds are the biggest threat to democracy, leading to the "disintegration of the general will" and "polarization that drives populism," abound, hard evidence is more difficult to find.

The Myth of the Echo Chamber

The mechanism that is most often offered for this state of events is the existence of echo chambers or filter bubbles. The argument goes that first social media platforms feed people the news that is closest to their own ideological standpoint (estimated from their previous patterns of consumption) and second, that people create their own personalized information environments through their online behavior, selecting friends and news sources that back up their world view.

Once in these ideological bubbles, people are prey to fake news and political bots that further reinforce their views. So, some argue, social media reinforces people's current views and acts as a polarizing force on politics, meaning that "random exposure to content is gone from our diets of news and information."

Really? Is exposure less random than before? Surely, the most perfect echo chamber would be the one occupied by someone who only read the *Daily Mail* in the 1930s—with little possibility of other news—or someone who just watches Fox News? Can our new habitat on social media really be as closed off as these environments, when our digital networks are so very much larger and more heterogeneous than anything we've had before?

Research suggests not. A recent large-scale survey (of 50,000 news consumers in 26 countries) shows how those who do not use social media on average come across news from significantly fewer different online sources than those who do. Social media users, it found, receive an additional "boost" in the number of news sources they use each week, even if they are not actually trying to consume more news. These findings are reinforced by an analysis of Facebook data, where 8.8 billion posts, likes, and comments were posted through the US election.

Recent research published in *Science* shows that algorithms play less of a role in exposure to attitude-challenging content than individuals' own choices and that "on average, more than 20 percent of an individual's Facebook friends who report an ideological affiliation are from the opposing party," meaning that social media exposes individuals to at least some ideologically crosscutting viewpoints: "24 percent of the hard content shared by liberals' friends is crosscutting, compared to 35 percent for conservatives" (the equivalent figures would be 40 percent and 45 percent if random).

. . .

In fact, companies have no incentive to create hermetically sealed (as I have heard one commentator claim) echo chambers. Most of the social media content is not about politics (sorry guys)—most of that £5 billion advertising revenue does not come from political organizations. So any incentives that companies have to create echo chambers—for the purposes of targeted advertising, for example—are most likely to relate to lifestyle choices or entertainment preferences, rather than political attitudes.

And where filter bubbles do exist they are constantly shifting and sliding—easily punctured by a trending cross-issue item (anybody looking at #Election2016 shortly before polling day would have seen a rich mix of views, while having little doubt about Trump's impending victory).

And of course, even if political echo chambers were as efficient as some seem to think, there is little evidence that this is what actually shapes election results. After all, by definition, echo chambers preach to the converted. It is the undecided people who (for example) the Leave and Trump campaigns needed to reach.

And from the research, it looks like they managed to do just that. A barrage of evidence suggests that such advertising was effective in the 2015 UK general election (where the Conservatives spent 10 times as much as Labour on Facebook advertising), in the EU referendum (where the Leave campaign also focused on paid Facebook ads), and in the presidential election, where Facebook advertising has been credited for Trump's victory, while the Clinton campaign focused on TV ads. And of course, advanced advertising techniques might actually focus on those undecided voters from their conversations. This is not the bottom-up political mobilization that fired off support for Podemos or Bernie Sanders. It is massive top-down advertising dollars.

Ironically, however, these huge top-down political advertising campaigns have some of the same characteristics as the bottom-up movements discussed above, particularly sustainability. Former New York Governor Mario Cuomo's dictum that candidates "campaign in poetry and govern in prose" may need an update. Barack Obama's innovative campaigns of online social networks, micro-donations, and matching support were miraculous, but the extent to which he developed digital government or data-driven policy-making in office was disappointing. Campaign digitally, govern in analogue might be the new mantra.

Chaotic Pluralism

Politics is a lot messier in the social media era than it used to be—whether something takes off and succeeds in gaining critical mass is far more random than it appears to be from a casual glance, where we see only those that succeed.

In *Political Turbulence*, we wanted to identify the model of democracy that best encapsulates politics intertwined with social media. The dynamics we observed seem to be leading us to a model of "chaotic pluralism," characterized by diversity and heterogeneity—similar to early pluralist models—but also by nonlinearity and high interconnectivity, making liberal democracies far more disorganized, unstable, and unpredictable than the architects of pluralist political thought ever envisaged.

Perhaps rather than blaming social media for undermining democracy, we should be thinking about how we can improve the (inevitably major) part that it plays.

. . .

Within chaotic pluralism, there is an urgent need for redesigning democratic institutions that can accommodate new forms of political engagement and respond to the discontent, inequalities, and feelings of exclusion—even anger and alienation—that are at the root of the new populism. We should be using social media to listen to (rather than merely talk at) the expression of these public sentiments and not just at election time.

Many political institutions—for example, the British Labour Party, the US Republican Party, and the first-past-the-post electoral system shared by both countries—are in crisis, precisely because they have become so far removed from the concerns and needs of citizens. Redesign will need to include social media platforms themselves, which have rapidly become established as institutions of democracy and will be at the heart of any democratic revival.

As these platforms finally start to admit to being media companies (rather than tech companies), we will need to demand human intervention and transparency over algorithms that determine trending news; fact-checking (where Google took the lead); algorithms that detect fake news; and possibly even "public interest" bots to counteract the rise of computational propaganda.

Meanwhile, the only thing we can really predict with certainty is that unpredictable things will happen and that social media will be part of our political future.

Discussing the echoes of the 1930s in today's politics, the *Wall Street Journal* points out how Roosevelt managed to steer between the extremes of left and right because he knew that "public sentiments of anger and alienation aren't to be belittled or dismissed, for their causes can be legitimate and their consequences powerful." The path through populism and polarization may involve using the opportunity that social media presents to listen, understand, and respond to these sentiments.

HELEN MARGETTS is a professor of Society and the Internet, a political scientist specializing in digital government and politics.

EXPLORING THE ISSUE

Is the Power of Social Media Undermining Democracy?

Critical Thinking and Reflection

1. What are the dimensions of social media that make it a powerful force?
2. What actors seem most adept at using it to further their political goals?
3. Is social media an inherent good or evil or is it simply a tool and its character is shaped by the actor using it?
4. Can governments control the impact of social media on their own citizens?

Is There Common Ground?

Determining the relative power of social media when compared to other forces in global politics is certainly debatable and a moving target. The evolution of technology to communicate, disseminate, shield, and secure is rapidly changing on an almost weekly basis. What most analysts can agree on is that social media has empowered millions more people and groups within the international system to engage in both good works, political organization along with crime and violence. This explosion of access for millions has made the international system more volatile, more fluid, and potentially more dangerous.

Additional Resources

Pariser, Eli, *The Filter Bubble: What the Internet Is Hiding from You* (Penguin Press, 2011).

Vaidhyanathan, Siva, *Antisocial Media: How Facebook Disconnects Us and Undermines Democracy* (Oxford University Press, 2018).

Sunstein, Cass, *#Republic: Divided Democracy in the Age of Social Media* (Princeton University Press, 2017).

Noble, Safiya Umoja, *Algorithms of Oppression: How Search Engines Reinforce Racism* (NYU Press, 2018).

Barberá, Pablo and Thomas Zeitzoff. "The New Public Address System: Why Do World Leaders Adopt Social Media?" *International Studies Quarterly*, (Mar. 2018).

Tucker, Joshua, et al. "Analysis: This Explains How Social Media Can Both Weaken – and Strengthen – Democracy." *The Washington Post*, WP Company, Dec. 6, 2017, www.washingtonpost.com/news/monkey-cage/wp/2017/12/06/this-explains-how-social-media-can-both-weaken-and-strengthen-democracy/?noredirect=on&utm_term=.2d295409ac95.

Hull, Gordon. "Why Social Media May Not Be so Good for Democracy." *The Conversation*, June 14, 2018, theconversation.com/why-social-media-may-not-be-so-good-for-democracy-86285.

"New Report - Freedom on the Net 2017: Manipulating Social Media to Undermine Democracy." *Freedom House*, Jan. 16, 2018, freedomhouse.org/article/new-report-freedom-net-2017-manipulating-social-media-undermine-democracy.

Internet References . . .

Foreign Affairs

    https://www.foreignaffairs.com

Foreign Policy

    http://foreignpolicy.com

Freedom House

    https://freedomhouse.org

The Conversation

    https://theconversation.com/us

The Washington Post

    https://www.washingtonpost.com

Unit 3

UNIT

The New Global Security Agenda

*W*ith the end of the cold war, the concept of security was freed from the constraints of bipolar power politics and a purely state-centric focus. No longer were issues framed simply in terms of the United States–Soviet Union conflict (Vietnam, Afghanistan, and the Middle East) but rather analyzed in more complex ways related to issues of ethnicity, religious fundamentalism, cultural division, nuclear proliferation, and new asymmetrical forms of conflict driven not the least of which by technological evolution. What is clear over the ensuing three decades is that the global security agenda is becoming more complicated and the issues more numerous as new actor, issues, modes of communication, warfare, and ideologies take center stage.

This new security agenda poses difficult challenges for state and nonstate actors alike in terms of how to respond, when or if they should use force, how they can survive challenges, and whether their ways of promoting a more peaceful world are working. Issues from the role of social media to cyberwarfare to nuclear proliferation in Iran and North Korea and the likelihood of nuclear war to the emergence of China and a resurgent Russia now hold sway over the discourse. Add to these problems the civil war in Syria with intervention from many outside countries and the continuing struggle to find a lasting solution to the Israeli–Palestinian conflict. When examined within the accelerating forces of globalization and technology, however, these challenges take on new and at times more frightening manifestations.

Selected, Edited, and with Issue Framing Material by:
Marie E. Harf, *U.S. Department of State (2013–2017),*
Central Intelligence Agency (2006–2011)

ISSUE

Were Efforts to Withdraw the United States from the Iran Nuclear Agreement Misguided?*

Yes: Philip Gordon and Richard Nephew, from "The 'Worst Deal Ever' That Actually Wasn't," *The Atlantic,* (2017)

No: "Remarks by President Trump on the Joint Comprehensive Plan of Action," *The White House* (2018)

Learning Outcomes

After reading this issue, you will be able to:

- Describe the history of the relationship between the United States and Iran, and of Iran's nuclear program.
- Describe the path of negotiations over Iran's nuclear program.
- Outline the main components in the agreement on Iran's nuclear program.
- Describe the issues that have defined the debate over the agreement, including the specific views of President Donald Trump.
- Describe what implications President Trump's decision to withdraw from the agreement might have.

ISSUE SUMMARY

Yes: The authors, both policy makers who were part of the team that negotiated the Iran nuclear deal, argue it is achieving its objective of preventing Iran from acquiring enough fissile material for a nuclear weapon and therefore blocking Iran's pathways to the bomb. They argue that the myth of a "better deal" is simply wishful thinking and paint a bleak picture of how much stronger Iran's program would be without the deal in place. Therefore, they argue, efforts to walk away from the agreement are misguided.

No: In announcing that the United States was leaving the Iran nuclear agreement, President Trump argued that the deal "allowed Iran to continue enriching uranium and, over time, reach the brink of a nuclear breakout." He further stated that Iran's claim it desired a peaceful nuclear program "was a lie." Furthermore, the President also suggested that the deal failed to address Iran's development of ballistic missiles and provides "inadequate mechanisms to prevent, detect, and punish cheating . . . ."

On May 8, 2018, President Donald Trump announced that the United States was leaving the Joint Comprehensive Plan of Action (JCPOA), the multinational agreement to limit Iran's nuclear program. Keeping a campaign promise, Trump also said that he would reimpose U.S. nuclear sanctions on Iran that had been lifted as part of the deal between Tehran and the major Western powers, Russia,

---

Note to the Reader: *One of this book's coeditors, Marie E. Harf, worked on the Iran nuclear negotiations at the U.S. Department of State from 2013 until 2017.*

and China. Iran can now either continue working with the remaining signatories as part of the deal or abandon the agreement and resume its nuclear activity that the JCPOA had constrained.

President Trump's action is the latest chapter in the long-standing saga between Iran and the United States. Most Americans today view Iran primarily through the prism of the 1979 Iranian Revolution and the subsequent hostage crisis, when 52 U.S. diplomats and civilians were held for 444 days. The United States and Iran have not had diplomatic relations since 1980, and Iran has for decades supported actors opposed to America's and to its partners' interests in the region. Before the revolution, however, the United States and Iran were close allies. In fact, the United States provided Iran with key nuclear technology and education under President Eisenhower's Atoms for Peace Program, and in 1967, gave Iran a 5-megawatt nuclear research reactor (its first) and the necessary fuel for it.

Postrevolution, Iran began more secretive nuclear work, viewing its nuclear capability as a deterrent against the United States, Israel, and Iraq. Within decades, Iran had developed a vast network of nuclear-related facilities. The public exposure of covert nuclear sites led countries, individually and collectively, to sanction Iran. But despite this international pressure, Iran continued to expand the size and capability of its program, moving dangerously close to having enough fissile material for a nuclear weapon.

In 2009, President Barack Obama took office pledging to press Iran to come into compliance with its international obligations and to explore whether the nuclear issue could be resolved diplomatically. This openness finally paid off in 2013 when Iran elected a more moderate president, Hassan Rouhani, who called for serious negotiations over its nuclear program to relieve the country's crippling economic sanctions. The U.S. Secretary of State met with the Iranian Foreign Minister for the first time in decades that fall, and the two countries' presidents spoke by phone, ushering in a new era of diplomacy.

The P5+1 coalition (composed of the United States, the United Kingdom, France, Germany, China, and Russia), the European Union (EU), and Iran agreed to an interim deal in Fall 2013, halting the progress of Iran's nuclear program while giving negotiators time and space to hammer out a final agreement to cut off Iran's pathways to a nuclear weapon. For the next 19 months, negotiators worked through all the complicated technical and political issues, and on July 14, 2015, the JCPOA was announced in Vienna. The deal took effect in January 2016 after Iran had completed its nuclear commitments, at which point nuclear-related sanctions on Iran were lifted.

Exactly what was agreed to in the JCPOA? In sum, Iran accepted strict limitations on and monitoring of its nuclear program in return for the lifting of extensive nuclear-related economic sanctions. Iran agreed to reduce its installed centrifuges by ⅔ and its enriched uranium stockpile by 98 percent and to cap its enrichment at 3.67 percent, well below the level necessary for a bomb. It accepted limits on research and development of advanced centrifuges and filled the core of its plutonium reactor with concrete, rendering it unusable. Iran agreed to allow International Atomic Energy Agency (IAEA) inspectors to monitor its declared sites and visit nondeclared sites and said it would adhere to the Additional Protocol, a lifetime safeguards agreement that gives the IAEA access to Iran's nuclear facilities. Tehran also reaffirmed that it will never seek, develop, or acquire any nuclear weapons. In return, once Iran verifiably completed those steps, the P5+1 and the EU agreed to suspend or cancel nuclear-related sanctions.

Since the JCPOA was signed, there have been heated debates between supporters and critics, which form the backdrop of the discussion about whether the United States should withdraw. Both among analysts who believe the deal is a good one and those who do not, the conversation about U.S. withdrawal has focused on (1) the best ways to combat perceived deal weaknesses and (2) the impact such a move would have. But let us turn first to the wider debates about the deal itself.

Proponents of the JCPOA, including top scientists, have argued the deal's technical aspects shut off Iran's pathways to accumulate enough fissile material to make a nuclear weapon and, through the most stringent set of verification ever negotiated, established the monitoring and transparency mechanisms necessary to ensure Iran's compliance. They assert that the agreement is the best of the options available to deal with Iran's nuclear program and that without it, the world could be forced either to accept Iran becoming a nuclear weapons power or to prevent that eventuality by force. Two of the deal's U.S. negotiators, Philip Gordon and Richard Nephew, outline what Iran's current program would look like without the deal in our YES article: "Iran today would likely be only weeks from possessing enough weapons-usable material for a bomb. And without the verification procedures Iran committed to in the agreement, the international community would have no reliable way of knowing if it was stockpiling that material, until it was too late" (*The Atlantic*, July 14, 2017).

Deal opponents have a variety of criticisms. Some argue that any agreement is unwise because Iran will always cheat, and the international community should not confer legitimacy on a rogue state. Critics such as President Trump's third National Security Advisor John Bolton have argued the deal should not have allowed Iran any uranium enrichment whatsoever, even though Iran had already mastered the technology and JCPOA negotiators judged it impossible to completely destroy that know-how.

The primary technical issue that deal opponents have criticized involves its "sunset provisions," the fact that some of the JCPOA's restrictions expire in set time frames. As a result, these commentators argue the deal only delays, instead of destroys, Iran's ability to acquire a nuclear weapon (Mark Dubowitz, *Foundation for the Defense of Democracies*, July 14, 2016). They do not credit deal supporters' arguments that the JCPOA has many "forever" restrictions and that the best response to a concern about sunsets is to negotiate to extend them, not to move those sunset timelines up to today by withdrawing. On the sanctions side, a disagreement has raged over the amount of relief Iran received. Under the deal, Iran regained access to billions of dollars-worth of its currency that had been frozen by sanctions. While the exact dollar figures and how Iran has used them are debatable, it is worth keeping in mind that a diplomatic solution always rested on the concept of swapping nuclear restrictions for sanctions relief. The question was what the details of that relief would look like.

Another overarching critique of the JCPOA is that it should have also tackled Iran's other problematic nonnuclear behavior, such as its support for terrorism, its ballistic missile program, its dismal human rights record, and its ongoing unjust detention of American citizens. Critics argue that the agreement's singular focus on nuclear issues constrained the ability of the United States and its allies to counter Iran's other nefarious activities and actually emboldened Iran to be more aggressive in the region. Conversely, deal proponents dispute that the JCPOA took any options off the table in responding to Iranian malfeasance, which they point out would be much more dangerous if backed up by a nuclear deterrent that the deal prevents. Moreover, negotiators question whether an all-encompassing agreement was achievable, given the world was only united on one issue regarding Iran: its nuclear capability. Attempting to expand the negotiations beyond the nuclear file risked devolving into a paralyzing internal fight among the U.S. side and its partners (Colin Kahl, *Foreign Policy*, September 26, 2017).

While these (and other) disagreements have continued, the IAEA and the U.S. Intelligence Community have repeatedly confirmed that Iran is complying with the JCPOA.

Whatever the merits of the agreement, what are the potential consequences of the U.S. withdrawal? First, commentators have argued it will lead to a loss of American influence globally and undercut years of U.S. leadership on nonproliferation. America's partners in the deal and in much of the global community are unhappy with the U.S. decision, with the notable exception of Israeli Prime Minister Benjamin Netanyahu. This reduced standing could, for starters, complicate attempts to forge the kind of new agreement on Iran the Trump administration says it wants to work toward. John Bolton, before he became National Security advisor, wrote that if the United States did withdraw, it should undertake a robust international campaign to explain the decision and detail its plan to ratchet up pressure on Iran (*National Review*, August 28, 2017). Even with that kind of outreach, rebuilding essential international support for this pressure campaign—especially asking other countries to take actions that are tough on their economies—could prove difficult amid widespread international frustration with the United States.

The diplomatic fallout could also extend to North Korea, where the Trump administration is pursuing a reinvigorated diplomatic process over that country's nuclear program. The idea that the United States does not adhere to its own international agreements on nuclear weapons may well complicate those negotiations, as could frustration on the part of JCPOA-signatory China, just as the United States needs Beijing to help with Pyongyang.

Finally, there is a concern that the American withdrawal could empower Iran's hard-liners and undercut its moderates—the opposite of what the Trump administration seeks—because those moderates who supported the negotiations will be accused by the more skeptical hard-liners of naively believing U.S. promises. This could in turn make future negotiations more difficult.

Having decided to withdraw the United States from the JCPOA, the Trump administration will now be judged on how well it contains the fallout from that decision and whether it can create a more effective approach to address Iran's misbehavior (nuclear and otherwise) than the one it jettisoned. Whether President Trump and his team can pass this test remains to be seen. One immediate issue is whether the Trump administration will leave space for the other signatories to sustain the deal or take steps to ensure it does not survive the U.S. withdrawal. That too is an unanswered question—one of many that will remain as the world continues in its quest to prevent Iran from obtaining a nuclear weapon.

In the YES selection, former U.S. policy makers Philip Gordon and Richard Nephew argue the deal "is doing exactly what it was supposed to do," namely, to keep Iran from acquiring sufficient fissile material to build a nuclear weapon. In the NO selection, President Trump argues that that Iran nuclear program agreement is fatally flawed, believing that it allowed Iran to continue on the path toward nuclear weapons as well as to the development of missiles capable of delivering these weapons great distances. Furthermore, he argues that it does "nothing to constrain Iran's destabilizing activities, including its support of terrorism."

YES

Philip Gordon and Richard Nephew

The "Worst Deal Ever" That Actually Wasn't

It Is True That Iran's Behavior in the Region Has Not Improved.
But It Is Also True That This Behavior Cannot Be Attributed to the Nuclear Deal.

Today, the Iran nuclear deal turns two years old. In its critics' eyes, it has already failed. President Donald Trump and many of his supporters complain that it has not changed Iran's regional behavior, pointing to Tehran's continued support for regional proxies and ongoing ballistic missile tests as proof. Other critics, including Senators Tom Cotton, Ted Cruz, David Perdue, and Marco Rubio, who wrote a letter to the administration denouncing the deal just this week, suggest that Iran may actually be violating it. They allege a range of technical violations, even though the International Atomic Energy Agency—and Trump's State Department, for that matter—have confirmed Iran's compliance.

In fact, the deal is doing exactly what is was supposed to do: prevent Iran from acquiring enough fissile material for a nuclear weapon, demonstrate to the Iranian public the benefits of cooperation with the international community, and buy time for potential changes in Iranian politics and foreign policy.

Anyone who thought a deal would immediately change Iran's regional agenda or who maintains that, if only America and its partners had insisted on such changes in the talks they would have materialized, has a misguided sense of what sanctions and diplomatic pressure can accomplish. Having been deeply involved in the negotiations, we think it's important to be clear about the purpose, enduring benefits, and inevitable limitations of the agreement.

The chief benefit of the agreement was to block Iran's pathways to the bomb by freezing or reducing its capacity to produce the amounts of fissile materials required to do so—the most difficult step in the bomb-making process. Thus, as we know from the additional IAEA inspectors and 24/7 on-site cameras deployed as part of the agreement,

Iran today operates only some 5,000 older-model centrifuges, maintains a much reduced stockpile of enriched uranium, limits its centrifuge research and development programs, and has filled the core of its heavy-water nuclear reactor with concrete. Whereas experts assessed that, at the time of the deal, Iran was only months from being able to produce enough nuclear material for a bomb; under these new terms, it is now at least a year away—plenty of time for the international community to anticipate any oncoming danger and respond accordingly.

Where would Iran be today without the agreement? It's hard to know for sure, but even if Tehran had continued only to steadily expand its nuclear program as it had for the previous two decades, it would today likely be operating the more than 20,000 centrifuges it had at the time of the agreement. Iran would have continued enriching uranium and building its stockpiles, and it would've been operating a fully functional heavy-water nuclear reactor capable of producing enough plutonium for one or two nuclear weapons per year, all without the additional verification provisions put in place to ensure this was *all* it was doing.

What that means: Without the deal, Iran would today likely be only weeks from possessing enough weapons-usable material for a bomb. And without the verification procedures Iran committed to in the agreement, the international community would have no reliable way of knowing if it was stockpiling that material—until it was too late.

Critics assert that tougher sanctions and the threat of military force could have prevented Iran from arriving at this point. This argument does not hold up to scrutiny. Economic sanctions, even when progressively tightened over the years, never halted Iran's program. When George W. Bush took office in 2001, Iran possessed only a few hundred centrifuges and no stockpile of enriched uranium. In the years that followed, Bush expanded U.S. sanctions and obtained three UN Security Council resolutions that all imposed real pressure on Iran. Yet when he left office in 2009, Iran had nearly 6,000 centrifuges, over 2,000 pounds of low enriched uranium, a partly built heavy-water reactor, and a secret underground enrichment facility.

Even after international sanctions were dramatically expanded and toughened in 2010 through 2012 under Obama, Iran continued expanding the quantity of its centrifuges, grew its enriched-uranium stock to more than 30,000 pounds, and build its heavy-water reactor—right up until the November 2013 Joint Plan of Action froze that program, paving the way for negotiations. It is wishful thinking to imagine that Iran, after expanding its program for decades despite heavy sanctions, would have miraculously decided in 2016 or 2017 to suddenly unilaterally refrain from any further nuclear advances, or even abandon its program altogether.

Critics also claim that the threat of force could have deterred Iran from expanding its program—another case of wishful thinking. Under Bush, who had a demonstrated willingness to use force in the Middle East, the United States refrained from any military strikes against Iran, even as it developed its nuclear program and killed U.S. soldiers in Iraq. As Obama's critics accurately point out, it is not enough to threaten to use force: you actually have to follow through if your red lines are crossed.

If the nuclear deal went away, would the Trump administration, or any administration for that matter, bomb Iran if it expanded its uranium stockpile once again to, say, 1,000 pounds? What about 2,000? And what about ballistic missile tests? It is legitimate to argue the risk of an Iranian bomb is so high that the United States should use force to prevent it and accept the consequences. But it is not persuasive to simply assert that Iran would have walked away from its entire nuclear program in the face of a more credible threat.

None of this means that the Iran negotiations were perfect. Of course, it's possible that the Obama administration and its partners could have gotten more in certain areas from Iran; just as easily, holding out could have scuttled a deal. What seems unlikely, though, is that Iran would have accepted any of the critics' proposed "improvements." The deal that many of them say they wanted—where Iran not only abandoned its entire nuclear program but also agreed to stop interfering in the Middle East—was never in the cards.

It is true that Iran's behavior in the region has not improved. It continues to prop up the murderous Assad regime in Syria and to fuel sectarianism by supporting proxies in Yemen, Lebanon, Iraq, and Bahrain. But it is also true that this behavior, which has gone on for years, including when Iran was under the toughest sanctions, cannot be attributed to the nuclear deal. Making Iran's regional interference part of the agreement would have been a recipe for failure, resulting in both an increased nuclear threat *and* persistent Iranian meddling in the region. The reality is that, for Iran, supporting its regional proxies is relatively cheap, and absent a broader policy change (which should remain a U.S. goal) is likely to continue regardless of the regime's economic health, which remains mediocre.

While a boost in revenues from unfrozen assets and increased oil sales obviously provides some scope for additional spending on military activities or terrorism, the regime also has a strong interest in allocating the bulk of any new revenues to its growing population, whose potential discontent is ultimately a greater threat to the regime than any Sunni neighbor. While the regime will seek to distribute some financial gains from the nuclear deal to its security forces, the "preponderance of the money [from sanctions relief] has gone to economic development and infrastructure," according to General Vincent Stewart, director of the Defense Intelligence Agency.

The idea that a windfall from sanctions relief has turned Iran into an economic powerhouse fails to take into account the degree to which collapsing oil prices have undercut some of the financial benefits Iran has received. While the lifting of sanctions has allowed Iran to increase its oil exports by some 730,000 barrels per day since the agreement was reached, the price of oil since the negotiations began fell by around $40 per barrel—some 50 percent compared with average prices over the decade preceding the deal. As a result, Iran is earning less from its annual oil sales now than it did every year of the entire period from 2001 to 2011, even if it is selling around the same amount of oil.

While access to once-frozen revenue provides Iran with additional resources to spend on destabilizing activities—witness the recent, modest increase in the Iranian Revolutionary Guards Corps's budget—the overall revenue stream is not nearly what it was prior to 2011. And given the new realities of the global oil market, it is unlikely to return to the previous levels. Iran's foreign policy is a big problem, but not primarily because of new resources from the Iran deal.

The debate over how the nuclear agreement is faring will shape the Trump administration's Iran policy. As a candidate, Trump called it the "worst agreement ever negotiated" and promised to "dismantle" it. Upon taking office, however, he seemed to realize there were no good alternatives, and that a unilateral breach would pave the way for Iran to resume its nuclear program and turn America into the pariah that facilitated that outcome. In April 2017, Secretary of State Rex Tillerson grudgingly certified that Iran was complying with the deal while denouncing its behavior and announcing a comprehensive Iran policy review.

Options for altering the nuclear deal, however, remain limited. Unilateral abrogation now is no more appealing than it was in January. Meaningful renegotiation—of an agreement negotiated by six international powers and endorsed by the entire Security Council—is a fantasy. More likely, then, will be pledges to confront Iran and enforce further sanctions (such as those in a new bill targeting Iran's ballistic missile program, conventional weapons acquisition, and the IRGC). The nuclear deal permits such sanctions, which remain an important tool of U.S. policy. But the risk will be the temptation to impose "backdoor" nuclear sanctions that Iran and others would consider a violation of the agreement. Supporters of the deal should be wary of sanctions designed to try to destroy it.

There are also reports that some within the Trump administration and outside groups are advocating for an explicit policy of regime change despite America's dubious track record in the region. That Iran and the region could use a new government in Tehran is not in doubt. Significant anecdotal evidence and repeated electoral results suggest that the Iranian regime is unpopular and the country's youth are desperate for change. But it is far from clear that an explicit U.S. policy to bring about that change—let alone overt or covert U.S. support for Iranian minority groups—(suggested recently by Senator Cotton) will bring a transition to a more democratic, peaceful, and pro-Western regime.

What the deal has done, at least for the next decade, is to remove any realistic threat of a near-term Iranian nuclear weapon. The United States should use that decade wisely: standing up to and imposing costs on Iranian transgressions, supporting U.S. allies in the region, making clear to the Iranian public that the West is not an enemy, and preparing for the day when some of the deal's restrictions will no longer apply. If, by 2030, Iran has not demonstrated that its nuclear program is exclusively peaceful and that it is willing to live in peace with its neighbors, the United States and its international partners will have difficult decisions to make about how to handle the issue going forward.

But since there is a chance that Iran will have different leaders or policies by then—the current Supreme Leader will almost certainly be gone, and a new generation may have come to power—why make those difficult decisions now? The Iran deal has bought valuable time. Squandering that time without a better plan would be foolish.

Philip Gordon and Richard Nephew were policy makers who served as part of the U.S. negotiating team for the Iran nuclear agreement.

 **NO**

Remarks by President Trump on the Joint Comprehensive Plan of Action

THE PRESIDENT: My fellow Americans: Today, I want to update the world on our efforts to prevent Iran from acquiring a nuclear weapon.

The Iranian regime is the leading state sponsor of terror. It exports dangerous missiles, fuels conflicts across the Middle East, and supports terrorist proxies and militias such as Hezbollah, Hamas, the Taliban, and al Qaeda.

Over the years, Iran and its proxies have bombed American embassies and military installations, murdered hundreds of American service members, and kidnapped, imprisoned, and tortured American citizens. The Iranian regime has funded its long reign of chaos and terror by plundering the wealth of its own people.

No action taken by the regime has been more dangerous than its pursuit of nuclear weapons and the means of delivering them.

In 2015, the previous administration joined with other nations in a deal regarding Iran's nuclear program. This agreement was known as the Joint Comprehensive Plan of Action (JCPOA).

In theory, the so-called "Iran deal" was supposed to protect the United States and our allies from the lunacy of an Iranian nuclear bomb, a weapon that will only endanger the survival of the Iranian regime. In fact, the deal allowed Iran to continue enriching uranium and, over time, reach the brink of a nuclear breakout.

The deal lifted crippling economic sanctions on Iran in exchange for very weak limits on the regime's nuclear activity, and no limits at all on its other malign behavior, including its sinister activities in Syria, Yemen, and other places all around the world.

In other words, at the point when the United States had maximum leverage, this disastrous deal gave this regime—and it's a regime of great terror—many billions of dollars, some of it in actual cash—a great embarrassment to me as a citizen and to all citizens of the United States.

A constructive deal could easily have been struck at the time, but it wasn't. At the heart of the Iran deal was a giant fiction that a murderous regime desired only a peaceful nuclear energy program.

Today, we have definitive proof that this Iranian promise was a lie. Last week, Israel published intelligence documents long concealed by Iran, conclusively showing the Iranian regime and its history of pursuing nuclear weapons.

The fact is this was a horrible, one-sided deal that should have never, ever been made. It didn't bring calm, it didn't bring peace, and it never will.

In the years since the deal was reached, Iran's military budget has grown by almost 40 percent, while its economy is doing very badly. After the sanctions were lifted, the dictatorship used its new funds to build nuclear-capable missiles, support terrorism, and cause havoc throughout the Middle East and beyond.

The agreement was so poorly negotiated that even if Iran fully complies, the regime can still be on the verge of a nuclear breakout in just a short period of time. The deal's sunset provisions are totally unacceptable. If I allowed this deal to stand, there would soon be a nuclear arms race in the Middle East. Everyone would want their weapons ready by the time Iran had theirs.

Making matters worse, the deal's inspection provisions lack adequate mechanisms to prevent, detect, and punish cheating, and don't even have the unqualified right to inspect many important locations, including military facilities.

Not only does the deal fail to halt Iran's nuclear ambitions, but it also fails to address the regime's development of ballistic missiles that could deliver nuclear warheads.

Finally, the deal does nothing to constrain Iran's destabilizing activities, including its support for terrorism. Since the agreement, Iran's bloody ambitions have grown only more brazen.

In light of these glaring flaws, I announced last October that the Iran deal must either be renegotiated or terminated.

Three months later, on January 12, I repeated these conditions. I made clear that if the deal could not be

Trump, Donald, Remarks by President Trump on the Joint Comprehensive Plan of Action, May 8, 2018, Diplomatic Reception Room.

fixed, the United States would no longer be a party to the agreement.

Over the past few months, we have engaged extensively with our allies and partners around the world, including France, Germany, and the United Kingdom. We have also consulted with our friends from across the Middle East. We are unified in our understanding of the threat and in our conviction that Iran must never acquire a nuclear weapon.

After these consultations, it is clear to me that we cannot prevent an Iranian nuclear bomb under the decaying and rotten structure of the current agreement.

The Iran deal is defective at its core. If we do nothing, we know exactly what will happen. In just a short period of time, the world's leading state sponsor of terror will be on the cusp of acquiring the world's most dangerous weapons.

Therefore, I am announcing today that the United States will withdraw from the Iran nuclear deal.

In a few moments, I will sign a presidential memorandum to begin reinstating U.S. nuclear sanctions on the Iranian regime. We will be instituting the highest level of economic sanction. Any nation that helps Iran in its quest for nuclear weapons could also be strongly sanctioned by the United States.

America will not be held hostage to nuclear blackmail. We will not allow American cities to be threatened with destruction. And we will not allow a regime that chants "Death to America" to gain access to the most deadly weapons on Earth.

Today's action sends a critical message: The United States no longer makes empty threats. When I make promises, I keep them. In fact, at this very moment, Secretary Pompeo is on his way to North Korea in preparation for my upcoming meeting with Kim Jong-un. Plans are being made. Relationships are building. Hopefully, a deal will happen and, with the help of China, South Korea, and Japan, a future of great prosperity and security can be achieved for everyone.

As we exit the Iran deal, we will be working with our allies to find a real, comprehensive, and lasting solution to the Iranian nuclear threat. This will include efforts to eliminate the threat of Iran's ballistic missile program, to stop its terrorist activities worldwide, and to block its menacing activity across the Middle East. In the meantime, powerful sanctions will go into full effect. If the regime continues its nuclear aspirations, it will have bigger problems than it has ever had before.

Finally, I want to deliver a message to the long-suffering people of Iran: The people of America stand with you. It has now been almost 40 years since this dictatorship seized power and took a proud nation hostage. Most of Iran's 80 million citizens have sadly never known an Iran that prospered in peace with its neighbors and commanded the admiration of the world.

But the future of Iran belongs to its people. They are the rightful heirs to a rich culture and an ancient land. And they deserve a nation that does justice to their dreams, honor to their history, and glory to God.

Iran's leaders will naturally say that they refuse to negotiate a new deal; they refuse. And that's fine. I'd probably say the same thing if I was in their position. But the fact is they are going to want to make a new and lasting deal, one that benefits all of Iran and the Iranian people. When they do, I am ready, willing, and able.

Great things can happen for Iran, and great things can happen for the peace and stability that we all want in the Middle East.

There has been enough suffering, death, and destruction. Let it end now.

Thank you. God bless you. Thank you.

(The presidential memorandum is signed.)

Q Mr. President, how does this make America safer? How does this make America safer?

THE PRESIDENT: Thank you very much. This will make America much safer. Thank you very much.

Q Is Secretary Pompeo bringing the detainees home?

THE PRESIDENT: Thank you. Secretary Pompeo is, right now, going to North Korea. He will be there very shortly in a matter of virtual—probably an hour. He's got meetings set up. We have our meeting scheduled. We have our meeting set. The location is picked—the time and the date. Everything is picked. And we look forward to having a very great success.

We think relationships are building with North Korea. We'll see how it all works out. Maybe it will, maybe it won't. But it can be a great thing for North Korea, South Korea, Japan, and the entire world. We hope it all works out.

Thank you very much.

Q Are the Americans being freed?

Q Are the Americans coming home, Mr. President?

THE PRESIDENT: We'll all soon be finding out. We will soon be finding out. It would be a great thing if they are. We'll soon be finding out. Thank you very much.

Donald Trump is the 45th president of the United States.

EXPLORING THE ISSUE

Were Efforts to Withdraw the United States from the Iran Nuclear Agreement Misguided?

Critical Thinking and Reflection

1. Does Iran's history of developing a nuclear program lead one to be suspicious of Iran's stated desire to forego nuclear weapons?
2. Did the P5+1 and the Obama administration specifically make too many concessions in their efforts to secure the deal?
3. Do the components of the agreement seem to provide a reasonable set of restrictions and monitoring to prevent Iran from developing nuclear weapons?
4. Since the agreement was approved in July 2015, do you have any reason or evidence to feel less safe against Iran's aggressive moves outside its borders?
5. Is there a cumulative impact on U.S. leadership because of America's withdrawal not just from the Iran deal but also from the Paris climate accord and the Trans-Pacific Trade Partnership?

Is There Common Ground?

Much of the disagreement over the Iran nuclear program deal has focused on the nontechnical aspects of the accord, such as whether issues outside the nuclear file should have been included in the negotiations. There are three major areas of agreement, however. At the heart of one consensus are the science-related aspects and the nuclear technology pieces of the deal; there is a wide agreement that the technical nuclear details (i.e., that you cannot build a nuclear weapon with only 300 kilograms of highly enriched uranium and while enriching only to 3.67 percent) are sound. There has also been agreement among the IAEA and various countries' intelligence communities that Iran has been in compliance with the agreement. Finally, there is widespread agreement that Iran is a bad actor in a complicated region and therefore needs to be checked; the question is how best to do so.

Additional Resources

Arms Control Association, "Timeline of Nuclear Diplomacy with Iran" (Updated March 2018).

British Broadcasting Company, "Iran Nuclear Deal: Key Details" (May 8, 2018).

Kahl, Colin, "The Myth of a 'Better' Deal Iran," *Foreign Policy* (September 26, 2017).

Kerry, John, "The Iran deal is working. Here's how we know," *The Washington Post* (September 29, 2017).

Laub, Zachary, "The Impact of the Iran Nuclear Agreement," *Council on Foreign Relations Backgrounder* (May 8, 2018).

Rowberry, Ariana, "Sixty Years of Atoms for Peace and Iran's Nuclear Program," *Brookings* (December 18, 2013).

Sherman, Wendy and Richard Nephew, "As an Expert: The Iran Deal Two Years Later," The Center for Arms Control and Non-Proliferation" (undated).

Smith, Lee "Tearing Up the Joint Comprehensive Plan of Action," from *Walking Away from the Bad Deal with Iran*, Friends of Israel Initiative (September 2017).

Tabatabai, Ariane, "Preserving the Iran Nuclear Deal," Cato Institute (August 15, 2017).

"What's Wrong with the Iran Nuclear Deal and What Can We Do Now?, United Against Nuclear Iran (undated).

Internet References . . .

Belfer Center for Science and International Affairs, Harvard Kennedy School

http://belfercenter.ksg.harvard.edu/publication/25599/
iran_nuclear_deal.html

Cato Institute

www.cato.org/

Ploughshares Fund

www.ploughshares.org/

The Iran Project

www.iranprojectfcsny.org

Selected, Edited, and with Issue Framing Material by:
Marie E. Harf, *U.S. Department of State (2013–2017),*
Central Intelligence Agency (2006–2011)

ISSUE

Has the Assad Regime Won the Syrian Civil War?

YES: **Daniel R. DePetris,** from "How Bashar al-Assad Won the War in Syria," *The National Interest* (2017)

NO: **Krishnadev Calamur,** from "No One Is Winning the Syrian Civil War," *The Atlantic* (2018)

Learning Outcomes
After reading this issue, you will be able to:
• Describe the history and complex dynamics of the Syrian civil war.
• Understand how Syrian President Bashar al-Assad has stayed in power who has supported him, and what the military situation on the ground looks like seven years into the conflict.
• Discuss why and how outside powers have intervened, and what the results have been.
• Understand the challenges Syria faces going forward.

ISSUE SUMMARY

YES: Daniel R. DePetris, an analyst at Wikistrat, writes that early in the Syrian conflict, many analysts assessed that President Bashar al-Assad was on his way out because of opposition military advances and perceived weaknesses. But now, after Assad has ruthlessly crushed military opposition to his rule, while murdering hundreds of thousands of civilians, the world has come to understand "how wily, clever, and street-smart" the government had been all along, leaving Assad in power with the crucial help of Russian and Iranian support.

NO: Krishnadev Calamur, a senior editor at *The Atlantic*, argues that President Assad and his regime have not won the war. It is more accurate to say that Russian, Iranian, and Kurdish forces have emerged as the victors. He writes that Assad would not be able to survive in power on his own without his outside backers. And Assad's goal to regain control of the entire country has failed, as Syria as a unified nation has effectively collapsed, and it is unlikely that he will ever rule over the entirety of the country again.

The current Syrian civil war began in 2011 against the backdrop of the wider Arab Spring. As citizens across the Middle East stood up against decades of repressive authoritarian rule, their governments responded with everything from abdication to token reform gestures to violent crackdowns. In Syria, when peaceful protestors began speaking out, they were met with brute force from the regime of President Bashar al-Assad, starting a cycle that spiraled into full blown civil war. After over seven years of fighting, the results are staggering: hundreds of thousands of Syrians have been killed. More than half of the country's prewar population has become refugees or internally displaced—helping to create the world's worst refugee crisis since World War II. The security vacuum gave rise to the nihilist terrorist group ISIS, which rampaged through Iraq and Syria murdering civilians and taking territory, prompting an aggressive international military response. Numerous outside countries and groups intervened in various ways, essentially turning the country into a local battleground for competing regional and global interests to fight their own proxy wars.

The 2011 protests have their roots in the oppressive behavior of a Syrian regime that has terrorized its citizens since Hafez al-Assad, Bashar's father, took control of the government in 1970. Hafez, a member of Syria's minority Alawi sect, forged an autocratic regime at home that rewarded loyalists and destroyed dissenters. In 1982, Hafez brutally put down an uprising in the city of Hama, killing 25,000, an event that would later be used as a rallying cry in the 2011 uprising against his son. Bashar assumed power in 2000 upon his father's death. His older brother had actually been groomed for the role, but after he was killed in a car accident, Bashar (a Western-trained ophthalmologist) was thrust into the spotlight. He came into office promising reforms, especially in the economic sector, but soon adopted his father's autocratic playbook.

In December 2010, a fruit vendor in Tunisia, fed up with his government, set himself on fire, a single act that touched off waves of protests demanding change across the Middle East. Syria was not immune to this movement. Fifteen boys in the city of Deraa, inspired by the protests elsewhere, spray-painted a wall with anti-government slogans and were subsequently arrested and tortured. Their abuse prompted additional protests, which was met by further Syrian government aggression. Before long, the Syrian army was firing on and killing unarmed protestors, the security services were making mass indiscriminate arrests and reports of torture and extrajudicial executions began to appear.

Various opposition groups emerged in response to the crackdown and eventually took up arms against the regime's escalating actions. In July 2011, defectors from the Syrian army announced the formation of the Free Syrian Army (FSA), which became the nominal military leader among opposition groups (especially in the eyes of outside supporters like the United States). The FSA's political counterpart, the Syrian National Coalition, was established in mid-2011 as a sort of "government in exile." Other anti-regime armed extremist groups joined the fight as well. As the protests spread throughout the country, Assad promised reform but instead violently cracked down. The conflict escalated into a full-blown civil war, mired in increasing complexity, as Assad fought to regain control of what had become an ungovernable chaotic state. In 2013, as the civil war raged, the Islamic State—a reincarnation of al-Qaeda in Iraq—which had been active during the second U.S. war there, began capturing large swaths of territory in Syria and Iraq and brutally terrorizing civilians.

Outside powers have also intervened in Syria to pursue or safeguard their own interests. Russia has backed the regime diplomatically at the United Nations and militarily in Syria to bolster its ally, to maintain a strategic foothold in the region, and, it claims, to fight terrorism. Iran has both backed the Assad regime and fought ISIS. Meanwhile, the Gulf States, which are primarily concerned about Iranian expansionism in the Arab world, have backed all manner of groups fighting Assad, including some that the United States considers extremists. The United States, for its part, has overtly and covertly supported more moderate opposition elements, intervened militarily to fight ISIS, and pursued diplomatic initiatives to end the conflict.

Those initiatives, most notably a UN-led process, have thus far been unsuccessful. There are significant disagreements about almost everything: which groups should be included in the official Syrian opposition, how and when to replace the current regime, including if and when Assad must go, and how to maintain Syrian territorial integrity.

Meanwhile, the conflict has dragged on, and the continuing violence has produced massive humanitarian challenges. Nearby countries have struggled to absorb millions of refugees, forcing debates among and within major Western powers over how to address the overflows and what moral responsibility the world has to help those Syrians fleeing such chaos.

The question faced by the world in 2018 is this: after the initial optimism that the Arab Spring could bring positive change to Syria, has this bloody civil war essentially ended in a victory for the brutal dictator Assad? There is a strong military case that the Assad regime has effectively stamped out the armed opposition and therefore "won" the civil war. Contrary to many analysts' early assessments that Assad was militarily vulnerable and might soon be deposed, he has been able to mobilize his most loyal forces and crucial outside support to retake significant territory from opposition groups and from ISIS. Also critical to his success has been his willingness to channel his father and resort to increasingly ruthless tactics, including the use of sieges, barrel bombs, and chemical weapons against his own people.

Assad's military success was by no means preordained. In fact, he seemed doomed to failure until Russia directly intervened in 2015, and Iran and Hezbollah significantly upped their support with additional weapons and man power. With those reinforcements, Assad slowly started taking territory back from a divided opposition; most notably, in 2016, the regime began capturing the last opposition-held areas of Aleppo, the nation's economic powerhouse that had been fiercely contested since 2012. Throughout 2017 and early 2018, Assad continued his military advances into rebel-held areas in the Damascus suburbs and central Syria. As a result, "the prospect of the opposition displacing the Assad regime, or even securing representation in a national government, is long gone" (Scott Lucas, *The Conversation*, January 25, 2018).

Assad has succeeded militarily not just because of his side's strength but also because of the opposition's weaknesses. There has been little cohesion among the dozens of anti-Assad factions in terms of command and control, military strategy, or ideology. Robert Ford, former U.S. Ambassador to Syria, has detailed a fairly devastating "series of blunders" by the opposition that aided Assad in his victory: murderous leadership rivalries, a failure to reach out to parts of the regime's support base who might have been sympathetic to the opposition cause, a slowness to reject extremist groups, and never punishing those within their ranks who committed atrocities (*Foreign Affairs*, November/December 2017). Moreover, official foreign support for the opposition has been unsteady and uncoordinated, leaving the FSA and its cohorts significantly outgunned. Little political will has existed in other countries to seriously invest in arming the opposition, even when those weapons would have been necessary in achieving those countries' declaration that "Assad must go" (Nickolas Van Dam, *Foreign Policy*, August 22, 2017). As a result, absent a credible alternative with the strength and the legitimacy to rally the Syrian people around one unified opposition force, Assad has to some degree won by forfeit or default.

The case that Assad has not, in fact, "won" the Syrian civil war rests on two arguments. First, he would not be able to stay in power without the direct intervention and support of outside powers such as Russia and Iran; second, the country of "Syria" as defined by its prewar borders is unlikely to ever be put back together in its entirety under one ruler again. In sum, while Assad may continue to rule Damascus and various strongholds throughout the country, he has not won the war to control "Syria," and he would not control anything without his patrons outside his own borders.

Turning first to Assad's reliance on outside actors, many analysts believe Assad could not survive in power without significant continued assistance from Russia, Iran, and Hezbollah. Moscow and Tehran provide Assad with much needed economic support, despite being subject to international sanctions themselves. Just as critical is their military assistance. As a result of defections and battlefield casualties, the Syrian Army has shrunk from a prewar strength of 220,000 troops to as few as 25,000 troops in a 2017 estimate, forcing Assad increasingly to rely on

foreign fighters to fill that gap (Alaa Faqir, *Council on Foreign Relations*, April 2018). Indeed, Russia, Iran, and Hezbollah all have tens of thousands of fighters in Syria today. These foreign fighters do not answer to Assad, and their sponsors are primarily fighting for their own geostrategic interests that may not always overlap with his. In other words, "Assad is hardly in charge of what happens on the ground militarily" (Malak Chabkoun, *Al Jazeera*, November 3, 2017).

The second argument against an Assad "victory" is that the government will never have the capacity to control the whole of the country and its population again. The country has fragmented into distinct regions and subregions controlled by oppositionists, warlords, and external powers. A free-for-all is happening in the country's Eastern territory recently liberated from ISIS, and Syria's Kurds are unlikely to give up their hard-won autonomy in the country's north. And, given the fact that at least half of Syria's population has fled the country, Assad does not control anything close to a majority of the Syrian people.

Even just retaking Syrian territory would require fighters and resources that Assad lacks and his external patrons will not provide. In addition to the vast physical destruction from the war, the state is bankrupt, its economy has been destroyed, and the price tag to rebuild it is estimated in the hundreds of billions of dollars. Syria as a nation has effectively collapsed. As analyst Daniel DePetris writes, "It is clear that an Assad victory does not correlate into a healthy and functioning state that has control over its sovereign borders or can survive independently" (*The National Interest*, December 19, 2017).

As we debate whether Assad has won the Syrian civil war, we should not lose focus on the Syrian people themselves who have tragically lost so much since 2011. As Noura al-Yafi, a Damascene who works with refugee women in Beirut, told *The Independent* newspaper, "No one will ever achieve what they see as victory now. Whichever side you're on, we have all lost our country forever" (Bethan McKernan, *The Independent*, March 18, 2017).

In the YES selection, Daniel DePetris argues that Syrian President Bashar al-Assad has steadily stamped out his armed opposition, with the help of Russian and Iranian support, and therefore, he has won the country's civil war. In the NO selection, Krishnadev Calamur argues that Assad would not be able to stay in power on his own without the help of the Russians and Iranians and that Syria as a unified nation has collapsed—leaving no one a "winner" in the civil war.

YES ⤶

Daniel R. DePetris

How Bashar al-Assad Won the War in Syria

On August 21, 2013, the international community awoke to a scene of absolute terror. Broadcasted on television screens around the world were pictures and video of men, women, and even small babies sprawled on the floor, gasping for breath. Many were already dead from exposure to the Sarin gas that was delivered from the Syrian army's surface-to-surface missiles. The attack in the rebel-held suburbs of Damascus, which left an estimated 1,400 people dead according to U.S. intelligence community assessments, was the most gruesome chemical weapons strike since former Iraqi dictator Saddam Hussein gassed Kurdish civilians in the town of Halabja in 1988. Four years later, I still remember the *New York Post* cover page the next morning, dead Syrian children on one side and a grinning Bashar al-Assad on the other.

To the world's credit, the 2013 chemical attack was so visually upsetting and such an appalling violation of international law that the United States and Russia, by then in complete opposition to how to manage the Syrian dictator, came together (with the endorsement of the U.N. Security Council) to force Assad to give up his declared chemical weapons stockpile and to enlist Syria as a signatory to the Chemical Weapons Convention. The first international chemical weapons inspectors were deployed on Syrian soil a short time later—and despite the enormous stress of working in a war zone and dealing with Syrian government officials who were less than truthful, managed to remove and destroy 1,300 tons of chemical weapons. "Never before," the OPCW's director boasted at the time, "has an entire arsenal of a category of weapons of mass destruction been removed from a country experiencing a state of internal armed conflict."

Of course, what we now know—and should have recognized when the chemical weapons were being transported to ships in the Mediterranean—was that the Assad government didn't declare all of its stockpile. Indeed, Damascus may still be producing chemical munitions somewhere in the country. As an exhaustive investigation from Reuters last week showed with alarming precision,

Assad's regime has lied, obfuscated, deceived, and provided international inspectors with so much inaccurate information that the world will never know the full extent of the Syrian government's chemical weapons program. In one case, OPCW inspectors were made to wait outside a facility, while the government was suspected of cleaning the building of chemical remnants. In another instance, Syrian military officials told government witnesses being interviewed by the OPCW to change their stories.

The account described in Reuters has all the hallmarks of a regime so intent on saving its own skin and winning the war against its armed opponents that it's willing to use some of the world's most indiscriminate weapons in the field, regardless of the target—and then go to great lengths to cover it up and largely get away with it.

And yet, while all of this is a disturbing indictment of Bashar al-Assad's leadership and his regime's criminal behavior, it also exposes how wily, clever, and street-smart Assad's government has been since the civil war began in 2011. Assad has been nothing but a survivor; President Barack Obama's numerous warnings that it was only a matter of time before the dictator fled into exile have proved to be a wildly rosy assessment about as accurate as the Bush administration's allegations of a Saddam Hussein connection with Osama Bin Laden.

In the summer of 2012, it did look as if Assad was on his way out. Thousands of Syrian troops were deserting the army out of disgust for the regime's tactics or out of an abiding sense of fear that they would be killed or captured by the rebels they were sent to fight. Aleppo, the country's cultural and economic capital, went from a regime-held city somewhat insulated from the revolution to one that was divided and on the frontline. The only thing keeping the regime afloat during this period were foreign Shia militia volunteers, discounted fuel prices from Iran, the overstretched 4th Armored Division led by Assad's younger brother and constant Iranian weapons shipments.

Five years later, Aleppo is back in Assad's control and it is the armed opposition now at its weakest point in the conflict. Whether we like it or not, the UN Security

Council's internal division, Iran's organization and training of pro-Assad militias and Russia's bombing campaign have produced a situation where the Assad family clan will be in charge for some time to come.

However, as critical as Russia and Iran's military and financial support has been, Assad himself deserves much of the credit for staying in power. The way he has prosecuted the war has been as effective as it has been inhumane. So desperate he is to perpetuate the political order his father has built that he has pulled out all the stops, from deliberately releasing hardcore Islamists out of prison in order to infect the rebellion to destroying entire cities. Understanding that they had far too few troops to occupy rebel-held cities and towns after clearing them out, Assad's generals and field commanders decided instead to adopt the kind of medieval starve-and-siege tactics that requires less man power. Surrounding entire city districts, depriving everybody inside of the food, water, and medicine to survive, and bombarding them relentlessly until they surrender unconditionally turned out to be a faster way to reclaim ground. As illegal as these tactics are, the mass displacement of civilians, forced depopulation and the repopulation of that newly acquired territory with regime supporters worked. If they didn't, Assad would either be dead, facing a war crimes tribunal, or enjoying a new life in Russia.

At the present time, the United States, Europe, and most of the Arab world who would rightly prefer a more democratic and peaceful alternative to the current administration in Damascus are now forced to reckon with the hard reality that Bashar al-Assad will continue to be Syria's president. Regime change in Syria, partly due to Washington's unwillingness to get fully involved in a proxy war with combatants that increasingly operate with similar brutality, partly due to the support of Syria's allies, and partly due to Assad's tactics, is now a dead letter.

The Trump administration has no choice but to figure out a policy that addresses these realities. Whatever that policy turns out to be, Syria will be a fractured, broken, chaotic, and violent country for a long time to come.

DANIEL R. DePETRIS is an analyst at Wikistrat, Inc., a geostrategic consulting firm, and a freelance researcher. He has also written for CNN.com.

Krishnadev Calamur

No One Is Winning the Syrian Civil War

Bashar al-Assad is only in power because of Russia's support. His country is devastated.

Seven years ago, when Syrian protesters called for "a day of rage" against Bashar al-Assad, there were few signs that they would have an impact. Three years later, as the protests transformed into a civil war, one that would eventually draw in the region's powers, it seemed a matter of when, not if, Assad would go the way of his fellow strongmen in Tunisia and Egypt. But on March 15, 2018, which by some accounts marks the seventh anniversary of the start of the conflict, Assad appears no closer to leaving office than he was seven years ago.*

Assad's has kept his position, at great cost to Syria. But it would be wrong to say he is in control. It's true that he, with the support of Russia and Iran, has held on to Syria's major cities, including Damascus and Aleppo, as well as much of the West of the country. (Russia's military intervention in the conflict in late 2015 gave Assad a decisive edge.) Most of the Syrian population that didn't flee the country now lives in areas controlled by the government. But Syria as a whole has effectively collapsed. Before the civil war, the country was, by Arab standards, solidly middle income. It is estimated that it will take another two decades after the fighting ends, whenever that happens, for Syria to regain its prewar economic status. The price tag to rebuild the country is estimated at $200 billion or more if the conflict endures—money neither Assad nor his patrons in Moscow or Tehran have to spare.

Then, there is the human cost: more than 500,000 people killed, 5 million refugees, entire cities flattened. There are few signs the fighting is close to stopping—despite a 30-day, UN-mandated cease-fire that went into effect last month. Assad continues to bomb Eastern Ghouta, the region outside Damascus held by rebels including anti-Assad Islamists. The death toll there since the most recent assault began last month exceeds 1,000. With the international community doing nothing to stop him, it is all but certain Assad will sooner or later capture

the area. When he does that, he will have defeated one of the last major pockets of resistance. But even then, it will be hard to say that he "won" the war.

"It's very difficult for us, as Syrians, who have watched this from the beginning of the revolution. For us it feels like . . . there's nothing really being done to help the people have been suffering for over seven years," said Lina Attar, a Syrian American architect from Aleppo who is the cofounder of the Karam Foundation, an aid organization that works with displaced Syrians. "And so when you hear the words 'Assad has won,' they are very difficult words to hear. As a Syrian you think, 'Won over what?'"

It's unclear—and highly unlikely—that Assad can survive in power without Russian, Iranian, and Hezbollah support. He says he wants to regain control of all of Syria but may have to settle for only a bit more than he has now. The Kurds, for example, are unlikely to give up the autonomous territory they've gained in the northeast of the country. And though ISIS has largely been defeated in the country, its enemies are now turning their guns on each other in at least three more potential conflicts playing out on Syrian territory, that pit Turkey against the Syrian Kurds, Israel against Iran, and the United States against Russia.

"The way we look at it is Assad won the war, but the rest of the region doesn't see it that way," Andrew Tabler, an expert on Syria at the Washington Institute, said in a recent interview. "They see the outcome very differently. They see Iranian activities there. They see Russian activity. They see Kurdish activities."

Syria was once the power broker in Lebanon and a major force in the region but is now dependent on the largesse of its few allies. Assad's military forces are depleted. The most effective pro-Assad fighting forces are militia members and foreign fighters. And Tabler argues that an outcome in which Assad remains in power is unacceptable to both Turkey and Israel. "That threatens to morph the

Syrian civil war into the Syria war," he said. "This is very similar to what happened in Lebanon in the 1980s—where you had a civil war, initially driven by Palestinian activities there, and then after they departed the scene, the war continued. International players became involved in the Lebanon war—and it tends to prolong wars and makes the outcome far more difficult to obtain." In Syria's case, Israel is threatened by the presence of Iranian forces in a country on its border; in Turkey's, it sees the Kurds as menacing its own territorial integrity. Both powers have been drawn further into Syria's fighting in recent weeks.

The world looks much different now than it did in the 1980s, however. For one, the countries in the region are embroiled in other regional conflicts: the Iranians and Saudis are engaged in a devastating proxy war in Yemen; Turkey is perennially worried about Kurds, including in Iraq, and external foes, real and perceived; the Trump administration's decision to move the U.S. Embassy in Israel to Jerusalem has not yet set off the kind of violence that many feared, but given the political realities in the region there's no assurance it won't. Nor does the United States seem particularly interested in doing anything more in Syria than fight ISIS—a policy that has carried over from the Obama years when the president declined to enforce a "red line" on Assad's use of chemical weapons on civilians. Assad has now done so multiple times.

On the other hand, other countries in the region are preparing for life with Assad staying in place—no matter how distasteful that may sound to them. "Those countries that directly border Syria, I think you are beginning to see capitalized into their strategic calculation this notion of Assad staying," Mona Yacoubian, the senior adviser for Syria, Middle East, and North Africa at the U.S. Institute for Peace, told me. "And I think that's most apparent in Jordan where actions by the Jordanian government suggest that they do believe he is there to stay at least for the short- to medium term." The country has moved toward opening the official crossing with Syria, is providing less support for Syrian rebels in the south, and has been pushing to get Syrian refugees (currently in Jordan) to return to de-escalation zones negotiated with the Russians.

As for the population that's left in Syria, four years ago, the UN estimated that 80 percent of the country lived in poverty and that life expectancy had fallen by 20 years, to a little over 55 years. Nor does Syria have hope for the kind of international financing poured into Iraq and Afghanistan for reconstruction, with mixed results. International funders are reluctant to spend that kind of money in Syria for fear it will benefit a regime accused of war crimes. "And when you look at the United Nations, the Security Council, the large aid agencies, and everybody saying . . . whatever is happening right now needs to stop, but there's no true action to intervene to end this war, that's very disheartening," Attar said. "And if Assad survives all of this, it's really because of the world's inaction."

KRISHNADEV CALAMUR is a senior editor at *The Atlantic* and a former editor and reporter at NPR.

EXPLORING THE ISSUE

Has the Assad Regime Won the Syrian Civil War?

Critical Thinking and Reflection

1. How has Syrian President Assad been able to have so much military success?
2. Would a better-organized or supported opposition have been more successful in fighting the Assad regime?
3. Why have different outside powers invested resources fighting proxy wars in Syria?
4. Should outside powers have more directly worked to oust Assad, especially when he was weaker militarily?
5. How should the rest of the world deal with the situation in Syria today, given Assad's military advances and the catastrophic humanitarian challenges?

Is There Common Ground?

In the debate over whether President Assad has "won" his country's civil war, there is broad agreement on the military facts on the ground: that the regime has been able to take back significant swathes of territory from rebels, and the opposition is not well-enough equipped to seriously challenge the regime. The disagreements tend to focus on the degree to which Assad could maintain control of these areas without continued support from outside powers like Russia and Iran. Further, the debate continues about what it means that Assad control only a portion of the country—while large areas are now controlled by the semiautonomous Kurds, for example. Even a decisive military victory over a portion of a country one previously controlled in its entirety doesn't really sound like a resounding success. And, of course, the biggest debates about Syria continue to surround the issues of what to do next. The world agrees it is a humanitarian catastrophe, but how to deal with the millions of refugees and work to try to get a diplomatic solution remain challenges without easy answers.

Additional Resources

Cambanis, Thanassis et al., "Four Perspectives on the War in Syria," *The Century Foundation*, (July 26, 2016)

Collin, Katy, "7 Years into the Syrian War, Is There a Way Out?" *Brookings Institution* (March 16, 2018)

Collard, Rebecca, "Civil War in Syria Has Entered a Dangerous New Phase," *Time* (February 15, 2018)

Faqir, Alaa, "Who's Who in Syria's Civil War," *Council on Foreign Relations* (April 28, 2017)

Feldman, Noah, "Syria Is the New Afghanistan, Where War Won't End," *Bloomberg View* (February 15, 2018)

Jenkins, Brian Michael, "The Dynamics of Syria's Civil War," *Rand Corporation* (2014)

Laub, Zachary, "Syria's War: The Descent into Horror," *Council on Foreign Relations* (April 2018)

Trenin, Dmitri, "Putin's Plan for Syria," *Foreign Affairs* (December 13, 2017)

Internet References . . .

Kathy Gilsinan

http://theAtlantic.com/internatuional/archive/2015/10/
Syrian-civil-war-guide-isis/410746/

Liveupmap

http://syria.liveyamap.com/

Migration Policy Centre, European
University Institute

http://syrianrefugees.eu/

Selected, Edited, and with Issue Framing Material by:
Marie E. Harf, *U.S. Department of State (2013–2017),*
Central Intelligence Agency (2006–2011)

ISSUE

Is a Two-state Diplomatic Solution to the Israeli–Palestinian Conflict Possible or Likely in the Near Future?

YES: **Mara Rudman and Brian Katulis,** from "A Practical Plan on the Israeli–Palestinian Front," *Center for American Progress* (2016)

NO: **Nickolay Mladenov,** from "Security Council Briefing on the Situation in the Middle East," *UNESCO* (2018)

Learning Outcomes

After reading this issue, you will be able to:

- Describe the historical events that have driven the Israeli–Palestinian conflict.
- Understand the role played by the territorial results of the 1948 Arab–Israeli War and the 1967 Six-Day War in peace negotiations between the Israelis and the Palestinians.
- Outline the six building blocks advanced by the Center for American Progress study for a two-state solution to the Israeli–Palestinian problem.
- Describe why there is much pessimism among analysts for the likelihood of successful peace negotiations.
- Understand the possible effects of moving the American Embassy to Jerusalem.

ISSUE SUMMARY

YES: The Center for American Progress study, authored by two experienced analysts who served in Democratic administrations, suggests six building blocks for a two-state solution to the Israeli–Palestinian conflict. The study's authors, respected scholars of Middle East affairs, argue that despite a number of factors making a solution more difficult, progress toward a two-state solution can be made if attention is paid to these building blocks.

NO: Nicolay Mladenov, the UN Special Coordinator for the Middle East Peace Process, suggests that it is a grim time for those seeking peace in the region. For him, "much of the Middle East continues to be in the grips of an ongoing human tragedy of immense proportions." He argues that those opposed to peace are gaining confidence with each passing day, and they are hindering progress by pushing unilateral facts on the ground that are "blocking the pathway back to the negotiating table."

On May 14, 2018, the 70th anniversary of Israel's independence, two events took place that captured the complexity of the Israeli–Palestinian conflict. Split screens and photo montages displayed the dichotomy. On one side, viewers observed Israeli and American political leaders participating in a carefully orchestrated ceremony celebrating the controversial move of the U.S. Embassy from Tel Aviv to Jerusalem. On the other side were images of a major demonstration by Palestinians near the border between the Gaza Strip and Israel, resulting in clashes where more than 2,700 Palestinians were injured (including over 1,350 by gunfire) and around 60 were killed by Israeli security forces. The bloody carnage and protests stood in stark contrast to the jubilant Embassy ceremony occurring simultaneously.

Sadly, events juxtaposed against each other are not a new phenomenon in the area comprising Israel and the Palestinian territories in Gaza and the West Bank, land that holds religious significance for Jews, Christians, and Muslims. Controversy and clashes have fueled this conflict for decades. After World War I, the United Kingdom gained control of what would become Israel, the West Bank, Gaza, and Jordan. In November 1947, in the wake of World War II and the Holocaust (which led to a surge in Jewish immigration, in addition to those Jews who had immigrated to the territory beginning in the 1880s), the newly created United Nations recommended the partition of British-mandate Palestine into two separate states, one Jewish and the other Arab. The plan was rejected, however, by Arab countries and the Palestinians. On May 14, 1948, Israel declared its independence, and immediately the armies of the Arab Legion, Egypt, Lebanon, Iraq, and Syria attacked the newly proclaimed Jewish state. Israel prevailed militarily, and as a result, controlled both the land it had been promised by the UN and also a large majority of what was supposed to have been a Palestinian state. Approximately 750,000 Palestinian refugees were rendered stateless.

In 1967, Israel attacked Egypt and then went to war with Jordan and Syria, after months of escalation and skirmishes, and Israeli fears that the Arab states were preparing to attack to regain lost territory. Israel again had the military upper hand, and as a result in only six days of fighting gained control of the Golan Heights, the West Bank, the Sinai Peninsula, the Gaza Strip, and East Jerusalem—making Israel three times larger than it had been in 1949. In 1973, Egypt and Syria attacked Israel to make up for their crushing defeat in 1967, but the conflict essentially ended in a stalemate, and the Arab states were unable to recoup the lost land. Subsequent negotiations orchestrated by U.S. President Jimmy Carter resulted in a breakthrough in 1978 with the signing of the Camp David Accords between Israel, Egypt, and the United States. Israel returned the Sinai to Egypt and the two countries normalized relations, and a framework was outlined for future negotiations among Egypt, Jordan, Israel, and the Palestinians.

As the conflict continued without any resolution for the Palestinians, they increasingly turned to more violent resistance, embarking on the First Intifada, or uprising, from 1987 until 1993 and the Second Intifada from 2000 until 2005. Negotiations occurred in fits and starts, with the most prominent being secret talks between the two sides that led to the Oslo Accords in the mid-1990s.

Oslo included recognition by the Palestinian Liberation Organization (PLO) of the State of Israel and the recognition by Israel of the PLO as the representative of the Palestinian people and a partner in negotiations. Since Oslo, diplomatic efforts to resolve the final status issues have all stalled, and today, the Oslo-created Palestinian Authority (PA) runs the government in the West Bank, while Islamist group (and U.S.-designated terrorist organization) Hamas controls the Gaza Strip, which is in the midst of a severe humanitarian crisis. The PA negotiates with Israel but often is hampered in its ability to implement any agreements because of Hamas resistance. The PA and Hamas have been attempting to form a united government but have thus far been unsuccessful.

The Palestinians want their own state and the opportunity to function in a viable economic, social, and political environment; the Israelis need acceptance and guarantees of their safe existence from its neighbors. The broad outlines of what a two-state solution would have to cover are generally known: defined borders (likely based on the pre-1967 lines with mutually agreed land swaps), a shared capital in Jerusalem, a resolution to the Palestinian refugee issue, and security for both states. However, the devil is really in the details, and negotiations have proven unable to overcome stalemates on issues laden with such history, religion, emotion, and politics. Over the past decades, the Israeli government has moved further to the right politically, hardening many of its positions, and the Palestinian leadership has been deeply divided between two governments that cannot figure out how to reconcile among themselves, let alone negotiate with Israel. U.S. Secretary of State John Kerry, who worked to bring the parties back to the negotiating table in an effort that ultimately led to yet another breakdown in talks, summed up today's challenges: "Despite our best efforts over the years, the two-state solution is now in serious jeopardy. The truth is that trends on the ground—violence, terrorism, incitement, settlement expansion, and the seemingly endless occupation—are destroying hopes for peace on both sides" (*Remarks on Middle East Peace*, December 28, 2016). Every U.S. president since Israel's founding has come into office pledging to renew peace efforts, and Donald Trump is no exception. As of mid-2018, the Trump administration had not yet released its promised peace plan, but his team says they are working to develop their proposals now.

Is a two-state peace agreement still possible or even likely? On the more optimistic side, there is a school of thought that fresh eyes and new policy ideas of the sort that might come from the Trump administration could shake something loose in the negotiating process. Further, some analysts argue that the increasing dialogue and cooperation between Sunni Arab states and Israel—borne from a shared hatred of Iran and ISIS, as well as common interests on energy issues—could improve the conditions for Israeli–Palestinian negotiations. While the Arab world in general has shifted its focus away from the plight of the Palestinians toward other more pressing security issues—and many Arab leaders are frustrated by Palestinian infighting—this shift toward Arab–Israeli cooperation could paradoxically help reinvigorate the peace process if there is more pragmatism injected into the talks. If both the Arab states and Israel recognize the real gains to be made by increased cooperation in security, economic, and energy issues, this changing geopolitical dynamic could spur more movement toward resolving the Israeli–Palestinian issue because without a resolution, there will always be upper bounds on how much of this desired cooperation can really take place.

Many observers of the peace process have argued that, in order to gain some momentum toward a possible final agreement, a number of more modest confidence-building measures should and could be initiated now. These include encouraging Israel to provide Palestinians economic access to Area "C" of the West Bank and promoting Palestinian leadership reform (*WINEP*, February 14, 2018). Further, helping to alleviate the dire humanitarian crisis in the Gaza Strip, including pushing the Israelis to lessen the restrictions on the movement of people and goods like medical supplies in and out of Gaza, could give the process a boost.

Finally, those who express optimism for a two-state solution argue that there are no realistic policy alternatives; any proposals that do not include two states or involve the maintenance of the status quo carry unacceptably high costs, including an unavoidable demographic problem for Israel. Secretary Kerry outlined this challenge: "If the choice is one state, Israel can either be Jewish or democratic—it cannot be both—and it won't ever really be at peace. Moreover, the Palestinians will never fully realize their vast potential in a homeland of their own with a one state solution . . . if there is only one state, you would have millions of Palestinians permanently living in segregated enclaves in the middle of the West Bank, with no real political rights, separate legal, education, and transportation systems, vast income disparities, under a permanent military occupation that deprives of them of the most basic freedoms—separate but unequal" (*Remarks on Middle East Peace*, December 28, 2016).

Despite the above considerations, there are many obstacles that make Israeli–Palestinian peace seem unlikely. Israeli settlement activity has pushed deeper into areas that will almost certainly have to be a part of a future Palestinian state. That reality on the ground, combined with continued Palestinian infighting, have led many observers to believe there is little hope for a breakthrough. Because of these developments, and decades of failure, both the Israeli and Palestinian publics are increasingly negative about the prospects for peace (*Foreign Policy*, December 11, 2017). The status quo for most Israelis has also become relatively peaceful and bearable, according to the *New York Times'* Max Fisher (December 29, 2016). As a result, both sides have little room for the kind of political maneuvering necessary to get a peace process back on track. PA President Mahmoud Abbas is deeply unpopular, and as Israeli public pressure for a deal has declined (in part because of the continued rise of the powerful settler movement), there are few incentives for Israeli Prime Minister Benjamin Netanyahu to take political risks either.

The continued Israeli settlement activity in the West Bank has, according to many observers, done two things: first, looked like bad faith on the part of the Israelis and, second, changed the facts on the ground so much that it is becoming increasingly difficult to carve out a contiguous Palestinian state. The settler population in the West Bank alone (not including East Jerusalem) has increased by nearly 270,000 since the signing of the Oslo Accords, including 100,000 just since 2009. Today, estimates place the overall settler population at upward of 435,000 Israelis, many of whom are living in areas that will likely be part of Palestinian territory under any agreement, and therefore, they will have to be relocated. But the more entrenched and deeper into future Palestinian territory these settlements go, the more logistically and politically difficult that process becomes.

Further, the Arab states' increasing work with Israel discussed above as a possible positive catalyst for movement in the peace process could also have the opposite impact. The Palestinian cause is no longer a priority for the Arab states in the face of wars in Syria, Yemen, and Libya, as well as the ongoing threat of ISIS; and an aggressive Iran. As a result, many observers believe the Palestinians may have lost a powerful point of leverage. If the Arab states are already willing to work with Israel, despite no resolution to the Palestinian issue, then the geopolitical incentives for Israel to make peace may have lessened.

How President Trump's decision to move the U.S. embassy to Jerusalem will impact the potential for peace talks remains unknown. The move was something U.S. presidents of both parties have long promised but never followed through on because of concerns that it would reduce America's ability to be seen as an honest broker in the peace process and prejudice one of the final status issues that must be worked out between the parties themselves. In the immediate wake of the embassy move, several things stood out. First, many people predicted the Arab states would be furious and respond aggressively to the move. But while many made critical public statements, there was not massive upheaval or outcry. PA President Abbas' job, already difficult, has been made even harder. And the question remains whether the United States can be seen as a partner for peace or is now viewed as too biased in favor of Israel—and if it is the latter, will anyone else step up instead?

As the Israelis and Palestinians enter the eighth decade of their conflict, the cost of failure seems to keep rising. As Israeli commentator Akiva Eldar notes: "with every failure comes more disappointment. More disappointment generates further radicalization" (*Al-Monitor*, March 6, 2018). Or, as analyst Nathan Thrall argues: "perpetuating the status quo is the most frightening of the possibilities" (*New York Times*, December 29, 2016).

In the YES selection, two experienced government analysts suggest six building blocks for a two-state solution to the long-standing Israeli–Palestinian conflict. The first is to enhance teamwork with regional partners by creating a range of incentives and "tools of persuasion" for various actors. Second, support the political leadership, particularly on the Palestinian side. Third, ensure security for both sides. Fourth, create a vision for Jerusalem that includes an administrative structure for Palestinian villages and Jerusalem neighborhoods. Fifth, prioritize improved services such as water and electricity. And sixth, allow Palestinians to operate businesses on land that they own. In the NO selection, the UN Special Coordinator for the Middle East Peace Process presented quite a negative view in a speech before the UN Security Council. In short, he said that the Middle East "continues to be in the grips of an ongoing human tragedy of immense proportions." He argues that opponents of peace are deliberately working to make the conditions on the ground less conducive to a resolution and that "the enemies of peace are growing more confident by the day."

YES

Mara Rudman and Brian Katulis

A Practical Plan on the Israeli–Palestinian Front

Introduction and Summary

The incoming U.S. administration has an opportunity to increase stability and advance U.S. security interests in the Middle East by outlining a framework for Israelis and Palestinians to make independent, coordinated, and constructive steps toward a two-state solution. This solution would support a safe and secure Israel and a sustainable, contiguous, and sovereign Palestine. At a time when the broader region continues to experience threats from civil wars, state fragmentation, and terrorist networks, the Israeli–Palestinian front is one area where the incoming administration can build on decades of investments to help enhance security and construct lasting institutions to achieve a sustainable resolution to the Israeli–Palestinian conflict.

President-elect Donald Trump has declared that he wants "to be the one that made peace with Israel and the Palestinians." Direct negotiations between Israelis and Palestinians are unworkable right now, but Trump can move toward this goal if he starts to lay the groundwork with five key steps:

1. **Outline** a vision that includes a nonmilitarized Palestine and a territorial point framed as 1967 lines with mutually agreed swaps. This vision would highlight a horizon that advances America's interests, reflects bipartisan U.S. precedent and the positions of key international actors, reassures partners, and addresses existential Israeli and Palestinian concerns.

2. **Lead** an international effort that incentivizes Israelis and Palestinians to take parallel but mutually reinforcing routes toward the vision, rather than expecting either to be able to start negotiating immediately.

3. **Follow-up** on the White House invitation received by Israeli Prime Minister Benjamin Netanyahu with invitations to key Arab leaders for meetings. All of these meetings should be scheduled for the first half of 2017.

4. **Ensure** that preparatory meetings leading up to these White House sessions are used to see that a coordinated approach is in place.

5. **Recognize** that the United States may be most effective when it operates as a trusted partner between and among critical players, able to advise on what can be realistically delivered and how it can occur. It will be important to appreciate what Israel most wants and needs from its Arab neighbors and what they in turn seek from a relationship with Israel.

To make progress toward the two-state solution, six building blocks are essential:

1. **Enhance teamwork with regional partners.** Deploying a range of incentives and tools of persuasion to various actors, depending on relationships, will make a difference. Messages and work must remain coordinated, however, to leverage each country's strengths. Major shifts in long-standing U.S. policies on the Israeli–Palestinian conflict could undermine the incoming U.S. administration's credibility and leverage to shape the actions of key regional powers on this front.

2. **Support political leadership.** Accompanying the task of making Palestinian Authority (PA) President Mahmoud Abbas sufficiently secure in his role and position must be an effort to convince him of the value and import of a reliable supporting bench.

3. **Ensure security.** Israelis and Palestinians need to feel safe from threats for successful conflict resolution. Palestinian security forces coordinate closely with Israeli military

and security operations in the context of their complexly intertwined population and geography; east of the security barrier, there are 110,000 Israeli settlers and 2.6 million Palestinians. The U.S. security coordinator, a three-star officer who engages with the Israelis and Palestinians on security initiatives that build trust and confidence, will offer important continuity through this role, reinforcing the Palestinian security force's structural core work and strengthening force sustainability.

4. **Put forward a vision for Jerusalem.** Within the existing Jerusalem municipality structure, an administrative subdivision for Palestinian villages and Jerusalem neighborhoods could be established. It would be "managed as a separate municipal framework within the city." East Jerusalem residents would collect their locality's taxes and pensions and administer finances; they also would develop, implement, and respond to services needed by their neighbors. Unexpected and unprecedented U.S. policy shifts on the status of Jerusalem could have broad regional implications with reliable partners like Jordan, which plays an important role in the administration of the Muslim holy sites in Jerusalem.

5. **Prioritize unity in improved services.** More reliable delivery of quality water and electricity can provide a cornerstone for better jobs, homes, schools, and futures. Increasing water access, and the electricity to deliver it, for farmers in the northern West Bank—particularly in areas where there are fewer settlements—would be a reasonable place to start in project portfolios linked to Gaza water efforts. Having a common approach to service delivery—and being seen as taking responsibility for Gaza and West Bank Palestinians alike—is as critical to unifying the West Bank and Gaza as is reaching political understandings between Fatah and Hamas, understandings that must recognize the Quartet Principles to be viable internationally.

6. **Link territory and economy.** Palestinians should be able to run and operate businesses, such as farms and stone and marble quarries, on land they own. If permitted to do so, they could add nearly $1 billion to the PA's gross domestic product (GDP) as long as they had access to land and water in previously inaccessible areas and committed to maximizing the use of recycled water and other sustainable use techniques. U.S. efforts to accelerate work, partnerships, and engagement between the Palestinian information and communications technology sector, Israelis, and the international market also could increase economic growth significantly.

This report examines the Israeli–Palestinian predicament in the context of today's Middle East and the efforts by the United States and other global and regional powers to resolve this conflict over the past several years. It makes the case for the incoming Trump administration to adopt a pragmatic approach that brings Israel and the PA closer to resolving the conflict through coordinated actions on the security, economic, and political fronts. This formula would bring the parties closer to a sustainable agreement without direct negotiations at the outset. It outlines the six key building blocks aimed at fostering a more favorable environment to maintain a safe and secure Israel and achieve a sustainable, contiguous, and sovereign Palestine. This practical plan offers the best formula for progress.

The incoming Trump administration has indicated that it may adopt an impractical approach, which could end up producing greater instability in the region. Moving the U.S. embassy from Tel Aviv to Jerusalem—which some Trump senior advisors have suggested as a top priority—could end up isolating both Israel and the United States in the broader Middle East, where the issue of Jerusalem's status remains an unresolved question subject to negotiations. Furthermore, Trump's nominee for U.S. ambassador to Israel would contradict his predecessors, appointed by U.S. presidents since 1967, in his support for Israel to annex disputed territory in the West Bank and build more settlements there. These moves could inflame a fragile situation unnecessarily.

The Middle East is experiencing tremendous challenges—from the rise of the Islamic State to Iran's ongoing destabilizing regional actions and turmoil in Syria and Iraq to a refugee crisis with no end in sight. As the Center for American Progress recently outlined, the United States maintains a unique position to shape and influence trends in the region toward a more positive trajectory. The Israeli–Palestinian front is one area where the incoming Trump administration could have an impact if it adopts an approach centered on coordinated unilateral moves by the parties. By outlining a horizon to resolve the Israeli–Palestinian conflict and creating incentives for the parties to move toward a two-state solution, the incoming U.S. administration can focus the energies of the parties in a way that safeguards against the outbreak of another

Is a Two-state Diplomatic Solution to the Israeli-Palestinian Conflict Possible or Likely in the Near Future? by Harf, Harf, and Lombardi

223

military conflict along Israel's borders, such as the 2008, 2012, and 2014 wars in Gaza.

The new administration has an opportunity to align America's interests and strengths with those of Israel and key Arab countries and lay the groundwork toward a sustainable two-state resolution and broader U.S. strategy in the Middle East. This route acknowledges that direct negotiations between Israelis and Palestinians are not workable right now. It offers more opportunities for much needed gains in security, economics, governance, and the trust necessary to negotiate any agreement's final steps. This would represent a major shift from what has become the ever-constricting space of the status quo. President-elect Trump could bring this opportunity to America, Israel, the Palestinians, and the region.

Making a Deal: Analyzing the Current Context

A sustainable Palestinian state with clearly demarcated borders would make Israel more secure and enhance regional and global stability. The incoming U.S. administration has an opportunity to lay the groundwork while advancing Middle East and U.S. security interests. It can do this by outlining a framework for Israelis and Palestinians to take independent, coordinated, and constructive steps toward a two-state solution. The president-elect can build on decades of investments to help enhance security and lasting institutions to achieve a sustainable resolution to the Israeli–Palestinian conflict. Doing so with a pragmatic vision and coordination can bring together critical actors acting as a force for stability and security, even as the broader region experiences threats from civil wars, state fragmentation, and terrorist networks.

The Trump administration enters office on January 20, 2017. It will be a year with momentous anniversaries: June will mark the 50th year of the 1967 war when Israel's occupation of the West Bank and Gaza started; November will mark 100 years since the Balfour Declaration was signed. Under the Balfour Declaration, Britain promised Israel land in Palestine for a state.

Recognizing the challenge that it represents, President-elect Trump has stated that he wants "to be the one that made peace with Israel and the Palestinians." As president, Trump could expand opportunities for United States, Israeli, and regional security in making a deal. Direct negotiations between Israelis and Palestinians are not possible immediately, but the United States can move toward this goal, with an effort supported by Israeli, Palestinian, and regional security, political, and business leaders. The

United States can help lead a properly scoped and shaped endeavor, strategically leveraging resources, relationships, and skills. The incoming administration should learn from its predecessors' gains and miscalculations. Such an assessment would conclude that there is sound logic, premised on U.S. national security interests, in the convergence of Republican and Democratic presidents' views on the following:

- The need for a two-state solution, defined as a safe and secure Israel and a sustainable, contiguous, and sovereign Palestine.
- Significant reforms to continue building the future Palestine, and some good investment to date on governance and economic fronts.
- Regional participation as critical to any plausible resolution.

Relations between Israel and the Arab Quartet—Jordan, Egypt, Saudi Arabia, and the United Arab Emirates—have been quietly warming, as have those, to a lesser degree, with Turkey and Qatar. This is a result of shared interests and concerns, including what several commonly perceive as the more threatening regional status of Iran as a result of the nuclear agreement. Within areas of potential partnership, however, the Palestinian situation status remains "like a thorn." Countries such as Jordan and Egypt also face heightened concern about direct impact on their own security from instability in the West Bank and Gaza. Conversely, they would benefit from an effectively functioning Palestinian state that could be counted as a reliable partner.

President Trump would be on firm ground, and most likely to achieve results, if he makes an early statement that: (1) reaffirms his commitment to working with the parties and regional players to resolve conflict and (2) frames his goal as a nonmilitarized Palestine and 1967 lines with mutually agreed swaps. In doing so, Trump would be building on a framework grounded in long-standing U.S. policy positions to advance the interests of the United States, Israel, and the United States' closest partners in the Middle East.

Two key existing elements that could help in constructing a new framework include U.S. positions on territory and security and the Arab Peace Initiative.

U.S. Positions on Territory and Security

The U.S. position on territory and security with respect to Israeli–Palestinian framework issues has remained consistent over nearly two decades. President Bill Clinton, President George W. Bush, and President Barack Obama have each cited the absolute of Israel's right to self-defense against any threat, required robust provisions to prevent terrorism, and stated that the future Palestinian state be nonmilitarized. Each described a U.S. commitment to a negotiated two-state resolution that would result in a sovereign, sustainable Palestine, and a secure Israel, with borders based on 1967 lines with mutually agreed swaps.

Arab Peace Initiative

The Arab Peace Initiative, launched in 2002 by the late King Abdullah of Saudi Arabia, calls for withdrawal to 1967 lines—and from the Golan—as well as "a just solution to the Palestinian refugee problem to be agreed upon in accordance with UN General Assembly Resolution 194." It also calls for accepting a sovereign and independent Palestinian state in the West Bank and Gaza with East Jerusalem as the capital. The Arab League endorsed the initiative in 2002 at its Beirut Summit and re-endorsed it in 2007. The latest version, endorsed in 2013, calls for the initiative to be based on the two-state solution on the basis of 1967 lines, with the possibility of comparable and mutually agreed-upon minor swaps of the land between Israel and Palestine. Israel's ambassador to the United States described the 2013 Arab Peace Initiative as "version 1.25" but in the context of openness to conversations toward a version 2.0.

Moving forward, resolving the Israeli–Palestinian conflict requires advancing a framework that includes the desired destination but also captures the coordinated and simultaneous steps necessary to achieve progress on several fronts to improve the lives and security of Israelis and Palestinians alike. The framework should focus on four areas: security, politics and governance, water and electricity service delivery, and economic progress.

Security

Grappling with security is a daily worry. Palestinian security forces coordinate closely with Israeli military and security operations on their complexly intertwined population and geography and the ever more volatile region that they face together. Consider that in the West Bank, Palestinians number 2.6 million and Israelis number 570,000. In the West Bank, 19.3 percent of Israelis are living beyond the 1967 line, but this includes nearly 200,000 living within greater Jerusalem, and another 150,000 living in three major settlements surrounding Jerusalem: Beitar Illit,

Modi'in Illit, and Ma'ale Adumim. East of the security barrier, there are 110,000 Israelis or 4.5 percent of the total population.

Palestinian law enforcement is constrained in its ability to operate freely only within the limited and noncontiguous area A jurisdictions. The Israel Defense Forces is responsible for a widely dispersed Israeli settler population and, significantly, for working with Jordan and Egypt to defend against other regional threats. The Center for a New American Security (CNAS) worked with Commanders for Israel's Security (CIS) to tackle how a security system might be developed to promote a two-state solution that meets the needs of Israelis and Palestinians. In doing so, CNAS included guidance on steps that could be taken immediately to lead to security improvements for both parties. The CNAS and CIS work on security solutions, both long-term and interim, supports the two-state destination approach.

Politics and Governance

Appreciating that security concerns must and can be addressed, President Trump would make his framing statement recognizing that Palestinian and Israeli politics are consumed by internal matters that need to be tackled before direct negotiations will be productive. This internal work can occur even as they each progress on parallel coordinated paths toward the two-state destination.

In recent years, President Abbas has been subject to intense speculation about his tenure. He is 81 years old, has threatened to resign several times, and last faced a PA election in 2005. He convened the first Fatah congress in seven years in late November 2016, with restricted participation terms, to support his position as Fatah leader and chairman of the Palestine Liberation Organization (PLO). He believes, not without reason, that he is in a precarious political position domestically and that he lacks sufficient external backing. He is unlikely to be the Palestinian leader who seals a deal with Israel; instead, he is a transition leader. President-elect Trump should consider what kind of transition this will be and what is in America's interests for Palestinians and Israelis to transition toward. If the United States is best protected and most secure with a Middle East in which Israel and its Arab Quartet neighbors are strongly allied—and more united than not with Turkey and Qatar—it will be best served by continuing to make gains toward Palestinian statehood.

It seems likely Prime Minister Netanyahu has made the same calculation within his own country and that he is assessing how to execute it given his position within his

Is a Two-state Diplomatic Solution to the Israeli-Palestinian Conflict Possible or Likely in the Near Future? by Harf, Harf, and Lombardi

225

rightward leaning coalition. Since the 2016 U.S. presidential election, he has more than once made statements to remind his ministers—and others—that he speaks for the state of Israel. He has done so to leave options on the table with the Palestinians and Arab states, and with the incoming U.S. administration.

The political turmoil among Palestinian leaders precludes focus on challenging governance and negotiation issues. Resolving high politics could lead to a stronger foundation for negotiations. Arguably, faith in functioning governing institutions should undergird any future state. Such institutions should be able to deliver services that people need and be seen to be to delivering such services. These all should be key for the viability of a future Palestine. So too is unifying Palestinians in the West Bank and Gaza and getting people the basic services they need: water, electricity, food, shelter, schooling, and rule of law.

Having a government that delivers on its promises to its people is an important component of building and retaining political legitimacy. In laying out his state-building vision in 2010, then-PA Prime Minister Salam Fayyad said, "It's the power of ideas translated into facts on the ground . . . putting institutions together and getting them to coordinate their activities, getting them to be better able to provide services like medical care and security—that's what statehood is about." The PA has made some gains since its initial major internal reform and restructuring effort, but it also has suffered some setbacks.

Service Delivery: Water and Electricity Critical

Any Palestinian governance stocktaking requires focus on water and electricity. The PA is neither solely responsible for these services nor is it completely free of burden. In Gaza, the water situation is dire. Its population could run out of reasonable water supplies as soon as 2020. Israel shares the interests of Palestinians in Gaza to stave off this crisis and put longer-term solutions in place. The Palestinian Water Authority, run by the PA, and the Gaza Coastal Municipalities Water Utility—operated by technicians but on which Hamas-elected mayors may retain a governing majority—share control of water distribution. Israel, Egypt, and/or a privately owned Gaza facility contracted by the PA provide the electricity needed to meet water demands. Water issues also are complicated in the West Bank. Most new water

resources require application by permit to Israeli authorities and funding assistance from international donors. The approval process for Palestinians has not been smooth.

Economic Progress

In April 2016, the Center for American Progress published a report discussing specific measures to bolster the Palestinian economy. Particular areas offer the most opportunity for outside actors to leverage their resources to the greatest advantage:

- The Palestinian Information Communications Technologies (ICT) sector could capture a growing percentage of the Palestinian GDP. It has the basis for natural partnership with Israeli offices of multinational companies, such as Cisco, Microsoft, Google, Hewlett-Packard, and Intel. But Palestinians anxious to work in the ICT sector need skills that match the current needs of the companies from which they seek work.

- The new U.S. administration is well-positioned to encourage the direct input and commitment of high-level executives at the leading companies, whose regional offices in Israel are eager to support outreach to Palestinian ICT companies for contracts that meet current and future market needs.

- U.S. efforts to accelerate work, partnerships, and engagement between the Palestinian ICT sector, Israelis, and the international market could increase economic growth beyond that sector. Technological gains in sustainable water use, for example, would revolutionize Palestinian farming, particularly if combined with smart access to previously unavailable land or water resources.

- President-elect Trump's White House will appreciate that land use planning and other related rule of law efforts are critical to real estate development. The PA needs rules of the road that will impact actors operating now. Laying the foundation for a functioning state that controls the desired destination—land within 1967 lines with mutually agreed swaps, where currently, Palestinian property options and zoning are often haphazard—means restructuring property taxes and seeking stewardship accountability opportunities to incentivize the most appropriate land use in a given municipality.

Game Plan to Make a Deal: Building Blocks for Progress

First, President-elect Trump should lay out a vision for resolving the conflict. Next, to make progress toward a two-state solution with a sustainable Palestinian state while maintaining a safe and secure Israel, the Trump administration should focus on the following six initial building blocks.

1. **Advance teamwork with regional partners.** The United States should work with Israelis and Palestinians who live the realities daily. It also should work with regional actors who have direct and immediate interests in building a sustainable state that will be a good neighbor and an overall asset in a tough neighborhood and with European and multilateral partners who have long been active contributors.

   - Follow-up on the White House's invitation to Prime Minister Netanyahu with invitations to key Arab leaders. All meetings should occur within the first half of 2017.

   - Preparatory meetings leading up to the president's White House sessions should ensure that an integrated approach is in place.

   - Each country shares an interest in building long-term stability for Palestinians in the West Bank and Gaza. It will be important to deploy a variety of tools of persuasion and incentives with different actors, depending on relationships. Messages and work must remain coordinated, however, to leverage each country's strengths.

2. **Support political leadership.** To progress toward Palestinian statehood, the United States, Israel, and regional and international partners need to make a conscious choice to support PA President Abbas. This means recognizing him as the transition leader that he is, with an appreciation of his strengths and the limits of his capabilities. Accompanying the task of making President Abbas sufficiently secure in his role and position must be convincing him of the value and import of a reliable supporting bench.

   - With these assurances, President Abbas should be encouraged to return his focus to daily governance and the broader political horizon required for peace negotiations.

   - Included in regular discussions should be transparent planning for a development process for next generation leaders within Fatah and, separately, in the PA.

   - Hamas also is undergoing leadership turmoil. Khaled Mashal, the political leader based in Qatar, has said that he will step down by year's end. Ismail Haniyeh, the political leader within Gaza, may be his logical successor, but significant power also lies within the security and militia wings. More extreme jihadist groups within Gaza, augmented by Sinai groups, are further destabilizing. Arab partners need to bring Hamas toward the Quartet Principles and reconciliation with the PLO.

3. **Ensure security.** Israelis and Palestinians need to feel safe from threats to resolve conflicts successfully. The U.S. security coordinator, a three-star officer who engages with Israelis and Palestinians on security initiatives that build trust and confidence, will offer important continuity through this role. The security coordinator's work reinforces the structural core work of the Palestinian security force, strengthening sustainability.

   - To strengthen the Palestinian legal system, CNAS has suggested building counterterror expertise, including a special court system, combined with working on the overall Palestinian court system and rule of law.

   - The political dynamics are not steady state. Interactions could improve through working on commonly designated tasks that yield concrete results, designed to suit the strengths of each partner, as has been the case on security coordination.

4. **Outline a vision for Jerusalem.** The boundaries of Greater Jerusalem were expanded significantly in 1967. Palestinians now comprise some 40 percent of all city residents. Jerusalem residents pay municipal taxes and depend on Israeli services, but routine administration work, trash pickup, and other services function less effectively in Arab areas. Certain Arab neighborhoods lack access to law enforcement; Israeli police do not enter them, and Palestinian security cannot enter. The housing market also is tight, particularly for Arab residents.

   - Within Jerusalem's existing municipality structure, an administrative subdivision for Palestinian villages and Jerusalem neighborhoods could be established. It would be "managed as a separate municipal framework within the city." East Jerusalem residents would collect their locality's taxes and pensions, and administer finances; they also would develop, implement, and respond to services needed by their neighbors.

- Arab residents of East Jerusalem should be sought, through transparent competitive hiring processes, for the senior municipality positions, intended for professionals who will assist Arab residents of East Jerusalem.

- To address law and order concerns, a new unit of police could be created to work throughout East Jerusalem. It could be composed entirely of East Jerusalem residents or, at least initially, of East Jerusalem residents and Israeli police forces. Alternatively, Israelis might consider asking the U.S. security coordinator to develop training for a joint East Jerusalem force, with Palestinian security forces. These structures would address concerns about services and law and order, while also testing some aspects of possible options on separation and unification.

5. **Work toward unity in improved services.** More reliable delivery of quality water and electricity can provide a cornerstone for better jobs, homes, schools, and futures. Increasing water access—and the electricity to deliver it—for farmers in the northern West Bank, particularly in areas where there are fewer settlements, would be a reasonable place to start in project portfolios linked to Gaza water efforts. Having a common approach to delivering services, and being seen as taking responsibility for both Gaza and West Bank Palestinians, is as critical to unifying West Bank and Gaza as reaching political understandings between Fatah and Hamas, understandings that must recognize the Quartet Principles to be viable internationally.

- Palestinians in Gaza can be overwhelmed and isolated by the lack of opportunity and horizon and also may feel forgotten or cast aside by a world consumed with crises elsewhere. Too often, they may get this sense from Palestinians as close as the West Bank. But when clean water flows and lights work—whether in Gaza or the West Bank—Palestinians should be able to credit the PA, with pride, for getting it done. The United Arab Emirates, Qatar, Oman, and Turkey share expertise that could be useful, particularly if they provide support for service delivery in both West Bank and Gaza.

- In September 2016, the PA signed an electricity agreement intended to resolve its outstanding $530 million debt to the Israel Electric Corporation and frame a path forward. The agreement created an Israeli–Palestinian committee that will oversee transfer of responsibility to the PA for power lines that supply electricity to West Bank Palestinian cities. There is challenging work ahead for Palestinians in running this service effectively and collecting user fees. An appropriate international actor should help mentor the PA as it assumes this key state role.

- International actors helping support and ensure service delivery will be better situated to grapple with intraparty politics and constituencies when they have on-the-ground experience.

- The West Bank and Gaza need to be able to operate and act as one en route to statehood. For Hamas, elements interested in any long-term prospects for leading within an entity that can achieve international support, this means recognizing Israel and buying into a nonmilitarized Palestine.

- Israel must be able to negotiate with a unified Palestinian partner, to perceive and treat the West Bank and Gaza as a single unit, to reach the desired two-state resolution.

6. **Link territory and economy.** Palestinians should be able to run and operate businesses, such as farms or stone and marble quarries, on land they own. If permitted to do so in area C locations, for example, they could add nearly $1 billion dollars to the Palestinian GDP, according to World Bank estimates, as long as they had the land and water access to commit to maximizing use of recycled water and other sustainable use techniques. U.S. efforts to accelerate work, partnerships, and engagement between the Palestinian information and communications technology sector, Israelis, and the international

market also could increase economic growth significantly.

- Israel could consider addressing the lack of building permits for area C's growing Palestinian population by allowing construction on the small segments in separate locations adjacent to area B Palestinian villages. Making this policy change would affect less than 1 percent of total area C territory but would remove demolition threats for 11,000 homes in which 200,000 Palestinians live.

- Israeli citizens pay an economic price in the taxes that subsidize settlement expenditures. They also suffer lost opportunity costs with respect to investment and economic activity for trade with Palestinians; the Arab world; and, increasingly, with Europe.

- Israeli organizations have proposed voluntary compensation legislation that would provide funds and other services for settlers who wish to relocate from a settlement east of the barrier to anywhere west of it. Were Israel to move forward with such a paradigm-shifting approach, it would clear space—literally and figuratively—in the northern West Bank, removing concern about friction points between Palestinians and Israeli settlers. This would give Palestinian leaders, working cooperatively with their Israeli counterparts, the ability to test political and governance structures on much larger expanses of contiguous territory than has been the case previously.

- Palestinian businesses in the West Bank and Gaza sell 80 percent of their products in Israel across agriculture, textiles, and light manufacturing sectors. When borders, and the secure transit of people and goods, are regularized, economies will benefit, as will the region. The crossing at Gilboa–Jalameh between Northern Israel and the Northern West Bank provides an illustrative pilot program. Located north of the city of Jenin at the green line, Israel operates it for Palestinians and Israeli Arabs who transit by vehicles and on foot. The United States funded its upgrade to handle commercial transit and vehicles of all types. Since the vehicle crossing opened in 2009 and through the end of 2014, the estimated benefit to Jenin's economy totaled $230 million.

- This demonstrates the potential of that city's economy, which had previously been isolated from regional markets. As the economy in the northern West Bank has expanded, so has the demand for facilities at crossing points. Today, Jalameh is promoted for its safe, secure, and expanded access for people and trade; few people can recall how challenging it was initially to convince counterparts to proceed.

Conclusion

From the rise of the Islamic State to Iran's ongoing actions destabilizing the region, turmoil in Syria and Iraq, and a refugee crisis with no end in sight, some see the Middle East as spinning out of control, with the Israeli–Palestinian conflict an ever more remote component in the regional diorama and the United States a less consequential player. President-elect Trump has an opportunity to align America's interests and strengths with those of Israel and key Arab countries and lay the groundwork for a sustainable two-state resolution and a broader U.S.–Middle East strategy.

This route acknowledges that direct negotiations between Israelis and Palestinians are not workable right now, though such negotiations will be needed in the last steps of any agreement. Many factors currently stand in the way, including mutual mistrust, political stasis, and division among Palestinians and Israelis. At the same time, however, disengagement could leave a vacuum that, given history's lessons, will not lead anywhere good. President-elect Trump could add fuel to a combustible arena unless he finds a way to change the trajectory he has laid with his nominee for ambassador to Israel. But should President-elect Trump desire to make a deal, he can seize the moment, by encouraging coordinated and constructive steps that bring Israelis and Palestinians much closer to a two-state solution that supports a secure Israel and a sovereign, contiguous Palestine. Forward progress on key fronts—including security, governance, and the economy—can help set the conditions for a deal that enhances security and stability across the Middle East and in the United States.

MARA RUDMAN is a diplomat in residence at American University, having served in senior positions dealing with the Middle East in the Obama and Clinton National Security Councils, at the State Department, and at USAID.

BRIAN KATULIS is a senior fellow at the Center for American Progress and previously worked on national security issues in the Clinton Administration's NSC and Departments of State and Defense.

Nickolay Mladenov

Security Council Briefing on the Situation in the Middle East

Mr. President,

Your Excellency President Mahmoud Abbas, President of the State of Palestine; Ladies and Gentlemen,

We meet this month as regional tensions are taking an increasingly perilous turn. Fighting in Syria is increasing, endangering de-escalation arrangements and regional stability, as well as undermining efforts for a political solution.

Despite the positive news from Iraq and the defeat of Da'esh, much of the Middle East continues to be in the grips of an ongoing human tragedy of immense proportions.

Mr. President,

Against this backdrop and after over a century of hostilities including 50 years of continued military occupation, Israelis and Palestinians are still no closer to peace; many have lost hope that they will see it in their lifetimes.

The enemies of peace are growing more confident by the day.

They see every failure of the forces of moderation as a win for the forces of radicalization.

They believe the political odds are turning in their favor. Day after day they are emboldened.

Hindering peace are also those who push facts on the ground, who promote unilateral moves blocking the pathway back to the negotiating table.

None of this will bring us closer to resolving the conflict. None of it will respond to the inalienable right of the Palestinian people to statehood or the Israeli longing for security. It will only drive us farther down the road of confrontation, suffering, and a one-state reality of perpetual occupation.

Mr. President,

Last month the international community discussed key priorities to advance the goal of peace at the extraordinary ministerial meeting of the Ad Hoc Liaison Committee.

At the meeting, I was encouraged by widespread, unequivocal messages reaffirming support for the two-state solution, in line with relevant UN resolutions, and the need to resume meaningful negotiations over all final status issues, including the status of Jerusalem.

Participants also made a critical commitment to undertake efforts to address the humanitarian crisis in Gaza, including support for projects focused on water, electricity, and economic recovery.

My message to all was clear: first, we must clearly reaffirm that sustainable peace requires a two-state solution, one that can only be achieved through a negotiated process. Israelis and Palestinians have defined the final status issues and only they, together, can determine their resolution.

Second, efforts must continue to seek implementation of concrete and transformative steps on the ground—including ending Israeli settlement expansion and advancing policy shifts particularly in area C of the West Bank—consistent with a transition to greater Palestinian civil authority, as called for in the 2016 report of the Middle East Quartet.

Third, the Palestinian Authority (PA) must continue to advance institution-building and service delivery to the Palestinian people and work toward bringing Gaza back under its control.

And lastly, it is critical that any future peace proposal focus on the two-state solution and all final status issues as per prior agreements and relevant United Nations resolutions. A failure to do so could have dangerous repercussions.

Mr. President,

Maintaining support for Palestine refugees is fundamental to the pursuit of peace and stability in the region. I reiterate my ongoing concern over UNRWA's sizable funding shortfall, despite the welcome flexibility of some member states in accelerating the disbursement of their funding commitments. In addition, the emergency appeals launched on January 30 seek to raise US$ 800 million for the West Bank and Gaza, as well as for the Syria regional crisis, to meet the essential needs of some

1.5 million highly vulnerable people. I encourage member states to consider urgently providing new funding for UNRWA's critical requirements.

As the peace process falters and the gulf between the two sides widens, Palestinians and Israelis continue to suffer the violent consequences on the ground.

Seven Palestinians were killed by Israeli security forces in various incidents across the occupied Palestinian territory and one Israeli civilian was stabbed and killed by a Palestinian in the West Bank.

Three of the Palestinians killed died during violent clashes with security forces, one a 16-year-old was shot near Ramallah. He was the fourth child killed under such circumstances since the beginning of the year.

I once again emphasize that the use of force must be calibrated and that lethal force should only be used as a last resort, with any resulting fatalities properly investigated by the authorities. I urge Israeli security forces to exercise maximum restraint to avoid casualties under such circumstances.

I call upon all sides to reject violence, condemn terror, ensure accountability, and work to reduce tensions.

In recent days, we have also witnessed dangerous security incidents in and around Gaza. On February 17, four Israeli soldiers were wounded by an improvised explosive device placed at the Gaza fence. This was followed by Israeli airstrikes on some 18 Hamas targets, while Palestinian militants fired two rockets into Israel—one causing damage to a house in the Sha'ar HaNegev Regional Council. Two Palestinian teens were killed by Israeli security forces while reportedly attempting to approach the fence.

Prior to this latest flare-up during the course of the past month, three more rockets were fired toward Israel, with two Israeli retaliatory strikes, all without injuries.

I encourage the international community to join the UN in calling on militants in Gaza to refrain from such provocations and end the building of tunnels and the firing of rockets toward Israel. Such actions, and the response they elicit, only risk the lives of Palestinians and Israelis, undermine peace efforts, and increase the likelihood of another devastating conflict.

I also take the opportunity to note the need to resolve the matter of the missing Israeli soldiers and civilians that are being held in Gaza.

Two additional incidents, Mr. President, highlight the risk of escalation and the need for continued Israeli–Palestinian security coordination. These were the discovery of 12 roadside bombs in the West Bank on January 26 and the foiled attempt on February 4 to smuggle a dual-use component used to make explosives into Gaza within a shipment of medical equipment.

I also note that the trial of 17-year-old Palestinian girl Ahed Tamimi started on February 13 behind closed doors. She has been detained on remand for two months to date. As stated in my last briefing, the detention of a child must only be used as a measure of last resort and for the shortest possible time.

Mr. President,

Throughout the reporting period, Israel's illegal settlement-related activities continued unabated. In response to last month's killing of a resident of the illegal Havat Gilad outpost, on February 4, Israel approved the establishment of a new settlement to absorb its residents. I strongly denounce the expansion of the settlement enterprise as compensation for Israeli deaths.

Settlement construction is not a morally appropriate way to respond to murder.

On February 12, Israel also advanced two settlement plans for some 85 housing units near Bethlehem. I reiterate the long-standing UN position that all settlement-related activities are illegal under international law and are a substantial obstacle to peace; and I call on Israel to seize and reverse such policies.

Mr. President,

Demolition and seizure of Palestinian-owned structures also continued, with 31 structures affected, resulting in 33 Palestinians displaced. Particularly concerning was the demolition of two donor-funded classrooms serving Palestinian children in the Bedouin community of Abu Nuwar. This is the sixth demolition or confiscation in the school since February 2016.

Overall, according to OCHA, 44 schools in the occupied West Bank are currently at risk of demolition. I urge Israel to cease this practice.

Mr. President,

I briefed you last week on the situation in Gaza. Month after month, we have raised the alarm about the humanitarian, economic, and ecological calamity underway. It bears repeating that the situation is unsustainable.

Continuing power cuts of up to 20 hours per day severely undermine the provision of basic services. Without additional immediate fuel deliveries, the situation could deteriorate with dramatic consequences.

I reiterate the Secretary-General's appreciation to the United Arab Emirates and to the State of Qatar for their support to deal with this emergency. Their immediate response to our appeal has helped stave off a further deterioration.

I am encouraged by the trilateral meeting I had last week with Palestinian Prime Minister Hamdallah and Israel's Coordinator of Government Activities in the Territories, Major General Mordechai in which we focused on the humanitarian problems in Gaza. Both sides reaffirmed their commitment to the temporary Gaza Reconstruction Mechanism and agreed on the need for a joint review to improve its functionality, transparency, and predictability.

Mr. President,

As the humanitarian crisis in Gaza escalates, the implementation of the Egyptian-brokered intra-Palestinian agreement has stalled. Absent immediate steps to address the humanitarian crisis and to revive the economy, we will face a total institutional and economic collapse in Gaza. This is not an alarmist prediction Mr. President—it is a fact.

I welcome the proposal of the Palestinian Government to incorporate into its 2018 budget some 20,000 civil service employees in Gaza. A positive outcome, however, is contingent, *inter alia*, upon the collection of taxes, the payment of salaries, the return of the Government administration, and ultimately, security control of Gaza.

I urge all sides to intensify their engagement and to move forward in this process.

Mr. President,

For a decade, two million people have lived under the full control of Hamas with crippling Israeli closures and movement and access restrictions. Throughout this period, the international community has provided aid and humanitarian assistance to alleviate the suffering and to rebuild what was destroyed in three devastating conflicts.

It is time to break this cycle. It is time to return Gaza back to the control of the legitimate PA, for there can be no Palestinian state without Palestinian unity.

Those who stand in the way of reconciliation hurt the Palestinian national cause, and the price will be paid by generations of ordinary people.

Mr. President,

The security situation on the Golan is also of growing concern. A worrying escalation occurred on February 10, when Israeli Defense Forces destroyed what they identified as an Iranian Unmanned Aerial Vehicle which had reportedly entered its airspace from Syria. Shortly thereafter, Israeli aircraft targeted a Syrian airbase. During the attack, one Israeli jet was hit injuring two pilots, which further prompted Israel to attack what it described as "12 military objectives" inside Syria. I urge all sides to work toward easing tensions in this highly volatile area.

Turning briefly to Lebanon. Heightened rhetoric was exchanged between Israel and Lebanon over disputed maritime areas. The United Nations continues to call on the sides to act responsibly, avoid security risks, and explore with the support of the United Nations ways to resolve the issue.

Preparations continue for May parliamentary elections in Lebanon and for the upcoming Rome II and CEDRE conferences to support the security sector and economy, respectively on March 15 and April 5.

While the situation was generally quiet in the UNIFIL area of operation, heightened rhetoric relating to the Israeli Defense Forces proposed constructions in Lebanese "reservation areas" south of the Blue Line continued. The planned construction commenced in nonreservation areas on February 7 with no incidents reported.

Mr. President,

Returning to the Israeli–Palestinian conflict, let me reiterate in closing that we in the international community must continue advocating for substantial Israeli policy changes related to the situation in the West Bank, including a halt to settlement construction, demolition of structures and prevention of Palestinian development in Area C. On Gaza, we must collectively work to alleviate the humanitarian disaster and provide full support to Egyptian reconciliation efforts. Our support to UNRWA also remains vital.

I also hope that we will be able to look beyond the closed, dark negotiating rooms that are currently empty of diplomats and politicians, to see that there are Israeli and Palestinian advocates for peace working tirelessly to promote change: civil society organizations, youth and women's groups, religious and community leaders—they all have a critical role to play and must be supported and allowed to express their views freely. We rarely discuss their role, we don't speak often enough of the challenges they face, but their efforts must be recognized and supported.

In this Chamber, Mr. President, we have often spoken of the need for leadership on both sides to reach a deal, a compromise, through negotiations that would allow Israelis and Palestinians to separate and be masters of their own fate.

But Mr. President, these negotiations would not be negotiations between equals.

For one side is under military occupation. Its leadership has committed to a peaceful solution to the conflict through negotiation. I urge the international community not to give up on support for the moderate Palestinian leadership or on building up the institutions that will increase the chances of success. Our window of opportunity is closing and, if we do not seize it quickly, the Israeli–Palestinian conflict will be engulfed in the whirlwind of religious radicalization that remains present in the region.

Thank you.

Nickolay Mladenov is the UN special coordinator for the Middle East Peace Process.

EXPLORING THE ISSUE

Is a Two-state Diplomatic Solution to the Israeli–Palestinian Conflict Possible or Likely in the Near Future?

Critical Thinking and Reflection

1. How can the two sides work to overcome such troubled history to work to make peace?
2. How can the Arab states or other outside actors (the United States, the U.N., etc.) play a role in reinvigorating negotiations between the Israelis and the Palestinians?
3. How do the changing dynamics in the Middle East impact the Israeli–Palestinian conflict?
4. Was the American decision to move its embassy to Jerusalem without extracting some benefits or concessions from Israel a good example of President Trump's *The Art of the Deal* or, as some have argued, *The Art of the Giveaway*?
5. Did the American decision to move its embassy to Jerusalem lessen the likelihood of Middle East peace in the foreseeable future?

Is There Common Ground?

Moderates on both sides of the issue believe that a solution of two states for two peoples, living side-by-side in peace and security is the best outcome for the Israeli–Palestinian conflict. There is also general agreement about the issues that will have to comprise any final agreement—borders, refugees, Jerusalem, and security—as well as the broad contours of how those issues might be addressed. Finally, there tends to be agreement that outside actors will need to play a positive role in helping achieve peace, whether it is the United States, the U.N., the Arab states, or the Quartet, because the two sides need mediators to help bridge the gaps.

Additional Resources

"A Brief History of the Key Events and People That Shaped the Arab-Israeli Conflict," *The Guardian* (August 16, 2009)

Al-Omari, Ghaith, "Israel, the Palestinians, and the Administration's Peace Plan," *Washington Institute for Near East Policy* (February 14, 2018)

Anthony, C. Ross, et al., "*The Costs of the Israeli-Palestinian Conflict,*" The Rand Corporation (2015)

Hammond, Jeremy R., "The No-State Solution to the Israeli-Palestine Conflict," *Foreign Policy Journal* (July 9, 2016)

Amr, Hady, "Jerusalem: After 30 Years of Hope and Failure, What's Next for Israel/Palestine?," *Foreign Policy* (December 11, 2017)

Report to the Ad Hoc Liaison Committee's Office of the United Nations Special Coordinator for the Middle East Peace Process, United Nations (Brussels, March 20, 2018)

Yaalon, Moshe and Leehe Friedman, "Israel and the Arab State," *Foreign Affairs* (January 26, 2018)

Internet References . . .

Columbia University Libraries

https://library.edu/locations/global/virtual-libraries/
middle_east_studies/israeli-palestinian-conflict

Council on Foreign Relations

https://www.cfr.org/interactives/crisis-guide-israeli-
palestinian-conflict

PBS "Shattered Dreams of Peace: The Road from Oslo" Series

https://pbs.org/wgbh/pages/frontline/shows/oslo/

ISSUE

Selected, Edited, and with Issue Framing Material by:
Marie E. Harf, *U.S. Department of State (2013–2017),*
Central Intelligence Agency (2006–2011)

Is Russia Increasingly Pursuing a Strategy to Threaten Democratic Regimes throughout Europe and the Western World?

YES: **Larry Diamond**, from "Russia and the Threat to Liberal Democracy," *The Atlantic* (2016)

NO: **Mark Lawrence Schrad**, from "Vladimir Putin Isn't a Supervillain," *Foreign Policy* (2017)

Learning Outcomes

After reading this issue, you will be able to:

- Describe why Russian President Vladimir Putin believes his country is threatened by Western democracies and institutions, including the underlying historical context.
- Outline the kinds of activities Russia has engaged in to undermine Western democracies, according to those who believe this has been the Russian intent.
- Understand why Russia has focused on information warfare and elections as prime targets of its activities.
- Understand the position of those analysts who believe Russia does not have the capacity to adversely affect Western democracies and that it is Western weakness instead that enables this outside activity to be successful.

ISSUE SUMMARY

YES: Larry Diamond, a senior fellow at Stanford University's Hoover Institution and Freeman Spogli Institute for International Studies, argues that Putin "has embraced an opportunistic but sophisticated campaign to sabotage democracy." Diamond says this new Russian assault has occurred with a speed and scope that few in the West fully understand, which "puts the future of liberal democracy in the world . . . in doubt and on the defensive."

NO: Mark Lawrence Schrad, a Villanova University professor, suggests that Western commentary on Russia's foreign policy can be placed into two rather extreme camps. One approach says Putin is 10-feet-tall, while the other sees a country falling apart. Schrad argues that the reality is somewhere in between. "Russia is not nearly the global menace that many fear nor is it doomed to collapse." Accordingly, he believes that any analysis must be a "sober assessment of the country's capabilities and limitations" and not a rush to see Russian interference everywhere.

This issue addresses the question of whether Russia under the leadership of Vladimir Putin is increasingly pursuing a foreign policy strategy designed to threaten democratic regimes in Europe and the Western world. Given the history of relations between the two sides throughout the Cold War, this question is not a new one. Recently, however, it has taken on an increased urgency, made especially acute by Russia's interference in the 2016 U.S. presidential election as well as similar meddling in the affairs of other democracies throughout Europe.

As far back as the end of World War II, Soviet behavior patterns had convinced the West that Moscow was intent on undermining if not destroying the government systems of those countries that were either established democracies or aspiring ones. At the beginning of the Cold War, the Soviets took advantage of the geopolitical terrain to fight their ideological battles: Europe was devastated, effective governing was sporadic, and Soviet troops positioned throughout Eastern and Central Europe were well-placed to meddle in other countries' affairs. Moscow bolstered friendly regimes and parties with military and financial assistance, and when any of these regimes came under threat, the Soviet Union did what it could to push back. "Spheres of influence" became the international system's *modus operandi*, and the Soviet Union worked hard to maintain the nondemocratic ideology in its aligned countries.

When the Soviet Union fell and its successor states, including Russia, emerged, Western hopes were high that these new countries would experiment with their own forms of democracy. But after an arguably disastrous post–Cold War Russian administration led by Boris Yeltsin, authoritarian tendencies that had been the hallmark of the former Communist regime reemerged as a nod to restoring stability. A new autocratic leader, Vladimir Putin, rose to power with the goal of making Russia a great power again, and he has ruled in one form or another for almost two decades, solidifying and maintaining his position by all manner of nondemocratic means. The current regime in Moscow, still led by former KGB officer Putin, today looks and acts very much like the former Soviet Union, absent the public allegiance to Marxist–Leninist ideology.

Putin's strategy from day 1 has been to restore what he views as unfairly lost Soviet power and prestige. He has called the Soviet Union's collapse "the greatest geopolitical catastrophe of the century" and he blames the United States for toppling the USSR and humiliating Russia. Putin sees the European Union and NATO as adversaries who keep pushing Western-style democracy and their military forces closer and closer to Russia's borders. As a result, "Moscow's long-term strategy is to break these institutions from within" because they support the liberal international order that Russia views as a threat (*Politico*, March 17, 2017).

Russia's territorial advantages of the Cold War are no longer quite so stark, and nuclear parity has made direct military confrontation too dangerous. But modern technology has made the flow of information and money both easier and more deniable, which has opened up new avenues of potential influence, and the Russians have been eager to exploit them.

There is mounting evidence that the Russian government has adopted a new strategy of hybrid warfare, outlined publicly by one of its top generals, centered around the government and its shadowy friends undertaking deniable offensive measures against its adversaries. Whether it is covert information warfare or special forces operating without any government insignia, Russia has developed tools that can affect outcomes without deploying traditional military resources or using visible arms of the state.

A cornerstone of this strategy is intense information warfare: spreading fake news through official Russian media such as *Russia Today* and *Sputnik*; running troll farms that propagate myths, lies, and distortions and engage in character assassination of adversaries; and launching cyberattacks against governments, democracy advocates, and political parties across the West. Russia has arguably married the art of deception with modern technology and is directing it at populations in ways that bypass our usual critical thinking faculties because this content looks real and often seems plausible. The spread of fake news is key; Russia appears to believe that by peddling believable falsehoods or distortions, sometimes based on a kernel of truth, it can sow mistrust between citizens and their governments and undermine the social contract that underpins basic principles of democracy (Julie Lenarz, *Telegraph*, January 26, 2017). The information does not have to be true; it just has to be believable enough to muddy the waters.

The technology revolution has made this kind of Russian propaganda even more dangerous today than in the past. Widespread Internet access has allowed Russian disinformation to more directly, quickly, and covertly reach a much wider audience. The use of big data and online marketing by Western political parties has left doors wide open for Russian actors to run through with their messages. These factors, combined with a crisis of traditional media among many in the West and a rise in excessive partisanship, have left democracies vulnerable to this type of warfare. And it is extremely difficult to get a handle on the sheer size of the Russian effort in terms of online accounts or people reached.

A recent study by the Council on Foreign Relations (Robert D. Blackwell and Philip H. Gordon, *Containing Russia*, January 2018) outlined a litany of Russian behavior beyond online meddling that underscores the fears of policy makers and analysts alike about Russia's intentions: Russia's invasion and annexation of Crimea, its occupation of parts of Eastern Ukraine, its substantial military presence and increased bombings in Syria, and its threats to cut off gas supplies to intimidate European countries. Further, Russia funds and works with far right political parties in the West, such as the National Front in France, the United Kingdom's Independence Party and its pro-Brexit effort, led by Nigel Farage, and the Alternative for Germany. All of these actions share the goal of upending the postwar liberal order.

Why did President Putin decide to embrace these activities, and why now? To begin, the popular uprisings against autocrats in several former Soviet states in the 2000s, in the Arab Spring starting in 2011, and in places like Ukraine in 2013 made Putin increasingly threatened, especially because he (incorrectly) believed American or Western actors were fueling those movements. He has also accused the United States, and then-Secretary of State Hillary Clinton specifically, of promoting the domestic protests against his regime that erupted in 2011. In response, Putin is trying to "erode rules-based institutions that have established democratic norms and cemented the postwar liberal order, check the reform ambitions of aspiring democracies and subvert the vitality of young democracies, and systematically assail the established democracies and central ideas associated with them as [he] seeks to reshape the manner in which the world thinks about democracy" (*World Affairs Journal*, May/June 2015). Or, as Blackwill and Gordon write, "Putin is a career intelligence officer who is deeply hostile to democratic change anywhere near Russia, paranoid about what he believes to be U.S. efforts to oust him, and resentful of American domination of the post–Cold War world" (*Foreign Affairs*, January 18, 2018). Much of Putin's war on Western democracies can arguably be attributed to these deep-seated feelings borne out of a messy post-Soviet legacy that he himself is trying to rectify, turning Russia from the victim of the West to the victor.

The question of whether Putin's activities represent a new or fundamental shift in Russian behavior is a good one. For example, Russia began interfering in the domestic politics of the "near abroad"—the countries that comprised the former Soviet Union—shortly after the breakup of the USSR in the 1990s. But those activities appeared to be designed more to support pro-Russian candidates than to bolster authoritarianism per se. In contrast, the current wave of meddling that began in 2014 has "expanded dramatically to include a range of established democracies in the West and utilized a variety of novel strategies," according to a study by two University of Toronto academics. For the authors, Russia is now "engaged in a virtually unprecedented assault on Western democracy" (Way and Casey, November 2017).

While most Western observers accept that Russia does desire to diminish the power and influence of Western democracies and has acted aggressively to affect such a goal, not all analysts agree. Perhaps the loudest dissenting voice is that of Stephen F. Cohen, an academic at New York University and Princeton University. A longtime scholar of Soviet and Russian behavior, Cohen has repeatedly advanced an alternative explanation for Putin's behavior. For Cohen, it is the United States rather than Russia that has been the aggressor (see, e.g., "Does Putin Really Want to 'Destabilize' the West'?" *The Nation*, September 6, 2017). Putin's charge when he assumed the presidency, according to Cohen, was to rebuild a country that had fallen on severely hard times. His strategy was to do so "through expanding good political and profitable economic relations with democratic Europe and particularly through commercial market relations." Cohen then asks why Putin would "want to destabilize Western democracies that were substantially funding Russia's rebirth at home and as a great power abroad while accepting him as their legitimate counterpart"?

Other analysts argue a version of "whataboutism"—that all countries use these kinds of shadowy tactics to influence outcomes overseas, and therefore, they are not unique to Russia or Putin. Some commentators assert that this is not a new strategic doctrine for Russia; instead, it is an old doctrine updated with new tools. And others believe that the Russian government is not undertaking a strategic plan at all, but rather these activities are the work of a loose, disorganized configuration of activists with small resources probing for Western weaknesses (Heer, *The New Republic*, February 20, 2018).

A somewhat-related theory is advanced both by analysts who believe Moscow is undertaking a concerted campaign and those who do not: that Russian strategy is not the problem, the West's current political systems are. In other words, Russia is not 10-feet-tall, and Moscow cannot push on a door that's not already open. As some scholars have argued, "Russia is better thought of as a symptom, rather than the cause of democratic crisis in the West. . . . The fact that Russia's threat must be taken seriously is more of an outgrowth of deep underlying problems in Western democracy rather than any real threat" (Way and Casey, November 2017). Or, as another analyst writes: "the problem is not that American democracy was hacked, but that it is hackable, that there was enough fragility in American democracy for a few crude memes to have an outside influence" (Heer, February 20, 2018). In exploiting tensions that already exist over issues like immigration and Islam, Russia simply uses the fact that Western societies are distracted by polarization, extremism, and domestic political problems to sow chaos.

And this fundamental question remains: Is Russia's current behavior an existential threat to the West? Princeton scholar Stephen Kotkin tries to put that complex query into some context: "Russia today is not a great revolutionary power threatening to overthrow the international order. Moscow operates within a familiar great-power school of international relations, one that priorities room for maneuver over morality and assumes the inevitability of conflict, the supremacy of hard power, and

the cynicism of others' motives. In certain places and on certain issues, Russia has the ability to thwart U.S. interests, but it does not even remotely approach the scale of the threat posed by the Soviet Union" (Stephen Kotkin, *Foreign Affairs*, May/June 2016).

In the YES selection, Larry Diamond suggests that Vladimir Putin has embarked on a campaign to "sabotage democracy" and has been relentless in its pursuit of policies that threaten the very core of Western political beliefs. In the NO selection, Mark Lawrence Schrad suggests that Russia is not "nearly the global menace" many fear but rather a country somewhere between a global menace and a country trying to avoid collapse.

YES ⤶

Larry Diamond

Russia and the Threat to Liberal Democracy

How Vladimir Putin Is Making the World Safe for Autocracy

Since the end of World War II, the most crucial underpinning of freedom in the world has been the vigor of the advanced liberal democracies and the alliances that bound them together. Through the Cold War, the key multilateral anchors were NATO, the expanding European Union, and the U.S.–Japan security alliance. With the end of the Cold War and the expansion of NATO and the EU to virtually all of Central and Eastern Europe, liberal democracy seemed ascendant and *secure* as never before in history.

Under the shrewd and relentless assault of a resurgent Russian authoritarian state, all of this has come under strain with a speed and scope that few in the West have fully comprehended and that puts the future of liberal democracy in the world squarely where Vladimir Putin wants it: in doubt and on the defensive.

On the global chessboard, there has been no more deft and brilliant (and of late, lucky) player than Putin. From the early days of his presidency a decade and a half ago, he began to signal that he intended to make Russia great again and that he saw this imperative as a zero-sum game: as the West gained friendships among postcommunist states, Russia lost, and so everything possible had to be done to force Georgia, Ukraine, Moldova, and the Balkan states out of a Western liberal orientation and back into the greater Russian orbit.

The first dramatic salvo came in the summer of 2008, when Russia intervened militarily to back separatist forces in the enclaves of Abkhazia and South Ossetia seeking to break away from Georgia. Russia's military assault was brief but brutal and involved bombing civilian populations both in the disputed areas and in the rest of Georgia, as well as attacking fleeing civilians. The overconfident pro-Western president of Georgia, Mikheil Saakashvili, was dealt a painful lesson courtesy of Putin, and the two breakaway "republics" remain under Russian occupation to this day. It was the first time since the end of the Soviet Union that Russia's military violated the sovereignty of an independent state, but it would not be the last.

Since huge swaths of society rose up in color revolutions in the former Yugoslavia in 2000, in Georgia in 2003, and in Ukraine in 2004–2005—all to protest electoral fraud and bring about a transition from authoritarianism to democracy—Putin has behaved as if obsessed with fear that the virus of mass democratic mobilization might spread to Russia itself. Neither was he prepared to condone the "loss" of key parts of the former Soviet Union, such as Georgia and Ukraine, to any potential alliance structure with the West. As the forces of Ukraine's Orange Revolution squandered their miraculous victory in corruption and political squabbling, Putin won another victory in 2010, when the pro-Russian villain of the rigged election that prompted the 2004 uprising, Viktor Yanukovych, finally won the presidency.

But Yanukovych's authoritarianism and pro-Russia orientation—which led him to scuttle a much hoped-for association agreement between Ukraine and the EU—increasingly outraged the Ukrainian people who ousted him in a second people-power revolution (the Euromaidan) in February 2014. Soon thereafter, Russian troops without insignias infiltrated Crimea and, with sympathetic local actors, seized control of its infrastructure. Militarily weak and bereft of Western military support—which in any case was difficult to deliver quickly and effectively due to the distance relative to Russia's proximity—Ukraine watched helplessly as Putin consolidated his conquest with a pseudo-referendum that endorsed Crimea's reabsorption into Russia.

It was the first time since the Nazis marauded across Europe in World War II that the boundaries of a European country had been altered by military aggression. But Putin did not stop there. In a replay of its shadowy campaign of aggression against Georgia, Russia infiltrated its troops and equipment into the Donbas region of far Eastern Ukraine, in support (and probably orchestration) of separatist forces there. It was one of those Eastern Ukrainian armed groups that used a Soviet-era missile system to shoot down Malaysia Airlines Flight 17 on July 17, 2014. More blatant Russian military intervention followed, with Russia denying any involvement of its own soldiers, despite abundant evidence to the contrary. Today, Russia still occupies a portion of the Donbas region. A major swing state between West and East has been militarily violated and partially dismantled, and the story isn't over yet.

Like President Bush with respect to the Georgia crisis in 2008, President Obama did not respond militarily to this aggression. But he was not passive. Together with the European Union, the United States imposed several rounds of painful economic and financial sanctions on key Russian officials, banks, and businesses. As the sanctions have broadened, they have hurt important Russian elites and seriously impaired the functioning of the Russian financial, energy, and defense sectors—not exactly a great formula for making Russia great again.

Putin has embraced an opportunistic but sophisticated campaign to sabotage democracy.

Putin has been desperate to get out from under these sanctions so that his regime can thrive domestically and internationally. His goals appear to be twofold. First, he seeks to restore some form of Russian empire—with at least informal dominion over all the territories of the former Soviet Union—while forcing the West to accept this new balance of power and treat Russia as a superpower once again. Second, he seeks to invert Woodrow Wilson's famous call to arms and instead "make the world safe for autocracy." Democracy is his enemy. He is smart enough to know that he cannot undermine it everywhere, but he will subvert, corrupt, and confuse it wherever he can.

And so Putin's regime has been embarked for some years now on an opportunistic but sophisticated campaign to sabotage democracy and bend it toward his interests, not just in some marginal, fragile places but at the very core of the liberal democratic order, Europe and the United States. As *The Telegraph* reported in January, Western intelligence agencies have been monitoring a Russian campaign on a Cold War scale to support a wide range of European parties and actors—illiberal parties and politicians of both the far left and far right—that are sympathetic to Russia and Putin. This includes not just newer neofascist parties, but anti-immigrant far-right parties like the National Front of France—which obtained a 9 million euro loan from a Russian bank in 2014—and the Freedom Party of Austria, both of which have been gaining popularity for some time. While the Freedom Party lost the election for Austria's ceremonial presidency last Sunday, its candidate, Norbert Hofer, won over 46 percent of the vote, and it remains the third largest party in the parliament, poised to do better in the next elections.

Hofer's defeat may temporarily slow the right-wing populist momentum across Europe, but National Front leader Marine Le Pen, who endorsed Putin's annexation of Crimea and has called for an end to Western sanctions on Russia, could well be elected the next president of France next spring. And even if she loses, Putin is likely to be sitting pretty with the next French president. Le Pen's principal rival, former French Prime Minister François Fillon, who recently won the conservative presidential primaries in France, has for years been calling for an end to sanctions on Putin and a closer relationship between France and Russia.

The romance between far-right, anti-immigrant European parties and Vladimir Putin's Russia springs not just from practical ties of support but a shared conservative reaction against liberalism, globalization, and multiculturalism, and a celebration of Putin, in the words of the scholar Alina Polyakova, as "as a staunch defender of national sovereignty and conservative values who has challenged US influence and the idea of 'Europe' in a way that mirrors their own convictions." This same spirit suffused the Brexit campaign in the United Kingdom, whose longtime populist champion, Nigel Farage, has combined fierce demands for British independence from Europe with fawning admiration for Putin. Yet the Russian boost to Brexit did not come only from the right. Russian media lavishly praised the successful campaign for Labour Party leadership of the far-left candidate Jeremy Corbyn, an NATO and EU skeptic whose extremely tepid support for the Remain campaign contributed to the narrow victory of Brexit.

Meanwhile, the damage to liberalism in Europe was also being driven by a more brutal form of Russian intervention—in Syria. Russia's bombing campaign there has not only tilted the war in favor of the dictator, Bashar al-Assad, who along with his allies has killed more civilians than either ISIS fighters or rebels but it also dramatically accelerated the flow of Syrian refugees (now nearing 5 million) into other countries, including European ones. While Europe's refugee crisis has many sources and causes, roughly 30 percent of European asylum-seekers last year were Syrian refugees, and the human exodus from that civil war has incidentally further helped to feed right-wing (pro-Putin) populist parties and movements across Europe while undermining liberal leaders like Angela Merkel of Germany.

The destabilizing effects of the refugee crisis in Europe have been a kind of dividend of Putin's campaign to defend his Middle East ally. But Putin has also attempted to destabilize democracies directly through methods more reminiscent of the Cold War. After Montenegro's parliamentary elections on October 16 (which saw Putin pouring money into the pro-Russian opposition party and sympathetic media and NGOs, in an unsuccessful attempt to defeat the pro-NATO prime minister), evidence emerged of a plot involving three Russian citizens (alleged in the Montenegrin news media to be agents of the GRU, Russian military intelligence) and some 20 right-wing Serbian nationalists. Montenegrin authorities now allege they planned to stage a terrorist attack that would discredit the election outcome, assassinate the pro-Western prime minister, and topple his government.

As these political dramas and tensions have unfolded in democratic Europe, Putin's Russia has made brilliant use of old and new forms of propaganda to exploit political divisions. The leading element of this has been Russia Today (RT) which is not only one of the most widely watched (and heavily subsidized) global sources of state television propaganda—and which claims 70 million weekly viewers and 35 million daily—but a vast social-media machinery as well. Added to this is the hidden influence of a vast network of Russian trolls—agents paid to spread disinformation and Russian propaganda points by posing as authentic and spontaneous commentators.

What began as a somewhat preposterous effusion of fake news reports spreading panic, for example, about an Ebola outbreak in the United States, morphed into something more sinister, sophisticated, and profoundly consequential: a dedicated campaign to discredit Hillary Clinton and tilt the U.S. presidential election to Donald Trump. The army of Russian trolls started infiltrating U.S. media with conservative commentaries, playing up Clinton's scandals and weaknesses and widely diffusing other right-wing narratives against Clinton. The Russian government (America's own intelligence agencies believe) hacked into the e-mails of the Democratic Party and of Clinton campaign Chairman John Podesta and passed them on to WikiLeaks to dispense in a devastating drip-drip-drip of divisive and unflattering revelations. In *The Washington Post*'s words, the campaign portrayed "Clinton as a criminal hiding potentially fatal health problems and preparing to hand control of the nation to a shadowy cabal of global financiers." All of this gave Trump significantly more political traction while dispiriting and discouraging possible Clinton voters (many of whom simply stayed home in disgust). Given how close the U.S. election outcome was, it is easy to imagine that this intervention might have provided Trump with his margin of victory in the Electoral College.

We stand now at the most dangerous moment for liberal democracy since the end of World War II. There are still many more democracies worldwide today than when the Cold War ended. But outside the West, many of them are fragile or rapidly declining. Turkey is in the grip of full authoritarianism, the Philippines is sliding in that direction, and Korea and Brazil have both seen their first women presidents disgraced in eruptions of public anger over corruption and misuse of power. Some 200,000 Muslim Indonesians have flooded the streets of Jakarta demanding that the Christian governor be arrested for insulting Islam. In much of Africa, the people still overwhelmingly want democracy, but leaders in numerous countries are dragging their systems in the opposite direction.

Geopolitics does not have to be a zero-sum game. But great powers must recognize and defend vital interests.

The greatest danger, however, is not what is happening in Asia, Africa, or Latin America. It is the alarming decay of liberal democracy in Europe and the United States, accelerated by escalating Russian efforts at subversion. Putin's forces are on such a roll that they can no longer contain their glee. One pro-Putin Russian governor recently declared in a radio interview, "It turns out that United Russia [Putin's political party] won the elections in America."

Donald Trump's election victory was an extraordinary political achievement for someone who has never held or sought political office. It drew the support of many tens of millions of voters who rallied to his themes of controlling immigration, changing the way things are done in Washington, generating economic opportunity for those left behind by globalization, or somehow just "making American great again." But it probably would not have happened without Russia's hacking of America's political process—and on behalf of a candidate who had said he wanted good relations with Vladimir Putin.

Geopolitics does not have to be a zero-sum game. But great powers must recognize and defend vital interests. Having a Europe that is whole and free is a vital American interest. Enforcing the principle that established borders cannot be eviscerated by military aggression is a vital American interest—and nowhere more so than in Europe.

Ensuring that an authoritarian Russian regime does not replicate its values and expand its power by subverting democracy in the heart of Europe is also a vital American interest.

The most urgent foreign-policy question now is how America will respond to the mounting threat that Putin's Russia poses to freedom and its most important anchor, the Western alliance. Nothing will more profoundly shape the kind of world we live in than how the Trump administration responds to that challenge.

LARRY DIAMOND is a senior fellow at the Hoover Institution and at the Freeman Spogli Institute at Stanford University.

Mark Lawrence Schrad

Vladimir Putin Isn't a Supervillain

Russia is neither the global menace nor dying superpower of America's increasingly hysterical fantasies.

America's hysteria over Russian President Vladimir Putin is mounting, and there's no reason to think the fever will break anytime soon. At this point, it's only tangentially related to the accusations that Putin has made President Donald Trump his "puppet" or that Trump—or Attorney General Jeff Sessions, or any number of other administration officials—is in cahoots with Russian oligarchs.

Perhaps you've heard about the sudden death of Russia's U.N. ambassador, Vitaly Churkin? It's all nefarious Kremlin intrigues—or so we're told. In fact, a lot of Russian diplomats have died recently—isn't that suspicious? And don't look now, but while you were fixated on Russia's subversion of American society through psychological warfare, you may have missed that Russia's expanding its influence in Syria. And provoking Japan. And meddling with Britain. And it's sowing "chaos" in the Balkans. And the Baltics. And Ukraine. And may invade Belarus. And Finland. And if that weren't enough, Putin has a "master plan" for overthrowing the entire European and world democratic order. We might as well give up: Russia "runs the world now."

With such bombast dominating American political discourse, citizens and pundits rightly worry about the potential for geopolitical competition from Russia. But is Putin's regime really as threatening and omnipresent as it is cracked up to be?

Western commentary on Kremlin's foreign-policy ambitions tends to fall into two opposing camps, each with different starting points: one begins with Russia's foreign policy and the other with Russian domestic politics. Both are prone to hyperbole in their appraisals and conclusions, albeit in different directions. And neither is useful for understanding, or responding to, the reality of Russian ambitions.

I call the first camp "Putler," a mash-up of Putin and Adolf Hitler, the two leaders whom Western commentators seem most fond of pairing. Largely a result of Russia's 2014 annexation of Crimea and intervention in the Donbass, this lens portrays Russia as the foremost threat to liberal democracy: a scary, aggressive, expansionist, revanchist reincarnation of the Soviet Union, equating Putin with the worst excesses of authoritarianism. Rooted in 20th-century historical analogies, specifically World War II, this camp implicitly prescribes military confrontation: anything less, including economic sanctions, is weak-kneed, Chamberlainesque appeasement, to evoke the Hitlerite comparison.

Another favored historical analogy for Putler adherents is the Cold War. For many observers, it is given that we are already grappling in a life-and-death "Cold War 2.0" (just without, they neglect to mention, the ideology of communism, the nuclear arms race, realist power balancing, global competition for proxies, or any of the other elements that defined the original Cold War). House Speaker Paul Ryan's recent reference to Russia as a "global menace led by a man who is menacing" falls squarely within this school of thinking, along with his rejoinder that President Barack Obama's sanctions followed "too much of an appeasement policy."

Turning from geopolitical ambitions to Russian domestic policy, the Putler worldview tends to highlight Putin's consolidation of autocratic control, fraudulent elections, his harassment and murder of opposition journalists, curtailing of civil liberties, and his use of disinformation through state-run media to disorient and control the public. It is a portrait of Putin as an unrestrained totalitarian, intent on weaponizing "absurdity and unreality." Such appraisals often border on the hysterical, but one imagines they draw a lot of Internet traffic.

At the other end of the spectrum from the Putler worldview is the "Dying Bear" camp. This approach is dismissive of Russia as a threat; its adherents instead presage stagnation, corruption, and decline. The term originated with demographers, discouraged by Russia's dim health prospects but could reasonably include its political, social, and economic limitations as well. To be sure, Russia's health and demographic statistics lag far behind those of Western Europe and the United States, with relatively high mortality rates, relatively low fertility rates, and average life expectancy on par with impoverished African countries. In the medium and long term, that means demographic decline: fewer Russians means fewer taxpayers, fewer conscripts, and fewer state resources; all exert downward pressure on Russia's growth potential. There are a bevy of other limitations on Russia's potential for future economic growth: an undiversified economy cursed with an overreliance on resource extraction; a lumbering, systematically corrupt, and growing state bureaucracy that impedes entrepreneurship; technological backwardness; and a kleptocratic political system that rewards cronyism and penalizes development. Without economic diversification and freedom, we're told, Russia's economy has hit "rock bottom." Groaning under the weight of Western sanctions and low global oil prices, Russia's own Economic Development Ministry is forecasting no real improvement in living standards until 2035.

For some in the Dying Bear camp, Russia's foreign-policy aggression—including its incursions into Ukraine and Syria—is just Putin's attempt to distract patriotic Russians from the misery of their own existence and have them rally around the flag of patriotism, since he can't deliver the performance legitimacy associated with the economic growth of the early 2000s, driven by sky-high global oil prices. While the Putler perspective calls for confrontation, Dying Bear prescribes management or marginalization, if not disengagement: Why bother taking Russia seriously if it's doomed anyway?

President Obama's dismissive public statements about Russia being at best a "regional power," or a "weaker country" that doesn't produce anything worth buying "except oil and gas and arms," and that its international interventions are borne "not out of strength but out of weakness" are all reflective of the Dying Bear position.

The reality, of course, is somewhere between these extremes. Russia is not nearly the global menace that many fear nor is it doomed to collapse.

Russia's geopolitical strength is indeed constrained by its demographic, economic, social, and political weaknesses, but those aren't as catastrophic as they're often made to be. Russians today are healthier and living longer than they ever have. Though having ever fewer women of childbearing age presages long-term demographic decline, with births outpacing deaths, Russia's population has recently registered natural growth for the first time since the collapse of communism.

Economically, the ruble has stabilized following the collapse of late 2014, and the recession of 2014–2015 is statistically over. However, Russia isn't out of the woods, with low oil prices leading to dwindling state revenue, and little private investment for the foreseeable future, which will inevitably mean stagnation and low growth. Russia's economic performance is so intimately tied to public spending that any curtailment of spending despite dwindling oil receipts would reverberate throughout the economy. And the economy ultimately constrains its political options. Although Putin's geopolitical gambits in Ukraine and Syria can boost his approval ratings, they come at the expense of increasing poverty and unpaid wages, which are fueling a notable rise in labor protests nationwide. While presently manageable, the Kremlin will need to address these socioeconomic issues in order to maintain domestic tranquility, limiting its resources for foreign adventurism in Syria, Ukraine, and beyond, to say nothing of investments in health care, education, science, and infrastructure. Russia can't have it all.

So, despite its high-level meddling in American affairs, for the foreseeable future, Russia is poised to continue to muddle through, with economic and demographic stagnation constraining its lofty geopolitical ambitions. Unsurprisingly, the Russia of 2020 will look more like the Russia of 2012 or 2016, rather than the expansionist Soviet Union of 1944 or the collapsing Soviet Union of 1991. Accordingly, American foreign policy toward Russia should not be given to the militarization and conflict of the Putler camp, nor to the marginalization of the Dying Bear view, but rather a respectful engagement, recognizing the interconnectedness of Russia's varied strategic interests, which may conflict with Washington's own.

The problem, though, is that stasis isn't a particularly sexy prognosis, which means it is not a frequently made one. There are two reasons for this. First is a lack of nuanced understanding of Russian governance. Most experts know what liberal democracy looks like and—if we believe democratization scholarship (and there is good reason for skepticism, especially in the Trump era)—that once "consolidated," democracies are robust and durable. We also understand that autocracies can be reasonably stable, too: just look at the longevity of Fidel Castro's reign in Cuba or the Kim dynasty in North Korea. But we have a harder time understanding a polity like present-day Russia, which is neither fully democratic nor fully autocratic. For a long time, democratization theorists have struggled to understand this sort of neither/nor "illiberal democracy" or "competitive authoritarian" regimes like Russia that combine democratic and nondemocratic elements. If liberal democracy is understood to be the optimal endpoint, then it is understandable to assume that Russia is just "stuck" in transition, rather than having achieved something of a stable equilibrium in its own right.

Second, still haunted by Kremlinologists' fabled inability to foresee one of the most significant geopolitical events of the 20th century—the collapse of communism and the Soviet Union—Russia watchers now appear to be hypersensitive to any economic or social clue that may portend trouble for the Putin regime. When the global financial crisis rocked Russia in 2008, we were told it was "the end of the Putin era." When popular protests opposed his reelection in 2011–2012, experts called it "the beginning of the end of Putin." The Euromaidan revolution in next-door Ukraine likewise allegedly portended "the end of Vladimir Putin." As it turns out, competitive authoritarian regimes in general, and Putin's Russia in particular, tend to be surprisingly durable.

With Russia's new prominence in American political discourse, it is necessary to have a sober assessment of the country's capabilities and limitations. Russia is neither the juggernaut nor basket case it is varyingly made out to be. A well-reasoned Russian policy begins by quelling one's hysteria long enough to recognize this and then engaging it accordingly.

MARK LAWRENCE SCHRAD is a professor at Villanova University.

EXPLORING THE ISSUE

Is Russia Increasingly Pursuing a Strategy to Threaten Democratic Regimes throughout Europe and the Western World?

Critical Thinking and Reflection

1. Why do you think Vladimir Putin has felt a need to undermine Western democracies?
2. How can consumers of Internet information ensure what they're reading is accurate and they're not falling prey to fake news or propaganda?
3. Why do you believe that Russia might be emphasizing elections as one of the most vulnerable targets in democratic countries?
4. Do you believe that those smaller number of analysts who believe Russia is not trying to undermine Western democracies have any valid points for their position?
5. Do you think Russia today is a bigger threat to the West than the Soviet Union was?

Is There Common Ground?

Both the United States and the Soviet Union/Russia have viewed each other as a principle adversary since the end of World War II, particularly during the Cold War. Most analysts agree that the fall of the Soviet empire and its system of communism left Russia with a need to reassert itself in some fashion in the new global order that followed. Most Western analysts also agree that Russia meddled in the U.S. presidential election in 2016 and in many other elections over the decades as well, although there is debate about how successful that meddling has been.

Additional Resources

Blackwill, Robert D. and Gordon, Philip H., *Containing Russia*, Council Special Report No. 80, Council on Foreign Relations (January 2018)

Choksy, Jamsheed K., "The New Containment: Undermining Democracy," *World Affairs Journal* (May/June 2015)

GLOBESEC, "Four Factors Threatening Our Freedom and Democracy" (March 12, 2017)

Gude, Ken, "How Putin Undermines Democracy in the West, Chapter and Verse," Center for American Progress (March 18, 2017)

"Is Democracy Dying?," A Global Report, *Foreign Affairs* (May/June 2018)

Kirchick, James, "Russia's Plot against the West," *Politico* (March 17, 2017)

Putin's Asymmetric Assault on Democracy in Russia and Europe: Implications for U.S. National Security, Minority Staff Report, Committee on Foreign Relations, United States Senate (January 10, 2018)

Rosenberger, Laura and Jamie Fly, "Lessons from France for Fighting Russian Interference in Democracy," *German Marshall Fund* (July 17, 2017)

Way, Lucan Ahmad and Casey, Adam, "Is Russia a Threat to Western Democracy? Russian Intervention in Foreign Elections, 1991-2017," Draft Memo for Global Populism as a Threat to Democracy?, Stanford University (November 2017)

Internet References . . .

Brookings Institution

https://www.brookings.edu/topic/Russia/

Center for Strategic and International Studies

https://www.csis.or

Chatham House

https://www.chathamhouse.org/about/structure/rus-sia-eurasia-programme/russian-foreign-policy-report

Rand Corporation

https:// www.rand.org/topics/international-affairs.html

The Jamestown Foundation

https://jamestown.org

Selected, Edited, and with Issue Framing Material by:
Mark Owen Lombardi, *Maryville University*

ISSUE

Will China Be the Next Global Superpower?

YES: **Kenneth Rapoza**, from "The Future: China's Rise, America's Decline," *Forbes* (2017)

NO: **Alan Dupont**, from "Will China Rule the World? Asian Superpower Faces Uncertain Future," *The Australian* (2016)

Learning Outcomes
After reading this issue, you will be able to: • Understand China's rise to economic giant and how that has impacted the global system.   • Be able to evaluate China's strengths and weaknesses as it relates to its potential superpower status.   • Be able to understand what the traits of a superpower are.   • Evaluate whether China is a superpower or is on the road to such status eventually.

ISSUE SUMMARY

YES: *Forbes* writer Kenneth Rapoza argues that most economic and social indicators point to both a steady rise for China and a decline for the United States. When the crossover point will be is anyone's guess.

NO: Dupont contends that despite China's enormous gifs and potential, it still faces great obstacles in its quest to move from regional dominance to true superpower status.

In 1979, Deng Xiaoping emerged as the leader of China after a prolonged power struggle following the death of Mao Tse Tung. The resulting shift in power within and among the communist party of China led to Deng's emergence and over the next several years, as he solidified his power over the party and the country. Deng was a communist, but he also believed that Mao's brand of revolution had hurt China's development economically, politically, and socially. This led to a new set of policies that to one degree or another are still in place today. These policies reflected a fusion of sorts that essentially meant that China would stay as one-party authoritarian state, but its economy would be opened up to capitalism and foreign investment. This was also combined with a drive to modernize the Chinese military combined with technological enhancements consistent with the emerging information age. Thus, China's vast economic potential was unleashed. The results were and remain staggering. No economy on earth has expanded more,

produced more goods, or exported more products during that time. A few macro statistics tell part of the story. Chinas growth rates from the 1980s to today average just under 10 percent per year. China's GDP per capita rose from less than $1,000/year to over $13,000/year. Real GDP growth adjusted for inflation has averaged 7–10 percent per year for over two decades. China's production has outstripped almost all other nations, and it is difficult to fund any nation on earth, where China is not a primary trading partner in some or many sectors of the economy.

Today, we live in a world where China' economy is second only to the United States, and projections are that within 30 years at current levels, China will surpass the United States as the largest economy in the world. This growth and development has led scholars to speculate about China as a global superpower for the past 15 years. Since the collapse of the Soviet Union, many have argued that it is just a matter of time before China becomes the next superpower to rival the United States.

In this century, the debate has raged. One side argues that it is not a question of if but when. That viewpoint tends to rely upon China's sheer economic size and growth, and the fact that they are beginning to leverage that economic influence in international trade negotiations and with various region of the world, particularly, Asia, East Africa, the Middle East, and Latin America. Their argument is that economic influence will lead to strategic superpower status.

The other side points out a number of factors that they believe mitigate China's rise to superpower status. They argue that while the standard of living has risen dramatically for some 350 million of its citizens, another 1 billion still live in relative poverty. While its economic output is impressive, its level of inventiveness and technological sophistication still lags behind the United States and the West. And while their military has modernized, China lacks the power projection capability to influence conflicts and events outside the Asian theater. All of these mean that while it is a formidable economic power, its status as true superpower on a par with the United States is far off if attainable at all.

Rapoza argues that a steady consistent rise of China economically and militarily combined with America's decline will lead to natural superpower status. When that occurs is probably anyone's guess.

Dupont contends that China has made great strides in asserting economic development and influence commensurate with that growth. But he also argues that China has great obstacles to its further development including its centralized government, lack of innovation in education, and the demographics of its size and population.

YES ⤶

Kenneth Rapoza

The Future: China's Rise, America's Decline

In the big scheme of things, the new grand chessboard isn't Western capitalism versus Soviet communism; it's the West versus the East, and China is in the pole position. Slap China with trade tariffs, they dump Treasury bonds and send interest rates higher for American corporations. Play hardball with China on disputed islands in the South China Sea and you need every old Asian Tiger plus Japan on your team, countries one-and-all that are more dependent on China for growth than they are on the United States. In this topsy turvey world, the United States has the military and the money. China has the money . . . and the military. Barring gunfire, we all know you follow the money.

The idea that the era of Westernization is coming to a close is most evident in cities like Shanghai and Singapore. Shanghai is fast becoming the new Hong Kong, which is already the new Tokyo. Rich Singapore is a world trade hub thanks to China, a dominant force still in nearly every container sitting on the deck of Hyundai merchant marine ship. China is used to the fall of dynasties. The United States is not. The history of the United States has moved only one way toward greater riches and military might. The notion that the United States falls from power is much stranger to Americans than it is to the Chinese. America . . . get used to it?

Gideon Rachman is not the only man to have this idea about the post-Western world being led by the Chinese. Ruchir Sharma, a global strategist for Morgan Stanley, has made his writing career out of how the West was—mostly—lost. Then there's *Financial Times* chief foreign affairs commentator Rachman sitting in London, the former capital of the old colonial world, looking over the bows of a rotting East Indiaman and seeing how the world has changed so radically not in the last 400 years but in the last 20 years.

"Easternization: Asia's Rise and America's Decline from Obama to Trump and Beyond," published late last year, is his second stab at America's decline. His first was six years ago, titled *"Zero Sum Future."* Both take a long historical book of the Western powers, from how they got their gilded do me rooftops and drove their rivals into submission to how they're now starting to look a bit more like the keystone cops. This might not be true yet for the United States, but China surely has more power than the old colonists in France and Portugal in every way imaginable.

Shanghai now gleams with the tallest buildings in Asia. This coming June, the MSCI indexers might include Shanghai stocks in their biggest emerging market benchmarks, mandating more American money into the mainland.

Shanghai is a microcosm of greater China: a city within a city, in a world within a world. The world it straddles is communism and uber-rich capitalism; new China and old-China with remnants of its semicolonial past. Back then, Shanghai and China made concessions to the Western imperial powers. White Europeans lived under their own laws. The Chinese, in their own country, were second-class citizens. Imagine how a New Yorker would feel if every time they looked up at the Empire State building, they were reminded that it was built by a foreign power who had lived their hundreds of years ago, while Americans cleaned their toilet bowls and weren't allowed to take in the shows on 42nd Street. Most Americans cannot fathom such a thing.

That past is eroding quick. China is rising. The West is merely an economic system; the Chinese have adopted and hybridized into something the world is still trying to. to fgure out.

Attitudes toward the West, and the United States in particular, are mixed. Nationalists are inclined to dismiss criticism from the Democracy nuns (my term, not Rachman's) in Washington, who hammer on about human rights and territorial disputes, forgetting wholeheartedly that they brought the world such wonderful things as Abu Ghraib and the implosion of Libya and Iraq (with Syria waiting in the wings, if not for Russians getting in the way).

Liberal Chinese, meanwhile, are very sceptical if not fearful of one-party rule in Beijing. They view the past colonial days as more positive than negative. This is particularly true in Hong Kong, where there is a strong pro-democracy movement that does not want to be controlled by Beijing.

Yet, even as Hong Kong prefers the lifestyle, and a more open market democracy that it inherited from British colonizers, there is little doubt that widespread "Easternization" is happening, Rachman argues in his book.

Opinion polls show that the Americans believe China is to blame for the destruction of manufacturing labor. They also think, by and large, that China will one day surpass the United States as global economic superpower. As it is now, many U.S. companies are becoming dependent on China for future growth. If not, they are betting on China to help drive growth in the future. This is as true for Amazon, with its favorite side kick in China, FORBES billionaire Jack Ma's e-commerce juggernaut Alibaba, as it is for Hollywood.

Five years ago, neoconservative Robert Kagan from the Foreign Policy Initiative (the spin-off of the WMD story tellers over at the defunct Project for a New American Century, aka PNAC) wrote *"The World America Made"* where he argued for more American soft power, more American military power, to counter who? Not ISIS, China. Kagan wrote that China would surpass the United States in GDP terms by 2050. China's GDP is around $9.5 trillion. The U.S. GDP is closer to $17 trillion. China has a long way to go to catch up. It's GDP growth rate is triple that of the United States today but is expected to slow down considerably. China is getting older, however. And the United States, meanwhile, is getting younger with a new baby boom generation called the millennials, which will help the United States stay strong. It's not a straight line to the top for China, in other words.

Still, there is no turning back the clock on this one. China is nobody's lapdog. It cannot be used as a foot rest. Secretary of State Rex Tillerson and President Donald Trump cannot demand it to fetch their newspaper and slippers. The political implications of China's rise in economic power are profound. Rachman lays them all out in a few key chapters in his book, which is not solely China-centric.

He looks at the United States and the Korean dilemmas, the impacts of a failed Middle East policy on the United States, and—in a positive nod to the West—how American (and, believe it or not, European!) institutions will save us from a one world government ruled from Beijing.

The United States became the world's largest economy in 1871 and holds that title to this day, though I think Rachman disputes this mainly because he includes the much wealthier (and smaller) autonomous regions of China. In terms of both purchasing power parity and overall economic output, the United States wins the day over mainland China. Outside of the wealthy eastern cities, China has a lot more poor people than the United States.

As a stand-alone, however, Hong Kong is on par today with the United States in terms of purchasing power parity, according to World Bank data. And Macao, the former Portuguese colony now home to China's casinos and also a special administrative region like Hong Kong, is actually far wealthier than the United States. It certainly blows Portugal out of the water. In fact, the roughly half a million people who live in Macao have more wealth than those in Boston, a similar sized city, based on GDP per capita and purchasing power parity.

After World War II, the United States was about 30 percent of world economic output. We've been the sole economic superpower since we beat the Soviet Union in 1991. The United States will always be a go-to economy. The Chinese want to sell us their Lenovos and maybe someday their zoomlions. They want to buy Gerber baby food. Nike needs China's NBA fans. They love our real estate. But the rise of China in the geopolitical sense "clearly raises the question of how long the United States can continue to dominate global politics," says Rachman. Thus, the post-Western world has already begun. Like an angry dog boxed into a corner, it begs the question what this all means and how the United States might react to counter it. Rachman lays out the possibilities.

KENNETH RAPOZA has spent the last five years covering all aspects of the country for the *Wall Street Journal* and Dow Jones.

Alan Dupont

 **NO**

Will China Rule the World?
Asian Superpower Faces Uncertain Future

Given China's emergence from a century of relative weakness and "national humiliation" at the hands of foreigners in an otherwise extended period of preeminence in Asia going back millennia, it is understandable a lot of Chinese may be thinking that their nation's time has come. Will China rule the world?

For these Chinese, the natural order is being restored. More surprising, perhaps, is how many non-Chinese agree and either welcome, or are resigned to, the seeming inevitability that an emerging China-centric order will soon supplant a visibly crumbling West.

Seven years ago, British scholar and journalist Martin Jacques wrote a book with the provocative title *When China Rules the World*. Jacques says China's remarkable economic transformation will provide the platform for political, military, and cultural influence that would rival and surpass that of the United States and provide an alternative path to modernity as well as a very different world order.

Echoes of this thinking can be found in Australia's intensifying debate about whether it is possible to accommodate China's reemergence as a great power without an unacceptable loss of independence, sovereignty, and a dilution of the values that define Australia's liberal democracy.

This is not solely an Australian dilemma, but one we share with the rest of the world. Sentiment, however, is firmly shifting toward acceptance of the Jacques's thesis.

Before falling on his own Brexian sword, former British Prime Minister David Cameron flung open the doors of what remains of the British Empire to the new emperor from the East. He royally feted his Chinese counterpart in a glittering display of British soft power designed to position Britain as China's best friend in Europe, a policy critics derided as a servile kowtow to a country it once lorded over.

Independently minded southeast Asians, once proud of the leading role ASEAN had secured for itself in the region during the heady, benign 1990s and noughties, seem powerless to resist China's will in the South China Sea, fearful of Beijing's military clout and seduced by its economic and financial blandishments.

Only last month, Philippines President Rodrigo Duterte directly challenged the notion that the United States is still the dominant Pacific power. Announcing the end of joint naval patrols with his erstwhile ally, Duterte asserted that "China is now in power and they have military superiority in the region."

Is it time for Australia to bow to the inevitable and get on board the Chinese train, whatever our reservations about its ultimate destination or the likelihood that the keys to the first-class coach will be given only to those who sign up to Beijing's loyalty program?

It's hard to think of a more important question for Australia. Answering it, however, requires a close examination of the common assumption that China is on the fast track to becoming the preeminent global power by 2030. If this assumption is false, then it substantially weakens the argument for a more intimate and uncritical relationship with China as the best way of ensuring Australia's future prosperity and security.

It's not difficult to understand why so many people believe that China's rise to the top is preordained. Everything about China is big—its geography, reach, population, buildings, and, above all, vaulting ambition. This unique combination of size, ambition, and focused capability is the key to China's success, along with a strategy that harmonizes the country's formidable hard and soft power assets in a way that no other state can match.

The story of modern China's meteoric rise from underdeveloped backwater to emerging superpower has been well chronicled. Undeniably, the most impressive national socioeconomic transformation in history, the Chinese surge shows few visible signs of abating. In many areas, it seems to be accelerating.

China Inc is a leading, or aspiring, player in just about every sphere imaginable, from the economic and geopolitical to the technological and educational. Thirsty for knowledge and wanting to improve their lot in life, Chinese students dominate foreign student intakes in just about every developed country, including Australia, and their own universities are rapidly moving up international league tables of excellence.

In contrast to its complacent, energy-rich neighbor—Russia—China has invested enormous resources in the enabling technologies of the 21st century in an audacious bid to seize the commanding heights of the future economy.

And it's not fussy about how it gets there, empowering the military and contracted netizens to hoover up intellectual property from around the world in what amounts to the greatest secret heist of all time. At the top of the list are information and communications technology, health care, pharmaceuticals, military technologies, robotics, agricultural, and renewable energy technologies, natural resources, and advanced materials and manufacturing techniques. Strategic milestones are clicking over. China recently secured bragging rights to owning the most powerful computer in the world. In August, it launched the world's first quantum satellite in an effort to leap ahead in the high stakes competition to develop unhackable encryption technology. What was once a yawning military capability gap with the United States is closing fast as the modernizing People's Liberation Army shows the benefits of more than two decades of double-digit increases in defense spending. Arms exports have increased 143 percent over the past five years, and China is poised to become the world leader in unmanned military aircraft by 2023.

Chinese workers, entrepreneurs, diplomats, and technicians are ubiquitously present in every corner of the globe promoting China Inc.

Nonagenarian Zimbabwean dictator Robert Mugabe might be a pariah in the West, but his regime has been sustained by regular infusions of Chinese cash as part of a wider strategy to cement Beijing's position in Africa that is beginning to pay handsome dividends. Trade has increased 150 percent in just over a decade to make China Africa's largest trading partner.

The Chinese military also seems to be everywhere. During the past 18 months, the navy has sailed through the Bering Straits for the first time, held joint exercises with Russia in the Mediterranean, sent submarines to Sri Lanka, and accessed new military support facilities at the strategically located former French colony of Djibouti, adjacent to the mouth of the Red Sea.

A secret space facility in Argentina, ostensibly for civilian purposes but with potential military application, underlines just how intertwined China's commercial and national security objectives have become in the country's quest for superpower status.

Soft power strategies are also deployed to increasing effect, reinforcing China's desired image that it is a nation of standing and influence in world affairs and the heir apparent to a declining United States.

The Dastyari affair was a salutary lesson for Australia in how China uses institutional and diaspora soft power to buy influence and curry favor with politicians and opinion leaders, but it was merely a chapter in a larger, grand narrative to convince the world that China's rise to the top is unstoppable.

There is much more to come. Only last week, China's richest man, Wang Jianlin, bought into an icon of Hollywood soft power by taking a stake in Sony Pictures, declaring that he wants to change the rules "set by foreigners."

The undoubted centerpiece of President Xi Jinping's quest to position China at the center of global affairs is his visionary new Silk Road concept, officially dubbed "One *Belt One Road*." OBOR's aim is simple but bold. Its central purpose is the extension and consolidation of China's economic and geopolitical influence across Central Asia to Europe by land and within the countries that border the Indian and Pacific oceans by sea. Xi sees Australia as an integral part of OBOR, which is linked to the Coalition's northern development plan and partly explains the current enthusiasm for acquiring Australian ports, infrastructure, and land.

Given the nearly $3 trillion in capital at China's disposal, dwarfing the $120 billion (in today's dollars) spent by the United States in the Marshall Plan's reconstruction of war-torn Europe, OBOR is a serious—if not unprecedented—undertaking by a nation state. Should OBOR succeed, China may well rule the world. But there are many reasons to think that it won't.

The first is economic. It is increasingly obvious that China will be unable to reach its annual growth target of 6.5–7 percent, and there is no guarantee the country will be able to seamlessly transition from an export-oriented economy to one fuelled by domestic consumption. Many experienced economists believe real GDP growth this year may be only half that of the official projections. Debt is rising twice as fast as economic growth, raising the prospect that China's overexposed banking sector could be forced to write off bad debts four times larger than those of US banks during the devastating 2008 financial crisis.

The Australian's China correspondent, Rowan Callick, belled the cat on the health of the Chinese economy in

July, writing that the unanimous verdict of top China economists is that a debt crisis is approaching, "there are no signs of policy renewal and a recession is almost inevitable—either sharp and possibly calamitous or drawn out." Although this may not occur in the next few years, some kind of financial crisis appears unavoidable in the medium term.

As for OBOR, there is widespread skepticism that the initiative's more ambitious goals can be met, and OBOR's soft power gains could be reversed by negative international reaction to China's assertive nationalism in the South China Sea.

Geopolitical risk could compound Beijing's economic problems in other ways, should the ability to protect its far-flung investments and expanding diaspora exceed the nation's resources, which is a distinct possibility. Aside from established Chinese communities in more than 30 countries, there are an estimated 5 million Chinese nationals working internationally, including up to 2 million in Africa, who need to be protected from terrorism, kidnappings, and potential anti-Chinese pogroms of the kind witnessed in Indonesia during the mid-1960s.

A second challenge is resisting hubris and avoiding the imperial overstretch that eventually brings all empires down. China is especially vulnerable to external shocks because of the rapidity of its expansion and mounting challenges on its periphery from a nuclear-armed North Korea, pro-independence sentiment in Taiwan and Hong Kong and the hedging activities of anxious neighbors who worry about their potential loss of freedom and autonomy in a China-dominated Asia. The leadership is also acutely aware that a Donald Trump or Hillary Clinton administration in Washington next year will be far less accepting of China's interests than Barack Obama's.

A third challenge is demographic. Demography might not always be destiny, but demographic decline has eliminated the once seemingly inexhaustible supply of cheap labor that turbocharged China's growth after 1980. By 2012, this demographic dividend had reversed with fertility rates in free fall due to the one child policy. As a result, China has aged more rapidly than any other country and more than three times the rate of Germany, Russia, and Italy in the past century.

By 2020, there will be nearly 170 million Chinese over the age of 65, a majority of whom don't have pensions, underlining the fact that China is still a developing country for all its impressive advances. Whether China grows old before, it gets rich depends on one's definition of rich. But as their people's aspirations grow, Chinese leaders will have to divert more of the national budget toward aged care, putting added pressure on revenue just

as the labor pool shrinks, a problem with which developed Australia is only too familiar. China has the highest take-up of industrial robots in the world, so robots may be able to fill some of the labor gap and stimulate productivity. But you wouldn't want to bet your house on it.

The fourth great challenge, domestic political instability, is the most difficult to assess because of the opacity of Chinese politics. Some broad trends are identifiable, however, and none of them augur well for the country's long-term stability or its relations with the wider world. After a period of relative openness and collective leadership under the presidencies of Jiang Zemin and Hu Jintao, Xi Jinping has ruthlessly suppressed internal dissent, prioritized the military, centralized bureaucratic power in his hands, strengthened the government's control over the media, and the Internet and fostered a prickly nationalism which has done little to ease concerns China's rise may not be peaceful.

Fordham University academic Carl Minzner says Xi has broken with the post-1978 past in other important ways, principally in his revival of an ethnonationalist ideology rooted in imperial history and tradition and the Maoist era tactics of rule by fear. The risk is that in seeking to emulate Mao, Xi will succeed only in cannabilizing the Chinese political system, visiting upon his country, the anarchy, and internal chaos that would destroy not only Xi's dream of a great China but the more humble aspirations of millions of his fellow citizens. This bleaker, alternative future is no less plausible than Jacques's prognosis.

Midway between these two polar opposites is a third credible alternative—that China has already peaked. Although the country will continue to be among the group of leading nations for the next two decades because of economic momentum, it will not become more powerful than the United States and it certainly won't rule the world.

Given the uncertainty surrounding China's future, a smart Australia would hedge its bets and not be seduced by questionable assertions that China's ascendancy is irreversible.

We should also be alive to the self-serving role of the Chinese communist "party-state" which uses its soft power to exaggerate and amplify the country's achievements, influence, and power, inducing a kind of fatalistic acceptance among targeted audiences that China's momentum is unstoppable and resistance futile.

Hedging our bets does not preclude us from having a constructive, profitable relationship with China. But it does mean we need options and choices should things go wrong or our core interests and values are threatened as they are in the South China Sea and by unacceptable interference in our domestic affairs. These options include trade diversification to prevent overreliance on China; enhancing our strategic relationships with other states, especially Japan, India, and Indonesia; and strengthening the US alliance and our independent defense and intelligence capabilities.

The China challenge is as much about values as it is interests. If Xi takes China further down an authoritarian, expansionist path, the differences between our two countries will multiply and eventually overwhelm centripetal impulses, creating a trust deficit that could prove insurmountable.

Nobody expects China to become a Jeffersonian democracy. But unless the current leadership learns to tolerate more pluralism at home, open up to criticism, and accommodate smaller countries' legitimate concerns, there will be trouble ahead and hardening resistance to the idea of a China-centric world.

ALAN DUPONT is the founder and CEO of Cognoscenti Group, a political and strategic risk consultancy. Following 25 years of service in government as an army officer, defense intelligence analyst, and diplomat Alan distinguished himself as an academic entrepreneur and scholar. He holds a PhD in international relations from the Australian National University and is a graduate of the Royal Military College Duntroon and the US Foreign Service Institute. He is currently an adjunct professor at the University of NSW in Sydney and a nonresident senior fellow at the Atlantic Council in Washington.

EXPLORING THE ISSUE

Will China Be the Next Global Superpower?

Critical Thinking and Reflection

1. Does China possess the necessary attributes of a superpower or are their areas where it has yet to achieve such status?
2. Does China have superpower ambitions or is it merely trying to maximize its influence in Asia alone?
3. What policies does China pursue that either proves their superpower status or calls into question that position?
4. What are the implications of China as a superpower for the global community?

Is There Common Ground?

There seems to be great debate about the classification of China as a full-fledged superpower given the traditional definitions of such. Analysts differ on the relative strengths and weaknesses of China in that role and appear that this will continue in the years ahead. What analysts can agree on is that China is a very influential economic actor in the global community both in terms of trade, productivity, expansion, and influence. That power does not seem to be a temporary or ephemeral thing but will grow and endure throughout the early half of the twenty-first century.

Additional Resources

Fishman, Ted, China, Inc.: How the Rise of the Next Superpower Challenges America and the World (Scribner, 2005).

Fallows, James, Postcards from Tomorrow Square: Reports from China (Vintage Books, 2009).

Mahbubani, et al, Asia: The Next Higher Education Superpower (Global Education Research Reports,

Report Nine) (The Institute of International Education, 2015).

Nathan, Andrew J. "The Hundred-Year Marathon: China's Secret Strategy to Replace America as the Global Superpower/Fire on the Water: China, America, and the Future of the Pacific/The South China Sea: The Struggle for Power in Asia." *Foreign Affairs* (Jan/Feb2015).

Ghitis, Frida. "Will China Challenge U.S. as Global Superpower?." *World Politics Review (Selective Content)* (October 21, 2010).

Williams, Armstrong. "Walking the Yellow Brick Road: China's Rise to Global Superpower Took Brains, Heart and Courage." *New York Amsterdam News* (August 28, 2008).

Garver, John W. "America's Debate over the Rise of China." *China Quarterly* (June 2016).

Hsu, Sara. "Why China Won't Replace The U.S. As The World's Superpower." *Forbes, Forbes Magazine*, February 3, 2017, www.forbes.com/sites/sarahsu/2017/02/02/why-china-wont-replace-the-u-s-as-the-worlds-superpower/#3c5151b7234d

Internet References . . .

CNN

www.cnn.com

Forbes

https://www.forbes.com

Foreign Affairs

https://www.foreignaffairs.com

Foreign Policy

http://foreignpolicy.com

The Diplomat

https://thediplomat.com

Selected, Edited, and with Issue Framing Material by:
Marie E. Harf, *U.S. Department of State (2013–2017),*
Central Intelligence Agency (2006–2011)

ISSUE

Can Diplomacy, Rather than Military Action, Result in North Korea Denuclearizing?

YES: **Uri Friedman**, from "Here's What Trump Actually Achieved with North Korea," *The Atlantic* (2018)

NO: **Brian Barrett**, from "All the Times North Korea Promised to Denuclearize," *WIRED* (2018)

Learning Outcomes

After reading this issue, you will be able to:

- Describe the options the United States has for dealing with North Korea's nuclear program, including preemption and diplomacy.
- Describe the basic policy dilemmas facing the United States because North Korea already has nuclear weapons and increasingly capable missile systems.
- Discuss the complications involved with taking military action against North Korea's nuclear program.
- Understand the arguments advanced that this new round of negotiations led by U.S. President Donald Trump and North Korean leader Kim Jong-un might finally have the right conditions in place for a diplomatic resolution to the issue.
- Appreciate the difficulties of diplomacy as the preferred tool for solving the American–North Korean conflict.

ISSUE SUMMARY

YES: Uri Freidman, global affairs staff writer at *The Atlantic*, argues a case can be made that diplomacy might finally work this time in getting North Korea to denuclearize after the latest round of negotiations at the leader level. Among the author's six reasons for optimism is the fact that the two countries are talking to each other at a political decision-maker level—putting the politics first and at a very high level—and that any North Korean denuclearization pledge such as this latest one is significant.

NO: Brian Barrett, News Editor at WIRED, is not hopeful, suggesting that this is simply another example of the pattern where North Korea promises to "abandon nuclear efforts" with "surprising regularity" and then does not follow through on its promises. He argues that North Korea uses the promise of denuclearization as a "bargaining chip in times of desperation" and details the multiple rounds of negotiations over the past several decades that have all ended in failure.

Throughout 2017 and 2018, the conflict between the United States and North Korea whiplashed between two diametrically opposed tones. The first—an escalation of threatening behavior and language on both sides—began early in the Trump administration and grew in response to North Korea's continued testing of its most recent advances in nuclear weapons and missile technologies. President Trump upped his rhetoric, calling North Korean leader Kim Jong-un "Little Rocket Man," bragging that American nuclear weapons were bigger and more plentiful than those of North Korea and threatening "fire and fury" if Pyongyang continued its actions. Kim responded with his own personal insults of President Trump and more aggressive moves. Given the general perception that both leaders are capable of impulsive decision-making, observers around the world—including North Korea's neighbors, U.S.-allied South Korea and Japan—became increasingly nervous about the real possibility that military conflict between the two countries was not only becoming more likely but was dangerously close to crossing over into a state of inevitability.

But then, beginning in early 2018, several events occurred that opened a new path for diplomacy and lowered the temperature of the conflict. First, South Korea hosted the Winter Olympics, and its leader, Moon Jae-in, reached out to North Korea, inviting its athletes to march with South Korean athletes under one flag. This olive branch led to reinvigorated talks between the two Koreas and ultimately to an invitation from the North Korean leader to President Trump, delivered through the South Koreans, to meet in a leader summit. Kim also announced he was suspending nuclear and missile tests, and Trump reciprocated with a corresponding lowering of his verbal rhetoric in advance of the summit.

The meeting between President Trump and Kim Jong-un, the first-ever between sitting heads of states of the United States and North Korea, took place amid much media frenzy in Singapore on June 12, 2018. After about five hours of talks, the two leaders signed a joint statement consisting of four general points, but with no attached specifics about either the substance or follow-up timetables. First, both countries agreed to establish new bilateral "relations in accordance with the desire of the peoples of the two countries for peace and prosperity." Second, both countries will join "to build a lasting and stable peace regime on the Korea Peninsula." Third, North Korea "commits to work toward complete denuclearization of the Korean Peninsula," reaffirming an April 27, 2018, declaration. And fourth, both countries "commit to recovering POW/MIA remains" as well as the immediate reparation of those who have already been identified. While the document was vague, it represents the first step in what could become a multiyear process of complex negotiations on each of the points outlined. President Trump also announced in a subsequent press conference that the United States would be temporarily suspending military exercises with ally South Korea, routine military activities the North Koreans have repeatedly called "war games" and asked to be stopped. In the aftermath of the summit, President Trump, who only mere months before was personally insulting the North Korean leader

on Twitter, now described the dictator in Pyongyang as "strong," "very smart," and "very talented."

This is not the first time that North Korea and the United States have left the negotiating table with a signed statement about "denuclearization" in hand. The debate over Pyongyang's nuclear program should be viewed in the context of the wider conflict between the two countries, including the Korean War, which was waged between 1950 and 1953. The war ended with a truce between all parties—but never a peace treaty—and Korea has since remained partitioned between the North and the South, countries that developed in drastically different ways following the war, with the South becoming an economic, modern, democratic powerhouse, and the North being ruled by a family of despotic leaders who have starved, imprisoned, and tortured their own people and left the country as one of the most underdeveloped in the world.

Throughout the history of North Korea's nuclear program, the international community has used both threats and promises to try to change the regime's behavior: threats of economic sanctions and at times military action, and promises of aid or security guarantees. Neither has succeeded in stopping the North's nuclear program. Negotiations over the program have resulted in various agreements over the decades, most notably the 1994 Agreed Framework where North Korea agreed to freeze operation of nuclear reactors suspected of being part of a covert nuclear weapons program in exchange for two proliferation-resistant nuclear power reactors. The Framework succeeded in temporarily freezing North Korea's plutonium production capabilities and placing it under IAEA safeguards, but it unraveled in 2002 after a covert North Korean uranium enrichment program was discovered. During these and other rounds of negotiations, the regime continued moving ahead with its nuclear program and ultimately conducted its first nuclear test in 2006, breaking the promises it had made throughout the years. Today, the U.S. intelligence community believes North Korea has as many as 60 nuclear warheads.

When President Obama met with President-elect Trump in the Oval Office shortly after the 2016 election, he warned the incoming president that North Korea would be the most urgent national security problem he would face. Several months later in 2017, North Korea claimed it had tested its first hydrogen bomb in its sixth nuclear test, which was followed by the testing of a new type of intercontinental ballistic missile it claimed could reach all of the continental United States. As a consequence, for the first time, it appeared that North Korea was getting dangerously close to possessing both nuclear weapons and the means to transport these weapons from North Korean launch sites to mainland America—a claim its leadership loudly proclaimed—and a threshold which has generally been agreed upon as the "red line" for U.S. policy makers. President Trump, like no U.S. president before him, was thus confronted with a more immediate dilemma. In response, the U.S. has led a "maximum pressure" campaign designed to increase the costs to North Korea of its actions, including putting in place additional sanctions, which has had tangible negative effects on North Korea in part because of China's increased cooperation. This aggressive North Korean activity, combined with the ratcheting up of international pressure, is what led to the rhetorical back-and-forth mentioned earlier in this chapter, followed by the surprise reinvigorated diplomatic process that has brought the conflict back from what appeared to be an increasingly close brink. The world is now engaged in this diplomacy to see if the threat from Pyongyang's nuclear and missile programs can be rolled back—a process that could drag on for many months or years and which has a very uncertain end, especially given the history of failure.

As the United States and North Korea embark on yet another try at diplomacy, the U.S. faces a dilemma over how to most effectively remove the threat of a nuclear-armed North Korea. Should Washington pursue a harder line, with threats of a preemptive or preventative military strikes to convince North Korea to denuclearize, or else? Should it work to increase the economic pressure through sanctions even more, hoping that will change Pyongyang's calculations? Should it emphasize diplomacy and hope that this round of negotiations might be different? Should it engage in the kind of deterrence and containment strategy that the United States used effectively against the Soviet Union during the Cold War by making clear how grave the consequences would be for North Korea if they did in fact use their nuclear weapons? Or should it do all of the above?

President Trump's current national security advisor, John Bolton, an advocate of a hard line approach to North Korea, made a legal case for pre-emptively striking North Korea in an opinion piece in the *Wall Street Journal* in early 2018 (before being named to his White House position), arguing that North Korea represents an "imminent threat." Many analysts, on the other hand, view a pre-emptive U.S. strike as a recipe for catastrophic human and strategic consequences. Retired American military officer Daniel L. Davis warns that it "is difficult to overstate the negative consequences that would result" from a pre-emptive military strike against North Korea.

Because Pyongyang has made it a military priority to be able to survive an American first strike, it would be able to respond with nuclear and conventional weapons, in addition to its significant arsenal of chemical and biological weapons. The damage to South Korea and Japan done by a North Korean response could be devastating to the millions of civilians within range of North Korea's weapons, including approximately 230,000 Americans living in South Korea and 90,000 in Japan (Cha and Katz, *Foreign Affairs* May/June 2018). Not only would the humanitarian consequences be catastrophic, it is unlikely that any first strike by the United States would succeed in destroying all of North Korea's arsenal because of a lack of good intelligence about where all of it is located and the fact that Pyongyang uses mobile technology to move its weapons assets around. A strike would only delay, not destroy, North Korea's programs. As a result of these consequences, many analysts argue a first strike by the .United States should only be considered in the face of a truly imminent threat of an ICBM launch aimed at the United States from North Korea.

On the other hand, there is real disagreement about whether diplomacy can actually achieve the desired result of a denuclearized North Korea, with many analysts fairly negative about the willingness and ability of the regime in Pyongyang to abandon its nuclear weapons program through negotiations. Since the summit, there has been wide disagreement over whether the five-hour meeting between the two leaders will ultimately result in anything concrete. The Trump administration has also arguably boxed itself into a corner in the North Korea talks as a consequence of its withdrawal from the Iran nuclear deal because any agreement with North Korea must now have more stringent controls and tighter restrictions than what was achieved in the Iran deal, which raises the bar for negotiations and likely constrains the policy outcomes available to the United States. The Trump administration continues to insist the goal is "complete, verifiable, and irreversible" denuclearization of North Korea—a very high bar that will be an incredibly complicated goal to achieve.

One option some commentators argue could spur momentum on a diplomatic process is to focus on interim confidence-building measures designed to alleviate the greatest near-threat posed by North Korea against the United States. While the long-term goal of complete denuclearization should remain, experts like Robert Einhorn and Michael Fuchs argue there are steps that could significantly reduce the current threat, such as a freeze on North Korea's program and testing that is verified by international inspectors. In response, Fuchs says the United

States should consider ending the military exercises with South Korea and opening a diplomatic interest section in Pyongyang (*Foreign Affairs*, December 21, 2017). Einhorn, a long-time arms control and nuclear expert, outlines a "very demanding freeze" that halts the North's progress in exchange for a lessening of economic pressure (*Brookings*, April 18, 2017). At some point, this diplomacy will also likely have to include other countries who have equities in the issue, possibly in the format of the previous Six-Party Talks. Multilateral diplomacy is often more difficult because you have to address more points of view, but in the end, if it is successful, it often has more international buy-in and a greater likelihood of long-term viability.

As we evaluate the ongoing diplomacy, a key question to consider is why North Korea has invested so heavily in these weapons. Most analysts agree that the regime believes the nuclear program ensure its own political survival by deterring U.S. intervention and consolidating internal support. But is the North's posture only defensive, or does the regime have offensive intent in mind for these weapons (a much more dangerous prospect)? Is Kim Jong-un different than his grandfather or his father, neither of whom were ultimately willing to negotiate away their nuclear or missile programs and who both used past promises to "denuclearize" simply to relieve international pressure in times of desperation while secretly continuing their programs? Is there a diplomatic deal—possibly that includes security guarantees of the regime's survival, critically important to Kim—that would be enough for him to negotiate the end of their nuclear program? The Trump administration has been trying to send the message to Kim that this is a choice between a weapons program and a thriving economy—but would the U.S. taxpayer or international companies actually be willing to invest in a North Korea that remains a brutal dictatorship? And, given how critical personal relationships are to diplomacy, could President Trump's unique style based in part on flattery help convince Kim that they're both strong leaders who pride themselves on being the sole deciders, and therefore they should work together on a historic agreement? After all, President Trump's unpredictability arguably has already paid dividends in getting Kim to the negotiating table by possibly convincing the North Korean leader that he would in fact be willing to take the kind of military action that previous U.S. administrations were not.

As the talks proceed and these questions are all considered, it would be helpful for the United States to have a more accurate picture of how Kim thinks—and, importantly, whether the regime sees its nuclear capability as truly inextricable from its own survival and therefore something that needs to be held onto under any circumstances (Jervis and Rapp-Hooper, May/June 2018). Time is not on the U.S.' side, however, because the more technically advanced North Korea's program gets, the less leverage the United States will have and the less it will be able to demand in negotiations. It is harder to negotiate away things countries already have. The drama of the leader summit now has to be turned into actual policies by experts on both sides, and the world will continue watching to see if this time is truly any different.

As this book goes to press, the country and the world await the outcome of this new round of diplomacy. In the YES selection, Uri Friedman argues that there are now reasons in place why North Korea might just follow through this time on its promise to denuclearize. In the NO article, Brian Barrett suggests that North Korea has made and broken similar promises many times in the past, and there is no reason to believe this time is any different.

YES

Uri Friedman

Here's What Trump Actually Achieved with North Korea

It Wasn't What He Said. But It Was Much More Than Nothing

Donald Trump didn't get much in the way of North Korean denuclearization in Singapore. And that's not necessarily a bad thing.

In the days since the summit with Kim Jong-un, critics—including me—have pointed out how little the U.S. president got from North Korea's leader during their much-hyped meeting. And it's true that Trump fell far short in that meeting of his stated goal to fully dismantle North Korea's nuclear-weapons program and then wildly overstated his achievement by declaring the North Korean nuclear threat over. (It's not.) But the Trump administration racked up real accomplishments in Singapore that are perhaps best understood by setting aside the president's grand (and at times groundless) pronouncements. The summit's modest and provisional results are actually of considerable consequence.

Here's a rundown of why Trump can reasonably make the case that the Singapore summit was successful and that the United States and the world are safer now than they were before he decided to become the first American president to meet with North Korea's leader.

1) U.S. Concessions to North Korea so far Are Largely Reversible

If North Korea hasn't yet given up a lot in negotiations, neither has the United States. Trump can't retract his decision to hold a summit with and even speak admiringly of the dictatorial rule of Kim Jong-un, just like Kim can't walk back his decision to release American hostages ahead of the summit. But Trump is right to state that while he has suspended upcoming U.S.–South Korea military exercises that he considers "provocative," he can always reinstate the drills if nuclear talks collapse. Likewise, the Trump administration has refrained from imposing new

sanctions on North Korea as diplomacy proceeds and, in engaging North Korea, has potentially weakened the resolve of countries such as China and South Korea to enforce existing sanctions. But here again, there's been no easing of U.S. sanctions in exchange for North Korea's vague, noncommittal promise of denuclearization in Singapore.

This, of course, isn't all that surprising: goodwill gestures at the outset of negotiations, when there's little trust among the parties, tend to be provisional. Experts suspect, for instance, that the North Koreans may still be able to reopen the nuclear-test site that they claimed to have destroyed with great fanfare in the lead-up to the summit.

2) The United States and North Korea Are now Talking to each other Rather than Threatening War

It was just six months ago that Lindsey Graham, the Republican senator and Trump confidant, was telling me there was a 70-percent chance of the president launching an all-out war against the Kim regime if North Korea tested another nuclear device. A month later, Tammy Duckworth, the Democratic senator and military veteran, returned from South Korea and told me that U.S. forces appeared to be operating with the attitude that a conflict "will probably happen, and we better be ready to go." A Russian academic came back from Pyongyang with a chilling report: the North Korean government "is not bluffing when it says that "only one question remains: when will war break out?'" With each test of a bomb or long-range missile, the North moved closer to the capability to strike the United States with nuclear weapons—a development the Trump administration had vowed to prevent at all costs.

Whether or not hostilities were truly imminent, the military brinkmanship was real. And in this climate, people weren't exactly holding their breath for a swift, negotiated end to the North Korean nuclear program. Around the time that Trump threatened North Korea with "fire and fury" in August, the nuclear scientist Siegfried Hecker, who has visited North Korea's nuclear facilities several times, argued that the most immediate task for U.S. policy makers was not to address North Korea's nuclear weapons but to avoid stumbling into nuclear war on the Korean peninsula. He urged Trump to send military and diplomatic officials to Pyongyang to simply talk with and learn more about their North Korean counterparts and thereby reduce tensions and the risk of dangerous miscalculation. Graham, one of the leading North Korea hawks in Congress, surprisingly went further. When we spoke he wouldn't rule out a Kim-Trump summit, then a fanciful idea. "I'm not taking anything off the table to avoid a war," he said.

If these recommendations seemed prudent and urgent at the time, it's hard to argue only half a year later that the Singapore summit and the flurry of direct, lower-level talks preceding it are meaningless or even reckless. Within months of Duckworth warning darkly that the U.S. military had "seen the writing on the wall," Donald Trump and Kim Jong-un were signing a statement in which they pledged to jointly "build a lasting and stable peace regime on the Korean peninsula." That's astonishing.

3) Any North Korean Denuclearization Pledge Is Remarkable

Critics of Trump's North Korea summit have pointed out that Kim's commitment to "work toward complete denuclearization of the Korean peninsula" by some unspecified time—squishy wording that might entail the nuclear-armed United States ending its military alliance with South Korea and concluding a peace treaty with North Korea—is actually weaker than the North's vow in a 2005 statement to abandon "all nuclear weapons and existing nuclear programs" at "an early date" and pursue the goal of "verifiable denuclearization of the Korean peninsula."

But this is comparing apples to oranges—or several bombs' worth of plutonium to a bristling nuclear-weapons arsenal, as it were. While North Korea had declared itself a nuclear power in 2005, it hadn't yet tested a nuclear bomb. Thirteen years later, it has tested *six*, including most recently a suspected thermonuclear weapon 17 times as strong as the bomb that devastated Hiroshima—plus last year's successful tests of intercontinental ballistic missiles

that may be able to carry nuclear warheads to the United States. The deficiencies in the language notwithstanding, it's remarkable that a now nearly full-fledged nuclear power would agree in writing to *anything* involving the ceding of that status. (Granted, the parties to the international Treaty on the Non-Proliferation of Nuclear Weapons, which include the United States and other nuclear states, sign on to similarly aspirational disarmament goals.) Also notable: North Korean state media has released a documentary on the Singapore summit that shows viewers the agreed-to language on denuclearization.

The 2005 statement, moreover, came after years of negotiations, not mere months as in the case of the 2018 statement. And the 2005 denuclearization pledge was accompanied by written assurances from the Bush administration to not attack North Korea and to offer it energy and economic assistance. The 2018 denuclearization pledge was made without any such written assurances from the Trump administration, though the president and other U.S. officials verbally echoed these promises before the summit.

4) For the Moment, Some Conditions for a Realistic, Halfway-decent Nuclear Deal with North Korea Are in Place.

In March, just hours before Trump announced his intention to meet with Kim Jong-un, former U.S. Defense Secretary Bill Perry gave me a bleak assessment of what nuclear talks with North Korea could realistically achieve.

In the 1990s, Perry had spearheaded an effort by the Clinton administration to reach a comprehensive agreement for North Korea to abandon its nuclear program and its work on long-range missiles in return for a peace treaty formally ending the Korean War, the gradual normalization of United States–North Korean relations and other concessions. Had the 2000 U.S. presidential election not gotten in the way, the deal may well have succeeded. But Perry argued that what might have bought North Korean denuclearization a couple decades ago had much less purchase today. He suggested offering these same incentives to North Korea if it instituted a ban on nuclear and missile tests, which would be much easier to verify than a more sweeping agreement on the country's sprawling nuclear infrastructure. (We might not know if North Korea is disclosing all its nuclear weapons and facilities, but we do know when it explodes bombs underground or fires rockets into the Sea of Japan.)

"In 1999, we had a chance of getting denuclearization. I do not believe we will get that today," Perry told me. A moratorium on tests, while far from a grand bargain, "would be worth having," he argued, because it would keep Kim from refining the long-range nuclear capability that directly threatens the United States. The Trump administration, he added, could also try to get North Korea to limit the number of nuclear weapons in its arsenal, not build new and improved ones, and not transfer nuclear weapons and technology to other states or nonstate actors, though all of these moves would be more difficult to verify. Perry's proposal essentially aimed to keep a nuclear program that is already a fait accompli from growing more dangerous.

Diplomacy with North Korea hasn't yet produced even this limited nuclear deal. But as talks proceed, it has resulted in a de facto freeze of the North's tests of nuclear weapons and long-range missiles, which Kim announced in April. That means that for the time being, North Korea isn't experimenting (publicly at least) with its new intercontinental ballistic missiles, detonating nuclear devices, or test-firing nuclear-tipped missiles over the Pacific Ocean as it threatened to do last fall—all of which would signal advances in the North Korean nuclear program and bring the United States and North Korean closer to military conflict.

Tentatively suspending U.S.–South Korea military exercises while North Korea tentatively suspends its nuclear and missile tests is very far off from the "complete, verifiable, and irreversible" dismantling of North Korea's nuclear program that the Trump administration has demanded. But it's closer to what Perry has described as a workable outcome of negotiations.

5) Trump Is Experimenting with a Promising Politics-first Approach to the North Korean Nuclear Crisis

In jumpstarting talks with a head-of-state summit, Trump didn't only reverse the bottom-up process that has shaped inconclusive nuclear negotiations with North Korea over the last 25 years. He also appeared to be prioritizing the transformation of relations between the United States and North Korea over the technical details of constraining the North's nuclear capabilities. "President Trump places great faith in his own ability to relate to others on a personal basis, and so it does seem like he wants to bolster the political relationship (with Kim) and then trust that will lead to arms control," James Holmes of the U.S. Naval War College told me. "Politics leads, international law lags. We appear to be about to put this idea to the test."

And while we don't yet know the results of the test, this novel approach could potentially succeed in reducing the North Korean nuclear threat, if not eliminating it altogether. If the classic definition of a security threat is the combination of intent *and* capability to cause harm, U.S officials have tended to fixate on blunting North Korea's capabilities rather than addressing intent. But intent matters too. As the German political scientist Alexander Wendt once noted, "500 British nuclear weapons are less threatening to the United States than five North Korean nuclear weapons because the British are friends of the United States and the North Koreans are not."

If there's any chance of North Korea doing what only one country in history has done before—relinquishing nuclear weapons that it built and controls—it would probably be as a result of a massive shift in Kim Jong-un's perception of security threats and personal and political calculations. (North Korea claims that the purpose of its nuclear program is to deter U.S. aggression.) F. W. de Klerk, the former South African president who made that unprecedented decision to give up his nation's atomic bombs, told me that he did so in the early 1990s because he was personally opposed to nuclear weapons; because the Soviet Union, whose aggression South Africa was trying to deter, was disintegrating; and because South Africa was trying to end its international isolation as part of its political transition away from apartheid. (While some speculate that the country's white leaders didn't want the incoming black government to possess nuclear weapons, de Klerk denied that this informed his actions.)

George Perkovich, a nuclear-weapons expert at the Carnegie Endowment for International Peace, has identified a similar dynamic at play in United States—Russian nuclear-arms reduction agreements over the years. "When the political relationships changed and the types of war you were worried about being conducted changed . . . you could reduce nuclear weapons," he told me last fall.

6) It's Possible This Is the Small Start of Something Big

Reflecting on the significance of the Singapore summit in an interview with the BBC, the former South Korean military officer I-B Chun quoted a Korean saying: "a long journey starts with the first step. And when that first step is taken, the journey is half-finished." The journey to North Korea's denuclearization may be a long way from half-finished and may never finish or may even end abruptly at any moment, but Trump's meeting with Kim is certainly a first step in the right direction. And we simply don't know at this point where the next steps, which Secretary of State Mike Pompeo and his North Korean counterparts will now take, will lead.

"As risky and high-stakes as this entire process is, it makes sense because that's the way the North operates. Their regime is top-down," the Korea expert Duyeon Kim noted when we met in Seoul ahead of the Trump–Kim summit. She advised Trump and Kim to settle in Singapore "upon a very simple vision statement on end goals . . . and then have senior negotiators figure out the details, figure out timetables, figure out implementation."

That, in fact, is exactly what the two leaders did.

URI FRIEDMAN is senior associate editor at *The Atlantic* and deputy managing editor at *Foreign Policy*.

Brian Barrett

All the Times North Korea Promised to Denuclearize

The nuclear summit between President Donald Trump and North Korean leader Kim Jong-un has concluded, with each securing something they value. The United States will suspend the joint military exercises with South Korea that rattle the Hermit Kingdom. And North Korea has promised to denuclearize at some point, probably. But if the past is any sort of prologue, you shouldn't hold your breath.

On the face of it, the agreement signed by Trump and Kim seems promising. "President Trump committed to provide security guarantees to the DPRK, and Chairman Kim Jong-un reaffirmed his firm and unwavering commitment to complete denuclearization of the Korean Peninsula," the statement read.

But this is not the first time North Korea has promised to abandon its nuclear efforts. (In truth, even this was simply a reaffirmation of a denuclearization pledge Kim had already made in April.) Nor is it the second time or the third. The offer has resurfaced over the past several decades with surprising regularity. And it has never panned out so far.

"There's definitely a pattern where the North Koreans agree to denuclearize in theory, but then there's not really a substantive process that they agree to, to actually hammer it out," says James McKeon, a policy analyst at the Center for Arms Control and Non-Proliferation.

"Any notion that we're simply going to denuclearize North Korea now after the summit, or any time in the very near future, must be dispelled." says James McKeon, Center for Arms Control and Non-Proliferation.

Those failures don't necessarily come down to bad faith or at least not entirely. In fact, the 1994 Agreed Framework between the United States and North Korea, in which the North gave up its plutonium enrichment in exchange for aid, resulted in a roughly eight-year stretch of calm. That eventually collapsed too, though, as North Korea's pursuit of enriched uranium and the George W. Bush administration's hawkish stance imploded the already shaky scaffolding.

But in general, North Korea uses denuclearization as a bargaining chip in times of desperation. "Usually they suffer some kind of internal crisis and then start acting in a really threatening way to try to get people to give them stuff," says Mieke Eoyang, a national security analyst for center-left think tank Third Way.

In this instance, Eoyang argues, Trump gave the longtime US adversary far too much. "It's substantively worse than what any other president has done," she says, noting that the joint exercises aren't just for show. The United States rotates troops in and out of South Korea every few years; training with local counterparts helps newly stationed units prepare for potential North Korean aggression.

In return for that real loss, the United States gained the same promise North Korea has made since 1985, without a single specific about how to accomplish it. There's no agreement on inspections. North Korea doesn't have to declare the facilities it has, much less dismantle them, to say nothing of destroying actual warheads.

"It is much messier at the working level, particularly when it comes to verification," says John Carl Baker, a political engagement specialist at Ploughshares Fund, a grantmaking foundation that focuses on denuclearization. "As an analyst, I'm skeptical that this is the time that it's finally going to come together. I'm certainly skeptical of the fact that the North is going to completely denuclearize itself."

Add to this uncertain stew the fact that Trump very recently tore up a nuclear inspection framework that was actually working in Iran, and it's hard to see how or why North Korea would go through with a promise that it has broken time and again. Especially this time.

"It sent the absolute wrong message," says CACNP's McKeon of scrapping the Iran deal. "Any notion that we're simply going to denuclearize North Korea now after the summit, or any time in the very near future, must be dispelled."

Some North Korea observers did strike hopeful notes; both McKeon and Baker think the summit was an important first step, however symbolic. And it was certainly an improvement over the overt nuclear threats of a few months ago. But this script has been written before and always with the same ending. See for yourself (and for a more thorough dissection, check out the Arms Control Association's comprehensive time line):

What: Treaty on the Nonproliferation of Nuclear Weapons
When: December 12, 1985
What happened? North Korea signs onto this landmark treaty—190 countries are currently members—but makes its membership contingent on the United States withdrawing nuclear weapons from South Korea, which doesn't happen for several years, buying North Korea time to build its nuclear capabilities.

What: Joint Declaration of the Denuclearization of the Korean Peninsula
When: January 20, 1992
What happened? North and South Korea sign an agreement that "the South and the North shall not test, manufacture, produce, receive, possess, store, deploy, or use nuclear weapons." In February 1993, suspicion that North Korea is violating its commitments creates tension over inspections, leading to further delays.

What: Agreed Framework
When: October 21, 1994
What happened? North Korea promises to stop plutonium production in exchange for much-needed supplies. This mostly holds up until 2002, when the United States discovers that North Korea has secretly been enriching uranium for nuclear weapons. By the end of that year, Kim Jong Il kicks out all international inspectors. On January 10, 2003, North Korea officially withdraws from the 1985 nonproliferation treaty.

What: Six-Party Talks
When: September 19, 2005
What happened? After several rounds of intense talks with South Korea, China, Japan, the United States, and Russia, North Korea pledges to abandon "all nuclear weapons and existing nuclear programs." The United States and North Korea can't agree on verification details, though, leading to increased hostilities.

What: Six-Party Talks (Again)
When: October 3, 2007
What happened? In a joint statement, North Korea agrees to declare all of its nuclear programs, shut down those affiliated with its weapons program, and not to transfer "nuclear materials, technology, or know-how." Once again, stakeholders can't agree on a verification process.

What: US Agreement
When: February 29, 2012
What happened? North Korea agrees to suspend nuclear tests and uranium enrichment, and said it will allow inspectors, in exchange for food aid. Two weeks later, North Korea announces plans to launch a satellite, which immediately unwinds the deal.

So yes, North Korea has gotten this far before. Trump and Kim haven't forged any new ground. "The parallels are apparent in the similarities between this statement and many of the previous ones, such as those from the 1990s," says Baker. "That's very clear."

The rest hinges on whether the two sides can iron out not just when North Korea will denuclearize, but how, and the manner in which the rest of the world can confirm it. Or maybe the more apt question is what happens when they don't.

BRIAN BARRETT is News Editor at *WIRED*.

EXPLORING THE ISSUE

Can Diplomacy, Rather Than Military Action, Result in North Korea Denuclearizing?

Critical Thinking and Reflection

1. Why do you think the North Korean regime has believed it was essential that they acquire nuclear weapons capability and advanced missile programs?
2. Do you think there are other policy options for the United States in addition to a pre-emptive strike or diplomacy to move North Korea toward denuclearization?
3. Do you believe that the United States could achieve security against North Korea even if the latter does not totally denuclearize—in other words, can North Korea be "contained"?
4. Do those who argue against a pre-emptive strike on North Korea overstate the likely negative consequences of such an action?
5. Do you believe that President Donald Trump is overly optimistic about his ability to achieve North Korean denuclearization through diplomacy?

Is There Common Ground?

Both the United States and North Korea now agree that the survival of the Kim Jong-un regime should be guaranteed as part of any agreement between the two countries. Both countries have also committed to denuclearization of the Korean Peninsula and to "a lasting and stable peace regime" on the Peninsula (although the details of what those terms mean have not been agreed on). A vast majority of American policy makers and analysts agree that a pre-emptive strike against North Korea would yield many costly consequences, particularly to South Korea. Most Western analysts also believe that reaching a diplomatic solution to the problem of North Korea's nuclear capability acceptable to both sides will not be easy but will require a long, sustained, patient negotiating process full of much give-and-take on both sides.

Additional Resources

Denmark, Abraham M., "The Myth of the Limited Strike on North Korea," *Foreign Affairs* (January 9, 2018).

Goldberg, Jonah, "Why North Korea Isn't Going to Give Up Its Nukes," *National Review* (April 25, 2018).

Jervis, Robert and Rapp-Hooper, Mira, "The Risks of Misperception in the Nuclear Standoff with North Korea," *Foreign Affairs* (May/June 2018).

Jones, Bruce (Interviewer), "Averting Catastrophe: US Policy Options for North Korea," *Brookings* (April 18, 2017).

Monroe, Robert, "The Case for a Hard, Preemptive American Strike on North Korea," *The Hill* (March 5, 2018).

Sevastopulo, Demetri, "Trump and North Korea: The Perils of a Pre-Emptive Strike," *Financial Times* (January 8, 2018).

Internet References . . .

Council on Foreign Relations

https://www.foreignaffairs.com/regions/north-korea

Harvard Kennedy School Belfer Center

https://www.belfercenter.org/nuclear-issues?f(0)=subtopic%3ANuclear+Issues--North+Korea+nuclear+program

Nuclear Threat Initiative

http://www.nti.org/learn/countries/north-korea/nuclear/

Rand Corporation

https://www.rand.org/topics/north-korea.html

Wilson Center

https://www.wilsoncenter.org/program/north-korea-international-documentation-project

Selected, Edited, and with Issue Framing Material by:
Mark Owen Lombardi, *Maryville University*

ISSUE

Is Cyberwar the Future of 21st-Century Conflict?

YES: Rick Stella, from "From Cyberwarfare to Drones, the Future of Conflict Is Electronic," *Digital Trends* (2016)

NO: Daniel Moore, from "Struggling with Cyber: A Critical Look at Waging War Online," *War on the Rocks* (2016)

Learning Outcomes
After reading this issue, you will be able to:
• Describe the elements that would make up a cyberwar.
• Examine the pros and cons of why a country would want to wage a largely cyberwar.
• Speculate as to whether cyberwar will replace conventional war in the future and if so why and if so why not.

ISSUE SUMMARY

YES: Rick Stella, Outdoor Editor of *Digital Trends*, makes the argument that in the aftermath of 9/11, innovation and technology in warfare became of paramount importance. As a result, cyberwarfare has become the dominant trend in weapons research, development, and ultimately application.

NO: Daniel Moore, a threat intelligence engineer, makes that case that it is too easy to simply argue that if technology is sophisticated, then it means that all warfare will be cyber. He maintains that one must define one's terms before hitting the default button that all warfare is moving in a cyber direction.

Drone strikes, cyber hacks, computer viruses, and robot soldiers. These are some of the tools being used today by both state and some nonstate actors in the prosecution of war. These new ways of waging conflict against adversaries are surgical, effective, often deadly, and greatly decrease the casualties on the attacking side. They are also direct manifestations of the computer, technological revolution that is upon us and accelerating on a daily basis.

For millennia, war has been waged by human beings directly. It involved the killing of another groups soldiers and the occupation of territory. Historically, it has always been impacted by technological advances, from the horse bringing mobility to the lance and later gunpowder, to rail and later airpower which expanded the theaters of war and of course the most significant advancement, the invention, and use of nuclear weaponry. At every level of "advancement" soldiers have been required to engage in attacks and occupy territory. In the computer age and particularly in the twenty-first century, a new form of warfare has emerged which is now called cyberwar. In this new environment, states and in selected areas, nonstate actors can attack power grids, water systems, information, and financial records. They can use robotics such as drones to kill or bomb, and they can even construct cybernetic soldiers to engage in selected attacks.

Today the United States uses cyberwar in its fight against terrorism and ISIS. Other states use cyberattacks to diminish, disrupt, and degrade their adversaries' economic and social systems. The sophistication of the technology makes aspects of its use difficult for only a few states, but the ability to hack systems and use cyberattacks is relatively simple and therefore poorer states like Syria, North Korea, and Iran are just as able to employ such tactics as wealthy states such as the United States, China, Britain, and Russia.

Analysts such as P. W. Singer and others have written about the future use of robotic soldiers, DNA signature–guided explosives, remote and undetectable weaponry, and other such "futuristic" devices. Each of these inventions expands the options for waging war while in some ways mitigating some of the previous negative effects of traditional warfare.

However, as we are learning with drone strikes and cyberattacks, cyberwar has a variety of effects that have heretofore been underexamined. Does it make war easier to wage and therefore more likely? Does it violate aspects of international law built around clear state boundaries? Does it inhibit individual freedoms and protections long honored by some societies? Can it empower actors who before were deterred by confronting directly states with enormous military advantages, like the United States, for example.

Stella contends that in this century, we have crossed over into the era of cyberwarfare. He contends that technological sophistication combined with societal vulnerability as a result of the interconnected world make cyberwar for all actors, states, nonstate, and individuals an inevitability.

Moore is more cautious and argues that to simply argue that technology means cyberwar is and will be dominant ignores actors' motives, threats, and of course political goals and tactics related to all warfare.

YES ⬅

Rick Stella

From Cyberwarfare to Drones, the Future of Conflict Is Electronic

Innovation can take many forms: today's computers are faster. Space travel is cheaper. Artificial intelligence is smarter than ever before. The military is . . . well . . .

While the details on Intel's latest processors or LG's new OLED technology remain a simple Google search away, the uniquely secretive processes of the US military make it tough to know what's truly cutting edge. Much of the work happens behind closed doors, and even when an innovation is made public, layers of classified details often prevent us from ever knowing the full story. We may learn about battery-powered exoskeletons for soldiers from the Defense Advanced Research Projects Agency (DARPA) or real-life rail guns that shoot hunks of metal at blistering speed, but the projects we don't learn about may be even wilder.

So what has true military innovation looked like over the past decade? How are our soldiers equipped today? And what should we expect a decade from now? Are our armed forces really as advanced as Tom Clancy novels would have you believe, or is reliance on an antiquated procurement process dramatically holding it back? What would military technology look like if a company like Apple or Microsoft were in charge?

To understand it all, you'll need to step back more than 10 years, to one fateful day in 2001, to witness the genesis of modern conflict, and the technology the military uses to fight it.

New enemy, new strategies

In the wake of the deadly terrorist attacks on September 11, 2001, the then U.S. President George W. Bush took less than a month to declare war on Osama bin Laden's militant Sunni Islamist organization, al-Qaida. A coordinated attack that claimed the lives of nearly 3,000 people, 9/11 heralded a dramatic shift in U.S. foreign policy that would send ripples throughout our country's armed forces for years.

The United States entered Operation Enduring Freedom, as it became known, with the strongest, most technologically advanced armed forces on the planet. From state-of-the-art jet fighters and automatic grenade launchers to mammoth personnel carriers and tanks, it seemed as though the U.S. military would have an enormous advantage over an army equipped with Soviet-era leftovers and Toyota Land Cruisers.

Yet that technology didn't prepare the United States for what it would actually encounter once it stepped foot on Afghan soil.

"Threat at that time directly informed innovation."

"The United States lacked a real threat," former naval aviation commander Ward Carroll who now serves as editor-in-chief of military news outlet. We Are The Mighty, told Digital Trends. "We were fighting an asymmetrical war after 9/11 and had to adapt to who we were fighting." And as Carroll put it, the "threat at that time directly informed innovation."

The prevalence of improvised explosive devices (IEDs) transformed the battlefield: decades of technological advancements and military might were no match for $10 worth of explosives, shoddy wiring, and a cell phone today's teens would be embarrassed to carry. These crippling booby traps changed the course of what was under development at home, leading to significant upgrades in body-armor technology and paving the way for sand-resistant gear, improved night vision, and a host of advancements for Humvees and other armored vehicles.

The Almighty Dollar

Innovation during the 2000s meant adapting to a new enemy and a new landscape—one that included Iraq by 2003 and Pakistan by 2004. But defense contractors like Lockheed Martin, Northrop Grumman, and others always face a bigger obstacle than merely engineering solutions: procurement budgets.

A DIZZYING AMOUNT OF MONEY STILL GETS SPENT

Though its budgets have decreased since reaching a high in 2011, the U.S. Armed Forces still saw its allocated defense budget sit at a steep $597 billion in 2015. For context, the United States' entire defense spending in 2015 equaled that of China, Saudi Arabia, Russia, the United Kingdom, India, France, and Japan combined. In other words, the U.S. military may often dwarf the rest of the world in terms of innovation but it is a foregone conclusion—one backed up by data—that it blows every other country out of the water in terms of spending.

So where does the money go these days? For starters, some of the annual budget allocated by the Pentagon flows into Lockheed Martin—the manufacturer of the innovative but headache inducing F-35s. In 2014 alone, the Pentagon inked a $4.7 billion deal with Lockheed on an eighth batch of fighter jets that was actually 3.5 percent less expensive than the previous batch and a staggering 57 percent cheaper than batch no. 1. Keep in mind that this contract covers just the F-35 jet built in its various forms and doesn't include the engine, which is separately manufactured by Pratt and Whitney.

Outside of the F-35, the military budget pie splits its funds (not evenly, mind you) between operations and maintenance, military personnel, procurement, research and development and testing, military construction, family housing, among others. All told, the U.S. Navy tends to request (and receive) the most funding of the various branches of military, slightly edging out the Army.

"Because the Pentagon is so constrained by its budget, it's always looking to do more with less," Carroll continued. "This is why drones are so huge today, the tech saves millions of dollars. And unfortunately, sometimes decisions on what to develop are made arbitrarily—there's always a huge political factor—or by third parties." Innovation, Carrol says, takes a back seat when you're working with taxpayer dollars.

Dr. Lawrence Schuette, director of research for the Navy's Office of Naval Research (ONR), agrees. "What

holds us back is that we are one of the great stewards of taxpayer's dollars," he told Digital Trends. "We are resource constrained, as is everybody, so you really don't want to be spending money on things at the wrong amount. But we definitely saw the IED threat in the 2000s and worked very hard with what we had to go after it."

Born from this threat were sand- and IED-resistant armored vehicles and weapons, efficient body armor capable of protecting soldiers while remaining lightweight, and strategically placed forward operating bases. As the wars in Afghanistan and Iraq plodded on, so did the ways of dealing with IEDs. The Foster-Miller TALON allowed soldiers to destroy IEDs from up to 1,000 meters away. Why put soldiers in harm's way when a remote-controlled robot could sift out danger instead?

But the IED still ruled both conflicts. According to the Iraq Coalition Casualty Count website, roughly 1,509 Americans have been killed by IEDs in Iraq since July of 2003. Clearly, there was a problem—and we threw money at it.

In 2001, before Bush launched operations in Afghanistan, Iraq, and Pakistan, the United States' annual defense budget sat at roughly $335 billion. It was a staggering figure, but as the years went on and America became embroiled in desert conflicts, the military budget ballooned. After entering Operation Enduring Freedom, the military's budget rose just slightly to $362 billion for the 2002 fiscal year. Each subsequent year saw a significant increase—anywhere from $60 to $70 billion—with spending topping out at a whopping $721 billion by 2010, more than double where it had been at the beginning of the decade.

Boots Off the Ground

As far back as the Cold War, the United States has employed unmanned aerial vehicles (UAVs), more popularly referred to today as drones. Though the first batches of these devices were used strictly for surveillance, a prevailing desire to get soldiers out of harm's way led to weaponizing them as well.

Enter the Predator drone, an unmanned aerial system from General Atomics introduced in 1995, but first armed with Lockheed Martin–manufactured Hellfire missiles in 2001. Predators and similar UAVs carried out swarms of coordinated attacks in Pakistan against al-Qaida and the Taliban: 2,341 fighters with these groups have reportedly been killed by drone strikes since 2004. By 2009—President Barack Obama's first year in office—drone strikes in Pakistan became as normal as any other operation carried out by the military.

"This goes back to the Pentagon always wanting to be able to accomplish more with less," Carroll explains. "They think, 'Why shoot one of something when you could shoot four?' Drone technology perfectly fits into this line of thinking."

Though drones had been used sparingly since the start of the wars in Afghanistan and Iraq, their perceived effectiveness—though controversial—kept the program thriving into 2010 and beyond. According to the Bureau of Investigative Journalism, more than 400 drone strikes have been carried out inside Pakistan's tribal areas since 2004, with the majority coming between 2009 and 2014.

Just as researchers saw a need for technology to take soldiers out of harm's way when dealing with IEDs, they saw drones as a way to take pilots out of potential danger. Operators on the ground could fly the drones without putting themselves in harm's way.

We Don't Need No Stinkin' Tanks

As drones become staples in the skies above the battlefield, tanks are getting harder to find. But other new weapons are filling the void.

"People are going away from the tank a bit but still want an armored vehicle," Jarrod Krull, Orbital ATK communications manager, told Digital Trends. "Tank-on-tank warfare is likely going away, but having the ability to defeat hardened targets and operate in a somewhat urban terrain is still necessary. This is why we have precision weapons like the XM395 Hatchet, for instance, which is a small, very precise gravity weapon."

Capable of being dropped directly from a UAV, the Hatchet is deadly accurate. Armed with a laser-guided and laser-seeking navigation system, it's an optimized warhead that provides a lot of punch in a very small package. Orbital began developing the weapon after seeing a need for small, propulsion-less weapons that are easily carried—and dropped—by UAVs, helicopters, or bombers. The Hatchet weighs no more than six pounds, so it's as easy to deploy one as it is 2 or 10, depending on the size of the target and the goal.

"While soldiers might have eyes on a moving target, it's hard to get assets on it quickly," Krull explained. "The target is gone before they can get to it. ATK came up with this weapon [the XM 395] that can see the target and get to it immediately."

Though Orbital is reacting to the almost inevitable transition in warfare away from armored vehicles toward drones, the company does still manufacture weaponized solutions for tanks. The Mk44 Bushmaster Automatic Cannon, for instance, is a 30-mm chain gun capable of firing a variety of ammunition types. It can even be modified to fire a 40-mm round, a new area of ammunition Krull said Orbital has shifted into. Boasting low life cycle costs and supreme reliability, if the military does need to be on the ground, the Mk44 is considered bleeding edge.

A $1.5 Trillion Eye in the Sky

Even as reliance on drones grows, the military hasn't moved away from its jet fighter program—quite the opposite, in fact. When Lockheed Martin was awarded the contract to develop and manufacture the next great aircraft, dubbed the Joint Strike Fighter, it was supposed to serve as the revolutionary next step for fighters and supplant the decades-old F-16. The project has taken some time: Lockheed won the contract in 2001, while the Air Force declared the new plane combat-ready on August 2, 2016.

Lockheed's F-35 Lightning II was to feature a combination of strong computational power, complete sensor fusion, unprecedented stealth capabilities, and an innovative new helmet to create a first-of-its-kind fighter experience. In other words, this is the futuristic military tech you were looking for.

"Having come over from other fifth-generation airplanes, I was incredibly curious to see what 'state-of-the-art' meant," F-35 chief test pilot Al Norman told Digital Trends. "We've seen a tremendous transition and acceleration of capabilities over the last five years. It's been an enormous leap in tech capability."

To make the project adaptable to different environments, Lockheed's F-35 comes in three different variations: a conventional takeoff and landing variant (F-35A), a short takeoff and vertical landing variant (F-35B), and a modified F-35A that boasts larger wings with foldable wing tips (F-35C). Norman was quick to point out that each model only takes off and lands differently; once they're in the air, the computer systems that help fly the jet, as well as the pilot interface, are all the same.

Short takeoffs and vertical landings are interesting, but the tech of the F-35 is where the craft truly shines. The new helmet is as innovative as they come, giving pilots a full range of view outside the jet. Furthermore, the head-up display from previous fighters has been completely upgraded to integrate fully with the new helmet.

"It basically gives pilots the ability to see through the eyeballs of the airplane," Norman continued. "An image is projected in a binocular sense through the visor of the helmet once it's plugged into the airplane, and this image is projected anywhere they look. It's got night vision, infrared, all sorts of sensors that switch seamlessly with one another. It basically allows who's flying to become the pilot and the machine; it achieves ultimate synergy."

By simply looking around in the helmet, pilots have the ability to easily designate targets or waypoints. The whole contraption is as if someone were plugging themselves into something out of James Cameron's *Avatar*.

That laundry list of state-of-the-art technology also comes with intense concerns from both Congress and the Department of Defense over inflated costs, performance issues, and changes in leadership. To date, the U.S. military has dumped roughly $1.5 trillion (yes, with a T) into the Joint Strike Fighter program, with each variation of the jet costing anywhere from three to five times more than the decades-old F-15 and F-16 planes. This isn't necessarily surprising—we're talking about cutting-edge tech versus something manufactured in the 1970s, after all. But even the Pentagon has admitted to the program's failures.

Throughout its life span, Lockheed Martin has maintained the F-35s competency, even going so far as to say it's "400 percent more effective in air-to-air combat capability than the best fighters currently available." Perhaps so, but in 2015, an investigation conducted by the Pentagon also found that the Joint Strike Fighter program inaccurately counted aircraft failures to boost statistics and neglected to address "wing drop" concerns, while the helmet continued to trigger too many false alarms and showed stability issues.

"Part of the job of flight tests is to test design to see how it's going. You know, 'What do we need to tweak or fix?'" Norman told us. "It's no different than making software and beta testing to refine it with better software. Many times we hit the nail right on the head—which is by and large what we find—but you just don't know some things until you test it. You can't replicate it until you put the craft through its paces."

Despite a projected annual cost of roughly $12.5 billion, the Department of Defense is pot committed to the Joint Strike Fighter program at this point. Whether it will help battle the enemies of today and tomorrow remains to be seen.

The Military Tech of Tomorrow

Based solely on Hollywood's portrayals, you'd surely picture future military squadrons stock full of robotic soldiers—and their drone counterparts, of course—equipped with concentrated laser weapons capable of incinerating anything on contact. It's not even that farfetched to think the U.S. military might soon consist of supersoldiers outfitted with brain-enhancing drugs or wearable exoskeletons.

In reality, however, this question of what military tech might consist of over the next decade boils down to politics and the threat at hand. As the last decade in the Middle East has shown, the tech we invested in wasn't always at the forefront of what's possible but rather, what was necessary.

But with laser-guided precision rockets, futuristic fighter jets, and an increased reliance on drones proving to be imperative fixtures of today's military, it's clear there's now a renewed interest in emerging technology. In the past, heavy-handed process had an uncanny knack of striking down innovation at every turn because there just wasn't a day-to-day need for it. Today, we have one. For the first time in 15 years, the U.S. military is utilizing science fiction to fight an asymmetrical enemy—and it just might work.

Though the conflict following 9/11 shined bright lights on the inadequacies of relying on old strategies and old technology, the battlefield of tomorrow already appears to be bringing an entirely different threat altogether.

All Signs Point to Cyberwarfare

When attempting to forecast a future U.S. military threat, it's hard to avoid mentioning cyberwarfare: digital attacks from abroad that can spill secrets, disable weapons, hijack key systems, or even shut down power grids. The means may be electronic, but the damage can be quite real.

Though the biggest battles are yet to come, back-office preparation for the change has reportedly been underway since George W. Bush's residency in presidential office. In an apparent effort to derail Iran's nuclear program, the United States (along with Israel) allegedly developed a piece of malware geared toward targeting programmable logic controllers—that is, the type of computers used for automating assembly lines, light fixtures, and in this case, nuclear centrifuges located in Iran. Dubbed Stuxnet, this malware-based cyberweapon was manufactured to destroy the centrifuges, sabotaging Iran's nuclear enrichment. Though neither the United States nor Israel have publicly verified their involvement, various U.S. officials all but confirmed its suspected origin to the *Washington Post* in 2012.

Obama's administration also says it's currently considering elevating the status of the Pentagon's cyberspace defense outfit, Cyber Command—which is currently just a branch of the National Security Agency. Essentially, it would become a sixth branch of the military. With NATO officially deeming cyberspace a potential "battlefield," the U.S. government granting more operational control to a division like Cyber Command seems like the logical next step.

Not only would this open the door for widespread development of cyber weaponry with fewer hurdles, but an elevation in status would also tighten network security across other Department of Defense branches.

This shift from boots on the ground to fingers on a keyboard means military innovation could see yet another dramatic transition over the next 10 years. Instead of developing the next autonomous robot capable of sniffing out IEDs or flying over an enemy camp unsuspected, a hardened focus on strengthening information systems and thwarting cyberterrorists may take precedence. The U.S. military, particularly the U.S. Navy, is already seeing a spike in jobs surrounding cyberwarfare, so preparation for this future threat is underway.

On that battlefield, brains may be more important than brawn.

"Instead of focusing on creating a supersoldier that's capable of increasing his strength, what's more likely to happen is a push to increase cognition and cognitive ability over an entire group of people," ONR's Schuette added. "Just imagine operating at 160 IQ during your entire day at work and what that would mean for productivity."

A dramatic increase in cognitive ability assures you're seven or eight steps ahead of the other side—think Bradley Cooper in *Limitless* without the terrible side effects. Futuristic? Check. Necessary? On a cyber battlefield, quite possibly.

Tech from Today That's Built for Tomorrow

Outside of wild theories and closed-off research, a few of the technological advances of today have specifically been built for use in the future.

DARPA's Sea Hunter, an autonomous submarine-hunting surface vessel, for instance, is essentially a drone for the open seas. A roughly $23 million project, this first-of-its-kind craft only began open-ocean testing this past year. It may still be a couple years from service, but it's loaded to the gills with futuristic tech.

For starters, the rig (dubbed ACTUV) has an abundance of sensors, antifire mechanisms, and fuel tanks that would make some think it was ready to launch into space as opposed to navigating the open ocean. An onboard computer made up of 31 blade servers is the only thing responsible for piloting the rig. Considering it can be out on the open ocean for up to three months at a time, it's paramount this computer works and works well.

"The ACTUV doesn't just answer one of the biggest challenges the Navy faces today, it launches an entirely new class of unmanned vessel with vast possibilities for the future," says Leidos—the company formerly known as Science Applications International Corporation that was contracted by DARPA to build Sea Hunter.

Soldiers, though less relied upon, will find themselves with new tools as well. Orbital's XM25 Counter Defilade Target Engagement System, designed for the U.S. Army, allows soldiers to engage enemies behind cover or targets at range without cover. It uses a 25-mm "airburst round" that sends shrapnel in different directions, striking combatants a soldier might not even be able to see.

"Our idea was 'how can you engage a target that was in a defilade, or hiding behind a wall or rock or car?'" Krull explains. "Or perhaps a sniper firing from a window, or crouched down below a window."

Striving for a Functional Future

After the dramatic rise of IED use in the 2000s, many returning veterans have faced a new battle: missing limbs. Finding a way to properly fit modern prosthetics to help them reenter civilian life is another ongoing area of research.

"Right now, I have an effort with a program officer who attempts to answer this question: 'How do you put a prosthetic limb on someone and actually have the mounting surface be titanium that works itself right into the bone?'" Schuette explained. "A prosthetic without a leather cup resting on the stump but rather something that goes right into the bone. Right now, we have departments analyzing the nanomolecular level and working to develop antirejection materials."

Though Schuette and ONR are searching for solutions to this issue in 2016, research and development of suitable prosthetics has occurred for more than a decade. Once again, however, innovation in this field transpired as a direct response to a need generated by the U.S. military's threat at hand. If roadside bombs weren't as common, amputees—and the needed prosthetics that go along with such an injury—wouldn't have experienced a similar widespread demand.

Utility Over Novelty

Conventional wisdom would suggest the U.S. military has tech readily available to it that an ordinary person wouldn't even be able to fathom; a weapon so destructive and mind-blowing it seems ripped straight from the pages of an Isaac Asimov novel. That may be the case behind closed research doors, but what's actually put into the hands of soldiers has much more to do with necessity and budget. Driven by the decisions made in Washington, a soldier in Afghanistan is given only what money allows and what the decision makers deem a requirement.

In an ever-changing sea of could-be innovation, necessary armaments, and fluctuating budgets, signing off on something shiny and futuristic doesn't always make sense. How do you prepare for the enemy of the future when you have a hard time fighting the enemy of today? Perhaps this is why military procurement often seems like a Catch-22.

Could a billion-dollar tech company like Apple do better? Maybe for comic-book fans. X-ray vision or a strength-enhancing supersuit would be astonishing and groundbreaking, no doubt, but if it didn't serve a direct purpose against the military's current threat, it would gather dust. For better or worse, our military's acquisition formula often quells innovation in favor of safety and current demand. For that reason, the next truly groundbreaking and awe-inspiring military innovation could have some application off the battlefield—think Schuette's comments about an IQ-boosting superdrug. In this world, the next big military contractor could be Pfizer, not General Dynamics.

Our military doesn't lack the tools (or minds) for innovation, but in a practical world, being on the bleeding edge often means finding a way to bleed less.

RICK STELLA is an associate editor for *Digital Trends*.

Daniel Moore  **NO**

Struggling with Cyber:
A Critical Look at Waging War Online

If media coverage is to be believed, we are in the midst of a cyberwar with daily attacks occurring across several theaters. Between dropping "cyber-bombs" on the Islamic State, Chinese intruders pilfering precious technology, and Russian information operations shaping the U.S. political process, it seems that the continuous power struggle between nations is now most commonly waged on the Internet. While there might be some truth to that narrative, the reality is—of course—more nuanced. It's difficult to define and explain attacks that are entirely virtual. To understand this, one must understand a few points about offensive network operations. First, cyber operations are not as novel as they appear. Rather, they draw heavily from the integration of electronic warfare into joint operations. Second, different nations have largely different perspectives on how to employ network capabilities to achieve political objectives. Third, most incidents we label as "cyberattacks" or "cyberwarfare" do not in fact merit being called such.

Cyber Evolution

The United States and NATO have declared networks to be a fifth domain of warfare, cementing the perception that it is novel and distinct. We have also seen massive investments and doctrinal updates toward cyber-related activities. But network operations are neither entirely novel nor do they necessarily constitute warfare. Perhaps then we should stop automatically defining them as such. Labeling an incident an "attack" can have tremendous consequences, especially when carried out by one nation against another. Indeed, NATO's secretary general just revealed that alliance's leaders "decided that a cyberattack can trigger Article 5." It is therefore crucial that everyone from the world leader to the average citizen have an informed understanding of what exactly constitutes an "attack."

Offensive network operations—essentially military cyberattacks—are a combination of information operations, intelligence collection, and electronic warfare. As such, they draw familiar characteristics from each of these, creating a unique but not altogether new activity. Much like their electronic predecessors, offensive network operations target the trust between operators and equipment. They do this by influencing the flow and presentation of data. If operators can't rely on their sensors, communication links, or autonomous platforms, they are not left with much else. Rather than physically targeting human beings or equipment, network operations can qualify as attacks when they seek to degrade, disrupt, or destroy software and networks.

Let's turn to a classic example of electronic warfare: targeting radars to cripple antiair defenses. This is traditionally done by flooding the radar image with false matches, interfering with the transmission itself, or influencing the radar waves returned by a hostile aircraft so it appears as something else. These are essentially all external means of making the radar less functional.

A modern network attack on the same air defense network may instead use internal means. By penetrating the air defense network, an adversary may alter the inner workings of the network's radars or targeting systems. Friendly aircraft could be recoded as hostile aircraft and vice versa or altogether wiped off the radar image. Targeting coordinates might be altered so that any missiles launched would hit empty space. Those are only a few of the possibilities for a nuanced but significant operation against an air defense system.

The myth of the high-impact high-availability cyberattack is pervasive but ultimately difficult to implement at scale. As with their predecessors in electronic warfare, network operations are voracious consumers of accurate intelligence. It is impossible to conduct high-quality, impactful offensive network operations without first gaining in-depth familiarity with the specific target. In most cases, in order to shut down military equipment by way of a cyberattack, an attacker would need to (a) obtain access to the platform or network, (b) analyze the system for specific vulnerabilities, (c) weaponize an exploit capable of achieving the operational goal, (d) maintain a covert foothold in the network until the attack is needed, and finally (e) successfully execute the attack and perform a bomb damage assessment—the digital equivalent of observing the impact of an armed attack on a target. This process will not only vary per type of military hardware but potentially even per different deployments of the same hardware. Even the same equipment deployed in other scenarios and configurations might call for a new operation.

Cyber capabilities that work "out of the box" often provide little more than good tactical value. In a recent publication, the U.S. Army detailed how its fire teams utilize cyber capabilities against the Islamic State's communication networks used by the Islamic State in the field. Much like classic jamming, Army operators attack the communication network itself rather than its electromagnetic transmissions. Network operations are therefore often viewed as a component of joint operations, contributing to warfighting efforts by supporting other domains and reducing adversary capability to do the same. They do not include all adversarial interactions in cyberspace.

Differing Perspectives

The West does not hold monopoly over all matters cyber, but it does seem to have a monopoly on its obsession with the terminology. While Western audiences obsess about "cyberattacks" and "cyberwar," other nations have been busily integrating network operations into their doctrine in unique ways. Different approaches to targeting networks represent varying requirements and doctrine. Where China might use network operations to offset conventional superiority of a highly connected force such as that of the U.S. military, Israel might view network operations as a set of tools that enable stealthier, less violent strikes.

Russia has an elaborate history of maneuvering to influence the flow and shape of information. However, it has no independent concept of "cyberwarfare." The Russian transliteration of the term "kibervoyna" is primarily used when discussing Western approaches to network operations. Instead, Russian military doctrine and official literature as analyzed by experts portray network attacks holistically, as another toolset used both in peace and in wartime to help facilitate political success. In this sense, cyberattacks are a specific set of capabilities on an expansive information operations spectrum. There are ample examples to perfectly encapsulate different facets of this approach. An earlier case is the 2007 Estonia incident, when the removal of a Soviet-era war memorial from a Tallinn square triggered a barrage of denial of service attacks against Estonian websites, ostensibly facilitated by Russia to signal its political displeasure. While the attack had minimal lasting effect or political value, it was heard loudly and clearly in Estonia and the rest of NATO. Both quickly proceeded to establish NATO's Cooperative Cyber Defense Center of Excellence in Tallinn.

The breach of the U.S. Democratic National Committee in 2016 and the clumsy but effective disinformation campaign that followed was an unprecedented breach of sovereignty perpetrated through a network intrusion. It embodied the Russian approach to information operations, which view them in part as a means of beneficially shaping the political landscape in peacetime, thereby creating more favorable outcomes befitting Russian grand strategy. In this sense, while the operation was not an attack or cyberwar by any meaningful metric, it indicated the type of operations for which network intrusions are often more suitable for when used strategically to pursue political objectives.

There are other operational Russian examples that show the usefulness of cyberattacks in political signaling. In December 2015, a portion of the Ukrainian power grid suffered several hours of outage. Ukrainian authorities quickly identified it as a Russian-perpetrated network attack. It caused minimal lasting damage and had dubious impact in the ongoing war in the country's east, but it, at the very least, sent an unmistakable message: if conflict escalates, attacks against critical infrastructure are both on the table and within Moscow's technical and operational reach. While we have no visibility into political messaging that may have accompanied the operation, it perhaps was an attempt at political coercion or deterrence by way of cyberattack.

A controversial report by the U.S. information security company CrowdStrike suggests that Russia also relies on cyber operations for direct battlefield assistance. A network operation tied to Russian intelligence by technical indicators successfully targeted a mobile phone application supposedly used by Ukrainian military forces to calculate and direct fire for a specific type of artillery. If the details are even partially true, it suggests that a network operation directly contributed to physically targeting military hardware. However, as the operation was only used to collect intelligence on artillery locations rather than tamper with guidance calculation, the operation would again fall more within the bounds of an intelligence maneuver than an actual attack. If the operation had also covertly altered the targeting information as to impact the accuracy of Ukrainian artillery fire, that could have constituted a cyberattack.

Alternatively, Chinese doctrine has gradually cemented the role of network operations as a key component in shattering conventional asymmetries. This approach permeates beyond the battlefield to economic and political agendas. Operations to illicitly acquire intellectual property can allow getting access to cutting edge technologies instead of expensively developing or purchasing them, thereby subverting the need for long and costly research processes. At the same time, vast outfits of indeterminably affiliated online users identify potential online political hotspots and troll via commentary to skew public opinion. Other units attempt to infiltrate adversary military networks to preposition for possible wartime efforts.

After the first Gulf War, the People's Liberation Army identified the unmistakable reality of the modern U.S. doctrine. It was made glaringly obvious that integrating joint warfare based on an unprecedented flow of networked sensory data allowed effective direction of resources and combat operations. Simultaneously, networked joint warfare created new t so-called centers of gravity. The dependence of American forces on continuous data means if one can reduce the availability of that data or corrupt it, one can severely impact U.S. military operations. Those writing Chinese military doctrine gradually responded, with increasing references to network attacks designed to hinder forward-deployed U.S. regional forces. If the Chinese military sought to move against Taiwan or targets in the South China Sea, targeting U.S. forces through cyberspace could presumably slow their ability to muster an effective response to defend an ally. China could do this by tampering with logistical data, undermining sensors, or disrupting communication.

Excluding for Clarity

An intelligence operation—no matter how successful—is not intrinsically an armed attack. When intruders breached the U.S. Office of Personnel Management in 2015 and made off with an exorbitant amount of sensitive information, some in the government elected to label the intrusion an attack on U.S. infrastructure. By contrast, the Chinese government—which was, according to Washington, responsible for the operation—quickly labeled the theft as a criminal incident and even claimed to arrest the perpetrators. Aside from sharp rhetoric, the United States had precious little recourse available that would not be disproportionately escalatory. The reason for this was simple: while undoubtedly an embarrassing loss of important, the OPM breach was by no means an attack. Valuable intelligence was stolen, but no system or network was impacted in any way.

Influence campaigns also do not automatically merit being called attacks. At times, nations seeking to change the political climate of other countries would seek to do so by trying to covertly shape public discourse and sharing of information. This particular brand of information operations is practiced by many nations and often referred to as "active measures" when wielded by Russia. Perhaps the most notable such case was the alleged intervention of Russian intelligence agencies in the contentious 2016 U.S. election process. The hack into the Democratic National Committee turned into an awkwardly spun web of disinformation seemingly intent on discrediting the Clinton-led Democratic campaign. Even a brazen operation that constituted a meaningful breach of national sovereignty did not eventually qualify as an actual attack by Russia on the United States. Could it have triggered hostilities between Russia and the United States under different circumstances? Perhaps. It was, after all, a blatant political intervention. Ironically, even official Russian doctrine specifically lists significant breaches of political sovereignty as one of its top military threats:

> Use of information and communication technologies for the military–political purposes to take actions which run counter to international law, being aimed against sovereignty, political independence, territorial integrity of states, and posing threat to the international peace, security, global, and regional stability.

But despite its significance, the operation against the Democratic National Convention did not truly qualify as network-enabled violence on its own. While documents were perhaps tampered with for political effect, no system, network, or platform were directly degraded or manipulated in the operation. As then-Director of National Intelligence Clapper confirmed, it was an aggressive influence operation, it was a successful espionage campaign, but it wasn't a cyberattack.

Lastly, intrusions and theft perpetrated for a financial motive—especially but not exclusively when carried out by criminal groups—are neither attacks nor do they constitute cyberwar. Even if a skilled malware group with possible links to the Russian government exclusively targets customers of Western banks, it does not indicate political will or a military circumstance. Similarly, a national effort by North Korea to target the SWIFT financial network in an elaborate network operation to steal vast amounts of money does not inherently mean it is an attack. Were the intruders to cripple SWIFT networks just as North Korean intruders previously targeted Sony, rather than just a theft of money, that could arguably be framed as an attack on the global financial order. Instead, it was an elaborate and illegal operation certainly in breach of international norms but otherwise nonviolent in nature. The operation was just a modern, networked version of criminal activities North Korea routinely undertakes to subvert crippling sanctions—a cyber-enabled bank robbery.

Focusing on Reality

It's crucial to pinpoint what cyberwarfare actually means. Definitions inform perception and discussion, which in turn affects the shaping of public policy. If all manners of network intrusions continue to be labeled as cyberattacks—or, worse, as warfare—the discussion around actual offensive network operation suffers immeasurably. Intelligence operations are not comfortably on the spectrum of war. Nor is crime. Nor are peacetime influence operations, as wildly successful and sovereignty-breaching as they may be. Taking the notion that intelligence operations constitute attacks risks further increasing already rising global tension levels. If an operation is perceived as an attack, the victim is then expected to respond with the toolset reserved for confronting attacks. Instead, intelligence campaigns are accepted as commonplace between rivals and allies alike. Victims may attempt to mitigate, pursue countermeasures, or even deter, but the playing field is decidedly calmer than that of the battlefield.

There are still plenty of visible instances in which network operations are integrated into actual military doctrine across all levels of warfare. From assisting combatants in degrading enemy communication infrastructure to disabling air defense networks, the potential for meaningful integration of network operations into joint doctrine is immense. For tactical value, these operations require extensive research and development to identify vulnerabilities in targeted adversary military hardware. For strategic operations, attacks must be predicated by elaborate peacetime intelligence operations designed to acquire access to the sensitive systems later targeted in conflict. This means that the more comprehensive and impactful the network attack seeks to be, the more prepositioning and accurate, consistent intelligence is required to enable success.

It is more constructive to view "cyberwarfare" as offensive network operations aimed at attaining military objectives. This is a thoroughly restrictive definition excluding the overwhelming majority of intrusions reported on daily, but it is meant to be so. It still leaves a wide range of possibilities, from the most tactical attacks against a local communication grid to operational attacks against defensive hardware, costly strategic operations meant to cripple joint warfare throughout a theater and even attacks against critical infrastructure to weaken populace resolve. Different capabilities and resources characterize each tier of operations, but they all reliably fall within the military gamut.

When next confronted with a network intrusion characterized as an attack, it is important to ask who was targeted and how were they impacted? If it's written up or described as cyberwarfare, it is even more important to ask who was involved on both sides? Was there a discernible military–political objective? Were victim assets degraded, disrupted, or destroyed in any meaningful way? Applying these simple questions to most of what is commonly labeled as cyberwarfare will immediately exclude almost all such cases. That's for the better.

DANIEL MOORE is a PhD candidate focusing on cyberwarfare at the Department of War.

EXPLORING THE ISSUE

Is Cyberwar the Future of 21st-Century Conflict?

Critical Thinking and Reflection

1. Can cyberwar eliminate the need for conventional war?
2. Will cyberwar be a constant factor in the behavior of states and other actors if it is made as "painless" as it appears to be?
3. What are the political ramifications of such an evolution?
4. Will it make warfare more or less likely?
5. Does it eliminate some of the deleterious effects of war on its combatants?

Is There Common Ground?

"Futurists and purists" will debate the nature of warfare for some time in the twenty-first century as they did in the twentieth with the advent of airpower and mechanized tanks. What all can agree upon is that technology has allowed warfare to develop high levels of precision that will shape and guide its prosecution for decades to come.

Additional Resources

"Dark Territory: The Secret History of Cyber War." By Fred Kaplan.

"Binary Bullets: The Ethics of Cyberwarfare" by Fritz Allhoff, Adam Hensacke, Bradley Jay Strawser.

"Cyber War Versus Cyber Realities: Cyber Conflict in the International System." by Brandon Valeriano and Ryan C. Maness.

"NEW Digital Age: Reshaping the Future of People, Nations & Business" by Jared A. Cohen, Eric Schmidt.

Yong-Soo, Eun and Judith Sita Aßmann. "Cyberwar: Taking Stock of Security and Warfare in the Digital Age." *International Studies Perspectives*, vol. 17, no. 3, Aug. 2016, pp. 343–360.

Cimbala, Stephen J. "Nuclear Cyberwar and Crisis Management." *Comparative Strategy*, vol. 35, no. 2, Apr. 2016, pp. 114–123.

Paletta, Damian, et al. "CYBERWAR IGNITES NEW ARMS RACE. (Cover Story)." *Wall Street Journal—Eastern Edition*, vol. 266, no. 87, 12 Oct. 2015, pp. A1–A12.

Zittrain, Jonathan. "Netwar": The Unwelcome Militarization of the Internet Has Arrived." *Bulletin of the Atomic Scientists*, vol. 73, no. 5, Sept. 2017, pp. 300–304.

Schmidt, Eric. "We Must Prepare Ourselves for the Cyberwars of the Future." *Time*, Time, time.com/4606057/cyberwars-of-the-future/.

Internet References . . .

Foreign Affairs

https://www.foreignaffairs.com

Foreign Policy

http://foreignpolicy.com

GLOBSEC

https://www.globsec.org

Time

http://time.com/

Selected, Edited, and with Issue Framing Material by:
Mark Owen Lombardi, *Maryville University*

ISSUE

Is Nuclear War More Likely in the Next Decade?

YES: **John F. Harris and Bryan Bender,** from "Bill Perry Is Terrified. Why Aren't You?" *Politico Magazine* (2017)

NO: **Stephen M. Walt,** from "The World Doesn't Need Any More Nuclear Strategies," *Foreign Policy* (2018)

Learning Outcomes

After reading this issue, you will be able to:

- Understand the availability of nuclear weapons and in what the relative stability is of the nonproliferation regime is.
- Determine where the crisis points may be and also evaluate the role of the nuclear states in preventing nuclear war.

ISSUE SUMMARY

YES: The authors, both writers at Politico, through working with former Secretary of Defense Bill Perry paint a pessimistic picture of the likelihood of a nuclear war in the coming years due to issues such as nuclear proliferation, great power rivalry, and increasing tensions among key global actors.

NO: Stephen Walt, Harvard professor at the JFK School of Government, articulates a nuanced critique of nuclear politics but still maintains that the use of the nuclear deterrent has and will continue to make nuclear war less likely over time despite changes dimensions in the current global landscape.

Since the development of nuclear weaponry and America's use of the nuclear bomb against the Japanese in World War II, the world has lived in the nuclear age. That age was characterized by the steady proliferation of nuclear weapons by first, the Soviet Union (1949), then Great Britain (1952), France (1960), China (1964), India (1974), Pakistan (1998), and North Korea (2006). In addition, Israel developed some 300 nuclear weapons in the early 1970s but has never claimed to have them.

The bulk of the nuclear age was dominated by the nuclear rivalry of the United States and the USSR personified by the policy of mutually assured destruction (MAD). This policy simply stated meant that each side possessed enough weapons to absorb an attack from the other and then retaliate thus insuring the destruction of the other. This has been surmised kept the peace between the two states. Ironically, despite the animus between the two states, they shared the policy goal of preventing other states from acquiring nuclear weapons, and this shared interest helped construct a strong nonproliferation regime by treaty. To date most but not all states are part of the agreement.

After the fall of the Soviet Union, the nuclear age entered a different somewhat more volatile phase. Issues such as the security of Russia's nuclear stockpiles combined with the dissemination of nuclear information and technology has led other states to actively pursue such weapons with varying degrees of success and failure. States such as North Korea were successful, while others such as Syria, Iraq, and Iran have not been able to cross the threshold.

When one adds the prevalence of terrorist groups attempting to procure weapons from various sources and you have a more unstable nuclear world than during the cold war. This is because of several factors. The first is the simple fact that more actors can gain the know-how to build a nuclear weapon no matter how rudimentary. Building a so-called dirty bomb (less sophisticated without an automatic delivery system) is easier than ever if one can procure the fissionable material and a triggering system. Second, purchasing such a weapon is more likely today because such weapons are theoretically more available if for no other reason than North Korea possesses such weapons and has never show a reticence to engage in anti-peaceful actions in the international community. They have already worked with Syria, for example, in such endeavors. Third, statistics tell us that with every year, the likelihood of some kind of nuclear attack by some state or groups increases. For example, Israel has already declared that were Iran to develop a bomb that they would consider that an existential threat and therefore have to act. Similarly, instability in Pakistan may lead India to act lest Pakistan nuclear weapons fall into radical fundamentalist hands.

Harris and Bender discuss the views of former defense secretary William Perry who argues that we have never been closer to nuclear war than at this time. He argues that we will see such an exchange in the next decade because of a host of factors alluded to above.

Walt sees the nuclear deterrent of the United States among others to still be a strong mitigating factor in the advent that any actor may consider a nuclear attack against another actor.

YES ←

John F. Harris and Bryan Bender

Bill Perry Is Terrified. Why Aren't You?

How an 89-Year-Old Cold Warrior became America's Nuclear Conscience.

At this naked moment in the American experiment, when many people perceive civilization on the verge of blowing up in some metaphorical sense, there is an elderly man in California hoping to seize your attention about another possibility.

It is that civilization is on the verge of blowing up in a nonmetaphorical sense.

William J. Perry is 89 now, at the tail end of one of his generation's most illustrious careers in national security. By all rights, the former U.S. secretary of Defense, a trained mathematician who served or advised nearly every administration since Eisenhower, should be filling out the remainder of his years in quiet reflection on his achievements. Instead, he has set out on an urgent pilgrimage.

Bill Perry has become, he says with a rueful smile, "a prophet of doom."

His life's work, most of it highly classified, was nuclear weapons—how to maximize the fearsome deterrent power of the U.S. arsenal, how to minimize the possibility that the old Soviet arsenal would obliterate the United States and much of the planet along the way. Perry played a supporting role in the Cuban Missile Crisis, during which he went back to his Washington hotel room each night, fearing he had only hours left to live. He later founded his own successful defense firm, helped revolutionize the American way of high-tech war, and honed his diplomatic skills seeking common ground on security issues with the Soviets and Chinese—all culminating as head of the Pentagon in the early years after the end of the Cold War.

Nuclear bombs are an area of expertise Perry had assumed would be largely obsolete by now, seven decades after Hiroshima, a quarter-century after the fall of the Soviet Union, and in the flickering light of his own life. Instead, nukes are suddenly—*insanely*, by Perry's estimate—once again a contemporary nightmare and an

emphatically ascendant one. At the dawn of 2017, there is a Russian president making bellicose boasts about his modernized arsenal. There is an American president-elect who breezily free-associates on Twitter about starting a new nuclear arms race. Decades of cooperation between the two nations on arms control is nearly at a standstill. And, unlike the original Cold War, this time there is a world of busy fanatics excited by the prospect of a planet with more bombs—people who have already demonstrated the desire to slaughter many thousands of people in an instant and are zealously pursuing ever more deadly means to do so.

And there's one other difference from the Cold War: Americans no longer think about the threat every day.

Nuclear war isn't the subtext of popular movies or novels; disarmament has fallen far from the top of the policy priority list. The largest upcoming generation, the millennials, were raised in a time when the problem felt largely solved, and it's easy for them to imagine it's still quietly fading into history. The problem is, it's no longer fading. "Today, the danger of some sort of a nuclear catastrophe is greater than it was during the Cold War," Perry said in an interview in his Stanford office, "and most people are blissfully unaware of this danger."

It is a turn of events that has an old man newly obsessed with a question: why isn't everyone as terrified as he is?

Perry's hypothesis for the disconnect is that much of the population, especially that rising portion with no clear memories of the first Cold War, is suffering from a deficit of comprehension. Even a single nuclear explosion in a major city would represent an abrupt and possibly irreversible turn in modern life, upending the global economy, forcing every open society to suspend traditional liberties and remake itself into a security state. "The political, economic, and social consequences are beyond what people understand," Perry says. And yet many people place this scenario in roughly the same category as the meteor strike that supposedly wiped out the dinosaurs—frightening, to be sure, but something of an abstraction.

So Perry regard his last great contribution of a 65-year career as a crusade to stimulate the public imagination—to share the vivid details of his own nightmares. He is doing so in a recent memoir, in a busy public speaking schedule, in half-empty hearing rooms on Capitol Hill, and increasingly with an online presence aimed especially at young people. He has enlisted the help of his 28-year-old granddaughter to figure out how to engage a new generation, including through a series of virtual lectures known as an MOOC, or massive open online course.

He is eagerly signing up for "Ask Me Anything" chats on Reddit, in which some people still confuse him with William "The Refrigerator" Perry of NFL fame. He posts his ruminations on YouTube, where they give Katy Perry no run for her money, even as the most popular are closing in on 100,000 views.

One of the nightmare scenarios Perry invokes most often is designed to roust policy makers who live and work in the nation's capital. The terrorists would need enriched uranium. Due to the elaborate and highly industrial nature of production, hard to conceal from surveillance, fissile material is still hard to come by—but, alas, far from impossible. Once it is procured, with help from conspirators in a poorly secured overseas commercial power centrifuge facility, the rest of the plot as Perry imagines it is no great technological or logistical feat. The mechanics of building a crude nuclear device are easily within the reach of well-educated and well-funded militants. The crate would arrive at Dulles International Airport, disguised as agricultural freight. The truck bomb that detonates on Pennsylvania Avenue between the White House and Capitol instantly kills the president, vice president, House speaker, and 80,000 others.

Where exactly is your office? Your house? And then, as Perry spins it forward, how credible would you find the warnings, soon delivered to news networks that five more bombs are set to explode in unnamed U.S. cities, once a week for the next month, unless all U.S. military personnel overseas are withdrawn immediately?

If this particular scenario does not resonate with you, Perry can easily rattle off a long roster of others—a regional war that escalates into a nuclear exchange, a miscalculation between Moscow and Washington, a computer glitch at the exact wrong moment. They are all ilks of the same theme—the dimly understood threat that the science of the 20th century is set to collide with the destructive passions of the 21st.

"We're going back to the kind of dangers we had during the Cold War," Perry said. "I really thought in 1990, 1991, 1992, that we left those behind us. We're starting to reinvent them. We and the Russians and others don't understand that what we're doing is recreating those dangers—or maybe they don't remember the dangers. For younger people, they didn't live through those dangers. But when you live through a Cuban Missile Crisis up close and you live through a false alarm up close, you do understand how dangerous it is, and you believe you should do everything you could possibly do to [avoid] going back."

***

For people who follow the national security priesthood, the dire scenarios are all the more alarming for who is delivering them. Through his long years in government, Perry invariably impressed colleagues as the calmest person in the room, relentlessly rational, such that people who did not know him well—his love of music and literature and travel—regarded his as a purely analytical mind, emotion subordinated to logic and duty.

Starting in the 1950s as a technology executive and entrepreneur in some of the most secretive precincts of the defense industry, he gradually took on a series of high-level government assignments that gave him one of the most quietly influential careers of the Cold War and its aftermath.

Fifteen years before serving as Bill Clinton's secretary of defense, Perry was the Pentagon official in charge of weapons research during the Carter administration. It was from this perch that he may have had his most far-reaching impact and left him in some circles as a legendary figure. He used his office to give an essential push to two ideas that transformed warfare over the next generation decisively to American advantage. One idea was stealth technology, which allowed U.S. warplanes to fly over enemy territory undetected. The other was precision-guided munitions, which allowed U.S. bombs to land with near-perfect accuracy.

During the Clinton years, Perry so prized his privacy that he initially turned down the job of Defense secretary—changing his mind only after Clinton and Al Gore pleaded with him that the news media scrutiny wouldn't be so bad.

The reputation he built over a life in the public sphere is starkly at odds with this latest highly impassioned chapter of Perry's career. Harold Brown, who also is 89, first recruited Perry into government and was Perry's boss while serving as Defense secretary in the Carter years. "No one would have thought of Bill Perry as a crusader," he says. "But he is on a crusade."

Lee Perry, his wife of nearly 70 years, is living in an elder care facility, her once buoyant presence now lost to dementia. Perry himself, lucid as ever, has seen his physical frame become frail and stooped. Rather than slowing his schedule, he has accelerated his travels to plead with people to awaken to the danger. A trip to Washington includes a dinner with national security reporters and testimony on Capitol Hill. Back home in California, he's at the Google campus to prod engineers to contemplate that their world may not last long enough for their dreams of technology riches to come true. He's created an advocacy group, the William J. Perry project, devoted to public education about nuclear weapons. He's enlisted both his granddaughter and his 64-year-old daughter, Robin Perry, in the cause.

But if his profile is rising, his style is essentially unchanged. He is a man known for self-effacement, trying to shape an era known for relentless self-promotion, a voice of quiet precision in a time of devil-take-the-hindmost bombast. The rational approach to problem-solving that propelled his career and won him adherents and friends in both political parties and even among some of America's erstwhile enemies remains his guide—in this case, by endeavoring to calculate the possibilities and probabilities of a terrorist attack, regional nuclear war, or horrible miscalculation with Russia.

"I want to be very clear," he said. "I do not think it is a probability this year or next year or anytime in the foreseeable future. But the consequence is so great, we have to take it seriously. And there are things to greatly lower those possibilities that we're simply not doing."

***

Perry really did not expect he would have to write this chapter of his public life. His official career closed with what seemed then an unambiguous sense of mission accomplished. By the time he arrived in the Pentagon's top job in 1994, the Cold War was over, and the main item on the nuclear agenda seemed to be cleaning up no-longer-needed arsenals. As defense secretary, Perry stood with his Russian counterpart, Pavel Grachev, as they jointly blew up missile silos in the former Soviet Union and tilled sunflower seeds in the dirt.

"I finally thought by the end of the '80s we lived through this horrible experience and it's behind us," Perry said. "When I was secretary, I fully believed it was behind us."

After leaving the Pentagon, he accepted an assignment from Clinton to negotiate an end to North Korea's nuclear development program—and seemed agonizingly close to a breakthrough as the last days of the president's term expired.

Now, he sees his grandchildren inheriting a planet possibly more dangerous than it was during his public career. No one could doubt that the September 11 terrorists would have gladly used nuclear bombs instead of airplanes if they had had them, and it seems only a matter of time until they try. Instead of a retreating threat in North Korea, that fanatical regime now possesses as many as eight nuclear bombs and is just one member of a growing nuclear club. Far from a new partnership with Russia, Vladimir Putin has given old antagonisms a malevolent new face. American policy makers talk of spending up to $1 trillion to modernize the nuclear arsenal. And now comes Donald Trump with a long trail of statements effectively shrugging his shoulders about a world newly bristling with bombs and people with reasons to use them.

Perry knew Hillary Clinton well professionally and says he admired both her and Bill Clinton for their professional judgment though he was never a personal intimate of either. He was prescient before the election in expressing skepticism about how voters would respond to the dynastic premise of the Clinton campaign—a healthy democracy should grow new voices—but was as surprised as everyone else on Election Day. Donald Trump was not the voice he was looking for, to put it mildly, but he has responded to the Trump cyclone with modulated restraint. Perry said he assumes his most truculent rhetoric isn't serious, the utterances of a man who assumed his words were for political effect only and had no real consequences.

Now that they do, Perry is hoping to serve as a kind of ambassador to rationality. He said he is hoping for audiences soon, with Trump if the incoming president will see him, and certainly Trump's national security team, which includes several people Perry knows, including Defense Secretary nominee James Mattis.

There is little doubt the message if the meeting comes. "We are starting a new Cold War," he says. "We seem to be sleepwalking into this new nuclear arms race. . . . We and the Russians and others don't understand what we are doing."

"I am not suggesting that this Cold War and this arms race are identical to the old one," Perry added. "But in many ways, it is just as bad, just as dangerous. And totally unnecessary."

***

Perry had been brooding over the question for a year. It was in the early 1950s, he was still in his 20s, and the subject was partial differential equations—the topic of his PhD thesis. A particular problem had been absorbing him, day in and day out, hours and hours on end. Then, out of nowhere, a light came on.

"I woke up in the middle of the night, and it was all there," Perry recalled. "It was all there, and I got out of bed and sat down. The next two or three hours, I wrote my thesis, and from the first word I wrote down, I never doubted what the last word was going to be: it was a magic moment."

The story is a reminder of something definitional about Bill Perry. Before he became in recent years an apostle of disarmament, before he sat atop the nation's war-making apparatus in the 1990s, before he was the executive of a defense contractor specializing in the most complex arenas of Cold War surveillance in the 1960s, he was a young man in love with mathematics.

In those days, Perry had planned on a career as a math professor. His attraction to math was not merely practical, in the way that engineers or architects rely on math. The appeal was just as much aesthetic, in ways that people who are not numbers people—political life tends to be dominated by word people—cannot easily comprehend. To Perry's mind, there was a purity to math, a beauty to the patterns and relationships, that was not unlike music. Math for Perry represented analytical discipline, a way of achieving mastery not only over numerical problems but any hard problem, by breaking it down into essential parts, distilling complexity into simplicity.

This trait was why Pentagon reporters in the 1990s liked spending time around Perry. When most public officials are asked a question, one studies the transcript later to decipher a succession of starts and stalls, sentence fragments, and ellipses that cumulatively convey an impressionistic sense of mind but no clear fixed meaning. Perry's sentences, by contrast, always cut with surgical precision. It was one reason Clinton White House officials often held their breath when he gave interviews—Perry might make news by being clear on subjects, such as ethnic warfare in the Balkans or a nuclear showdown in North Korea that the West Wing preferred to try to fog over.

"I've never been able to attack a policy problem with a mathematical formula," he recalled, "but I have always believed that the rigorous way of thinking about a problem was good. It separated the fact from the bullshit, and that's very important sometimes, to separate what you can from what you would *hope* you can do."

Perry wishes more people were familiar with the concept of "expected value." That is a statistical way of understanding events of very large magnitude that have a low probability. The large magnitude event could be something good, like winning a lottery ticket. Or it could be something bad, like a nuclear bomb exploding. Because the odds of winning the lottery are so low, the rational thing is to save your money and not buy the ticket. As for a nuclear explosion, by Perry's lights, the consequences are so grave that the rational thing would be for people in the United States and everywhere to be in a state of peak alarm about their vulnerability and for political debate to be dominated by discussion of how to reduce the risk.

And just how high is the risk? The answer of course is ultimately unknowable. Perry's point, though, is that it's a hell of a lot higher than you think.

Perry invites his listeners to consider all the various scenarios that might lead to a nuclear event. "Mathematically speaking, you add those all together in one year it is still just a possibility, not a probability," he reckons. "But then you go out 10, 20 years and each time this possibility repeats itself, and then it starts to become a probability. How much time we have to get those possibility numbers lower, I don't know. But sooner or later the odds are going to get us, I am afraid."

***

Almost uniquely among living Americans, Bill Perry has actually faced down the prospect of nuclear war before—twice.

In the fall of 1962, Bill Perry was 35, father of five young children, living in the Bay Area and serving as director of Sylvania's Electronic Defense Laboratories—driving his station wagon to recitals in between studying missile trajectories and the radius of nuclear detonations.

Where he resided was not then called Silicon Valley, but the exuberance and spirit of creative possibility we now associate with the region was already evident. The giants then were Bill Hewlett and David Packard, men Perry deeply admired and wished to emulate in his own business career. The innovation engine at that time, however, was not consumer technology; it was the government's appetite for advantage in a mortal struggle against a powerful Soviet foe. Perry was known as a star in the highly complex field of weapons surveillance and interpretation.

So it was not a surprise, one bright October day, for Perry to get a call from Albert "Bud" Wheelon, a friend at the Central Intelligence Agency. Wheelon said he wanted Perry in Washington for a consultation. Perry said he'd juggle his schedule and be there the next week.

"No," Wheelon responded. "I need to see you right away."

Perry caught the red-eye from San Francisco, and went straight to the CIA, where he was handed photographs whose meaning was instantly clear to him. They were of Soviet missiles stationed in Cuba. For the next couple weeks, Perry would stay up past midnight each evening poring over the latest reconnaissance photos and help write the analysis that senior officials would present the next morning to President Kennedy.

Perry experienced the crisis partly as ordinary citizen, hearing Kennedy on television draw an unambiguous line against Soviet missiles in this hemisphere and promising that any attack would be met with "a full retaliatory response." But he possessed context, about the capabilities of weapons and the daily state of play in the crisis, that gave him a vantage point superior to that of all but perhaps a few dozen people.

"I was part of a small team—six or eight people," he recounted of those days 54 years earlier. "Half of them technical experts, half of them intelligence analysts, or photo interpreters. It was a minor role, but I was seeing all the information coming in. I thought every day when I went back to the hotel, it was the last day of my life because I knew exactly what nuclear weapons could do. I knew it was not just a lot of people getting killed. It was the end of civilization and I thought it was about to happen."

It was years later that Perry, like other more senior participants in the crisis, learned how right that appraisal was. Nuclear bombs weren't only heading toward Cuba on Soviet ships, as Kennedy believed and announced to Americans at the time. Some of them were already there, and local commanders had been given authority to use them if Americans launched a preemptive raid on Cuba, as Kennedy was being urged, goaded even, by Air Force General Curtis LeMay and other military commanders. At the same time, Soviet submarines were armed and one commander had been on the verge of launching them until other officers on the vessel talked him out of it. Either event would have in turn sent U.S. missiles flying.

The Cuban Missile Crisis recounting is one of the dramatic peaks in *"My Journey on the Nuclear Brink,"* the memoir Perry published last fall. It is a book laced with other close calls—like November 9, 1979, when Perry was awakened in the middle of the night by a watch officer at the North American Aerospace and Defense Command reporting that his computers showed 200 Soviet missiles in flight toward the United States. For a frozen moment, Perry thought: This is it—This is how it ends.

The watch officer soon set him at ease. It was a computer error, and he was calling to see whether Perry, the technology expert, had any explanation. It took a couple days to discover the low-tech answer: someone had carelessly left a crisis-simulation training tape in the computer. All was well. But what if this blunder had happened in the middle of a real crisis, with leaders in Washington and Moscow already on high alert? The inescapable conclusion

was the same as it was in 1962: the world skirting nuclear Armageddon as much by good luck as by skilled crisis management.

Perry is part of a distinct cohort in American history, one that didn't come home with the large-living ethos of the World War II generation but took responsibility for cleaning up the world that the war bequeathed. He was a 14-year-old in Butler, Pennsylvania, when he heard the news of the Pearl Harbor attack in a friend's living room and had the disappointed realization that the war might be over by the time he was old enough to fight in it. That turned out to be true—he was just shy of 18 at war's end—a fact that places Perry in what demographers have called the "Silent Generation," too young for one war but already middle-aged by the time college campuses erupted over Vietnam. Like many in his generation, Perry was not so much silent as deeply dutiful, with an understated style that served as a genial, dry-witted exterior to a life in which success was defined by how faithfully one met his responsibilities.

Perry said he became aware, first gradually and over time profoundly, of the surreal contradictions of his professional life. His work—first at Sylvania and then at ESL, a highly successful defense contracting firm he cofounded in 1963—was relentlessly logical, analyzing Soviet threats and intentions and coming up with rational responses to deter them. But each rational move was part of a supremely irrational dynamic—"mutually assured destruction"—that placed the threat of massive casualties at the heart of America's basic strategic thinking. It was the kind of framework in which policy makers could accept that a mere 25 million people dead was good news. Also the kind that in one year alone led the United States to produce 8,000 nuclear bombs. By the end, the Cold War left the planet with about 70,000 bombs (a total that is now down to about 15,500).

"I think probably everybody who was involved in nuclear weapons in those days would see the two sides of it," Perry recalls, "the logic of deterrence and the madness of deterrence, and there was no mistake, I think, that the acronym was MAD."

***

Perry has been at the forefront of a movement that he considers the sane and only alternative, and he has joined forces with other leading Cold Warriors who in another era would likely have derided their vision as naive. In January 2007, he was a coauthor of a remarkable commentary that ran on the op-ed page of the *Wall Street Journal*. It was signed also by two former secretaries of state, George Schulz and Henry Kissinger and by Sam Nunn, a former chairman of the Senate Armed Services Committee—all leading military hawks and foreign policy realists who came together to argue for something radical: that the goal of U.S. policy should be not merely the reduction and control of atomic arms, it should be the ultimate elimination of all nuclear weapons.

This sounded like gauzy utopianism, especially bizarre coming from supremely pragmatic men. But Perry and the others always made clear they were describing a long-term ideal, one that would only be achieved through a series of more incremental steps. The vision was stirring enough that it was endorsed by President Obama in his opening weeks in office, in a March 2009 address in Prague.

In retrospect, Obama's speech may have been the high point for the vision of abolition. "A huge amount of progress was made," recalled Shultz, now 93. "Now it is going in the other direction."

"We have less danger of an all-out war with Russia," in Nunn's view. "But we have more danger of some type of accident, miscalculation, cyber interference, a terrorist group getting a nuclear weapon. It requires a lot more attention than world leaders are giving it." Perry's goal now is much more defensive than it was just a few years ago—halting what has become inexorable momentum toward reviving Cold War assumptions about the central role of nukes in national security.

More recently, he's added yet another recruit to his cause: California Governor Jerry Brown. Brown, now 78, met Perry a year ago, after deciding that he wanted to devote his remaining time in public service mainly to what he sees as civilization's two existential issues, climate change and nuclear weapons. Brown said he became fixated on spreading Perry's message after reading his memoir: he recently gave a copy to President Obama and is trying to bend the ear of others with influence in Washington.

If Bill Perry has a gift for understatement, Brown has a gift for the theatrical. In an interview at the governor's mansion in Sacramento, he wonders why everyone is not paying attention to his new friend and his warnings for mankind.

"He is at the brink! At the brink! Not *WAS* at the brink—*IS* at the brink," Brown exclaimed. "But no one else is."

A California governor can have more influence, at least indirectly, than one might think, due to the state's outsized role in policy debates and the fact that the University of California's Board of Regents helps manage some of the nation's top weapons laboratories, which study and design nuclear weapons. Brown, who was a vocal critic in

the 1980s of what he called America's "nuclear addiction," reviewed Perry's recent memoir in the *New York Review of Books*, and said he is determined to help his new friend spread his message.

"Everybody is, 'we are not at the brink,' and we have this guy Perry who says we are. It is the thesis that is being ignored."

Even if more influential people wake up to Perry's message—a nuclear event is more likely and will be more terrible than you realize—a hard questions remains: now what?

This is where Perry's pragmatism comes back into play. The smartest move, he thinks, is to eliminate the riskiest part of the system. If we can't eliminate all nukes, Perry argues, we could at least eliminate one leg of the so-called nuclear triad, intercontinental ballistic missiles. These are especially prone to an accidental nuclear war, if they are launched by accident or due to miscalculation by a leader operating with only minutes to spare. Nuclear weapons carried by submarines beneath the sea or aboard bomber planes, he argues, are logically more than enough to deter Russia.

The problem, he knows, is that logic is not necessarily the prevailing force in political debates. Psychology is, and this seems to be dictating not merely that we deter a Russian military force that is modernizing its weapons, but that we have a force that is self-evidently superior to them.

It is an argument that strikes Perry as drearily familiar to the old days. Which leads him the conclusion that the only long-term way out is to persuade a younger generation to make a different choice.

His granddaughter, Lisa Perry, is precisely in the cohort he needs to reach. At first she had some uncomfortable news for her grandfather: not many in her generation thought much about the issue.

"The more I learned from him about nuclear weapons, the more concerned I was that my generation had this massive and dangerous blind spot in our understanding of the world," she said in an interview. "Nuclear weapons are the biggest public health issue I can think of."

But she has not lost hope that their efforts can make a difference, and today she has put her graduate studies in public health on hold to work full time for the Perry Project as its social media and web manager. "It can be easy to get discouraged about being able to do anything to change our course," she said. "But the good news is that nuclear weapons are actually something that we as humans can control . . . but first we need to start the conversation."

It was with her help that Perry went on Reddit to field questions ranging from how his PhD in mathematics prepared him to what young people need to understand.

"As a 90s baby I never lived in the Cold War era," wrote one participant, with the Reddit username Bobin-ForApples. "What is one thing today's generations will never understand about life during the Cold War?"

Perry answered, as SecDef19: "because you were born in the 1990s, you did not experience the daily terror of 'duck and cover' drills as my children did. Therefore, the appropriate fear of nuclear weapons is not part of your heritage, but the danger is just as real now as it was then. It will be up to your generation to develop the policies to deal with the deadly nuclear legacy that is still very much with us."

For the former defense secretary, the task now is to finally—belatedly—prove Einstein wrong. The physicist said in 1946: "the unleashed power of the atom has changed everything save our modes of thinking and we thus drift toward unparalleled catastrophe."

In Perry's view, the only way to avoid it is by directly contemplating catastrophe—and doing so face to face with the world's largest nuclear power, Russia, as he recently did in a forum in Luxembourg with several like-minded Russians he says are brave enough to speak out about nuclear dangers in the era of Putin.

"We could solve it," he said. "When you're a prophet of doom, what keeps you going is not just prophesizing doom but saying there are things we do to avoid that doom. That's where the optimism is."

John Harris is *Politico's* editor-in-chief and author of The Survivor: Bill Clinton in the White House.

Bryan Bender is *Politico's* national security editor and author of You Are Not Forgotten. Both Harris and Bender covered the Pentagon during the tenure of Secretary of Defense William J. Perry.

Stephen M. Walt

The World Doesn't Need Any More Nuclear Strategies

The Trump Administration's Nuclear Posture Review Answers Questions Nobody should be Asking.

The non-use of nuclear weapons since 1945 is a great achievement that we take for granted all too often. Although the number of states possessing nuclear weapons has slowly increased over the past seven decades, no country has used a nuclear weapon since 1945, and despite some worrisome incidents, I know of no case where a nuclear-armed state ever came really close to firing a nuclear bomb at another country. Continuing this lucky streak for as long as possible—ideally, forever—should be a paramount goal for all human beings.

There are a number of obvious reasons why nuclear weapons have never been used. Attacking another nuclear-armed power is obviously foolhardy because it risks one's own destruction and because no political gains could possibly be worth the costs of being hit by even a handful of nuclear bombs in retaliation. It is possible to attack nuclear-armed countries with conventional forces—as Egypt and Syria did in the 1973 Yom Kippur War—but if you do, your aims had better be limited and you must take care not to threaten the survival or independence of the state you've attacked. Using a nuclear weapon to attack a nonnuclear state would also be very costly to the attacking country's reputation, unless the nonnuclear state had done something truly horrible and seemed likely to continue doing it. The good news is that one does not have to be very smart or perfectly rational to figure these things out.

The extensive efforts to prevent nuclear proliferation have also made nuclear use less likely. Although this campaign could not stop a few additional states from joining the nuclear club, it ensured that this process occurred gradually and allowed other states time to adjust. Over time, improved command-and-control and other security arrangements made accidental or unauthorized use

less likely, and the emerging "taboo" against nuclear use probably reinforced nonuse as well. Instead of thinking of nuclear weapons as just a bigger bomb, both politicians and weapons experts actively worked to place these fearsome weapons in a special conceptual category, thereby increasing the political costs of crossing that particular threshold. And humankind also got lucky, insofar as there have been a few moments since 1945 when things might have gone differently.

I raise all this because nuclear weapons are back in the news. One reason, of course, is the widespread concern about North Korea's advancing nuclear and missile capabilities. Officials in the Donald Trump administration have repeatedly said it is unacceptable for North Korea to have the capacity to strike the American homeland, and their attempts at saber-rattling—such as talk of a so-called bloody nose strike—have raised fears that a real shooting war might break out on the Korean Peninsula.

A second reason is the partial release of the Pentagon's new Nuclear Posture Review, which lays out an ambitious and costly proposal for modernizing the U.S. nuclear arsenal. The modernization plan is not intended merely to ensure that U.S. nuclear weapons remain reliable and secure (which is a perfectly reasonable objective); rather, the Pentagon also wants to develop a new generation of smaller nuclear weapons and more flexible targeting abilities, so that actual nuclear use becomes more feasible. This step is necessary, or so the planners say, to address an increasingly complicated strategic environment and certain low-level nuclear options that Russia is said to be developing. In short, the Posture Review is recommending not just the prudent preservation of an effective deterrent; it also wants the American taxpayer to pay for a lot of expensive new ways to use a nuclear bomb. Not because its authors want to fight a nuclear war, mind you, but because they believe having this capability will make their country more secure.

Full disclosure: I've always found such discussions slightly baffling. I used to spend a lot of time thinking about these issues, and I taught classes on nuclear strategy and arms control at the start of my teaching career. I don't focus as much on the subject nowadays—my bad—but I've kept up with a lot of the literature, and I have yet to read anything that has altered my belief that nuclear weapons have no real political value except as a deterrent against direct attacks against a state's home territory and/or truly vital overseas interests. They're no good for blackmail or coercion, they don't confer as much geopolitical status as proponents believe, and they certainly don't allow their possessors to dictate terms to weaker and nonnuclear-armed opponents. If nuclear weapons gave their possessors lots of leverage, for example, dealing with leaders like Slobodan Milosevic, Saddam Hussein, Muammar al-Qaddafi, or Bashar al-Assad (not to mention the Castros in Cuba or the Kims in North Korea) would have been a lot easier.

Moreover, I find the elaborate scenarios that nuclear strategists dream up to justify new weapons to be both militarily and politically unrealistic.

> I find the elaborate scenarios that nuclear strategists dream up to justify new weapons to be both militarily and politically unrealistic.

They tend to assume that complex military operations will go off without a hitch the very first time they are attempted (and in the crucible of a nuclear crisis), and they further assume that political leaders in the real world would be willing to order the slaughter of millions for something less than existential stakes. My main concern has been that some gullible politician would actually believe that one of these elaborate scenarios would actually work and might therefore be tempted to try it. Just as bad: an adversary might *think* the United States thought it could win such a war and might decide it had no choice but to try to hit it first.

I also find the obsession with matching capabilities at every rung of some hypothetical "escalation ladder" to be slightly absurd. Is it realistic to think that U.S. leaders defending vital interests against a possible Russian threat would be stymied because they didn't have a capability that exactly mirrored whatever Russia had or was threatening to do? Would a top advisor really say to the president: "Oh dear, sir, Russia just threatened to attack with a nuclear weapon with a yield of 7.2 kilotons. We have lots of 5-kiloton bombs and lots of 11-kiloton bombs all ready to go, but if we use the little one, they'll think we're

wimps, and if we use the big one, then the onus of escalation will be on us. I guess they've got us over the whingwhang, sir, and we'll just have to do whatever Putin says. *If only we had built more 7.2 kiloton bombs than they did!"*

With all that as background, I have a few questions about the new direction the Pentagon is proposing, along with a few provisional answers of my own.

Question 1: Exactly how does the more modern nuclear arsenal proposed by the Nuclear Posture Review make the United States safer?
Answer: Apart from ensuring that the U.S. arsenal remains reliable, it doesn't.

As things stand now, nobody really doubts America's deterrent capability: its arsenal is already a lot more potent than anyone else's. Moreover, nobody really doubts its ability to blow things up all over the world without using a nuclear bomb, including some pretty hard targets. The United States has been conducting drone, air, and cruise missile strikes in lots of places for many years now, and it has even used the GBU-43/B Massive Ordnance Air Blast (the largest conventional bomb in the U.S. arsenal) against the Islamic State in Afghanistan.

So, what is the strategic problem that these new capabilities are going to solve? Do they really expect Russia or China or Iran or other adversaries to give up vital interests because the United States acquires a slightly more flexible set of strategic capabilities? Is there any country on earth that is looking at the current U.S. arsenal and saying to itself: "Gosh, attacking America or one of its allies would be easy today, but if they get some smaller nukes and more flexible options, then we'll have to abandon our entire plan of world domination!" Are other countries likely to be significantly more intimidated by U.S. development of nuclear bombs that are bigger than the Massive Ordnance Air Blast but smaller than its existing nuclear weapons? Will violent extremists like al Qaeda or the Islamic State suddenly cease their activities after the United States upgrades its ability to put a thermonuclear weapon in more places more rapidly? Will any of these new features boost the U.S. economy, slow climate change, reduce inequality, make the United States more popular around the world, or restore the confidence in U.S. judgment that has been lost under Trump? The questions answer themselves.

Question 2: Why doesn't the United States have more faith in nuclear deterrence?
Answer: Because threat-inflators are more numerous than threat-deflators.

A striking irony in most discussions of America's nuclear posture is how little confidence Americans seem to have in it. No matter how much the United States spends on nuclear forces, official Washington doesn't really believe they will achieve the aim for which they were bought. The United States has spent several trillion dollars on nuclear weapons since the Manhattan Project, and today it has the world's most capable nuclear arsenal. Even if the United States were attacked first, the 1,500-plus warheads that are presently deployed are capable of destroying any society on earth in a retaliatory strike. Yet somehow these vast powers aren't enough to make the United States confident it can take on much weaker nuclear powers, such as North Korea. President Donald Trump boasts that his "button" is bigger than North Korean leader Kim Jong Un's, but official Washington acts as if the opposite were true.

This position has never made much sense. America's nuclear deterrent was apparently good enough to keep mass murderers and ideological zealots such as Josef Stalin, Mao Zedong, Nikita Khrushchev, and Kim Il Sung from attacking the United States, and it discouraged them from threatening key U.S. allies, but apparently the United States cannot quite believe that it is enough to convince a weaker adversary like Kim Jong Un. Kim is hardly someone to admire or trust, but he shows no signs of being suicidal, and there's no reason to think he isn't fully aware of what the consequences of attacking the United States (or South Korea) would be. Ironically, the more visibly Americans fret about it, the more he might be led to believe that maybe his modest arsenal really is politically potent. Needless to say, that is hardly the conclusion the United States wants him to reach.

Question 3: Why is it in the U.S. interest to *lower* the nuclear threshold?
Answer: It's not.

By calling for smaller-yield weapons and more flexible nuclear targeting abilities, the Nuclear Posture Review deliberately seeks to lower the nuclear threshold. It wants the United States to acquire capabilities that will make other states think the United States can use these weapons more readily in the future, in the hope that this capability will make those states more inclined to do what it wants (or not to do what it doesn't want).

But there are big risks to lowering the nuclear threshold. Rather obviously, making nuclear weapons more usable makes it more likely that they will in fact be used—sooner or later. And because the United States has no idea how other states will respond once the nuclear threshold

has been crossed, making nuclear use more likely is a social science experiment it really does not want to run.

More importantly, having an improved war-fighting capability—and in particular, the clear potential to disarm an adversary—risks putting that adversary in a "use or lose" situation. If an enemy thought the United States was willing to use nuclear weapons first and believed it had lots of options for doing so (including a disarming first strike), then it might be tempted to preempt, especially in a serious crisis. And remember: no one is likely to even think about using nuclear weapons unless the stakes are pretty high. If an adversary thinks its existence or even its long-term power position is at risk, does the United States really want it thinking it will lose big if it waits? As we have understood since the seminal writings of Albert Wohlstetter and Thomas Schelling, threatening an adversary's deterrent is a bad recipe for crisis stability, and making nuclear crises harder to control is hardly in America's interest.

Question 4: What does this mean for America's anti-proliferation efforts?
Answer: Nothing good.

The new Posture Review sends a clear message to the rest of the world. It says that even if you are a continent-sized superpower with the world's largest economy, the world's most powerful conventional forces, no enemies nearby, and no powerful adversaries openly seeking to overthrow your government, you still need lots and lots of highly sophisticated and expensive nuclear weapons in order to be secure. Unfortunately, that message will make it pretty damn hard to convince far weaker and more vulnerable countries like North Korea or Iran that they don't need nuclear weapons to be safe, and it will make it harder to convince countries like China or Russia that they have no need to build up sophisticated war-fighting capacities of their own. From a long-term perspective, this approach seems rather short-sighted.

And how's a country like Estonia or even Sweden supposed to feel?

To be clear: I don't expect to see radical nuclear disarmament in my lifetime, and I don't expect to see a nuclear bomb being fired, either. I think nuclear weapons have made large-scale war less likely, and I'd support a well-thought-out effort to ensure that U.S. nuclear forces are both reliable and safeguarded against interference, theft, or accidental use. (In this regard, it is worth remembering that the Barack Obama administration had also proposed a significant modernization program, albeit one that was less costly and dangerous than what Trump & Co. seem to have in mind.) But instead of giving the bomb a more prominent role in U.S. strategy, and taking steps that lower the nuclear threshold in dangerous ways, I'd like to see them reserved for the only task for which they are really suited: deterring direct attacks on the U.S. homeland and other vital U.S. interests. That's probably one of the many reasons why I don't occupy a prominent place in America's strategic nuclear priesthood.

Stephen M. Walt is the Robert and Renée Belfer professor of international relations at Harvard University.

EXPLORING THE ISSUE

Is Nuclear War More Likely in the Next Decade?

Critical Thinking and Reflection

1. Can the likelihood of nuclear war be reduced in the global community today?
2. What are the factors that may lead to nuclear war happening?
3. What states or actors have the best chance to rebuild the nuclear nonproliferation regime?
4. Do terrorist groups have a better chance to obtain and use nuclear weapons than before?

Is There Common Ground?

As long as nuclear weapons exist, there is a statistical threat of nuclear war. Also, as long as some states pursue the acquisition of such weapons that likelihood exists and has the chance to increase. In addition, as nonstate actors pursue such weapons in a variety of forms and have the means to procure them either through purchase or theft, the likelihood can and will exists. The factors that mitigate those odds include sophisticated electronic detection by countries with satellite capability, strong cooperation by nuclear weapons states to avoid proliferation and of course the relative deterrent capabilities of nuclear weapons states making an attack by another essentially suicide.

In the realm of nuclear war and its likelihood in the next decade, one can say that the factors listed above will determine its probability to occur or not and each factor must be monitored and weighed carefully moment to moment.

Additional Resources

Larsen, Jeffery A., Kartchner, Kenny M., On Limited Nuclear War in the 21st Century Stanford Security Studies, 2014.

Delpech, Thérèse. Nuclear Deterrence in the 21st Century: Lessons from the Cold War for a New Era of Strategic Piracy. Rand Corporation, 2012.

Johnstone, Dr. John H., Roberts, Paul Craig, From MAD to Madness: Inside Pentagon Nuclear War Planning. Clarity Press, 2017.

Wanlund, William. "Modernizing the Nuclear Arsenal: Is a New Arms Race Brewing?" *CQ Researcher.* July 29, 2016.

Kühn, Ulrich. "Introduction: Nuclear Disarmament and Arms Control for the Next Decade." *Bulletin of the Atomic Scientists.* July 2017.

Podvig, Pavel. "Blurring the Line between Nuclear and Nonnuclear Weapons: Increasing the Risk of Accidental Nuclear War?" *Bulletin of the Atomic Scientists.* May 2016.

Najarian, Jonathan. "Pressing the Wrong Button": Pynchon's Postmodernism and the Threat of Nuclear War in the Crying of Lot 49. *Critique.* January 2018.

Hsu, Sara. "Why China Won't Replace The U.S. as the World's Superpower." *Forbes. Forbes Magazine*, February 3, 2017, www.forbes.com/sites/sarahsu/2017/02/02/why-china-wont-replace-the-u-s-as-the-worlds-superpower/#3c5151b7234d

Internet References . . .

Forbes

https://www.forbes.com

Foreign Affairs

https://www.foreignaffairs.com

Foreign Policy

http://foreignpolicy.com

USA Today

https://www.usatoday.com